FACING A HOLOCAUST

THE POLISH

GOVERNMENT-IN-EXILE

AND THE JEWS,

1943-1945

THE UNIVERSITY OF NORTH CAROLINA PRESS

CHAPEL HILL & LONDON

FACING A HOLO-CAUST

BY DAVID ENGEL

Library of Congress Cataloging-in-Publication Data

Engel, David.

Facing a holocaust : the Polish government-in-exile and
the Jews, 1943–1945 / by David Engel.

p. cm.

Includes bibliographical references and index.

ISBN 0-8078-2069-5

1. Jews—Poland—Politics and government. 2. Holocaust,
Jewish (1939–1945)—Poland. 3. Poland—History—
Occupation, 1939–1945. 4. Rzeczpospolita Polska
(Government-in-exile)   I. Title.

DS135.P6E53   1993

943.8'004924—dc20   92-28289

CIP

97 96 95 94 93   5 4 3 2 1

FOR RONIT

Contents

This book is a sequel to an earlier work, *In the Shadow of Auschwitz: The Polish Government-in-Exile and the Jews, 1939–1942*, which appeared in 1987. As such it depends upon an infrastructure of evidence and analysis that cannot be easily repeated for readers unfamiliar with the earlier volume. To be sure, the first chapter presents the main features of that infrastructure in summary fashion. Nevertheless, because the story told by the two volumes comprises a whole that has been artificially divided in two, it has been necessary, in order to preserve the sense of flow between the two periods that the volumes represent, to intersperse that summary with features of the ongoing story.

Part of the infrastructure consists of the conventions regarding personal and place names and transliterations that were employed in the previous volume. All of those conventions remain in force in the present work; rather than repeat them here, I refer readers to the prefatory note in *In the Shadow of Auschwitz*.

Since the earlier book was written, several additional people have offered assistance, encouragement, or advice, and I recall their contributions with thanks (alphabetically, as before): Raya Adler, Hagar Fynne, Irit Kenan, Shlomo Netzer, Synaj Okręt, Annie Roberts, Anita Shapira, Hana Shlomi, and Ron Zweig. Upon reading this acknowledgment some of these people may be scratching their heads in wonder over what their contribution might have been, as did some who were thanked in the earlier volume. Suffice it to say that I remember how each of them helped and that without them this book would not have turned out as it did. I can only hope that they will regard that fact as a source of pride rather than embarrassment. Again, naming them does not imply that they agree with any statements or interpretations that follow, which are entirely my own.

Additional support for this volume was provided by the Diaspora Research Institute at Tel Aviv University, my academic home during most of the years in which this project was conducted. Special thanks are due the institute's director, Shlomo Simonsohn, for his consistent encouragement. Thanks are also due the Joseph Meyerhoff Chair in Modern Jewish History at the University of Pennsylvania and the Skirball Department of Hebrew and Judaic Studies at New York University for providing me with facilities during stays in the United States. The Skirball Department also contributed materially to the publication of this volume, thanks to the support of its chairman, Robert Chazan.

Without the dedicated labors of the staff of the University of North Carolina Press, and especially without the confidence shown in this project by editor Lewis Bateman, neither this book nor its predecessor would ever have seen the light of day. The business of producing a scholarly work with citations in more than a half-dozen languages is not a simple one, and the people at Chapel Hill have gone about it in a thoroughly competent and professional way.

Finally, as with this volume's predecessor, my greatest source of support has been my family, and especially my wife, Ronit. This book is for her.

Ramat Hasharon, Israel, 1990

Introduction

What follows is an examination of the thoughts and actions of the Polish government-in-exile on matters of primary concern to Jewish citizens of Poland from the end of 1942 until the conclusion of the European chapter of the Second World War in May 1945. Like its predecessor, *In the Shadow of Auschwitz*, which examined the same subject from the outbreak of war until the end of 1942, the present study endeavors, on the basis of as full and fair an exploration of the extant documentary traces of those thoughts and actions as possible, to uncover the considerations, both of principle and conjunctural, that influenced Polish policymakers in formulating their responses to those Jewish citizens' expressed needs at a time when both parties—the former in the political, the latter in the biological, sense—faced the challenge of life or death. In particular, this study inquires after the extent to which the news that the Jews of Nazi-occupied Poland were being subjected not merely to a regime of unspeakable hardship and brutality but to a systematic program aimed at taking the life of each and every Jewish man, woman, and child within the German conquerors' grasp—news that the government-in-exile had played a central role in bringing to the attention of the free world at the time the present study commences—altered the government's perceptions of its obligations or interests vis-à-vis its Jewish citizens and led it to act upon Jews' expressions of need differently than it had been accustomed to do before it was aware of the dire nature of the Jews' plight.

The results of this examination will be offered—as were the conclusions of *In the Shadow of Auschwitz*—exclusively as propositions of fact, with no attempt made to reflect upon their ethical or practical implications. It is emphatically *not* the purpose of this study to identify heroes and villains or to assign praise and blame, whether absolute or relative, to the various participants in the events described. Nor does this work stem from any sense of obligation to promote a positive

1

or negative image of either of the protagonists or to impel their descendants toward any particular assessment of responsibility for the annihilation of Polish Jewry. Of course, it may be difficult for many readers to approach a book about an aspect of Polish-Jewish relations with moral judgment suspended or to accept that the author of such a book might not be seeking to serve either a Polish or a Jewish cause, for discussions of those relations have often been conducted within the context of a highly charged public debate in which both Poles and Jews seem to feel that they have much at stake.[1] Yet one who reads the present volume or its predecessor with a mind to determining its possible effects upon the self-understanding of contemporary Poles and Jews or upon the efforts of both peoples to achieve their collective public goals today is liable to miss much and misconstrue more.[2]

Indeed, the public context in which current discussions of Polish-Jewish relations are taking place makes it necessary to insist so vociferously upon the present volume's purely factual, morally neutral aim. When the project to examine the subject under discussion was first conceived, in May 1980, Edward Gierek still held power in Poland, the Solidarity movement had yet to be formed, and few outside of the country had ever heard the name of Lech Wałęsa.[3] A short time later, however, an open struggle against Communist rule in Poland rattled the foundations of the regime. This struggle quickly captured the imagination of the West in a fashion that the leaders of the struggle must have found encouraging; not only was international pressure in favor of the opposition movement brought to bear upon the Polish government but the Western public began to develop a highly sympathetic curiosity about the history of the Polish people. This curiosity provided fertile ground for promulgating the view that the authentic voice of the Polish nation—a voice that had been silenced for more than thirty-five years by a repressive regime—was a voice that called for freedom and democracy, humanity and brotherhood, and an ethical orientation toward life that the Western world held dear. Indeed, the years following the outbreak of what quickly came to be dubbed the Polish revolution witnessed the publication in the West of a number of works on Polish history that served to promote this view.[4]

Moreover, the resistance to the regime helped many in the West to understand the enormity of the gulf that separated the Polish state from Polish society. The realization of this separation, in turn, heightened the perception that the Polish people themselves were victims of Communism and provided the Poles with a measure of the moral capital that of late has underwritten the struggles of so many of those whom history, as it were, has forced to suffer. Poles could claim that the Western Allies, by ignoring their pleas for assistance in preventing a Communist takeover of their country—pleas that formed the backdrop for many of the occurrences discussed in this book—bore a portion of the responsibility for their victimization and hence owed the Polish nation collective recompense. This theme was sounded in several publications appearing during the 1980s written mainly by emigré Poles or by Westerners with a strong affinity for Poland.[5]

Unfortunately for those with an interest in advancing such images of the Polish past, the history of the relations between Poles and Jews—or more precisely, a version of that history that had also gained currency among the Western public—stood to weaken the Poles' claim both to a legacy of the highest moral values and to victim status. In particular, common perceptions of Polish-Jewish relations during the Second World War presented themselves as potential impediments to the advancement of the Polish cause. Jewish spokesmen, both during the war and after, expressed—at times quite loudly and vehemently—dissatisfaction with the manner in which the Polish government, underground, and society as a whole responded to the placement of all Jews within the Nazi orbit under sentence of death. Some critics complained that the Poles did not demonstrate proper concern for Jewish suffering or sufficient readiness to extend effective succor to Jews; others went so far as to charge the Poles with actual complicity in the Nazi murder plan. Virtually all held, moreover, that the fundamental factor influencing Polish attitudes toward the Jewish plight was a tradition of antipathy toward Jews as such, to which the highly pejorative label of antisemitism was almost always attached. Eventually the gravamen of these charges was absorbed by the mass media and passed on to wide audiences through such television and cinematic productions as Gerald Green's *Holocaust*, Herman Wouk's *The Winds of War*, and Claude Lanzmann's *Shoah*. Clearly such a view of events was inconsistent with the image of Poles as fighters for the freedom of all peoples, and identifying Poles with the persecutors rather than with the persecuted made it difficult for them to be counted among the war's casualties.

Yet there appears to be another reason why the spread of such a view of wartime Polish-Jewish relations has been greeted by many Poles as a cause for grave concern. Not surprisingly, this reason is rooted in the very period under discussion. Indeed, the last time, prior to the 1980s, the Polish people carried on such an intensive struggle for the hearts and minds of the Western public was during the Second World War. During this period the Polish government-in-exile and the underground forces loyal to it sought to return to power in a liberated homeland occupying the Polish state's boundaries of 1 September 1939. This desire was opposed by the aim of the Soviet Union to retain the Ukrainian and White Russian border areas that it had occupied during the September campaign and had annexed shortly thereafter and—increasingly as the war progressed—to impose upon Poland a new government more amenable to Soviet interests. Many Polish leaders believed at the time that Jews in the free world could play a decisive role in this Polish-Soviet dispute; however, as both *In the Shadow of Auschwitz* and the following pages demonstrate, Jews were never prepared to provide the Poles with the type of assistance they desired. To many Poles, in fact, it appeared that the Jews had decided deliberately to use their purported power over Western public opinion in order to advance the Soviet cause at Poland's expense. Polish leaders were led to this conclusion by Jewish organizations' publication of complaints about alleged anti-Jewish discrimination by various official Polish agencies, especially by the Polish army, and by what was taken as an implicit threat to publicize charges about the Polish people's purported indifference to or complicity in the Nazi murder campaign. The purpose of such publication was, they frequently argued, to blacken Poland's good name, to create an impression of the Poles as a fundamentally intolerant and mean-spirited people unfit to guarantee the rights and welfare of the non-ethnic Poles who formed the majority of the inhabitants of the territories under dispute. Such an impression, of course, stood not only to undermine the moral force of Poland's claim to those territories but also to cast doubt upon the very legitimacy of the current Polish government in a world about to be liberated, ostensibly, from the scourge of racism and racial prejudice. In such a context, any Jewish expression of dissatisfaction over the tenor of Polish-Jewish relations could easily be interpreted as an expression of hostility or even as a potentially serious blow to the survival of a national Polish regime.

This sense of threat, this notion that any statement lending credence to the various complaints brought during the war by Jewish groups against the Polish government-in-exile, the Polish underground, or the Polish people as a whole must somehow work to prevent the Polish nation from realizing its collective political desires and be taken as an expression of enmity toward Poland, appears to have been carried forward by some Poles at least through the 1980s.[6] Perhaps the most ardent and serious recent exponent of this view is the Solidarity attorney Władysław Siła-Nowicki. In a reply to a by-now-famous article published by a leading Catholic intellectual and professor of Polish literature, Jan Błoński, in the independent Catholic weekly *Tygodnik Powszechny* in January 1987—an article that contended that the relations between Poles and Jews were often less than salubrious largely because of Polish prejudices and suggested that because of those prejudices Poles needed to consider that they might bear a measure of collective responsibility for the fate of their Jewish neighbors under the Nazi occupation[7]—Siła-Nowicki charged that Błoński's views "may unfortunately be understood as the affirmation and quintessence (unintended of course) of a virulent anti-Polish propaganda campaign conducted endlessly for dozens of years by the enemies not of the government, nor the economic or political system of present-day Poland, but simply of the Polish nation."[8] Siła-Nowicki's position was supported by, among others, the journalist Witold Rymanowski, who suggested that Błoński's article "contains statements of the type covered in article 178 of the penal code and is therefore guilty of the offence of slandering the Polish nation in accordance with article 270 of that code."[9] It also found an echo in a recent, posthumously published book by Stefan Korboński, who during the war headed the underground Polish Directorate of Civil Resistance and who for his activities in that position was recognized by Yad Vashem, the official Israeli authority for commemorating the martyrdom of European Jewry, as one who contributed materially to saving Jewish lives. Korboński wrote that "the charges leveled by the Jews against the Poles for allegedly sharing responsibility for the Holocaust by not preventing the slaughter of the Jews by the Nazis are," among other things, "slanderous."[10] He also contended that the propagation by American Jews of "a version blaming the Poles for the Holocaust almost to the same extent as the Nazis . . . , [which] charged the Poles with indifference and even collusion with the Germans," was motivated no more and no less than by the propagators' "hatred of Poland."[11]

The invocation of legal terms to characterize the views of those who find Poles to have been on the whole indifferent to the plight of their Jewish neighbors during the German occupation, together with the vehemence with which they are invoked, appears telling; it suggests the feeling that the Polish nation is somehow today [12] being forced to stand trial, perhaps even for its life,[13] because of allegations put forth by its enemies concerning its behavior during the Second World War. No wonder, then, that there are among the Poles those who approach the subject at hand in a fashion appropriate to a judicial proceeding: they assume a defensive position, present evidence selected for its ability to refute the various sections of the indictment ostensibly placed against them, and endeavor to impeach the testimony of opposition witnesses. In doing so, moreover, these contemporary defenders frequently echo the efforts of Polish spokesmen to ward off similar Jewish charges voiced during the war itself.

Their argument can be summarized roughly thus: during the Second World War the Poles themselves were victims of a Nazi reign of terror that threatened their own annihilation no less than the annihilation of the Jews. Under such conditions the Polish people were powerless to stop the German killing machine. Still, those who were able (a minority, to be sure, but a significant one nonetheless) strove to rescue as many Jews as they could, generally risking their lives and the lives of their families in the process and often paying with them for their efforts. Admittedly there were also those who cooperated with the Nazis in their murderous designs or who expressed satisfaction over the Jews' misfortune; but they were few in number, and their actions were not only condemned but even severely punished by the responsible leaders of the nation. If, despite these efforts, the overwhelming majority of prewar Polish Jewry fell victim to the German murder program, this result was not brought about by the actions or inactions of the Polish people. Real, effective aid for the threatened Jews could have come only from the major Allies, but the governments of those countries remained altogether apathetic to the Jewish plight, as did Jewish organizations in the free world. Their apathy persisted, moreover, despite the consistent efforts of the Polish leadership to inform them of the dimensions of the catastrophe the Jews faced. All of these facts were known to Jews in the free world at the time, and they are known to them today; but because of a complex of factors, including excessive affinity for Communism, a fundamental hatred of Poland, and a desire to magnify their own sufferings at the expense of those of others—feelings that they displayed repeatedly both during the war and after—they continue to distort the historical record and to represent the Polish victims of the Nazi behemoth as partners in the Germans' crime.[14]

Clearly this line of defense also contains elements of a counterattack, and as such it raises among many Jews the fear that some of their people's vital interests are being threatened. In particular, both the presentation of the Poles as no less victims of the war than the Jews and the tarring of the Jews with the double brush of prejudicial hatred and tendencies toward Communism stand to diminish that very moral capital that the Jewish people, and particularly the State of Israel, have known how to invest to their advantage ever since the end of the war—an accumulation of moral force that was perhaps the most important positive outcome of a war that brought the Jews the greatest losses they have ever known. Defensive Polish responses to Jewish complaints thus often invite hostile counterresponses from the Jewish side.[15] Moreover, because the Polish defense is rooted in justifications similar to those employed during the war to answer charges raised by Jews at that time, Jewish counterresponses also tend to echo the language of an earlier time. The result of such an ongoing exchange of thrusts and parries is thus a situation in which both sides, while viewing themselves as engaged in a struggle over contemporary interests and self-images, conduct this struggle with the help of arguments that were first sounded almost fifty years ago. In fact, persons familiar with wartime Polish-Jewish polemics who listen to such arguments being employed today sometimes feel as though they are in a time tunnel, in which the division between past and present has been erased and new and old contexts can be interchanged at will.

In such a situation, the pressure upon professional historians to enter the fray is enormous. Because both parties to this ongoing moral litigation require documentary material from the past in order to prove their cases, it is no wonder that each would turn to those qualified by disciplinary training and practice to handle such material with requests to provide the required evidence. Such requests, however, actually call upon historians to do much more than simple research in order to fulfill them; in the end they require researchers to enter a situation in which they can no longer operate according to the tenets of their discipline. For one thing, historians who endeavor to function in surroundings that do not recognize the existence of boundaries between past and present vitiate that awareness of the time dimension that permits them to operate as historians in the first place. For another, the quasi-judicial, adversarial tone of the public debate demands that historians who enter it search for and bring forth primarily such evidence as will demonstrate the argument of one or the other side, whereas professional canons require historians to locate and to expose all available evidence, no matter what its present implications. Finally, the object of moral judgment can impel historians to prefer a priori the ascription of motivations of principle to actions that documentary investigation may show to have been undertaken in fact for altogether pragmatic reasons.

The best way to avoid these pitfalls, of course, is to avoid the situation that generates them from the beginning—to resist the pressure and the temptation to write about Polish-Jewish relations as a participant in the current public debate and to report solely on the content of the available evidence and on its usefulness in establishing matters of fact. However, it appears insufficient for some historians to eschew participation in the effort to adjudicate the Polish-Jewish dispute if their readers—including other historians—are not prepared to read their works in this light.

Consider, for example, the comments of a distinguished student of Polish diplomacy who took issue with the contention put forth in *In the Shadow of Auschwitz* that the Polish government-in-exile, like its prewar predecessors, essentially excluded Jews from its universe of obligation.[16] This reader initially argued that the evidence presented in the book did not warrant such a conclusion. However, instead of analyzing the alleged inadequacies of that evidence, she supported her argument with the justification that "like any other government, the Polish one was concerned primarily with the majority of its people and not with the Jewish minority, a minority, moreover, that was both much larger than in any other country . . . and radically different from the assimilated Jews of Central and Western Europe and the United States in having a distinct culture and way of life." If indeed such is this scholar's assessment of the position of Jews in the Polish government's universe of obligation, then it would appear that, on the purely factual plane, she does not disagree substantially with the book whose thesis she pronounces objectionable. Yet if, nonetheless, she regarded her words as words of refutation or rebuttal, she must have been responding primarily to what she took to be the "negative evaluation" of Polish government policy that the disputed conclusion implied.[17] Her counterargument was not that the Polish government did not concern itself primarily with the welfare of ethnic Poles but merely that primary governmental concern for the welfare of a state's majority nationality is altogether understandable and hardly something to be condemned. *In the Shadow of Auschwitz*, however, never adopted the position that such an allocation of concern was not understandable and likewise never undertook to condemn it. Indeed, the question of whether or not a state ought to conceive of itself as an advocate for the needs of all its citizens equally, without regard to their ethnic origin, or, in contrast, principally as the spokesman for a dominant, pre-existing national group claiming to have created the state in order to advance its own particular collective needs and interests—a problem felt acutely by a number of countries today, including, perhaps ironically, the State of Israel—is a proposition of policy rather than one of fact; it refers to the present and the future rather than to the past, and for this reason historians can claim no special competence, by virtue of their professional training, to deal with it. *In the Shadow of Auschwitz* thus confined itself to a simple proposition of fact—that the available evidence indicates that the Polish government-in-exile "tended to view its obligations toward the Jewish citizens of the Polish Republic as of a lesser order than its obligations toward ethnic Poles."[18] This proposition can, of course, be disputed, either by demonstrating that the book did not analyze the available evidence properly or by pointing to additional evidence not considered in the book that suggests a different conclusion. Reading into this proposition an implied statement of policy or of value, however, merely diverts the discussion from the historian's bailiwick and leads to reactions that are not to the point.

Such a reading also obscures a key problem for analysis. The scholar in question followed her expression of understanding for the government-in-exile's primary concern with the Polish majority over the Jewish minority with the observation, "However, when the government received the first report of genocide—in a letter from Bund leaders in Poland—it took vigorous action to publicize it . . . in June–July 1942." This sentence appears to suggest the opinion that despite the government's primary concern for the welfare of Poles, it still looked out for the welfare of Jews when it became clear that that welfare was under serious threat and thus does not deserve the "negative evaluation" supposedly given it in the book. The problem with this argument is that the fact that the Polish government took steps to publicize the

Bund report in June–July 1942—a fact discussed in *In the Shadow of Auschwitz* at some length [19]—cannot be taken *by itself* as evidence that those steps were motivated by a genuine sense of concern for the Jewish fate. As it happens, there is no direct evidence (in the form of internal correspondence by government officials about the Bund letter) that can prove or disprove this assumption. The preponderance of circumstantial evidence, however, appears to indicate, as the book shows, that the steps that were taken were taken because they addressed a concern of the Polish government that had little to do with the sufferings of the Jews. Again, should someone adduce either new, direct evidence pointing to genuine concern as the principal motive for the government's action or an alternate, more compelling reading of the circumstantial evidence, then that conclusion would be refuted. But it cannot be refuted with the logically fallacious argument that an action from which Jews benefited had to have been caused by a desire to benefit them.

Indeed, simple consideration of the book's presentation of information at face value, without regard for its possible "negative" implications, might have suggested the perhaps more revealing question of why a Polish government that "was concerned primarily with the majority of its people and not with the Jewish minority" would take "vigorous action" on the Jews' behalf despite its lack of concern in principle. As *In the Shadow of Auschwitz* made clear, and as the following pages reaffirm, there were more than a few occasions when the government-in-exile *did* accede to Jewish demands or act to promote Jewish interests. Even more significantly, there were instances in which the government acceded to a particular Jewish demand after having refused to do so earlier. These facts point to the existence of other, conjunctural factors at work in the formation of the manner in which the Polish government dealt with matters of concern to Jews, factors in which the government's theoretical assessment of its obligations toward Jews was secondary in importance to the immediate context in which specific decisions were taken. Careful analysis of the instances in question in relation to the overall exigencies of Polish politics that impinged upon them can reveal what those factors were and lead to an appreciation of Polish political leaders as people who responded to Jewish needs with something more than elemental "unadorned antisemitism"[20] on the one hand or "sheer decency"[21] on the other. Such an analysis is obviated, however, within a discourse concerned primarily with determining whether Polish actions toward

Jews (and Jewish actions toward Poles, for that matter) ought to be viewed in a morally positive or negative light.

This difficulty was exemplified at a session of a recent international conference on Polish-Jewish relations. After an explication of the motives for the Polish government's frequent interventions on behalf of Henryk Erlich and Wiktor Alter and strenuous protests following confirmation that they had been executed by the Soviets—an explication included in the present volume[22]—a participant at the conference objected that, all disclaimers to the contrary, the Poles had been unfairly represented as "devious."[23] Why, this person inquired, was it not sufficient to indicate simply that the Polish government had done its duty in the wake of the murder of two innocent Polish citizens at the hands of a foreign state? The answer to this question, of course, is that the government's own internal correspondence about the Erlich-Alter affair (in this case such direct evidence of Polish thinking is extant) indicates that the government did not protest solely because it felt that it had to do so; on the contrary, it wanted to do so, because a vital Polish interest was involved. Evidently, however, the questioner felt that a protest made for reasons of self-interest ought to be regarded as somehow morally tainted; he seems to have preferred, for reasons that undoubtedly had to do more with the current public debate about Polish-Jewish relations than with his own understanding of the available evidence, that the Poles be represented as having included Jewish citizens of their country within their universe of obligation. Indeed, there appears room to wonder whether similar remarks about the role of a calculus of interests in guiding the response of British or American leaders to a matter of Jewish concern would have aroused such an objection. More likely it would have been understood that the discussion was about politicians and that politicians of all persuasions and nationalities are required by the job they do to act in accordance with political interests. However, because in this particular case the politicians under discussion were Polish politicians, a statement about the interests that demonstrably guided them was understood as somehow aimed at impugning their moral integrity. Not only was this understanding mistaken, but the moral discourse that generated it limited the willingness to consider an unpalatable possibility.

Those who are still bothered by the search for conjunctural factors as motivators of Polish government actions with regard to Jews, however, should note that that search cuts in the opposite direction as well: it imposes a brake upon the tendency to assume that any Polish refusal to grant a Jewish request or any government behavior that was not to the Jews' liking was the result of a purported fundamental Polish antipathy toward Jews. Just as documentary evidence of genuine concern is required in order to ascribe any government action that accorded with Jewish desires to such a motive, so must similar documentary evidence be present in order to attribute an action that aroused Jewish complaints to ill will. Careful readers will thus observe that the term *antisemitism* is not a significant category of analysis in the following pages. Indeed, it has not proven difficult to write this entire book without making use of the word at all, except in direct quotations or paraphrases of the remarks of participants in the story. This fact should make it possible to avoid the essentially semantic (not historical) argument over the types of behavior to which this term should be applied that has characterized much writing on Polish-Jewish relations in general.[24] Hopefully it will also facilitate the acceptance of the book's morally neutral character by eliminating the highly judgmental connotations that are attached to the word. Indeed, an effort has been made in the following pages to avoid labeling any actions or attitudes with abstractions—including terms frequently employed in the documentary record itself, such as *collaboration, loyalty, treason, racism,* or *fascism*—that convey more emotional valence than denotative precision and that tend to divert discussion from the phenomenon under study to the suitability of a particular word to describe it.[25]

If all of the strictures outlined here have in fact been successfully carried out in the pages that follow, there should be no textual grounds for reading this volume as if it were written in the service of any contemporary Polish or Jewish communal goals. There should be no cause to write, as was written with regard to *In the Shadow of Auschwitz*, that the book "clearly, if somewhat grudgingly, commends the London regime and the *Armia Krajowa* for their various efforts in notifying the world of the Holocaust."[26] It should be understood that the book is meant to contain neither commendations nor castigations of either Poles or Jews and that statements of fact about what Polish leaders did in order to bring news of the systematic mass murder of Polish Jewry to the attention of the free world are made neither more grudgingly nor more willingly than statements about anything else Polish leaders did. To be sure, these strictures represent an ideal that is difficult to achieve in practice, and careful readers will undoubtedly be able to point to lapses in their observance. Nevertheless, it is hoped that such readers will accept any lapses they might locate as no more than unintentional slips and will not find reason to doubt the sincerity of the effort to reconstruct the thinking of the Polish government-in-exile on matters of concern to Jewish citizens of Poland during the latter half of the Second World War without reference to the current public debate over the nature of Polish-Jewish relations.

This is not to say, of course, that those who feel that they have a vital stake in that debate will not find information in the pages that follow that they may regard as useful or damaging to their cause. No doubt some will be encouraged, others angered, by the statement below that even though the Polish government expressed "warm support" for one particular Jewish rescue proposal, its own internal correspondence on the matter actually reveals little warmth toward it.[27] By the same token, the reactions will probably be reversed upon reading that Jewish organizations in Palestine suborned the desertion of Jewish soldiers from Polish military units stationed in the country.[28] In neither case, though, will it be correct to infer that the statements in question were made in order to arouse those reactions or that the former was intended to portray the Poles as disingenuous and the latter to show the Jews as disloyal. Readers may wish to draw such value-laden conclusions from what they have read, but they must do so on their own responsibility; such readings may be inferred, but they are neither implied nor endorsed by this text.[29]

Those who do wish to employ the findings of this volume in reaching judgment in the current public controversy over Polish-Jewish relations should be cautioned, however, that the book tells only a small part of the story of those relations. It is concerned directly only with leaders and officials of the Polish government-in-exile and its agencies who maintained some connection with Jewish organizations during the latter half of the Second World War and with Jewish leaders and officials who carried on contacts with agencies of the Polish government outside of the occupied homeland. Relations between Poles and Jews in the occupied homeland itself are beyond the purview of this book, and they are considered only to the extent that an assessment of them entered into the thinking or decisions of one of the two sets of protagonists.[30] Even the most general conclusions of this text, then, pertain at most to several dozen persons and warrant no extrapolation from them with regard to the thinking that guided the Polish and Jewish underground leaderships or the various segments of the

Polish and Jewish communities at large about the Nazi campaign of total murder. To what extent the attitudes and actions of Polish and Jewish leaders abroad affected the attitudes and actions of Poles and Jews under Nazi rule is, to be sure, a most tantalizing question. Answering it, however, depends upon information whose presentation is within the scope neither of the present volume nor of its predecessor.

Demands

For Jews throughout the free world, December 1942 was a time to mourn. Black borders enclosing the front pages of Jewish newspapers and periodicals in the United States, Britain, and Palestine drew somber attention to the frightful news: in Nazi-occupied Europe 2 million persons had already fallen victim to a campaign to kill every Jewish man, woman, and child within reach, and 5 million more were in immediate danger that the same fate would soon be theirs.[1] In Jerusalem the General Council of the Jewish Community of Palestine (Va'ad Le'umi), with the agreement of the Jewish Agency Executive, set aside three days for "sounding the alarm, protest, and outcry" from 30 November to 2 December, including, on the final day, a twelve-hour work stoppage in all enterprises not deemed essential to the Allied war effort.[2] In New York, seven major American Jewish organizations declared Wednesday, 2 December, a day of prayer and fasting (a call ultimately answered by Jews in twenty-nine countries), and Jewish workers stopped production for ten minutes;[3] in London, Chief Rabbi of the British Commonwealth J. H. Hertz proclaimed a similar day of mourning for Sunday, 13 December.[4] One American Jewish publication greeted readers of its issue of 11 December with the cry, "How long, O Lord, wilt Thou forget me for ever?" echoing Psalm 13.[5] Another publication took its text from the Book of Lamentations: "Mine eye runneth down with rivers of water for the breach of the daughter of my people."[6]

The news that prompted such outpourings of grief—that the Jews under Nazi rule were being subjected not simply to a regime of violence and persecution but to a systematic program aimed at putting every one of them to death—was in itself not new at all. Notices of a German campaign of total murder had appeared in the Western and Palestinian press the previous summer,[7] but for the most part the Jewish leadership of the free world had not reacted strongly to them, at least not as strongly as it was to respond six months later.[8] What was new about the reports appearing at the end of 1942—aside from the figure of 2 million Jewish dead, a considerably larger toll than had ever been reported previously—was their firsthand confirmation by reliable eyewitnesses as well as the substantiation they received from the governments of the two Western Allies.[9] "A few months ago," stated the London *Zionist Review* in an editorial on 27 November, "the World Jewish Congress received reports . . . about Hitler's devilish plan to exterminate the Jewish population. The information seemed so fantastic that it was difficult to believe in its accuracy. In spite of the Nazis' policy of brutality and persecution, some people could not, even now, believe that they would embark on a policy deliberately calculated to exterminate millions of Jews."[10] Nevertheless, the newspaper reported, "inquiries have been instigated, and the results are shocking beyond all imagination." In similar fashion the *Jewish Chronicle* warned its readers that "to-day the very worst of the reports are confirmed. . . . No one now doubts—certainly not official circles—the reality of the extermination plan, and its progress towards completion."[11] If it had still been possible earlier to treat the awful communications emanating from Europe with a measure of hopeful disbelief, by the end of 1942 the threshold of denial had been emphatically crossed.

This change in attitude was reflected in the new operative conclusions that free-world Jewry drew from the latest reports. Jewish leaders realized that expressions of shock and anguish would now have to be followed by specific proposals for action directed at the Allied governments, who alone, they believed, had the power to stop the murder campaign. In particular, the recognition that the Nazis' total murder plan was already well on its way to completion appears to have driven home to these leaders that what had earlier been the primary thrust of their reaction to the news from Europe—prayers for a swift Allied victory and promises of retribution after the war— would no longer suffice. Jewish bodies in the United States, Britain, and Palestine thus began to press demands upon the Western Allies— foremost among them calls to find refuge for escapees from the Nazi death trap, to negotiate with Germany and other Axis states over the release of their Jews to the West, and to repeal the British White Paper of 1939, which had severely limited Jewish immigration to Palestine. These demands were voiced in newspaper advertisements and at public protest meetings as well as in memoranda and delegations to legislators and government officials.[12]

In addition to the two major Western Allies, Jewish organizations also directed demands concerning rescue to the Polish government-in-exile. Indeed, it made good sense for them to do so. The Nazis' murder program was being carried out primarily in Poland; the country held the largest concentration of Europe's Jews, and it was the site of the major killing centers to which Jews from many parts of the occupied continent were then being deported.[13] Much of the news about the progress of the so-called final solution had come from sources inside Poland, and the government-in-exile, which presided over a highly ramified underground organization that sent it frequent reports on the situation of Jews inside the country, had formed a significant link in transmitting the news of the Jewish fate to the free world.[14] In fact, on 10 December 1942, the Polish Foreign Ministry became the first governmental body publicly to confirm, on the basis of "fully authenticated information received from Poland in recent weeks," that the German authorities "aim with systematic deliberation at the total extermination of the Jewish population of Poland."[15] This statement in turn served as the catalyst for the declaration issued a week later by the eleven Allied governments and the French National Committee condemning "in the strongest possible terms" the "bestial [German] policy of cold-blooded extermination" and promising "to ensure that those responsible for these crimes shall not escape retribution, and to press on with practical measures to this end."[16] It thus seemed to Jewish leaders that the likelihood of Allied rescue action depended to a significant extent upon the manner in which the Polish government brought the information at its disposal to light.

Moreover, a large part of whatever rescue action was to be carried out would have to take place in Poland. The Allied governments could, of course, be called upon to provide havens for refugees from the Nazi inferno, but the initial acts that would allow the threatened Jews to become refugees in the first place—hiding the pursued from their pursuers and helping them across borders to countries where they were not in immediate danger[17]—would have to be undertaken by local elements. So, too, would most actions aimed at interfering with the deportations themselves, whether through sabotage or through direct armed confrontation with the deporters. In any such actions the attitude of the Polish underground leadership and of the Polish population at large stood to play a fundamental role. Because the underground movement was formally subordinate to the government-in-exile, and because the government-in-exile had

regularly stressed to the Western public the confidence that the con-
quered Polish people placed in their underground organization, Jewish leaders believed that the Polish authorities in London were in a
position to instill in the Poles of the occupied homeland a readiness
to come to the threatened Jews' aid.

Thus, beginning in late 1942, when the leaders of free-world Jewry
first placed the issue of immediate rescue on their public agenda in
notable measure,[18] Jewish organizations began to approach the Polish
government, calling upon it to undertake practical measures aimed
at helping as many Jews as possible avoid the sentence of death the
Nazis had placed upon them. The first organization to do so was
the Palestine-based Representation of Polish Jewry (Reprezentacja
Żydostwa Polskiego), a body consisting of representatives of most of
the major Jewish ethnic political parties that had functioned in Poland
between the wars.[19] On 19 November 1942 the Reprezentacja contacted the Polish consul-general in Tel Aviv, Henryk Rosmarin, with
a request to transmit to the government in London a cable containing
what was to become a basic demand made of the Polish authorities by
many Jewish groups:

> Further news received about the situation in the homeland re-
> ports the mass murder of Jews by Germans. The informants[20]
> report in addition that in some parts of the country the behavior
> of the Polish population during the bloody [anti-Jewish] actions
> was not beyond reproach. We are not in a position to control
> these reports; nevertheless we consider that the situation that has
> been created makes it necessary for authoritative Polish agents to
> intervene with the aim of calling the attention of the Polish popu-
> lation in the homeland to the necessity of resisting this exploit of
> Hitlerism. We note with pain that in the regular weekly broad-
> casts of the Ministry of Propaganda[21] to the homeland we do not
> find one word about the necessity for civil coexistence and mutual
> assistance between Poles and Jews, even at a time when the mur-
> der of Jews by Hitler has reached frightening proportions. Thus
> we turn to the government with the earnest request that in taking
> into consideration the situation of Polish Jews, which has become
> so much more acute, it launch immediately an action exhorting
> the Polish people in the homeland not to give in to the influence
> of the conquerors' anti-Jewish action and to resist it. We regard
> the matter as extremely important and urgent, for, as is appar-

ent from the aforementioned reports, Hitler has evidently begun the utter annihilation of Polish Jewry. We expect that the government will do everything with the aim of making the people of the homeland aware of what their reaction should be to these bestial plans of the enemy.[22]

Government officials soon heard the same demand from other sources as well. On 27 November 1942 a delegation from the British Section of the World Jewish Congress approached Polish Foreign Minister Edward Raczyński[23] with a suggestion that the government-in-exile issue, along with the other Allied governments, "an appeal to the people of the occupied countries, containing an expression of recognition for the help they have given individual Jews, especially Jewish children, and a call for the people to continue their efforts to rescue the innocent from death."[24] On 12 December Ignacy Schwarzbart, a Jewish member of the Polish National Council who spoke on behalf of Polish Jewish political groups affiliated with the World Zionist Organization, laid a demand for a similar government appeal to the Polish population before the secretary-general of the Polish prime minister's office, Adam Romer.[25] Schwarzbart repeated this demand three days later to Polish President Władysław Raczkiewicz[26] and subsequently to Deputy Prime Minister and Minister of the Interior Stanisław Mikołajczyk.[27] From Jerusalem, Polish Consul-General Witold Korsak notified his foreign ministry that the Hebrew-language newspapers in Palestine had been calling upon the government steadily and forcefully to broadcast to Poland about the German murder scheme and even to distribute flyers by airdrop to the Polish population urging it to take active measures to help the threatened Jews.[28] Indeed, at a meeting with representatives of the Palestine Jewish press held in Tel Aviv on 5 December, Stanisław Kot, the government-in-exile's former minister of the interior and ambassador to the Soviet Union, who was now about to take up a new post as Poland's government delegate in the Middle East, was asked by Zalman Rubashov, editor-in-chief of the influential daily organ of the General Federation of Jewish Workers, *Davar*, what the Polish government and underground had done "to counteract these [German] atrocities," and specifically whether Polish Information Minister Stanisław Stroński had broadcast a message to the homeland along these lines.[29] The next day, at a meeting with political leaders of the Palestinian Jewish community, Kot was requested by both Emil

Schmorak, a member of the Committee on Poland of the Jewish Agency, and by David ben Gurion, chairman of the Agency Executive and the single most powerful figure among Palestinian Jews, that "the Polish government, which gives aid to people in the Homeland, . . . tell the people in Poland to render aid to the Jews and to give them support."[30]

The demand that the government issue a formal instruction to the Polish people to come to the Jews' aid was not the only one that Jewish leaders placed before Polish officials at the end of 1942. The Palestinian spokesmen, the Reprezentacja, and the World Jewish Congress all called upon the Polish authorities, in the words of a cable from the Reprezentacja to Polish Prime Minister Władysław Sikorski dispatched on 7 December, to "do all in [their] power to cause the Allies to take immediate steps that could put an end to these [Nazi] crimes."[31] Among the specific steps mentioned by these groups were negotiations with the German government regarding further exchanges of Jews for German citizens located in Allied territory, creation of an international body to facilitate the transfer and support of Jews thus released, and opening the gates of the Allied and neutral countries and their overseas possessions, including Palestine, to Jewish refugees seeking temporary asylum.[32] With regard to the last measure the government was requested to issue a formal declaration guaranteeing "that after the war the evacuees will not be a burden upon the countries in which they will be staying" and that Jewish Polish citizens would be readmitted to Poland following liberation.[33] Other Jewish spokesmen asked for an announcement that Jews who managed to escape from occupied Poland would receive a maintenance stipend from the Polish government for the duration of the war.[34] In order to impress upon the Allied and neutral nations the urgency of these demands, the government was asked to provide a steady flow of information about the Jewish situation in Poland and especially to enlist the aid of the Vatican in giving credibility to these reports.[35] Jewish representatives also asked Polish government assistance in cajoling from the Allies a warning that all citizens of Axis countries and collaborators from the occupied states who participated in the killing or deportation of Jews would be punished after the war.[36] Some, most notably Szmul Zygielbojm, who represented the Jewish socialist party, the Bund, on the Polish National Council, even suggested that Jewish and Polish representatives together propose immediate Allied reprisals against German civilians.[37]

In addition to calling upon the government-in-exile to pressure the Allies with regard to rescue, Jewish leaders also petitioned the government to take certain concrete steps in its own right, even beyond issuing the proposed instruction to the Polish people. Already in its first meeting with Kot on 27 November 1942 the Reprezentacja specifically requested "that the Polish clergy be persuaded that it must raise its voice and protest against what is happening."[38] Later it asked in addition that the government facilitate contact and the transmission of aid between the Jews of Palestine and Poland by appointing Reprezentacja delegates to Polish diplomatic offices in Turkey, Sweden, Portugal, Switzerland, and Iran and that it keep the Reprezentacja apprised of news of the Jewish situation reaching the government from the occupied homeland.[39] Thinking about strengthening the connection between Palestinian and Polish Jewry in another way altogether, Ben Gurion inquired of Kot "whether the Polish Government would be in a position and would agree to send a number of confidential agents nominated by the Jewish Agency through their facilities [to Poland]" for the purpose of "mak[ing] contact with the Government delegates and send[ing] exact news about the situation of Jews in Poland through the channels available to the Polish Government."[40] Similarly, he informed the Polish minister that Palestinian Jewry was "interested in obtaining the help of the Polish Government in creating a Jewish army, made up of Jews who are under no obligation to serve in armies of other countries."[41] And Yitshak Gruenbaum, the doyen of Polish Jewish political leaders, a former deputy of the Polish Sejm then serving as head of the Jewish Agency's recently established Rescue Committee, placed before Kot a demand to create a special government ministry of Jewish affairs, "because Jews in general do not give weight to declarations but demand action."[42]

At the same time, the government was receiving demands from inside the occupied homeland as well. In mid-November 1942 Jan Karski, an emissary from the Polish underground, arrived in London bearing, among other things, messages for President Raczkiewicz, Prime Minister Sikorski, and Deputy Prime Minister Mikołajczyk from two Jewish political leaders—one a Zionist, the other from the socialist Bund—whom he had met in Warsaw prior to his departure. Essentially, Karski's Jewish contacts hoped that he might impress upon the Polish leadership in exile, and through it the Western Allies, the need to "adjust [the strategy of war] to include the rescue of a fraction of the unhappy Jewish people."[43] To this end

Karski reported that "the Polish Jews solemnly appeal to the Polish and Allied governments to undertake *extraordinary* measures in an attempt to stop the extermination," including retaliation bombing of German targets, reprisals against German prisoners of war and civilians, and threats of collective action against the entire German people should the murders not stop.[44] Such demands were, to be sure, largely the product of desperation, and it seems that neither their makers nor Karski really anticipated a favorable response.[45] However, Karski also carried requests for more modest measures that the Polish government could carry out on its own, without Allied assistance. He told Raczkiewicz that the Jewish leaders had asked him to call upon the Vatican to enforce "religious sanctions, excommunication included," against those who in any way assisted the murder program.[46] To Sikorski and Mikołajczyk (as well as to the Jewish members of the National Council, Schwarzbart and Zygielbojm) he passed on the Jewish hope that the government would order the underground authorities to take "punitive measures, executions included," against the "many Polish criminals [who] blackmail, denounce or even murder the Jews in hiding."[47] Sikorski was further advised that the Jewish leaders had demanded his intervention to direct the commander of the underground Home Army, Gen. Stefan Grot-Rowecki, to provide arms from the Home Army arsenal to the newly formed underground Jewish military organization.[48] Finally, Karski presented a general demand from the Jews of occupied Poland for money, food, medicines, clothing, and blank foreign passports—anything that might help them escape the country or remain alive in hiding.[49]

Yet another set of demands was laid before the government by a group of Polish underground activists who in September 1942 had created, with the consent of the office of the government delegate in the homeland,[50] the Civic Committee for Aiding the Jewish Population.[51] On 31 October the government delegate sent a radio message to London informing the government-in-exile of the establishment of this committee and requesting on its behalf an allocation of 500,000 zł. monthly.[52] Three further communications were dispatched to the government in January 1943, after the committee had been reconstituted on an expanded basis (incorporating representatives of Jewish as well as Polish political groups) and renamed the Council for Aid to Jews (Rada Pomocy Żydom). One message requested "the assignment from the budget of such amounts as will make it possible to carry out a program of relief action" encompassing the procurement of pecuniary aid, shelter, identity papers, and medical care for Jews attempting to hide from their pursuers.[53] The second indicated that "the Council has decided to approach the government in London about taking the initiative to convene a general committee to aid the Jews for the purpose of raising special funds and transmitting them to the homeland, beyond the amounts allocated from the budget for assistance to Jews." This cable, which like the one dispatched the previous October was signed by the government delegate, concluded with the statement that "the needs are enormous; substantial means are necessary."[54] The third message spelled out precisely what those needs and means were: in order to provide 10,000 children with assistance in even the paltry amount of 500 zł. (about $7.70) per month, the council would require a monthly allotment of 5 million zł. The signers of this dispatch indicated that they were requesting the government in London to transfer an appropriate sum, earmarked specifically for the council, through the delegate's office.[55]

Thus, in the wake of its seminal declaration of 10 December 1942, the Polish government-in-exile found itself pressed by a number of groups, both Jewish and Polish, both within the occupied homeland and abroad, to take a variety of concrete steps aimed at promoting the rescue of its Jewish citizens from the immediate threat to their lives posed by the Nazi conquerors. As 1942 turned to 1943, all of these groups anxiously awaited the government's response.

━━━━━━━━━

Demands that were presented orally and in person before government officials required, of course, an initial on-the-spot reaction. Such reactions were on the whole cautious, noncommittal, and to an extent defensive. Kot, for example, after receiving a list of four specific demands from a Reprezentacja delegation,[56] replied that "there is no need to put requests to us." The government, he stated, had already taken decisions on these matters and found that there was little that it could do beyond what it had already done on the Jews' behalf. He even chided the Jewish leadership for not being more active itself along these lines: "The Polish Government will gladly do everything [that it can]," he remarked, "but you too must not remain silent."[57]

In his discussions with other groups of Palestinian Jewish leaders Kot took essentially the same line.[58] In fact, the only demands with which the Polish minister expressed his unqualified agreement were the request to supply Jewish circles abroad with a steady flow of information about the situation of Polish Jewry and the call for the government to pledge that Jewish escapees from Poland would be readmitted into the country following liberation.[59] To the other demands presented to him during his stay in Palestine he replied in effect that although he was willing to look into them further, he did not hold out much hope for their realization.

In London, both Schwarzbart and the World Jewish Congress met similar responses. The latter, having requested the assistance of the Polish Foreign Ministry in presenting a comprehensive rescue program to the Allies as well as the Polish government's participation in certain of the steps it envisioned, was promised support by Raczyński, although at the time the foreign minister cautioned that a substantial rescue project could be carried out only at the initiative of the great powers.[60] In similar fashion Schwarzbart, who was concerned primarily with obtaining a government radio appeal to the Poles in the occupied homeland, noted that he was told initially by Adam Romer that a declaration of this sort might leave the unwelcome impression that the Polish people had not been helping the Jews all along; only after the Jewish representative suggested that the appeal call upon the Poles to increase the aid that they had already been providing did the Polish official agree to pursue the idea.[61] Nevertheless, two days later Antoni Serafiński of the Polish Interior Ministry reportedly informed the National Council member that no declaration would be issued.[62] Subsequently Schwarzbart was promised by Raczkiewicz that the Polish president himself would "take appropriate steps and consider in what form this [appeal] could be achieved."[63] Still, however, the Jewish leader remained less than sanguine about the prospects that an instruction such as he desired would ever be issued.[64]

It appears, though, that such essentially noncommittal responses were intended mainly as a temporary ploy until the government could consider the full ramifications of the various demands with which it was confronted. Alongside these initial oral replies, serious discussions aimed at considering the demands within the framework of the government-in-exile's overall political situation and long-range objectives were taking place behind the scenes. These discussions, in turn, proceeded in accordance with certain clear guidelines for dealing with Jewish matters that the government-in-exile had developed during the first three years of the war.

The first such guideline stemmed naturally from the Polish government's conception of itself as the defender first and foremost of the welfare and interests of the ethnic Polish community. This view of its purpose often led the government to relegate Jewish Polish citizens to the periphery of its universe of obligation or even to exclude them from that universe altogether.[65] To be sure, certain key government figures had stated from time to time that "the Polish Commonwealth belongs not only to the Polish nation . . . but also to the body of Polish citizens of different national origins";[66] but actually the government-in-exile had inherited from the twenty-year history of the Second Polish Republic the idea that the long-range interests and aspirations of ethnic Poles and Polish Jews were by and large opposed to one another. In the economic field, for example, most Polish government leaders appear to have believed—as Józef Retinger, Sikorski's personal secretary and a wielder of considerable influence in government circles behind the scenes, explained in 1941—that "the natural expansion of the Gentile population [in Poland] has been inhibited and stopped" by "the high percentage of Jews in its demographic organism" and that therefore Polish-Jewish tensions could ultimately be overcome only if the bulk of Polish Jewry left Poland.[67] This image of Poles and Jews as competitors for limited resources had found an echo during the first three years of the war in Polish-Jewish clashes over, among other things, the distribution of relief funds to refugees, recruitment into the exile Polish army in the Soviet Union, and inclusion of soldiers and civilians in the Polish military transports evacuated from the Soviet Union in 1942.[68]

Moreover, the government-in-exile was heir to an additional prewar perception that had been voiced with considerable vehemence during the early years of the Second Republic. This view held Jews to be for the most part subjectively ill-disposed toward the Polish cause.[69] During the first three years of the war Polish leaders often appear to have found putative proof of this axiom in Jewish behavior. When government officials learned, for example, that in September 1939 most Jews in eastern Poland had rejoiced at the invasion of the Red Army and, unlike most Poles, did not look upon the Soviet conquerors as equally opprobrious enemies as the Germans, they frequently tended to interpret this reception as an expression of hostility toward Poland.[70] The impression that Jews were not prepared to defend Polish independence was reinforced by reports reaching the government from the occupied homeland suggesting that whereas the primary goal of the Polish community vis-à-vis the occupiers was the reestablishment of Polish sovereignty, the Jews' goal was limited to physical survival.[71]

Some Polish officials also expressed the opinion that many Jewish citizens of Poland residing in the countries of Western Europe were evading their duty to serve in the exile Polish armed forces being mustered in France and Great Britain.[72] Finally, after Polish leaders had been stung on numerous occasions by Jewish charges that their behavior on issues of concern to Jews had demonstrated anti-Jewish prejudice, many appear to have tended more and more to believe in the existence of an ineluctable Jewish anti-Polonism.[73]

Such impressions led the government-in-exile to vitiate in practice its theoretical commitment to regard all Polish citizens equally, irrespective of their ethnic origins.[74] Instead of looking upon Polish Jews as citizens for whose well-being the Polish authorities bore the primary responsibility, the government-in-exile tended to treat them as members of a distinct national group whose needs and interests would be represented first of all by their own spokesmen, consisting not merely of Jewish citizens of Poland but of Jewish bodies throughout the world as well.[75]

The practical consequence of this view was that the Polish government did not for the most part feel itself duty bound to offer protection to Polish Jews in the same sense that it felt itself duty bound to protect ethnic Poles. Thus it tended on the whole to look upon action of any sort intended mainly for the benefit of Polish Jews not as something it was obligated to undertake by virtue of the fact that the Jews in question were citizens of the Polish state but, rather, as a voluntary activity in which it might take part should, for whatever reason, it appear desirable for it to do so. In other words, when the government-in-exile considered how it ought to respond to claims upon its resources put forward by Jewish spokesmen, the fundamental question it put to itself was one of utility: to what extent was the government's own interest, or that of the ethnic Polish community, likely to be served by accession to a particular Jewish demand?

The most important consideration that Polish leaders, in determining the answer to this question on a case-by-case basis, had raised during the first three years of the war had been the influence they believed Jews to hold over public opinion in Britain and the United States, especially with regard to the conflict between Poland and the Soviet Union over the status of the former Polish territories that had been occupied by Soviet forces in September 1939 and annexed by the USSR shortly thereafter.[76] From the outset of the war the Poles had been disconcerted by the hesitancy Allied leaders had shown in upholding the principle of Poland's territorial integrity vis-à-vis the Soviets. Their uneasiness had grown more pronounced following the failure of the Polish-Soviet agreement of 30 July 1941 to affirm the validity of the prewar boundary between the two countries. In light of the forceful role Britain had played in cajoling the Poles to acquiesce to such an inconclusive formulation and the refusal of the United States to become involved in territorial questions, the Polish government had come increasingly to suspect—with good reason, as things turned out—that its eastern territories were liable to be offered as a sacrifice on the altar of Allied unity by its two senior patrons. Thus Polish political leaders needed to find effective ways of influencing the formation of British and American foreign policy on the eastern border issue.

In this context the idea that world Jewry might be able to play a useful role had surfaced periodically in government circles. "The Jews," wrote a high-ranking Polish military intelligence officer, "are the best newspapermen in the world," concluding that "winning the Jewish world over [to the Polish cause] could facilitate our [propaganda] actions in the Allied countries tremendously."[77] On the other hand, it followed from the same premise that antagonizing Jewry might have an adverse effect upon Polish diplomacy, especially if it were true, as many Poles appear to have thought, that Jews tended by nature to be hostile to the Polish people's aspirations. Thus Polish government representatives had endeavored since late 1940 to win support for their position in the Polish-Soviet border dispute among the Jews of Britain, Palestine, and the United States, or at least to induce Jews to refrain from actions that might damage Poland's international image or even advance the Soviet cause more directly. During 1942 they had steadily intensified their efforts in this direction, even seeking ways to pressure Jewish organizations into compliance with their wishes. Although for the most part their advances had remained unrequited—thus giving further credence to the belief that Jews were incurably hostile toward their country—their perception of Jewish power had continued to inhibit them from writing the Jews off as irredeemable enemies.[78]

A further area in which Polish government leaders believed that Jewish influence over British and American public opinion might have a positive effect for the Polish community was the campaign for Allied action against Germany in retaliation for the persecution of Poles in the occupied homeland. The Polish government had been actively involved in this campaign at least since early 1941,[79] yet government officials appear to have felt that, despite intensive Polish propaganda efforts, the Western Allies remained insufficiently informed about the oppression of the Polish people under the German yoke. In this context some officials seem to have thought that statements about the Polish plight emanating from Jewish sources might have a greater impact in the West than statements made by Poles. Thus, for example, Olgierd Górka, head of the Nationalities Division of the Polish Ministry of Information, had made repeated efforts during 1941 to enlist the assistance of Jewish political leaders and representatives of the Jewish press in calling attention to the atrocities being perpetrated by the Nazis against both Poles and Jews.[80] A memorandum from an underground source, probably dating from mid-1942, had underscored the wisdom of this strategy; after pointing out that the Polish nation was involved in "a war of material and moral annihilation as victim of the most brutal German persecution," the memorandum suggested that "if Polish reports from the homeland do not meet with complete credence on the part of the English-speaking nations, because they are [regarded as] altogether improbable, then it will be necessary to get at their governments through Jewish reports," especially reports directly related to the slaughter of Polish Jewry.[81] Evidently the belief was common in Polish circles that the Allied countries might be more sensitive to the Jewish than to the Polish plight.

From this premise it followed that news of the suffering of the Jewish population in Poland could throw the barbarity of the Nazi regime in the country as a whole into sharper focus than could news of Polish suffering alone and perhaps even inspire the Allies to action that would redound to the Polish population's benefit. To that end during the first three years of the war the government periodically released news of the situation of Polish Jewry under occupation as part of more extensive statements about Nazi persecution of Poles, guided, apparently, by a strategy that called for the oppression of both groups to be presented under the same general rubric. In mid-1942 this strategy had even brought a tangible gain, as the government and the National Council, largely by calling attention to recently received information about the Jewish situation, managed to obtain public declarations from the British and American governments that Germans guilty of abusing civilian populations would be called to account for their crimes following the conclusion of hostilities.[82]

Some Polish leaders even appear to have believed that by drawing attention among the Western Allies to the Jewish plight the government-in-exile might open channels that could perhaps eventually be used to help Poles escape the horrors of Nazi occupation. Thinking along these lines had evidently crystallized in September 1942, following receipt of reports from unoccupied France that the Vichy government had begun to hand over non-French Jews (including some 6,000 Jewish citizens of Poland) to the Germans for deportation eastward.[83] On 5 September, for example, Sikorski had written to Raczyński that the Vichy regime's anti-Jewish actions had aroused anxiety among Polish emigrés and refugees in France,[84] who feared that "similar measures would be applied to them."[85] In calling attention to this situation, the prime minister had further noted that Polish agents familiar with the situation in France believed that a warning directed by the United States to the Vichy government against further deportation of Jews "would be the most effective means of providing safety for Poles located on the territory of unoccupied France." One week later Labor Minister Jan Stańczyk had suggested to Raczyński that "the news coming from unoccupied France about the arrest and planned delivery to the Germans of Jewish citizens of Poland demands that all steps be taken that . . . will give at least the tiniest hope of protection for those Polish citizens . . . from the massacre awaiting them in Germany," adding that he attached all the more importance to such measures out of fear "that the delivery of Jewish Polish citizens to the Germans may be a precedent that will subsequently lead to the handing over of all Polish citizens."[86] Specifically, Stańczyk had urged the foreign minister to request that one of the neutral countries or the United States extend legal protection to all Polish citizens in the unoccupied zone and also to call upon various Allied governments to issue entry visas to threatened Jews as a possible means of facilitating their exit from France; he had indicated that such steps were especially urgent because recent dispatches from the ranking Polish diplomat in France did "not rule out the possibility that the deportation procedure would be applied to Polish workers as well."[87]

For his part, Raczyński had already decided on 11 September "to embark upon a forceful *démarche* against the French government in this matter in the name of humanitarian principles," explaining to Sikorski that such action was desirable "both in order to give expression to our concern for the fate of Jewish Polish citizens and in order to warn Vichy of the consequences of widening the forced deportations to include Polish workers and soldiers."[88] Moreover, he had subsequently not only called upon the governments of the several Allied and neutral countries to declare their readiness to give asylum to limited numbers of Jewish refugees from France but had even begun to explore the possibility of providing Polish Jews in that country with papers falsely attesting to their and their parents' Catholicism, in order to help them gain exit visas from the country.[89] Apparently, in this situation at least, the threat that Jews and Poles might share a common fate at the hands of the Nazis had proven capable of moving Polish leaders to advocate and to take action aimed at rescuing Jews even before Jewish leaders themselves had demanded such action.[90]

In the end, the government-in-exile's efforts on behalf of Polish Jews in France had been unsuccessful, both because the Allied and neutral governments had for the most part flatly refused the Poles' calls for action and because, on 11 November 1942, German forces had taken direct control of the former unoccupied zone, effectively nullifying whatever power the Vichy government might previously have had to stop the deportations or to permit Jews to leave the country.[91] Nevertheless, the government's response to the deportations from the unoccupied zone indicated that under certain circumstances the Polish regime could be motivated to champion the cause of rescuing Jews. In order for it to do so, it evidently needed to be convinced that a critical Polish interest was threatened and that forthright advocacy of a matter of vital Jewish concern might somehow help to attenuate that threat. Polish leaders appear on the whole to have believed that in theory such ties between Polish and Jewish interests could exist, both in the campaign to guarantee the prewar frontier between Poland and the Soviet Union and in the struggle against German anti-Polish terror. In confronting Jewish demands for rescue at the end of 1942 and the beginning of 1943, then, they needed to ascertain first of all whether at that particular moment such a nexus existed in practice— whether a critical Polish interest was in that instant being threatened and whether accession to some or all of the Jewish demands might help push the immediate menace aside.

As it happened, when Jewish spokesmen had begun to press the Polish government on rescue, the situation facing the Poles in their battle against both of their major enemies—the Soviets and the Germans—was bleak. Poland's hopes for restoring its eastern border had been dealt a severe blow the previous summer with the evacuation of the Polish exile army from the Soviet Union to the Middle East.[92] Shortly thereafter a new point of friction had developed in Polish-Soviet relations, as the Soviet authorities arrested a sizable group of relief workers attached to the Polish Embassy in the country as spies.[93] Although the United States intervened on behalf of these Polish officials,[94] it was not prepared to press the Soviets on the territorial issue.[95] In late November 1942 Sikorski had set out for Washington in order to present the Polish case on boundaries to the Roosevelt administration, but his requests for support for his country's eastern border claims had been rebuffed.[96] Earlier Winston Churchill had put off a similar request from the Polish prime minister for British support.[97]

Following Sikorski's return from the United States in January 1943, the Polish predicament became even more acute. On 16 January the Soviets abruptly informed the Polish Embassy in Kuibyshev (the temporary Soviet capital) that they would no longer recognize the Polish citizenship of ethnic Poles from the annexed territories.[98] This step was undoubtedly aimed at further consolidation of Soviet rule in these provinces. In response Sikorski raised the possibility of traveling to Moscow to confront the territorial issue directly, but he evidently abandoned the idea when British Foreign Secretary Anthony Eden informed him that the British government was not prepared "to commit itself to support any particular frontier." Eden further suggested that the American position was identical to the British one[99]—a suggestion that may have been deceptive at the time it was made but one whose accuracy Roosevelt was to confirm to Eden less than two weeks later.[100]

Moreover, as Poland's diplomatic position vis-à-vis the Soviets was becoming increasingly precarious, political developments in the occupied homeland and the course of the war on the eastern front had combined to make the government-in-exile more dependent than ever on the good graces of the Western Allies. Moscow had already (in late 1941) catalyzed the establishment of the pro-Communist Polish Workers Party (Polska Partia Robotnicza—PPR), a body whose existence was a continual source of consternation to the underground organizations loyal to the government in London. These latter groups believed that the main purpose of PPR was to prevent the return of the exile leadership to the homeland following liberation and to replace it with a Communist regime.[101] In October 1942 underground Home Army Commander Grot-Rowecki had reported to Sikorski that PPR—together with its military arm, the People's Guard (Gwardia

Ludowa)—had made notable inroads among certain segments of the Polish population.[102] Earlier, in June, Grot-Rowecki had addressed to the prime minister a memorandum raising the possibility that the end of the war might see Soviet forces chasing the retreating Wehrmacht across Poland—a scenario that, with the growing Communist presence inside the country, would render the chances for restoring the 1939 frontiers, and perhaps even for avoiding a Communist takeover, precarious indeed. In such a situation, he observed, British and American support would represent virtually the only hope for the government-in-exile to achieve its most fundamental war aim.[103] Sikorski essentially agreed with this analysis (although he disagreed with the Home Army commander over how the underground armed forces ought to behave in such a situation); on the eve of his departure for Washington he reemphasized to Grot-Rowecki that the Polish-Soviet border dispute would ultimately be decided in the international arena.[104] In the meantime, moreover, the Red Army had launched its counterattack at Stalingrad and had begun its march westward. What had—when Grot-Rowecki first put forward his ideas about the consequences of the presence of Soviet troops on Polish soil at the end of the war—seemed like a doubtful course of events now appeared an ever more likely forecast.[105] On 12 January 1943 the Home Army commander suggested to Sikorski that once Russian troops entered Polish territory, airborne landings both by Polish troops in the west and by British and American forces would be necessary in order to prevent Soviet "acts of disloyalty" toward Poland.[106]

Sikorski was not about to press the Western Allies for what amounted to military action against the Soviets unless the acts of disloyalty referred to by Grot-Rowecki actually took place.[107] He did, however, continue to be interested in bringing about direct Allied military action in Poland in response to German atrocities against Poles.[108] No doubt his interest, and that of other government leaders, was heightened by the receipt of reports from the underground in late 1942 indicating a marked stepping up of German anti-Polish terror. A statement from a government courier delivered on 27 November 1942 noted that "mass murders of Polish intellectuals and Polish peasants . . . have assumed hitherto unknown proportions." [109] Four weeks later Grot-Rowecki radioed Sikorski that the Germans had begun systematically depopulating villages in the Generalgouvernement so that German colonists could settle there.[110] On the same day Stefan Korboński, head of the underground's Directorate of Civilian Resistance

(Kierownictwo Walki Cywilnej), notified Mikołajczyk that fifty-four villages in the Zamość region alone had been destroyed, including one in which 170 peasants had been murdered.[111] In such a situation many Poles evidently began to fear, as Grot-Rowecki indicated as early as 10 November 1942 in an order to Home Army soldiers, that "after the completion of this action [of destroying the Jews] the Germans will begin to liquidate the Poles in the same fashion."[112] Indeed, Korboński declared explicitly that "everything indicates that the occupier is moving toward the planned annihilation of the peasants."[113] Similarly, the government courier spoke of a German "plan for the complete extermination of the Polish people."[114]

Such apprehensions gave rise to a series of demands on the part of Poles in the homeland for measures to be taken on their behalf. Both Grot-Rowecki and Korboński reported that the Home Army would initiate some sort of armed action against continued deportations of Polish peasants and indicated that assistance from the West, in the form of arms, ammunition, and air support, would be necessary if such action were to have the desired effect.[115] Korboński also called upon the government to "alarm the world" and to "threaten retaliatory bombing of unarmed German cities."[116] This call was echoed in the courier's message, which also made so bold a demand as "an immediate Anglo-Saxon [military] offensive at any point in the European continent." "In the event that the Great Powers are able to contemplate calmly the frightful atrocities committed on Poles and on other peoples," the courier continued, "the underground leaders in Poland demand that our Polish air forces be organized into a separate unit and assigned to retaliation bombing."[117]

Thus far, however, the Western Allies had given no more indication of sensitivity to the outcry of the Polish people for salvation from German terror than they had of support for Poland's eastern border claims. At the end of 1942 and the beginning of 1943, then, the Polish government found itself searching ever more desperately for ways of influencing Britain and the United States on both fronts.[118] Critical Polish interests were indeed being threatened, and the immediacy of the threat called for a bold and imaginative Polish response.

Within this context the Jewish demands for action to rescue Polish Jewry were received by the government-in-exile in London. Jewish organizations in the free world appeared to Polish leaders to be in a position, should they be so inclined, to influence Allied policymakers in a direction that might help attenuate the peril to the Poles in both the international and the domestic arenas. The fact that these same organizations were now coming to the Polish government with demands that were a matter of life and death for millions of their own people stood, then, conceivably to be employed as a lever for extracting the desired behavior from them. Thus the idea began to circulate among some Polish officials that the best way to respond to the Jewish demands might be to offer the Jews of the free world a straightforward political deal: the Polish government would take action along the lines put forth by the various Jewish organizations, provided that those same organizations would use their supposed influence in the West both to advance the Polish cause on the diplomatic front and to encourage Allied action not only on behalf of threatened Jews but on behalf of threatened Poles as well.

This approach had first been tried by Stanisław Kot—apparently on his own initiative—during his discussions with Jewish leaders in Palestine.[119] In response to the Reprezentacja's demand that the government instruct Poles in the homeland to come to the aid of their Jewish fellow citizens, the ambassador had suggested that Jews ought to issue a public declaration calling for the return of Lwów and Wilno to Poland. He had also insisted that Jews cease publicizing allegations of anti-Jewish discrimination in the evacuation of the Polish army from the Soviet Union—allegations that the government-in-exile felt might seriously damage Poland's image in the West and thereby strengthen the Soviet hand.[120] Later he had told Yitshak Gruenbaum that the Polish government had certain demands of its own vis-à-vis the Jews, including one regarding organized Jewish support for Allied reprisals against the Germans and for Poland's territorial claims in both the east and the west.[121]

The initial Jewish response to Kot's demands had been negative. None of the Jewish leaders with whom the Polish diplomat had met had indicated any willingness to consider striking a bargain along the lines he had suggested.[122] This fact was reflected most starkly in a report prepared by the deputy chief of Polish military intelligence in Palestine shortly after a round of discussions between Kot and representatives of various Palestinian Jewish bodies. "With regard to Polish matters," the military official wrote, "the attitude of the Jewish Agency may be defined as indifferent if not hostile, and several of the Jewish Agency's moves are even downright damaging to the Polish cause."

In sum, he claimed, "the disposition of the Jewish Agency toward the Polish authorities can be reduced to the principle: 'Demand and take away whatever you can, but give nothing of yourself.'"[123] His conclusion was seconded by Consul-General Korsak from Jerusalem, who during January 1943 filed a series of reports with the Polish Foreign Ministry speaking of a "campaign by the Hebrew press concerning the alleged apathy of the Polish government in the face of the extermination of the Jews being carried out by the Germans"[124] and claiming that "during the past few weeks [Palestinian Jewish] public opinion with regard to Polish matters has taken a turn for the worse."[125]

The consul attributed this purported development in large measure to a deliberate Soviet attempt to drive a wedge between Poles and Jews. Indeed, Polish officials in the Middle East were aware that the Soviets had recently intensified their own efforts to win Palestinian Jewish public opinion to their side in their dispute with the Poles.[126] Only a short while earlier two officials of the Soviet Embassy in Ankara had visited Palestine with the purpose, among others, of organizing a council for cultural exchange with the USSR among the country's Jewish population, a development at which Korsak had looked askance.[127] To the consul's mind the Soviets were "tying the problem of Polish-Jewish relations to the question of our eastern territories," and he worried lest "exacerbating these relations play into their hands once it again becomes possible for the Red Army to gain position upon Polish territory."[128]

In considering their response to Jewish demands for rescue, then, Polish leaders needed to balance their hope that Jews would intervene diplomatically on Poland's behalf with their sense that the Jews were not likely to do so and with their fear that the Jews might even publicly support the Soviet side. In this situation Kot, for one, appears to have been willing to make a favorable gesture toward the Jews even without a positive response on their part to the conditions that he had raised in his talks with the leaders of Palestinian Jewry. In fact, it seems that he even tried to portray the results of his mission to Palestine in more optimistic terms than the actual course of his discussions warranted. In a cable to London dispatched on 2 February 1943 he stated that he had "devoted much time and patience to Jewish matters, hoping to alleviate the constant suspicion and ill feeling" that prevailed toward Poland in Palestine as well as "to remove the troublesome suggestions that go forth from here to America"; and he hinted that he would be transmitting to the government a number of recommendations about how it might be possible to secure Jewish cooperation in the future, including on the matter of Polish-Soviet relations. The most important of these recommendations, he declared, was to accede to the Jewish demand for the government to assure neutral countries that Polish Jews who found asylum in them would be readmitted to Poland once the war ended. He also expressed his support for the creation of a special bureau of Jewish affairs within the Polish prime minister's office, and he ended by observing that Palestinian Jewry would "gladly cooperate" with the newly appointed consul-general in Jerusalem, Jan Drohojowski, who, he claimed, "knew how to win them to his side." [129]

Kot was able nonetheless to adduce a substantive reason why the Polish government ought to respond favorably to at least two Jewish requests even without obtaining quid pro quo. As he stated in his cable of 2 February, "I request that this formality, which politically will pay us extremely well, be carried out, as it is connected with previous declarations by the government." [130] Evidently he believed that the measures he recommended possessed a propaganda value beyond whatever potential they might have for inducing a reciprocal gesture from world Jewry; indeed, they might actually demonstrate to the British and American public the Polish government's beneficent intentions toward the Jews even in the face of continuing Jewish complaints of Polish anti-Jewish discrimination. To this contention he added the negative argument that such steps would not extend the scope of the government's declared obligations toward Jews beyond that which the government had already acknowledged. [131]

Other Polish figures, however, appear to have perceived a danger in Kot's strategy no matter what the Jewish response to it. Some expressed concern lest the increased publicity that would necessarily be accorded the Jewish plight in consequence of Kot's proposals divert attention from the desperate situation of the Poles themselves. Thus, for example, Jerzy Kurcjusz, Poland's vice-consul in Istanbul and chief of Polish intelligence operations in the Balkans, who had been dispatched to his post by Kot in August 1940 and had accompanied him to Palestine, [132] noted, in a top secret memorandum of 4 February 1943, that although, in his view, "guaranteeing at least a neutral if not a friendly stance on the part of the Jews at the peace conference is a matter of paramount importance," the assignment of space to Jewish matters in Polish propaganda should be made "on condition that the sufferings of the Jewish people will not . . . overshadow the magnitude of the losses and sufferings of the Polish people, who are oppressed in Poland certainly no less than the Jews." For this reason, it seems, he hoped that the general expressions of goodwill that Kot had offered at a banquet given by the Reprezentacja in his honor two weeks earlier had been propagandistic rather than programmatic in nature.[133]

In the same memorandum Kurcjusz expressed additional objections to the strategy advanced by Kot. In his view, guaranteeing that Jews who escaped from the Nazi clutches would be readmitted to Poland after the war might run counter to the long-range interests of the Polish nation. "Promises and declarations now made to the Jews," he admonished, were liable to be "called in in such a way that not only the Polish Jews but also those [Jews] deported earlier from Austria, Germany, Slovakia, Croatia, and other places to Poland will claim the right to settle in Poland." He explained that should this happen, the number of Jews in the homeland following liberation might well, despite the continuing German butchery, reach a level approaching that of the immediate prewar years—a level that, in his words, "did damage to the Polish people." He hoped that after the war Poland's Jewish population would not exceed 600,000; any greater number, he believed, would interfere with "the normal development of the nation and state." Yet, according to his estimates, which he claimed to have derived from Jewish sources, there were in January 1943 some 700,000 Jews remaining in the Generalgouvernement alone, and he feared that a large additional number might be found in the eastern territories, the Ukraine, the Wilno region, and the areas along the Russian front. Hence it seemed to him that Poland was likely to emerge from the war with a "surplus" of Jews, who would—"both for the good of the Polish people and of the Jews themselves"—have to be induced to leave the country. In such a situation, it hardly seemed advisable to him to make public promises about taking back into Poland, following liberation, Jews who had already left the country.[134]

Kurcjusz's comments echoed warnings reaching the government-in-exile from the occupied homeland. A report from the underground carried to London by Jan Karski in November 1942 indicated that although German bestiality toward the Jews had aroused "sympathy [for the victims] and condemnation of the Hitlerite methods" among the Poles and had caused "antisemitic attitudes to become less pronounced," the demand for "rapid regulation of the Jewish question following the war along the lines of voluntary or forced emigration of the Jewish masses" remained "widespread."[135] Similarly, in his own evaluation of attitudes among the Polish population Karski noted that the underground press of the National Party (Stronnictwo Narodowe) continued to call for an "uncompromising struggle with Jewry," while extreme right-wing underground publications had adopted "a hostile attitude" toward the Jews, an attitude "not expressing any feeling at all with regard to the German terror against the Jewish population." These latter publications, he observed further, also tended to charge the government with "being dependent upon the Jews." On the other hand, he gave no indication that the underground press of any of the center or left-wing parties were especially concerned with the Jewish situation one way or another.[136]

All of these comments spoke directly to concerns that had been felt in government circles virtually since the exile regime had been created. From the first year of the war the government had been receiving periodic warnings from sources in the Polish underground not to appear overly solicitous of Jewish concerns, lest it lose credibility with the masses of Poles, who, the reports suggested, tended to view Jewish interests as, for the most part, inconsistent with their own.[137] Specifically, underground reports had consistently advised that in the liberated Poland of the future, "the Jewish problem can be solved only through a massive . . . emigration of Jews" leading to the removal of "Jewish supremacy in economic life"[138] and had indicated that "without . . . a minimal program" to accomplish this goal, "no government will be able to rule in Poland peacefully and for a long time."[139] Moreover, by the time the Jewish demands had been placed on the government's agenda, some of the regime's opponents in exile appear to have been attempting to advance their cause through allegations of undue Jewish influence in Polish policymaking circles.[140] In such a situation government officials must have been aware that accession to some of the Jewish demands—especially those concerning issuing instructions to the Polish population to assist the threatened Jews and declaring readiness to readmit Jewish refugees to Poland after the war—could involve significant political risk for them. They also appear to have demonstrated apprehension during the first three years of the war that giving publicity to the sufferings of Jews in Poland might divert public attention from the plight of the Poles.[141] Thus Kurcjusz's caveat not to assign too much space in Polish propaganda to the Jewish situation undoubtedly fell upon receptive ears.

Under these circumstances, some government leaders may actually have felt relieved that Jewish spokesmen appeared to be balking at Kot's tacit offer of a political exchange. Indeed, had Jews indicated a willingness to undertake the specific pro-Polish initiatives that Kot had sought from them, the Polish government might have found itself constrained to satisfy the Jewish demands in return—and thus to expose itself to the possibly serious side effects that such action entailed. As a result, the strategy of attempting to use its unique position as a link between potential Jewish victims of the Nazi murder campaign and the means of their rescue as a vehicle for influencing the behavior of Jewish organizations in the free world appears to have been contemplated with considerable hesitancy by the government-in-exile at the end of 1942 and the beginning of 1943. The government would no doubt rather have employed an alternate means of gaining at least the neutrality if not the support of Western Jewry with regard to the Polish-Soviet dispute and of enlisting Jewish energies in the campaign to elicit Allied action on behalf of the Poles in the occupied homeland. It also would undoubtedly have preferred to draw Allied attention to the plight of the Poles without making simultaneous reference to the Jewish situation. In this context government leaders would understandably be reluctant to give Jewish spokesmen a lever with which they could potentially move the Poles to take steps that the Poles really did not wish to take.

At the time, however, it appeared questionable whether the government would be able to find any alternate means of obtaining these objectives. Indeed, even as the proper response to the Jewish demands was being debated in government circles, Poland's ambassador in Washington, Jan Ciechanowski, warned that the American Jewish press was likely to use Sikorski's upcoming visit to the United States as an opportunity to score the Polish government's record on Jewish issues. Such action, he claimed, would be carried out "in conjunction with the efforts of Soviet propaganda . . . to accuse the Polish government of antisemitism on every occasion."[142] Similarly, recent attempts by the government to publicize German atrocities against Poles without referring to the murder of Jews had borne little fruit.[143] Thus the government could not permit itself to ignore either the rescue demands of Jews in the free world or the news of the systematic murder of Jews in Poland that had prompted those demands. It needed at least, as Anthony Eden observed in a note to his colleague, Information Minister Brendan Bracken, "to take a prominent part in condemning these German actions and . . . to show that they [*sic*] have no sympathy for anti-Semitic measures."[144] The question confronting Polish policymakers in determining the government's response to the Jewish demands, then, was how they could take such a part without undertaking steps that might create problems for them in other areas, while at the same time manipulating as effectively as possible the influence that free world Jewry appeared to them to hold over the future of the Polish cause.

The direction that Polish policy was to take in this regard was adumbrated on 3 December 1942 in a telegram from Raczyński to Chaim Weizmann, president of the World Zionist Organization. After acknowledging that the government had "recently obtained the confirmation of the monstrous slaughters carried on by the Germans on Jews in Poland" and conveying to the Zionist leader his "heartfelt compassion with the martyrdom which the German barbarians have inflicted on the Jewish nation," the foreign minister declared that "the Polish Government and the Polish nation have pilloried with horrified indignation these mass murders" and pledged that "the Polish Government is determined that the dehumanized perpetrators of these dreadful deeds shall receive a punishment commensurate with their crimes."[145] With this statement Raczyński, while clearly placing Poland in the forefront of the outcry against the systematic murder of European Jewry, actually committed his government to no action beyond verbal protest and intervention with the Allies on behalf of a measure that Poles had been demanding in their own cause for some time.[146]

Indeed, over the next two months the only steps that Jewish spokesmen had demanded that were actually undertaken by the Polish administration were those directed toward the Allied and neutral powers. In this regard, though, the Poles demonstrated considerable alacrity. They passed on a number of notes to the governments of Great Britain and the United States containing rather extensive descriptions of aspects of the German murder campaign and emphasizing that "it is the deliberate policy of the German Government to wipe out the Jewish race in Poland."[147] Additionally they called upon the two major Western Allies to reconvene the St. James's Palace Conference on German Atrocities, which had initially met in January 1942, in order to take note of the Jewish situation.[148] When the British government rejected this suggestion, the Poles pressed the Allies to issue a formal joint declaration condemning Germany's actions toward the Jews—a declaration that was in fact issued on 17 December.[149] They also requested and received time to broadcast information on the Jewish fate over the Home Service of the BBC.[150] They addressed a note to the Vatican about the murder of Jews and asked "that the Holy See . . . clearly and distinctly condemn" the German crimes.[151] They also prepared a brochure entitled *The Mass Extermination of Jews in German Occupied Poland*, containing, among other documents, the text of the Polish government's own formal diplomatic note of 10 December officially confirming the news of the Nazi murder program.[152] Some 200 copies of this brochure were distributed among twenty-three Polish diplomatic missions throughout the world for further circulation among interested institutions and individuals.[153]

Polish representatives also passed on to the Allied governments certain specific Jewish demands for rescue action. At a meeting of the foreign ministers of the European Allies held in London, at Eden's invitation, on 18 January 1943, Raczyński "mentioned steps that must be undertaken with the aim of having the United Nations and the neutrals receive Jews who may manage to escape Germany or the Germans' reach," including "a plan to challenge the Germans to release the Jews." In bringing up this plan he pointed out that "such a challenge would require . . . organized international cooperation in order to take in the Jews who would be resettled." [154] Two days later, in conjunction with demands presented to him by the World Jewish Congress, he instructed Ambassador Ciechanowski in Washington to explore the attitude of the U.S. government toward negotiating with Germany over evacuating Jewish women and children from occupied areas and toward arranging international assistance for Jewish refugees from the Nazi terror.[155] On 30 January Ciechanowski discussed these matters with the State Department.[156] Neither the British nor the U.S. government, however, indicated much enthusiasm for any of these ideas. In fact, the U.S. undersecretary of state told the Polish ambassador specifically that "there can be no discussion at the present time of any international action aiming at securing Germany's agreement to a large-scale evacuation of Jews." [157]

Such a response to their overtures does not appear to have surprised the Poles. In fact, in issuing his instruction to Ciechanowski on 20 January, Raczyński had even noted in an aside that "with regard to approaching Germany on the matter of evacuating the Jews, I have encountered among several Allied governments (including among their representatives of Jewish origin) objections motivated by the fear 'that the Germans will agree.'"[158] Perhaps in consideration of such objections, as well as in response to Kot's prodding,[159] the government even went so far as to adopt on 12 February the resolution long sought by Jewish spokesmen promising the Allied and neutral nations "that Poland will readmit all citizens of Poland who during the war have found or will find shelter in those countries."[160] In doing so, government leaders were undoubtedly aware that this step would be greeted negatively in certain Polish political circles. Evidently, however, the potential propaganda benefit of such action, which Kot had stressed in advocating it, outweighed the potential risks of which Kurcjusz had warned.[161]

On the other hand, the regime's policymakers appeared to have taken most seriously Kurcjusz's admonition not to let publicity given the Jewish situation eclipse the plight of the Poles. As forthright as government interventions on behalf of the Jews were, they were overshadowed by a simultaneous campaign to rouse the Allies to action on behalf of the Polish community. The government's intention not to permit the murder of Polish Jewry to occupy the spotlight of Western attention alone, or even to appear substantially more alarming than German anti-Polish terror, was in fact signaled somewhat ironically in a press bulletin prepared by the Polish Government Information Center in New York on 1 January 1943 for Yiddish-language newspapers in the United States. Following a notice of a published Swedish report that only 30,000 Jews remained in Warsaw, the bulletin presented a full-page release about "a new mass terror action against Poles that the Germans have begun," including a statement that "in the Lublin district the Germans are systematically and methodically annihilating the entire Polish population."[162] Similarly, the government-sponsored daily *Dziennik Polski* published regular reports throughout the month of January of a German program to "wipe out the Polish nation," while devoting far less attention to the ongoing slaughter of the Jews.[163] In the middle of the month Mikołajczyk called a special press conference to discuss recently received reports of mass arrests of Poles in Warsaw,[164] and on 27 January Sikorski issued a statement to the press urging "a plan of immediate reprisals against the Germans" for their "wholesale destruction of all classes of the Polish population."[165]

Simultaneous Polish diplomatic actions also stressed the Polish far more than the Jewish predicament. On 2 January, President Raczkiewicz prepared an appeal to the Vatican for intervention on the Poles' behalf, writing that "extermination of the Jews, which included many Christians of the Semitic race, turned out to be merely an attempt at pre-testing the methods of the scientifically designed and systematically implemented mass murder . . . [now being] applied against the native Polish population." [166] Five days later the National Council adopted two resolutions (one for publication, the other secret) stating that "all of the nations of the earth must be made aware that the liquidation of the Polish population is proceeding on Polish territory in districts selected by the Germans according to plan" and calling upon the government to "formulate and carry out, together with the Allies, a plan for immediate reprisals against the Germans." [167] Minister of Industry Jan Kwapiński passed on to the leadership of the British Labour Party a series of communications from Polish socialists in underground claiming that the German occupiers were now about to do to the Poles in the homeland what they had already done to the Jews.[168] On his visit to Washington in early January, Sikorski again raised the demand for retaliatory measures with U.S. government officials, as he did with the British government following his return to London in the middle of the month.[169]

To be sure, the lack of responsiveness demonstrated by Britain and the United States toward the Jewish demands conveyed to them by the Polish government cannot be attributed to the fact that Polish spokesmen were generally reluctant to present the Jewish situation without making simultaneous and greater reference to the sufferings of the Poles. Indeed, the Allies on the whole proved no more amenable to Polish than to Jewish demands for action on behalf of those in mortal danger from the Nazi occupiers, and they specifically rejected the concept of retaliatory bombing.[170] Nevertheless, the tacit insistence of Polish leaders that government references to the Jewish plight be surrounded as much as possible by discussion of the Polish people's distress strongly suggests that in passing on Jewish calls for rescue to the Allied governments Polish policymakers hoped primarily to heighten Allied sensitivity to the predicament of the Poles in the homeland and eventually to win Allied assent to their own demands for anti-German reprisals. Indeed, this objective of the government was explicitly acknowledged by a senior Foreign Ministry official in a confidential memorandum of 4 January 1943 to Polish diplomatic posts throughout the world. Commenting on Raczyński's note to the Allied governments of 10 December 1942 on the mass murder of Polish Jewry (the text of which had now been prepared for distribution in pamphlet form), this official stated that "the original intention of the Polish government was to introduce into the text of the declaration the principle of applying repressive measures (through bombardment, for example) against Germany for carrying out mass murders equally against the Christian population of the occupied countries, especially Poland." And although, he added, "our position did not find an echo in the joint [Allied] declaration [of 17 December 1942] . . . , the Polish government continues to strive for acceptance by the Allies of the principle of retaliation, in the conviction that it is . . . the most effective means of restraining Germany from applying barbaric methods of extermination against the peoples of the occupied countries." [171]

Indeed, when it came not to encouraging others to take action but to taking action on its own, the Poles proved hardly more forthcoming toward the Jews' entreaties than did the principal Allies. Specifically, the government did not agree, despite continued pressure from Jewish representatives, to issue any instructions or orders to the people of the occupied homeland to aid their Jewish fellow citizens. This position was first enunciated by Information Minister Stroński in a note to Raczyński on 27 November 1942 and was consistently maintained throughout the winter of 1943.[172] Evidently, however, the government, realizing no doubt that an unambiguous refusal might arouse unfavorable repercussions among the Jews of the free world, was loathe to state its stance on this matter explicitly. Thus on 14 December, Adam Romer suggested that the Palestinian Reprezentacja, the group that had first presented this demand to the Polish government, be informed in response merely that the government had been active in publicly condemning German barbarity and in mobilizing international public opinion against it; the Reprezentacja's specific demand was to be ignored.[173] In actuality Romer's suggestions were incorporated with minor modifications into the government's formal reply to the Reprezentacja's call for action,[174] and subsequent Jewish inquiries concerning the status of this demand were met with evasion.[175]

Similarly the government appears to have ignored the demands issuing from within the homeland for the assignment of special funds for the rescue of Jews. Although it had been asked to transmit a separate monthly allocation via the government delegate in the occupied homeland earmarked specifically for the Council for Aid to Jews, there is no evidence that it did so, at least until mid-1944.[176] Nor did it endeavor, as it had been requested to do, to organize a body to raise funds for rescue in the West. The most the government did in this regard until mid-1944 was to permit free-world Jewish organizations to use its airlift facilities to transmit to Jewish underground groups sums that they themselves had collected, and the government began to offer this service in earnest only in the latter half of 1943.[177] In the meantime, the principal source of funds for the council continued to be its monthly allotment from the regular budget of the government delegate, a sum that was always dependent upon the delegate's own financial resources and that of necessity severely circumscribed the scope of the council's operations.[178]

Nor does the government appear to have taken serious initiative in proffering nonfinancial help. There is no indication, for example, that following Karski's transmittal of the demand from Jewish leaders in underground for food, clothing, and medicines the government sought to provide such supplies. The proposal to send Jewish paratroopers from Palestine to Poland was kept alive in negotiations for several months but was finally rejected by Mikołajczyk.[179] General Grot-Rowecki of the Home Army was not ordered, as Jewish leaders had requested, to supply arms to underground Jewish military units, and a similar appeal from Zionist officials to the Polish Ministry of Defense on the eve of the Warsaw ghetto uprising was not acted upon.[180] To be sure, contact between Jews in the West and clandestine Jewish organizations in occupied Poland increased during the first half of 1943 thanks to the courier and radio connections maintained by the government delegate in the homeland, but the lead in this regard appears to have come from the underground rather than from London.[181] Moreover, the government, although agreeing to intervene on behalf of Reprezentacja leader Anshel Reiss, who was seeking an entry visa to Britain in order to facilitate communication between Jewish groups in London and in Palestine, ignored altogether the Reprezentacja's request to appoint its delegates to Polish diplomatic missions in the neutral countries of Europe and the Middle East.[182]

It seems that the only substantial action that the government took along the lines of Jewish demands that was not directed primarily toward the Allied and neutral nations was the creation of a new Division of Jewish Affairs under the auspices of the Interior Ministry.[183] Yet even in this regard the government's deeds fell far short of the cabinet-level ministry that Jewish spokesmen had sought. Moreover, the appointment of a rabbi from Łódź who was a member of the anti-Zionist orthodox religious party Agudas Yisroel to head this new department enraged Zionist circles in Palestine, who had expected to be consulted on its staffing. The Reprezentacja even went so far as to term this step "against the spirit [of] all our talks with Professor [Kot]" [184] and suggested that it did "not match [the] importance of Jewish problems in Poland." [185] Indeed, the division played no noticeable role in any future government discussions of Jewish issues, and Zionist spokesmen continued to demand the creation of a cabinet-level department.[186]

The same statements could apply as easily to the feelings of Jewish leaders with regard to the Polish response to their other demands as well. Although grateful to the government-in-exile for bringing the plight of Polish Jewry to the attention of the world through its diplomatic note of 10 December 1942, they were on the whole deeply disappointed by what seemed to them the Poles' lack of concrete action in matters of aid and rescue.[187] During subsequent months they were to repeat their same basic demands time and again, and each time they were to feel that their needs were ignored.[188] If Polish policymakers had hoped that mere intervention with the Allies on the Jews' behalf, without adopting a concomitant program for assistance and rescue of their own, would be sufficient by itself to call forth expressions of gratitude from the Jews of the free world that would eventually redound to Poland's benefit in its pursuit of its war aims, they too were bound to feel no small frustration.

2

Żydokomuna

The Poles' frustration was evident upon Sikorski's return from his diplomatic visit to North America in January 1943. This trip had not been a success for the prime minister: he had embarked on the journey hoping to obtain a guarantee of U.S. support for his position concerning Poland's postwar boundaries before raising the issue again with the Soviets, but he had been advised—"most explicitly," as one of his senior aides later reported—that the Americans wished the Poles to make territorial concessions on their eastern frontier.[1] Moreover, at a conference with Anthony Eden on the results of Sikorski's visit, held shortly following the prime minister's arrival in London, the British foreign secretary had criticized a memorandum that Sikorski had presented to Roosevelt at their meeting for its insistence upon maintaining the 1939 border.[2] If the Polish prime minister had expected earlier to be able to confront the Russians with the clear backing of the major Western Allies, he now found himself trying to fend off British and American pressure to negotiate a boundary settlement directly with Stalin.[3]

During his tour of the United States and Mexico Sikorski and his personal secretary, Józef Retinger, had taken time to meet with a number of Jewish groups, undoubtedly in the hope that these groups might use whatever influence they had to benefit Poland's cause. This hope, too, had proven illusory. In a confidential statement to the National Council on 1 February 1943 the prime minister reported that although he had "frequently raised the matter of the atrocities perpetrated in Poland, not excluding the Jewish persecutions," the Jewish press had not given the Polish government any favorable publicity.[4] Rather, he indicated, certain Jewish circles seemed more interested in calling attention to "the wild sophomoric extravagances [*wybryki sztubackie*] of a handful of Polish individuals" allegedly directed against Jews in the Polish armed forces—extravagances of which neither the Polish government nor the Polish army approved and which both bodies had long since brought under control.[5] These Jewish circles, primarily Zionist, he charged, were doing serious damage to the Polish cause by their actions, which in any case were "incomprehensible" to him in light of "the German atrocities and the well-known position of the Soviet government regarding Polish Jews."[6]

Polish officials had, of course, expressed such incredulity before,[7] but Sikorski's comments displayed an especially harsh edge. The prime minister bitterly castigated "Jewish solidarity and Jewish influence in the international press" and singled out Schwarzbart for condemnation ad hominem. His remarks also contained a new accusation—that Jews were now intentionally coordinating an anti-Polish campaign with Communist elements:

> In New York I warned those who needed to be warned that should this action, which is being conducted on a parallel line with the Communists and is directed against Poland, develop any further, the Polish government would be compelled to adopt an altogether clear position toward it . . . , in order to open people's eyes as to where the real source of trouble lies. . . . I shall supply you with materials as to how the Jews are conducting actions in common with the Communists. They claim that the Poles are carrying out mass murders against Jews, but when it comes to the Germans they cover up [their activities] with silence. We shall have to explode these [myths]. . . . We are not sheep meant to be slaughtered and consumed. . . . [My remarks] concern mainly American Jewry, but the Zionists in general follow this line, and the Bund and Gruenbaum[8] certainly second it.[9]

Such intemperate remarks by the Polish prime minister do not appear to have stemmed from his recent experiences in the United States alone. Indeed, the charge of Jewish-Communist political collaboration against Poland, symbolized by the catch phrase *Żydokomuna* (Jewish commune), had had a long history in Polish politics, dating from the first days of the Second Polish Republic.[10] Earlier in his career even Sikorski himself may have spoken in part under its influence, albeit quite obliquely, in an effort to extricate Poland from a serious political crisis.[11] Since mid-1942, however, the accusation had been surfacing in Polish political circles with increasing frequency, to the point where it had become a significant theme in Polish-Jewish contacts.[12] Now, it appeared, the prime minister had concluded that the charge ought to be taken seriously, to the point where he might actually be contemplating treating world Jewry as Poland's avowed enemy and confronting it as such in a propaganda war.

This exercise in brinksmanship, which implied a willingness to abandon the search for a common ground from which each group might help the other to attain its primary goals, was no doubt prompted in large measure by the Poles' discovery in January 1943 of a document that had been circulating among Jewish leaders since the previous September. The document had been prepared by an attorney acting on behalf of the Jewish Agency for Palestine, Eliahu Rudnicki, who in July 1942 had been dispatched to the Iranian port of Pahlevi on the Caspian Sea to meet Jewish soldiers and civilians being evacuated from Russia together with the Polish exile army.[13] Rudnicki's mission had undoubtedly been prompted, at least in part, by the arrival in Palestine in May and June of several hundred Jewish evacuees, who had brought with them tales of gross discrimination and maltreatment allegedly suffered by them at the hands of Polish military and civilian officials in the Soviet Union.[14] By sending a representative to the point at which the Polish military transports departed from Soviet territory the Jewish Agency hoped, among other things, to obtain firsthand evidence that would substantiate either the charges of the evacuees or the denials of the Poles, which had quickly followed.[15] Rudnicki had remained in Pahlevi over six weeks, visiting Polish facilities for the evacuees and taking depositions from the Jews arriving with the Polish troops. On 8 September 1942, following his return to Tehran, he presented the Jewish Agency with a lengthy written report of his findings—a report that, when brought to the attention of the Polish government four months later, was to make Sikorski and other Polish officials see red.[16]

Rudnicki stated explicitly in the introduction to his report that the information he had gathered in Tehran and at the Polish transit camp at Pahlevi was meant to serve as a basis for "orienting [the Jewish Agency's] relations both with the Polish government and with the Soviets."[17] It appears that he intended to provide direction in this regard mainly by assessing the relative degrees of Soviet and Polish responsibility for the seemingly small proportion of Jews—some 5–6 percent—that had been included among the Polish evacuees.[18] The Polish authorities claimed that the Soviet People's Commissariat of Internal Affairs (Narodnyi Komissariat Vnutrennykh Del—NKVD) had refused to permit Jews to take part in the evacuation, on the grounds that, under the terms by which the USSR had annexed the former eastern Polish territories in 1939, all Jews from those regions had automatically become Soviet citizens and were thus not entitled to partake of the special privilege of departing from Soviet territory—a privilege that had been granted to citizens of Poland alone.[19] The Soviets, on the other hand, denied that they had imposed any restrictions upon who might be included among the evacuees, insisting that the sole responsibility for assigning places in the evacuating transports rested with the Poles.[20]

In his analysis of these two conflicting positions Rudnicki came down firmly on the Soviet side. He cited two instances in which senior Soviet officials had announced publicly, in the presence of Polish military commanders, that they would permit the departure of anyone certified for evacuation by the Polish authorities.[21] Furthermore, he reported that "the antisemitism of the Polish refugees [in Russia] knows no bounds" and even made so bold as to label Lt. Gen. Władysław Anders, the commander of the exile Polish forces, "an antisemite conscious of his goal." During the evacuation, he claimed, "there were cases in which Jewish women were beaten and humiliated." In fact, so convinced did he appear of the essential beneficence of the Soviets as opposed to the fundamental malevolence of the Poles that he even expected the Soviet authorities to permit additional recruitment and evacuation of Polish troops. In light of this possibility, he advised, the Jewish Agency ought to "demand an assurance from the Polish authorities that the proportion of Jews evacuated will be appropriate to the number of Jews among the general body of refugees—that is, 40 percent," as well as to "obtain the assurance of the Polish authorities that they will no longer apply any limitations with regard to Jewish refugees who wish to enter military service in the Polish army."[22] He also suggested that the agency "lodge the most energetic protest against the manner in which the . . . evacuation was carried out and demand that those responsible be investigated and punished."

For reasons unclear from the available evidence, the Jewish Agency did not make public the specific content of the Rudnicki report, although Jewish leaders did repeat its gravamen in subsequent discussions with Polish officials, particularly with Stanisław Kot.[23] During Sikorski's visit to the United States, however, Arieh Tartakower, director of the central office of the World Jewish Congress and head of the American Branch of the Reprezentacja, sent the prime minister a Polish translation of the document. He also passed on additional copies to the Polish Embassy in Washington and the Polish Consulate-General in New York.[24] The Polish reaction to Rudnicki's findings was heated: the Washington embassy termed the report "offensively devoid of objectivity not only with regard to particulars . . . but in its entire conception of the situation of Jewish Polish citizens in Russia,"[25] while the Foreign Ministry set about gathering materials to refute the document's "unprecedentedly tendentious explication of the difficulties encountered in evacuating Jews [from Russia]."[26] Although similar complaints had been heard from Jewish circles before, stressed the Foreign Ministry in a memorandum to Defense Minister Marian Kukiel, "the tendency emanating from the entire [present] text—to ascribe all unfavorable incidents exclusively to the ill will of the Polish authorities (especially the military authorities) while simultaneously whitewashing the Soviet authorities of all responsibility—is most striking."[27] Kukiel was requested to launch an investigation of the Jewish charges so that evidence could be adduced to answer them.[28]

Some Polish observers appear to have believed that the author of the report (of whose name they were not yet aware) was no more than an innocent dupe of sophisticated information manipulation by the Soviets and might even be unaware that his statement provided Poland's enemies with ammunition that could be used against Poland.[29] Soviet agents, these observers claimed, had infiltrated the ranks of the Jewish evacuees and had delivered deliberately contrived testimony to the Jewish Agency's representative in Tehran.[30] Others, however, seem to have been inclined to assess his motives differently. Reports prepared by Polish military intelligence sources in Palestine pointed not only to a recent intensification of Soviet propaganda activities in the country but also to what appeared to them to be increasing obsequiousness toward the Russians on the part of Zionist leaders of most ideological shadings.[31] According to one of these reports, Zionist circles were convinced that the Soviet government was adopting a positive attitude toward the Jewish national movement in Palestine and might even be induced to support Zionist demands at the anticipated postwar peace conference. This hope was, according to the document, "an illusion," but nevertheless it "place[d] an obstacle in the way of Polish-Palestinian understanding, for many Zionists are unwilling to take sides against Soviet Russia."[32] Some observers went even further, suggesting that most Zionists were anxious actively to assist the Russians, in order "to seek a path toward Palestinian-Soviet understanding with the goal of fighting Soviet prejudices with regard to [the] Palestine [question]."³³ Thus, an intelligence officer claimed, Jews who had originally told Rudnicki in Tehran that they were grateful to the Polish authorities for extricating them from the Soviet Union had been instructed later to change their testimony and to voice complaints against the Poles.³⁴ The implication, of course, was that the Jewish complaints about discrimination in evacuation ought to be viewed as a conscious act of Jewish cooperation with the Soviets against the Poles. Indeed, in the words of yet another report prepared for the military, "the general conviction prevailing in Palestine is that Communist inspiration is behind the many anti-Polish statements and actions calling attention to incidents of Polish antisemitism."³⁵

Actually, however, the Rudnicki report appears more likely to have been the work neither of a dupe nor of a Communist fellow traveler nor even of an inveterate Polonophobe, but of a Zionist functionary acting in the service of his particular cause. In May 1942 a special conference of Zionist activists meeting at the Biltmore Hotel in New York had raised publicly for the first time the demand to open the gates of Palestine to unlimited Jewish immigration, under the supervision of the Jewish Agency, as a prelude toward establishing the country as "a Jewish Commonwealth integrated in the structure of the new democratic world."³⁶ This postulate, officially adopted by the Zionist Executive in Jerusalem the following October as an official statement of the program of the Zionist movement, had been inspired by the thought that at war's end millions of homeless Jewish refugees would provide the human material for the creation of a Jewish majority in Palestine upon which a Jewish claim to territorial sovereignty might be based.³⁷ Yet during the very months when the strategy embodied in the so-called Biltmore Program was gaining ascendancy in Zionist circles, the leaders of the movement were becoming increasingly aware that those anticipated millions of refugees might not be alive at the conclusion of hostilities and indeed might already have perished in the Nazi abyss. In such a situation those countries that could still provide significant manpower for the Jewish state in the making became objects of particular Zionist attention.³⁸ The Soviet Union was such a country, mainly because in addition to its own indigenous Jewish population (which was prevented from emigrating by Soviet law) it housed some 400,000 to 500,000 Jewish escapees from German-occupied Poland, whom the Soviet authorities might conceivably permit to leave.³⁹ The Jewish Agency was thus vitally interested in finding a way to bring as many of these Jews as possible out of Russia to Palestine,⁴⁰ especially because, as Rudnicki's report confirmed, many were living in the most abysmal conditions, lacking sufficient food, clothing, and shelter, and hence were in imminent danger of death.[41]

The evacuation of the Polish forces from Russian territory and the willingness of the Soviet government to permit relatives of the departing soldiers to accompany them had provided the Jews with a framework in which this goal could seemingly be achieved. Jewish leaders were thus determined to do all they could to make certain that among the evacuees the maximum number of Jews was included. In this connection they approached both the Polish and the Soviet authorities in the manner that they believed would evoke the most beneficial response from each side. They understood that the Polish government was concerned about its public image and that reports of anti-Jewish discrimination would prove embarrassing to it, so they gambled that in order to avoid publication of such reports the Polish authorities would make an effort to include more Jews in any future evacuations.[42] They also seem to have been genuinely convinced—with good reason[43]—that the testimonies that had been offered to Rudnicki and to other Jewish officials, indicating that more Jews might have been able to leave the Soviet Union had the Polish authorities been interested in seeing this happen, emanated from reliable sources and had been given in good faith.[44] It does not appear, in other words, that the heads of the Jewish Agency conceived of Rudnicki's mission—as some of the Polish commentary on the agency's handling of the complaints surrounding the evacuation suggested[45]—as a way to manufacture a lever with which to coerce the government-in-exile into fostering their own interests. Moreover, Jewish leaders appear to have apprehended—again quite accurately[46]—that the Soviets might not be any more anxious than the Poles to permit large numbers of Polish Jews to leave their territory[47] and that the possibility of additional Jewish refugees arriving from the USSR in Palestine depended in the first instance upon the Russians' disposition.[48] However, they also understood that under the prevailing wartime conditions the Soviets were virtually immune to the type of pressure that Jewish organizations were able to exert upon the Poles; where the Polish government could conceivably be pushed, the Russians could at most be coaxed. Given the Jews' objective, then, it made no sense to call attention to the Soviet government's possible role in keeping the Jewish refugees penned inside the USSR in the way that the Poles' known role in this situation might be profitably publicized. If the Jewish Agency or other Jewish organizations wished to exert any positive influence upon the Soviets, they could do so only by employing the utmost circumspection and discretion in commenting upon any feature of the behavior of the Soviet regime.[49]

Although some Polish officials seem to have comprehended the strategic position of the Jewish Agency and to have understood that Jewish complaints regarding the Polish authorities' handling of the evacuation from the Soviet Union were inspired by a far more complex set of considerations than the mere will to help the Soviets achieve their diplomatic objectives at Poland's expense,[50] it appears that the *Żydokomuna* stereotype influenced others, including Sikorski, to read the Rudnicki report as an indication that world Jewry, especially the Zionist movement, had irrevocably thrown in its lot with one of Poland's enemies. Drawing such a conclusion from this document was, of course, bound to have serious consequences for the future of Polish-Jewish relations and in particular for the manner in which the Polish government would respond to the ongoing Jewish demands to assist the threatened Jews of the occupied homeland. If the Poles were to believe that no rescue action on their part was likely to wean the Jews from their affinity for the Soviet cause, then they would possess no compelling strategic reason for embarking upon such action. On the other hand, most Jewish leaders appear to have been quite unwilling to see their relations with the government-in-exile reach the point of open breach. Following Sikorski's outburst in the National Council, Schwarzbart began an intensive effort to repair the rupture toward which the prime minister appeared headed: he told Sikorski that Zionists and Communists were "mortal enemies" and even indicated his own readiness to issue a public statement to that effect.[51] He also sought to clear the air on the issue of alleged Zionist-Communist cooperation with Interior Minister Mikołajczyk before repeating his "categorical demand" for a government declaration calling upon the Polish people to come to the aid of their Jewish fellow citizens.[52] He even enlisted the aid of Moshe Shertok, head of the Political Department of the Jewish Agency, in attempting to convince the prime minister of the groundlessness of the charges he had brought.[53]

The protests by Schwarzbart and Shertok against Sikorski's remarks indicated that the Poles still possessed some leverage over the Jews and may have suggested to the Polish leaders that they proceed cautiously before placing their relations with world Jewry on an undisguised war footing. No doubt in the wake of such protests they felt the need for some final test of Jewish intentions, a test that would demonstrate definitively the depth and firmness of the Jews' apparent anti-Polish, pro-Soviet orientation.

At the end of February the means to conduct such a test fell into their laps, as it were, from an entirely unexpected quarter.

On 23 February 1943 William Green, president of the American Federation of Labor, received a letter from Soviet Ambassador to the United States Maxim Litvinov informing him that two leaders of the Jewish socialist Bund in interwar Poland and members of the Warsaw City Council, Henryk Erlich and Wiktor Alter, refugees in the USSR who had been arrested by the NKVD in December 1941, had been executed for "hostile activities [to the Soviet Union], including appeals to the Soviet troops to stop bloodshed and immediately to conclude peace with Germany."[54] Litvinov's terse and perfunctory statement was issued in response to a telegram that had been sent by Green and other prominent figures in American public life a month earlier to Soviet Foreign Minister Vyacheslav Molotov. This telegram had pointed out that "most prominent representatives of freedom-loving people throughout the world . . . [have] repeatedly requested" the release of "these outstanding fighters against Fascism and Nazism" and had renewed that request "in [the] name of justice and humanity" at a time "when universal public opinion unites in condemnation of the Nazi criminals who are murdering in cold blood [the] entire Jewish population [of] Poland."[55] Indeed, during the fourteen months that had passed since their arrest, Erlich and Alter had become the object of widespread public attention in the United States and in Great Britain, and a campaign for their release had prompted political leaders in these two countries to intervene with Soviet officials—unsuccessfully—on their behalf.[56]

Evidently the Soviets released their announcement of the execution of the two Polish Jewish leaders—which appears to have taken place shortly following their arrest[57]—at a time when they expected it to have minimal public impact. Not only was Jewish attention in the free world focused primarily upon the news of the Nazis' systematic mass murders, which had only recently come to the fore, but the Soviet reputation was especially high following the victory at Stalingrad only a few weeks earlier. In such a situation the Russians undoubtedly hoped that the Western press would see fit to relegate the Erlich and Alter story to the back pages.[58]

In fact, the Soviet authorities had been well aware of the prestige the two Jews enjoyed in international circles even before the beginning of the public campaign to learn of their fate. Erlich and Alter had first fallen into Soviet hands in October 1939, after fleeing their homes in Warsaw eastward in the face of the invading German armies.[59] As central figures in a democratic socialist party known for its critical attitude toward the Stalinist regime[60] they had been regarded with suspicion from the moment they had come under Soviet occupation, and within a matter of weeks both had been taken into custody on charges of anti-Soviet activity.[61] Shortly thereafter they had been transported to separate prisons in Moscow, where they were held for almost two years until, in July and August 1941, they were tried in absentia and sentenced to death.[62] During this period Soviet leaders had first confronted the influence that Erlich and Alter seemed to command abroad; even before their trial, petitions had been addressed to the Soviet government demanding their release, and in conjunction with the negotiations surrounding Russia's entry into the war against Germany such petitions multiplied.[63]

No doubt in response to such pressure the Soviet authorities' treatment of the two Jews had undergone a sudden and radical reversal. Not only had the two been abruptly released from prison in mid-September, but the Soviet government, on the initiative of NKVD Chief Lavrentii Beria (who earlier had personally attended one of Erlich's numerous interrogations[64]), had asked them to assume the leadership of a planned worldwide "Jewish Anti-Hitlerite Committee," which would promote the organization of anti-German propaganda activities among Jews in the West. Evidently the Soviets believed that the international following that Erlich and Alter seemed to command would enable them to propel the projected committee into a leadership role among world Jewry and to use it as a vehicle for gaining Western sympathy for the Soviet cause.[65] For their own reasons the Jewish leaders, despite the harsh treatment that they had received during their incarceration, were prepared to cooperate with the Russians on this project.[66] During the ensuing weeks they had prepared a memorandum to be submitted to Stalin himself, outlining the rationale for the proposed committee and its planned method of operation.[67] In the meantime, while they awaited Stalin's response, they had been provided with as luxurious accommodations as were then available in wartime Russia, both in Moscow and in the temporary capital at Kuibyshev, ostensibly to make up for the time they had spent in prison, which the Soviets now professed to regard as a mistake.[68]

Against this background, Erlich and Alter's sudden rearrest a few months later must have come as a profound shock. At about 12:30 A.M. on 4 December 1941 the two, having been informed earlier by an official of the NKVD that Stalin was prepared to respond to their memorandum, had been summoned from their hotel in Kuibyshev, never to be heard from again.[69] The next day Erlich and Alter's companions, Lucjan Blit and Stanisław Natanson, who had been with them in the hotel at the time of their disappearance, had requested that the Polish Embassy attempt to ascertain their whereabouts. Stanisław Kot, who was serving at the time as Poland's ambassador to the Soviet Union, had raised the matter on 6 December with Soviet Deputy Commissar for Foreign Affairs Andrei Vyshinsky, who had told him that the two had been arrested on charges of working for Germany.[70] Kot regarded the accusation as "a pretext not to be taken seriously," but he did not speculate on what the actual reason for the arrest might have been.[71] Indeed, the motive for the Soviets' action remains a riddle.[72]

The Polish government, too, was aware of Erlich and Alter's international stature, and even before their disappearance the Polish Embassy in Kuibyshev had tried to co-opt them for several important tasks.[73] The Poles thus took considerable interest in their fate following their rearrest. Some Polish officials, most notably Foreign Minister Raczyński, even appear to have believed that the case might turn out to be the vehicle, for which the government-in-exile had long been searching, for mobilizing the support of free-world Jewry for Poland in its boundary dispute with the USSR. Along these lines the Foreign Ministry had briefly considered the prospect of actively encouraging Jewish groups in the United States and Palestine to protest openly against the Soviet regime, not merely for its arrest of Erlich and Alter but for its alleged overall mistreatment of Russian Jews as well.[74] Nevertheless, despite the importance that it attached to harnessing the Jews of the West to the Polish cause, the government had evidently decided not to pursue this tactic, largely, it seems, for fear of triggering a Soviet backlash against the large number of Polish refugees in the USSR or against the Polish military forces in that country.[75] Once the news had been made public that Erlich and Alter had been put to death by the Soviet authorities, however, the idea of approaching Jewish organizations with a proposal to speak out against the Soviet government was quickly revived. To be sure, the same anxiety over exacerbating the already considerable friction between the Poles and the Russians continued to influence the thinking of Polish diplomats, especially in view of Britain's determination to preserve the already tottering Polish-Soviet alliance.[76] Yet in the winter of 1943, with the Anders army already having left Soviet soil, the Poles' chances of regaining their former eastern territories appeared so much more precarious than they had a year before that the government was obliged to consider taking risks that it might have abjured in a more favorable diplomatic context. The government thus could not permit itself to forgo the opportunity presented by the slaying of the two Polish Jewish leaders for opening a major anti-Soviet, pro-Polish public relations campaign.[77] It could, however, minimize the potential risk to the Polish refugees who remained under Soviet jurisdiction by relinquishing the most visible public role in such a campaign to another party with a similar stake in the affair. Free-world Jewry was obviously such a party, and the idea of allowing Jewish organizations to carry the ball of protest against the Soviets was under the circumstances a sensible one— especially because, as Ciechanowski reported from Washington on 5 March 1943, until that time the only substantial condemnation of Erlich and Alter's execution had come in the form of a paid advertisement by the Bund in the *New York Times*.[78] Thus on 8 March, one day after the Soviet news agency TASS officially confirmed what Litvinov had told William Green two weeks earlier, Raczyński cabled Ciechanowski that "the government attaches importance to arousing the broadest reaction [to the Erlich-Alter affair] in the American press and public opinion by coopting mainly Jewish activists." Moreover, in order to insure that whatever anti-Soviet publicity was generated over the case would redound specifically to Poland's benefit, he instructed the Polish ambassador "confidentially to inform" Jewish leaders, "especially those having influence upon the press, that from the moment of A[lter] and E[rlich]'s arrest the government incessantly and vigorously intervened in their case, defending their Polish citizenship and demanding their release."[79]

Of course this ploy also entailed risks, especially in light of the augmented role that the *Żydokomuna* stereotype appears to have played at that time in the thinking of some government leaders. Indeed, in the weeks immediately following the revelation concerning Erlich and Alter's death the Polish Foreign Ministry does not seem to have received any concrete indication from most free-world Jewish organizations—with the obvious exception of the American and British branches of the Bund—that especially strong anti-Soviet sentiment was brewing among them. Even less did it have any basis for assuming that whatever anti-Soviet sentiment might develop would be accompanied by cessation of the complaints about Polish anti-Jewish discrimination that the Polish government was so anxious to suppress.[80] Nevertheless it must have appeared inconceivable to Polish policymakers that Jews could fail to turn against the USSR following the bald-faced murder of two of their leaders on the preposterous charges that the Soviet authorities had put forth. In any case, the behavior of the Jews in the wake of the affair could provide the litmus test of their seeming affinity for Communism that the Polish government appears then to have been seeking. Should they fail to live up to the Poles' expectations, the Jews would indicate that they had irrevocably sold their souls to Stalin. In the worst case, then, Polish leaders stood to gain information that could conceivably be of importance to them in determining how to conduct their relations with world Jewry.

Moreover, besides offering both a seemingly definitive indicator of Jewish attitudes and a lightning rod to draw away from the Poles the onus of publicly criticizing their Soviet allies, the strategy of encouraging Jewish organizations to take the lead in protesting Erlich and Alter's execution offered the Polish government yet another potentially significant benefit. In the best case the propaganda materials channeled by Poles through Jewish outlets stood to make the Jewish conduits themselves realize that their interests actually lay in supporting the Polish side in the Polish-Soviet conflict. Not only would such a realization prove valuable to the Poles in its own right, but—perhaps equally important—it might in turn forestall the need for the government-in-exile to become involved in rescue activities as a means of currying Jewish favor. The use of the promise of rescue assistance as a lever for obtaining Jewish political concessions had made many Polish policymakers uneasy,[81] and the thought that it might not be necessary to do so was undoubtedly welcome. In this sense, then, the news of Erlich and Alter's death could not have been released at a more opportune time for the Polish government.

The Poles, however, were to be disappointed by the results of their strategy. Jewish and non-Jewish socialist circles in the United States organized a mass protest meeting at Mecca Temple in New York on

30 March, but although most speakers condemned Erlich and Alter's execution as "judicial murder," all praised the heroism of the Red Army and the Russian people and expressed the desire to continue to collaborate with the Soviets both during and after the war. Moreover, in the words of Polish Consul Sylwin Strakacz, "not a single word of sympathy was spoken toward Poland and the Polish people, apparently out of regard for the political situation."[82] On 8 April, Ciechanowski reported from Washington that although the Soviets had received some adverse comment in the American press as a result of the affair, it was unlikely that they would be seriously hurt by it. "The pro-Soviet forces in the Unites States," he observed, "are very strong."[83]

Similarly disappointing were Jewish responses to the affair. Although the largest Jewish daily newspaper in the United States, the Yiddish-language *Forverts*—whose political orientation was close to that of the Bund—proclaimed in an editorial that "the Soviet leaders will never be able to wipe Erlich and Alter's blood off their hands," its leading competitor, *Der Tog*, urged that the execution of the two Jewish leaders not be used as the basis for an anti-Soviet campaign.[84] Other American Jewish publications tended more to follow the position of *Der Tog* on this issue than that of *Forverts*.[85] In Palestine, too, a military intelligence report from late March indicated that the Jewish Agency had not taken up the Polish-Soviet dispute and that the agency's president, David ben Gurion, did not regard the conflict as having any great significance for Palestinian Jewry.[86] Another report concluded that "the responsible members of the Jewish community . . . are to a large extent impotent in the face of mounting [Soviet] propaganda"—propaganda whose spread, the report charged, was being encouraged not only by the powerful left-wing elements among Palestinian Jewry but also by the British mandatory regime, which was allegedly interested, in order to weaken the effectiveness of Jewish opposition to its severe restrictions upon immigration into the country, in promoting internal Jewish discord.[87] Moreover, Palestinian Jewish leaders continued to accept the Soviet version of events concerning the exclusion of Jews from the evacuating Polish military transports, holding the Poles exclusively responsible for the small number of Jews permitted to travel with the Polish forces to Iran.[88] Thus it did not appear to Polish leaders that the Erlich-Alter affair had significantly weakened Soviet credibility in Jewish eyes.

Nonetheless, although many Poles may have felt that Jewish behavior in the wake of the Erlich-Alter affair had proven the validity of the *Żydokomuna* stereotype, they quickly discovered, no doubt to their consternation, that this litmus test, however definitive, still did not permit them to draw unambiguous operative conclusions. No matter how it might have wished to do so, the government remained unable to denounce the Jews' purported anti-Polish bias without inhibitions: the war against Hitler's Germany, and even more the news of the Nazi Holocaust, had done much to delegitimize public expressions that might be deemed antipathetic to Jews as a group. Moreover, the Soviets had based their claim to Poland's eastern territories largely upon the argument that the Polish government was not sufficiently mindful of the needs and interests of the non-Polish ethnic groups— Jews among them—that made up the majority of inhabitants of those lands. This consideration placed Polish spokesmen in a quandary. On one hand, unable to dissuade Jews from raising allegations of Polish discrimination against their fellows, they had to rebut those charges vigorously themselves; yet on the other, they needed to take care not to give any impression of hard feelings toward the Jews on their part while doing so. Thus it remained virtually impossible for the government openly to regard Jewry as Poland's enemy, as Sikorski had threatened to do in his remarks to the National Council the previous February.

Similarly, Polish policymakers could not afford to give Jewish organizations any cause to extend their complaints about the government's attitude toward them to other areas as well, including the area of rescue. This constraint appears to have been sensed by the Poles even as they were gauging Jewish responses to the news of Erlich and Alter's execution. During March and April 1943 Jewish spokesmen continued to press the Polish government for rescue action, not only repeating previously enunciated demands but adding new ones as well.[89] They also made it clear to Polish officials that they were not satisfied with the way in which the government had acted in this matter until then and that if the government wished to strengthen its influence in Jewish circles it would have to improve its record in this regard.[90] Although government leaders might at that very moment have been in the process of concluding that Jews would never become active supporters of Poland in its struggle with the Soviet Union, they could not but have been aware that, in the current political context, a charge of callous indifference to the Jewish plight raised by Jewish organizations in the West might further injure their standing in British and

U.S. public opinion and thus exacerbate their weakness vis-à-vis their erstwhile Eastern ally. The very failure of the Erlich-Alter affair to dissuade Jews from their seemingly pro-Soviet orientation thus meant ironically that the government had to continue to project an appearance of earnestness in response to Jewish rescue demands, despite the political risks involved from its perspective and despite its mounting conviction that no tangible positive political benefit would ensue from such an attitude in any case.

That this was in fact how government officials perceived the situation was revealed by the government's response to several specific rescue proposals placed before it by various Jewish spokesmen during the very months in which it was considering the lessons of Jewish behavior in the wake of the Erlich-Alter affair. The first such proposal was presented as a request from the chief rabbi's Religious Emergency Council in Great Britain for Polish government assistance in arranging for the evacuation of seven prominent Polish rabbis to one of Britain's overseas colonies. The idea of evacuating rabbis from areas under German occupation with the consent of the occupiers had initially been raised in late 1942 in discussions between Chief Rabbi Hertz and the British secretary of state for colonial affairs, Viscount Cranborne; in February 1943 Cranborne's successor, Oliver Stanley, had informed the Emergency Council's executive director, Solomon Schonfeld, that proper procedure called for "the various national Governments of these rabbis to approach the Foreign Office with a view to having them considered for rescue."[91] In accordance with this instruction Schonfeld contacted Foreign Minister Raczyński on 7 March and, ten days later, sent him a list of the seven candidates for evacuation who were Polish citizens.[92]

Schonfeld's request appears to have been discussed with great seriousness by the staff of the Polish Foreign Ministry. The first to evaluate it, Jan Marlewski, recommended a negative response, based upon the principle that the government should not deal with requests from or on behalf of individuals seeking to leave the occupied homeland.[93] He was overruled, however, by the Foreign Ministry's secretary-general, Karol Kraczkiewicz, who suggested that, because of the small number of people included in the request, the overwhelming probability that the entire scheme would come to nothing because the German authorities would not consent to the rabbis' departure, and the likelihood that an unfavorable Polish response would have undesirable consequences in the propaganda realm, "the entire matter be treated not on the level of principle but on [that of] opportunism [*nie na płaszczyźnie zasad, ale raczej oportunizmu*]."[94] In a further elaboration of his position Kraczkiewicz provided noteworthy insight into the nature of the opportunistic thinking he advocated:

> I call your attention to the fact that our role would be confined exclusively to formal support for the visa request . . . , whereas the responsibility for carrying out the initiative will fall entirely upon the Jewish side. . . . In contrast with our subsidiary role . . . a refusal on our part could easily be interpreted as an expression of an anti-Jewish tendency and be exploited as such in the press. Our possible [counter]argument that the government does not make efforts toward getting Poles out of the country could bring about an unwelcome press discussion comparing the suffering of Jews and Poles in the homeland.

Kraczkiewicz did not spell out the positive opportunity that he saw presented by Schonfeld's request, nor did he need to. His intent was transparent from the context of the discussion: here was a chance for the government-in-exile to appear to be actively assisting in a scheme to rescue threatened Jews from Nazi occupation when in fact its role would be limited to writing a letter to the British Foreign Office. On the other hand, the primary risk in becoming involved in this project—that the occupied homeland would react negatively to government efforts to extricate Jews from the country when no such efforts were made on behalf of ethnic Poles[95]—seemed to him negligible in light of the fact that the homeland would most likely never learn of the government's connection with the scheme.[96] Moreover, this risk became even less consequential when compared with the adverse effects liable to stem from a Polish refusal of assistance— foremost among them the prospect that, should the Poles base their refusal upon the principle of nonintervention on behalf of any individual Polish citizen under German occupation, Pole or Jew, the Western press would contend in response that Jewish suffering was incomparably greater than that of the Poles. As the government-in-exile considered it vital to blunt any such impression that might be formed in Western opinion, its course of action, at least as far as Kraczkiewicz was concerned, seemed clear.

A decision on the matter, however, was not Kraczkiewicz's, nor even the Foreign Ministry's, to make; because Schonfeld's request involved Polish citizens located in the occupied homeland, it fell under the purview of the Ministry of the Interior. Accordingly on 20 March, Kraczkiewicz forwarded a review of all correspondence on the proposal to date to Mikołajczyk, with a request that his ministry "weigh the usefulness [celowość] of our extending support" to it.[97] Six days later the interior minister replied, "I have solicited the opinion of K. S. K[raczkiewicz], and based upon it I hold that we should communicate to the British government that the Polish government supports every action aimed at protecting Polish citizens without regard to ethnic affiliation [narodowość] or religion that has as its purpose the defense of a person against violence, murder, and plunder."[98] Because, in his opinion, Schonfeld's proposal "embraced these postulates," he proclaimed official government support for it. The wording of his statement reflected how conscious the Polish government was of the propaganda implications of its decision; it represented an action taken explicitly on the basis of a clear political calculus as one taken instead on high principle. Similarly, Kraczkiewicz informed Schonfeld on 3 April that the government had decided to lend his request its "warm support," though in fact warmth had been conspicuously absent from the government's deliberations about it.[99]

As the Poles had expected, nothing ever came of the chief rabbi's scheme; it is doubtful whether it was ever raised with the German government, and at least some of the rabbis in question perished in the Nazi murder program.[100] There was a second rescue scheme, too, that was presented to the government-in-exile at approximately the same time and that appeared equally unlikely to bear the intended fruit; in this case as well the Poles exhibited the same sort of thinking. This project, however, involved not a handful of rabbis but a rather substantial number of children. In February an official of the Jewish Agency based in London, Solomon Adler-Rudel, traveled to Stockholm with a request that neutral Sweden declare its willingness to provide asylum for 20,000 Jewish refugee children, should a way be found to secure their exit from occupied Europe.[101] Swedish officials took the proposal under advisement, and their deliberations lasted over a month. The delay evidently caused Adler-Rudel to seek ways of bringing pressure to bear upon the Swedish government, and he shared his thoughts with, among others, Schwarzbart, with whom he had developed a close working relationship in London. Schwarzbart in turn wrote to Raczyński on 22 March, outlining the nature of Adler-

Rudel's mission, explaining that "in this case we are talking about rescuing Polish Jewish children as well as Jewish children deported to Poland for certain annihilation by Hitler's hand," and requesting that the Polish government intervene diplomatically with the Swedes and ask the U.S. and British governments to do the same.[102]

As in the case of the rabbis, Raczyński's Foreign Ministry passed the matter on to the Interior Ministry for decision. On 26 March the Section on Nationalities and Religions of the Ministry's Political Department considered the case and recommended that it be regarded in the same light as the request concerning the rabbis—that is, that the government, mindful of the negative propaganda consequences of refusal, ought to accede nominally to the Jewish wishes, in expectation that other parties would eventually bring about the plan's collapse.[103] The Interior Ministry accepted this recommendation and transmitted its decision to the Foreign Ministry on 1 April;[104] the next day Raczyński instructed Poland's legate in Stockholm to meet with Adler-Rudel to obtain further information, adding that should it appear to him that Sweden was indeed prepared to grant asylum to Jewish children from Poland for the duration of the war, he was to inform the Swedes of the Polish government's support for the idea.[105] However, as the Poles had expected, the Germans refused to negotiate with the Swedes on the matter, and the scheme to rescue the 20,000 children, like that involving the rabbis, came to naught.[106]

The idea of rescuing Jewish children through negotiation with the German authorities figured also at around the same time in a set of demands transmitted by the Polish government delegate in the occupied homeland on behalf of a Jewish underground body known as the Jewish National Committee (Żydowski Komitet Narodowy— ŻKN). In January 1943 this organization, made up of representatives of Zionist political parties and youth groups,[107] had dispatched a message to the government-in-exile with a request that it be forwarded to Jewish leaders in the United States.[108] As received in London, the dispatch called not only for the exchange of 10,000 children for German internees in Allied countries but also, among other things, for reprisals to be undertaken by the Allies against Germans, for assistance in opening contacts between the Jews in Poland and neutral countries, and for the transmission of $500,000 for assistance to those Jews who were still alive. Although these demands were not addressed directly to the Polish government, government leaders could not help but take note of them, and their comments on the ŻKN plea provide yet another indicator of their thinking regarding their government's proper role in responding to the Jewish plight.

The ŻKN cable reached London only on 22 February, more than a month after its transmission from Poland. Five days later Mikołajczyk passed it on to Raczyński with a covering letter.[109] This letter took no notice of any of the Jewish demands except the one regarding the transmission of funds; presumably Mikołajczyk did not contemplate a government offer of assistance to the intended recipients of the message in accomplishing the tasks that the leaders of occupied Polish Jewry had set before them.[110] He was quick to stress, however, that he "could not undertake an intermediary role in transferring additional funds—outside of the Polish budget—for the Jews if collections were to take place openly, for this would expose the cover of the [underground] work in the homeland." He noted that he had held a discussion with Schwarzbart and Zygielbojm on this matter (even without informing them that the ŻKN message had contained a plea for money[111]) and that the two had promised that they would attempt to carry out any future fund-raising activities in secret. Furthermore, he insisted that the cable be transmitted to the addressees only on condition that the demand for funds remain confidential, "for its publication will render the transmission of assistance to the homeland via the Polish government impossible." Should the recipients wish to publicize any other portion of the message, he declared, they might do so, although they should realize that "any publication of this sort may accelerate the tempo of the liquidation of the Jews in Poland."

Mikołajczyk thus appears to have displayed considerable trepidation about informing Jewish leaders of the demands—and, most likely, even of the existence[112]—of the Jewish National Committee in Poland. Raczyński, too, evidently shared his hesitancy, for he did not actually transmit the ŻKN message to the Polish Embassy in Washington for delivery to the addressees until 15 March.[113] In Washington, Ciechanowski did not turn over the full contents of the dispatch to all of its intended recipients; he decided that "in order to insure secrecy" he would not let Stephen S. Wise and Nahum Goldmann of the World Jewish Congress, the first two addressees listed, know of the request for funds.[114] When he advised Raczyński of this decision, the foreign minister did not instruct him to do otherwise.

The apprehensiveness of the Polish leaders seems to have stemmed primarily from the fear that the cry for help from the remnants of Polish Jewry would be given wide publicity in the West. To be sure,

Mikołajczyk offered a clear reason for wishing to avoid such publicity in the case of the demand to transfer funds, but, as he himself tacitly acknowledged, the same reason was not likely to hinder publication of the remaining demands—a development that he still seems to have wished to prevent. Moreover, his expressed worry that a public fund-raising campaign by U.S. Jews on behalf of their threatened coreligionists in Poland would expose sensitive Polish underground operations, while plausible on the face of things, seems to have been contradicted, or at least modified, in subsequent actions. In his instructions to Raczyński of 27 February, Mikołajczyk indicated his belief that the demand for money had actually originated with the Council for Aid to Jews, of whose existence Raczyński had evidently not previously been informed.[115] It can, then, be presumed that this was the body that Mikołajczyk ostensibly feared was liable to be exposed should the funds demanded in the ŻKN cable be collected openly. Yet on 15 March the Political Department of Mikołajczyk's own Interior Ministry suggested to the minister that "the news coming from the homeland of the existence of a Council for Aid to Jews of mixed Polish-Jewish composition, confirming active help [to the Jews] by the Polish community, must be widely exploited for propaganda purposes."[116] Mikołajczyk adopted this recommendation and passed it on to Raczyński on 19 April, together with a suggested text for an instruction that he asked be sent to the appropriate Polish diplomatic posts.[117] This instruction was to point out that although "the name, composition, organizational details, and sources of funds of the Council for Aid to Jews cannot be distributed in propaganda materials for security reasons, use should be broadly made in propaganda of the existence of an aid organization in which Poles are taking an active part."[118] It is difficult to understand, however, why it would have been necessary for the organizers of a general fund-raising campaign on behalf of Polish Jewry to reveal any of the information that Mikołajczyk regarded as sensitive, especially as the ŻKN message had never mentioned the Council for Aid to Jews and had asked for no more than the collection of a sum of money "for purposes of aid."[119]

This apparent inconsistency over revealing information about the existence of the Council for Aid to Jews gives cause to wonder whether the hesitancy of the Polish leaders to pass on the ŻKN message, or at least parts of it, to its intended recipients might not have been in the end merely another indication of the tendency to determine their responses to Jewish demands for rescue with an eye primarily to the propaganda implications of their actions. Indeed, these implications appear to have changed somewhat in the two-month interval between the receipt of the ŻKN cable and Mikołajczyk's recommendation. In late March Great Britain and the United States had announced that they would hold a bilateral conference on refugees—primarily potential Jewish refugees from Nazi-held Europe—at Bermuda.[120] This conference had been called in response to what the British Foreign Office had termed the "intense public interest" in the plight of Europe's Jews that had been generated by the Allied memorandum of December 1942.[121] Ever since that memorandum had been published, some Polish leaders had worried lest such mounting public concern divert notice from the sufferings of the ethnic Polish population in the homeland, and they had been steadily intensifying their efforts to draw the public spotlight more in their direction.[122] The fears demonstrated by Mikołajczyk, Raczyński, and Ciechanowski over publicizing the ŻKN message were thus consistent with a more general apprehension in Polish circles. But with the announcement of the convening of the Bermuda conference, scheduled for 19–29 April, it now appeared that, however much Polish spokesmen might have hoped that the tribulations of their own people would win greater public and governmental regard, the Jews commanded public sympathy far more than the Poles could hope to do at that point. Polish observers realized that it was public attention to the Jewish situation, not to their own, that had moved the two major Western Allies to examine possibilities for aid and rescue in detail.[123] In such a context the best course of action for them was undoubtedly to appear as sympathetic to Jewish suffering as possible, offering the impression that the people of the occupied homeland were already making every possible sacrifice on behalf of their threatened Jewish neighbors. Thus it might not have been coincidental that Mikołajczyk not only abandoned his previously expressed unwillingness to risk making public knowledge of the existence of the Council for Aid to Jews but actually chose to transmit his recommendation to Raczyński about publicizing the council's activities—a suggestion that had first been raised over a month earlier—on the very day on which the Bermuda conference opened. Spreading such news at the precise moment when attention was to be most closely focused on the dangers confronting European Jewry offered the Poles a way to capture a measure of that attention for themselves and thereby to salvage some small propaganda success from a situation in which their own plight was bound to be overshadowed.

Examination of this changing international context alongside developments in the occupied homeland can also contribute much to understanding an even more radical reversal in the Polish response to Jewish rescue demands—the issue on 4 May 1943, following a series of explicit refusals extending over half a year, of a government instruction to the Polish people to assist Jews in avoiding the fate that the Nazi regime had set for them. The instruction was included as part of a radio broadcast by the prime minister to the occupied homeland. The idea that it might eventually be necessary to issue such an order had been raised in the same internal Interior Ministry memorandum of 15 March that had suggested propagating information about the Council for Aid to Jews.[124] The author of the memorandum [125] noted that previous efforts by the government-in-exile to direct the attention of the world to the horrors being perpetrated by the Nazi occupiers against Polish Jewry and to induce the major Allied governments to render aid to the survivors, "no matter how gratefully Jewish opinion may have received them, have not quieted [the Jews] down at all"—a fact indicated by their call for a government appeal to the Polish population. Perhaps, he hinted in retrospect, it might have been a good idea to issue such an appeal in December 1942, immediately after the demand was first received, for now that several months had gone by any such instruction would likely appear as "a rebuke [nagana] to the Polish population in the homeland for an insufficiently proper attitude [niedość godne stanowisko] during the tragic days when the Jews were being murdered." In such circumstances, he warned, "the government could encounter the valid charge that the decision to issue an appeal had been taken at a time when there was already no one left to save." Nevertheless, he appears to have felt the need for taking some action to satisfy Jewish opinion, and he expressed his hope that this goal could be accomplished by disseminating basic information about the Council for Aid to Jews "without the necessity of issuing an appeal."

Still, however, the author of the memorandum evidently suspected that this action alone might not be sufficient, for he also recommended a follow-up measure. "In one of the occasional speeches by the government to the homeland," he wrote, "a passage must be found in which the government states the fact of active assistance by the Polish community and expresses the conviction that in spite of the most sophisticated methods of the occupier [aimed at] setting the two communities against one another, the Polish community will not deviate from the appointed path [z obranej drogi nie zboczy]." He then suggested a three-paragraph text for such a statement, according to which "neither equally savage persecutions [to those being meted out to the Jews], nor the occupier's most elaborate methods for arousing hatred in you [Poles] toward the Jewish population, nor even the threat of cruel death has been able to restrain you from rendering active and effective aid to the suffering, dying Jewish population."

Evidently the government accepted the advice that a statement of this sort should be made subsequent to release of information about the existence of the Council for Aid to Jews, for it was not until seven weeks after this suggestion that the government acted upon it. In the meantime, however, not only had the British and U.S. governments convened and adjourned the conference on refugees at Bermuda, but Jews in the Warsaw ghetto had confronted German troops in an armed uprising that was eventually to capture the imagination of the free world.[126] The first news of this uprising had reached the Western press on 22 April, three days after its outbreak, apparently from a source connected in some way with the Polish government,[127] but no official public notice of it was taken by a government spokesman until a radio broadcast by Sikorski to the homeland on 4 May.[128] This broadcast, to be sure, was not devoted exclusively, or even primarily, to the events in the Warsaw ghetto; in fact only 28 of 271 lines of its text concerned this subject.[129] It did, however, contain one passage that, although shorter than the statement suggested by the Interior Ministry memorandum of 15 March, actually exceeded the limits for a public declaration that that memorandum had endeavored to maintain:

> On April 16th [sic], at 4 A.M., the Hitlerite gangsters proceeded to "liquidate"—by means which we know already—the remnants of the Warsaw ghetto, in which a few tens of thousands of Jews were still vegetating; after having blocked all exits, they invaded the ghetto in armoured cars and light tanks in order to kill the remaining men and women and children with machine-guns. The Jewish population, driven to despair, offered heroic, armed resistance and the battle continues. The rattle of machine-guns, bomb explosions and fires have attracted the population of Warsaw, who, though overcome with horror, are helping wherever and however they can the helpless victims of a barbarism the like of which has never been known in history.

In the name of the Government and in my own name I wish to thank you, Countrymen, for this noble ministration and, while asking you to offer all succour and protection to the threatened victims, I condemn these cruelties before the whole of mankind, which has already been silent too long.[130]

Thus Sikorski finally issued an explicit appeal to the Polish population to aid threatened Jews, some six months after the demand for such an appeal had initially been raised by Jewish spokesmen and evidently without regard for the caveat in the Interior Ministry recommendation on the matter. The reasons for this striking turnabout in the behavior of the Polish government with regard to Jewish matters, however, are not difficult to fathom. At the time that Sikorski broadcast his statement, not only had the Bermuda conference and the uprising in the Warsaw ghetto focused much public attention on the sufferings of the Jews of Poland under Nazi rule and made it necessary, from the perspective of propaganda, for Polish spokesmen to express sympathy with the Jewish plight; the Polish government also found itself in the midst of a grave diplomatic crisis that stood to alter the entire fabric of its relations with both the Soviet Union and the Western Allies. On 13 April, Radio Berlin had broadcast a report that German military forces in the Katyn forest near Smolensk in the USSR had uncovered "a ditch . . . 28 metres long and 16 metres wide, in which the bodies of 3,000 Polish officers were piled up in twelve layers." The German broadcast charged that these officers had been shot by the Soviets in March 1940 and announced that the German forces expected to find additional pits containing up to 10,000 bodies.[131] Two days later the Soviet government had responded, claiming that the dead were "former Polish prisoners of war, who . . . fell into the hands of the German-Fascist hangmen in the summer of 1941."[132] Polish officials, though, had discounted the Soviet version of events, noting that their own repeated inquiries into the fate of these soldiers had consistently been evaded by the Soviet government, and on 16 April, Polish Defense Minister Marian Kukiel had issued a public statement strongly suggesting that the officers had met their deaths at Soviet hands.[133] The next day the Polish government had announced that it was officially requesting the International Red Cross to send a delegation to the site of the mass graves,[134] and on 20 April it had asked the Soviets for "detailed and precise information" on the matter.[135] The Polish suspicions appear to have been well founded,[136] but the Soviets had nonetheless proven able to use the situation to undermine the standing of the Polish government with Britain and the United States still further. On 21 April, Stalin had written to Churchill accusing the Sikorski regime of "collusion" with Germany against the USSR,[137] and on 25 April the Soviets had announced that they were officially breaking off relations with the Polish government.[138]

The Poles had initially expected the revelations of the discovery of the graves at Katyn to create a groundswell of sympathy for the Polish cause in Allied public opinion,[139] but such a favorable turn of events had not materialized. Instead the Polish government had found itself under attack in the Allied press for attempting to sow inter-Allied discord in a fashion that could only give comfort to the enemy.[140] Nor had the British and U.S. governments, despite their general sense that the Soviets had not only murdered the Polish officers but had deliberately precipitated the rupture in relations with the Polish government in order to further their own ambitions in Eastern Europe, shown much of an inclination to stand firmly behind the Poles in the present crisis.[141] The Polish government thus again found itself in the by now familiar position of needing to bolster its public image and to cultivate all possible sources of public support in order to prevent the Katyn affair from turning into a diplomatic fiasco.

Similar situations in previous years had led Polish leaders to consider the idea of a possible alliance with world Jewry.[142] The response of Jewish organizations to the murder of Erlich and Alter, however, had made it appear virtually certain that Jews would not now rush to Poland's defense. Nevertheless, in the face of Stalin's allegations of Polish-German collusion in suggesting that the Soviets were responsible for the deaths of the Polish officers, and with Soviet press organs publishing diatribes against "Hitler's Polish allies,"[143] it was essential that the Poles do everything possible to establish the unimpeachability of their anti-Nazi credentials.[144] One way to accomplish this goal was loudly and vigorously to condemn the horrors of the German occupation of Poland, and indeed, from the outset of the Katyn affair the Polish government had adopted this strategy. Its statement of 17 April announcing its request for a Red Cross investigation, for example, had stressed that "the Polish Government . . . denies to the Germans any right to base on a crime they ascribe to others, arguments in their own defence" and had gone on to list a series of German atrocities against Poles, including "the massacre of one-and-a-half-million people by executions or in concentration camps" and "the recent imprisonment of 80,000 people of military age, officers and men, and their torture and murder in the camps of Maydanek and Tremblinka [sic]."[145]

Such condemnation had made no explicit mention of German acts committed against Polish Jews; in fact, it appears doubtful that at the time the Polish government adopted this tactic it intended to condemn acts against Jews in future statements.[146] Even Sikorski's broadcast of 4 May, which contained the instruction to the Polish people to come to the assistance of Polish Jews, appears to have been meant primarily to excoriate German outrages, to present the Polish people as bearing the brunt of Hitler's iniquity, and to highlight the tenacity of Polish anti-Nazi resistance.[147] By the time of the broadcast, however, the Bermuda conference had been convened and adjourned; news of the uprising in the Warsaw ghetto had been reported in the West; and the situation of Polish Jewry was in any case before the public eye. If, then, the Polish government wished to place itself in the forefront of those exposing and condemning the evil being wrought by the Nazi regime, it could not permit itself to take no notice of these events. On the contrary, aware of Jewish dissatisfaction with its response to rescue demands and suspicious of organized Jewish-Soviet collaboration, the government needed to anticipate the eventuality that the Soviets (or their purported Jewish fellow travelers) would try to counter its propaganda efforts by alleging Polish callousness toward Jewish suffering. Meeting what had been the principal demand placed upon it by Jewish leaders for the past six months, on the other hand, offered the Poles a way of nipping such an eventuality in the bud. To be sure, the considerations that had made the Polish government unwilling to issue an appeal to assist in the past remained in force, and for that reason any such request would have to be given in as inconspicuous a fashion as possible (as, it turned out, it was).[148] For the government's purposes, however, it was not essential to call special attention to such an appeal at the time it was issued; all that was necessary was to place the government on record as having made its desire known to the Polish population that succor be rendered to threatened Jews. The government could then point out, whenever hostile propaganda attempted to score its record on rescue, that it had made such an appeal.

To be sure, no document has as yet been adduced showing prima facie that such was in fact the thinking that led to Sikorski's request to the Polish population. Both the form and the circumstances of the promulgation of the request, however, make this reconstruction appear likely, especially when it is considered against the background of the government-in-exile's demonstrable tendency during the months immediately preceding the 4 May broadcast to regard Jewish rescue demands primarily from the perspective of their propaganda implications and the growing conviction within its ranks that world Jewry had irrevocably chosen to cast its lot with the Soviets against the Poles. What does seem certain is that by the time of the Sikorski broadcast the Polish government had given up the hope that its actions or inactions with regard to Jewish rescue demands would have any substantial bearing upon the orientation of world Jewry with regard to the Polish-Soviet dispute. Government spokesmen do not appear to have made any effort in the wake of the broadcast, as they had on numerous occasions in the past, to elicit any public expression by Jews of support for the Polish cause. On the contrary, when, on the day following the broadcast, Irving Miller, secretary-general of the World Jewish Congress, told Raczyński, in Schwarzbart's presence, of his organization's "readiness to collaborate with the Polish government" and its "sincere attitude . . . toward a free, independent, and *integral* Poland," the Polish foreign minister was reported to have passed over the remark entirely.[149] Mention of Sikorski's appeal was not even included in the weekly Yiddish-language press bulletins prepared by the Polish Information Center in New York for distribution to Jewish publications in the United States.[150] The request cannot be seen, then, as a serious attempt by the government-in-exile to win Jewish support for its position in its crisis with the Soviets. By May 1943, in the wake of the Erlich-Alter affair, the Polish government appears to have effectively abandoned any notion that a Polish-Jewish community of interest might ever be found.

Indeed, there does not appear to be any indication that Jews in the free world were impressed by Sikorski's appeal or that they regarded it as a possible turning point in their relations with the Poles. Jewish newspapers in Britain, the United States, and Palestine either failed to report about the broadcast at all or mentioned Sikorski's request to the Polish population only in passing, in the context of articles devoted to other aspects of his speech.[151] Irving Miller expressed satisfaction with the appeal to Raczyński but then raised the issue of possible discrimination against Jews in the evacuation from

Russia and in the resettlement of the evacuees abroad, in precisely the same fashion as had been customary before the request.[152] At the same meeting Schwarzbart mentioned Sikorski's broadcast only to complain that the Polish Telegraphic Agency's press release about it had omitted all mention of Jews.[153] The Reprezentacja, which had been the first Jewish organization to demand a government appeal to the Polish population to come to the assistance of threatened Jews, took no notice of the speech at all, continuing throughout the ensuing months to reiterate its demands in telegrams, memoranda, and meetings with government officials.[154] In short, it appeared that as far as the leaders of free-world Jewry were concerned, their approach to dealing with the Polish government would remain unchanged.[155]

This conclusion seemed to the Poles to be firmly demonstrated by the response of free-world Jewish organizations to the rupture of Polish-Soviet diplomatic relations over the Katyn affair. On 27 April, two days after the break, Polish officials in Palestine called a meeting with representatives of the Hebrew press in order to explain the Polish position in the affair, but they met with little sympathy. On the contrary, a representative of the Political Department of the Jewish Agency who attended the meeting later indicated that in his opinion "there is no point in *our* taking any stand on the crisis or in our helping the Poles to turn the Hebrew press . . . or Jerusalem as a whole into a propaganda and information *center* in the Polish spirit."[156] A month later Polish military intelligence reported that at a meeting of Hebrew journalists held on 13 May, a correspondent from the independent daily *HaBoker* had declared the Soviet stand in the Polish-Soviet conflict "correct and proper" and had castigated the Poles for their purported desire to reestablish a "Greater Poland" after the war.[157] Similarly, an assessment of "the influence of Jewish opinion on changes in the attitudes of the American public concerning Russia" prepared by the Polish Embassy in Washington stated that both Zionists and assimilationists in the United States were on the whole favorably disposed toward Stalin's state, with only the Bund expressing reservations. However, the document warned, the Bund opposed Stalin primarily because of its own alleged affinity for Trotsky; by implication it could thus hardly be counted on as a reliable ally for Poland.[158] As this and other reports pointed out, the Bund's influence among Jewish circles was relatively weak compared with that of the Zionists, not only in the United States but in Britain as well.[159]

By the time this evaluation was prepared, moreover, the Bund had lost its foremost leader in exile. On 12 May, Szmul Zygielbojm, evidently despondent over the crushing of the Warsaw ghetto uprising and the lack of decisive action emanating from the Bermuda conference, and hoping through a dramatic gesture to rouse the Allied governments finally to take some "concrete action . . . that will at least save the 300,000 Jews remaining today in Poland,"[160] committed suicide in his London apartment. He left a note intended for Sikorski, Mikołajczyk, Kot, and President Raczkiewicz and requested that it also be transmitted to the press.[161] The note charged the Allied governments and peoples in general with "indirect responsibility" for the crimes being committed by Germany against the Jews of Europe, for in his words they had watched passively as millions of defenseless men, women, and children had been murdered. The letter also singled out the Polish government for reproach: "Although the Polish government has to a great extent helped to influence world public opinion, it has not done so sufficiently; it has done nothing to fit the enormous dimensions of the drama now being played in Poland."[162] The note ended with what was in effect yet another demand: "I am certain . . . that the Polish government will soon begin the appropriate actions in the diplomatic realm on behalf of those still alive." Sikorski's broadcast to the homeland a week before Zygielbojm's death thus seems to have made little impression on him.

It fell to Schwarzbart, Zygielbojm's colleague on the Polish National Council and rival on the internal Jewish political scene, to point out to the Polish government what sort of actions the late Bund leader might have regarded as appropriate. On 17 May he wrote Raczyński suggesting that Zygielbojm's final letter be distributed to members of the British cabinet and to the leaders of both houses of Parliament prior to a Commons debate scheduled for two days hence on the results of the Bermuda conference. He also requested that those same British leaders receive translations of sections from recent underground reports describing the operations of the Nazi death camps. "People still do not believe," he wrote. "If the remainder of Polish Jewry can still be saved, then everything must be done to rouse the politicians from their wariness. . . . Such a step will also be in accord with the will of Zygielbojm, who gave his life for the cause."[163]

Schwarzbart's plea, however, bore no fruit; the Polish government made no effort to influence the course of the Commons debate. Neither did the government act upon his subsequent request to call upon the South American states that had joined the war against Germany to offer to exchange interned German civilians being held on their soil for Jews from occupied Europe.[164] Indeed, the government's non-intervention with other countries over the rescue of Jews in these instances contrasted markedly with the willingness Polish leaders had shown during January and February to act as an advocate for Jewish rescue demands vis-à-vis the Allied powers. Apparently whatever leverage Jews had held with the government-in-exile during the earlier part of the year had been dissipated by mid-1943; Polish leaders do not seem to have attached nearly the same degree of political urgency to Jewish calls for rescue action as they had but a few months before.[165] Such a change, however, is not surprising in light of the reinforcement that the Żydokomuna stereotype had received from Jewish responses to the Erlich-Alter and Katyn affairs: if there was no reasonable possibility of inducing Jews to take public action that would redound to Poland's political benefit, then, given the balance of forces impinging upon the formation of Polish policy both in the occupied homeland and in the international arena, there was also no reason to try to curry Jewish favor. The lack of any significant positive Jewish response to Sikorski's broadcast to the Polish population of 4 May could only have underscored the wisdom of this conclusion in Polish policymakers' minds.

The irony in this situation, of course, lies in the fact that precisely at the moment when Jews appear to have lost all political leverage vis-à-vis the government-in-exile, they achieved what might on the surface be regarded as one of their greatest political successes—an appeal by the Polish prime minister to the people of the occupied homeland to render assistance to Jews threatened with murder at the hands of the Nazi conqueror. To be sure, Sikorski had cast his words in the form of a request rather than the firm instruction that Jewish leaders had demanded, and it was true as well that the appeal had been submerged among a host of other statements on different matters. On the other hand, though, the prime minister had gone further in response to this central Jewish demand than his advisors had thought prudent and in doing so had risked the government's standing in the eyes of important segments of the Polish population. That he had found it advisable to do so, however, reflected—again ironically—the fact that the sufferings of the Jews of Europe had now come to possess a symbolic importance in the Allied war effort far transcending the importance attached by any of the Allied governments to the actual Jews laboring under the Nazi death sentence. Whatever the vital national interests that were at stake in the war against the Axis, the Allied powers had consistently couched their involvement in moral terms, not merely as a fight against hostile governments but as one on behalf of righteous principles to which those governments stood opposed. One of the most notable statements of those principles, the Atlantic Charter promulgated by Churchill and Roosevelt in August 1941, had spoken of the ultimate establishment of "a peace which will afford to all nations the means of dwelling in safety within their own boundaries, and which will afford assurance that all the men in all the lands may live out their lives in freedom from fear and want."[166] Within this context Allied statesmen needed to create the impression that they were doing all in their power to prevent Germany from denying such means and assurances to Europe's Jews; condemnations of the Nazi murder thus became de rigueur for all Allied leaders, and a country that could point to positive action on behalf of the threatened Jews stood to acquire important moral credit. By the same token, though, a nation's moral credentials as a member of the anti-Nazi alliance could easily be undermined were it shown that that nation itself harbored hostility toward the Jewish people.

Repeated complaints about anti-Jewish discrimination on the part of the Polish government and its agencies virtually from the outset of the war had long made the Poles especially vulnerable to attack along these lines. Once the Soviet Union had broken off diplomatic relations with the government-in-exile, the vulnerability of the Poles had become greater than ever; now there was little to prevent the Russians from making full use of the Jewish issue as an anti-Polish propaganda weapon. Furthermore, with most of world Jewry showing what the Poles believed to be a clear affinity for the Soviets, even in the wake of the Erlich-Alter affair, Polish leaders undoubtedly feared that the Russians would now try to present themselves as the world's foremost champions of the Jewish cause, in order to heighten the appearance of their own moral superiority over the Poles.

As it happened, no sooner had the Polish-Soviet rift broken open than the Soviets launched precisely such a propaganda offensive, an offensive that was to leave the Poles bewildered and to expose how precarious their situation was in the battle for public opinion in the West.

3

Propaganda

The Soviets had notably increased their pressure upon the government-in-exile even before the break in diplomatic relations. In late February 1943 Stalin had sanctioned the establishment of a new political organization of Poles in the USSR, led by Communists and fellow travelers, known as the Union of Polish Patriots (Związek Patriotów Polskich). This new body proclaimed as its purpose "to unite all Poles living in wartime upon Soviet territory—without distinction with regard to political, social, or religious views—into a single patriotic camp for the struggle against Hitlerism."[1] In fact, however, it appears to have conceived of its task also as conducting propaganda within Polish circles in favor of the Soviet position in the Polish-Soviet dispute, in order to weaken the support of the Polish people for the London leadership.[2] Thus the group began to publish a weekly newspaper entitled *Wolna Polska* (Free Poland), with a circulation of 40,000, containing articles calling upon Poles of all political persuasions to rally behind it—rather than the government-in-exile—in the fight to restore Poland's independence.[3] It also called for Poland to relinquish its claim to the territories annexed by the Soviets in 1939.[4]

Following the rupture over Katyn, the Soviets escalated their efforts to undermine the standing and the authority of the exile regime. In occupied Poland itself Communist circles began to assert that the London government lacked legitimacy and that all laws enacted by it were invalid.[5] The Soviet government also authorized the establishment of an alternate Polish military force to replace the departed army of General Anders. This new formation, known as the Kościuszko Division and commanded by Col. Zygmunt Berling, a Polish officer captured in the 1939 campaign who had been co-opted by the NKVD in 1940 and had deserted the Anders army during its evacuation,[6] owed no allegiance to the government-in-exile and was clearly intended to serve primarily as an instrument of Soviet policy in the Polish-Soviet dispute.[7] That policy now appeared to be aimed not merely at negating the Polish claim to the annexed territories but actually at installing a new regime in liberated Poland to replace the government-in-exile, with whom the Soviets were no longer prepared to maintain relations. Indeed, by early May, Stalin had already made known to the British his conviction of the necessity of "taking measures to improve the composition of the present Polish Government."[8]

As it happened, the Polish government did undergo a reorganization during the summer of 1943, but hardly along lines acceptable to the Russians. On 4 July, Sikorski was killed in an airplane crash shortly after takeoff from the British airfield at Gibraltar. His death plunged the government into a protracted internal struggle for power, the outcome of which merely highlighted the divisions within the regime and made the Soviets more intractable than ever in dealing with the Polish issue. Sikorski's former dual position as prime minister and commander-in-chief was now divided in two, with Mikołajczyk assuming the reins of government and Gen. Kazimierz Sosnkowski, designated successor to President Raczkiewicz (and a former cabinet minister who had resigned his position in protest over the Polish-Soviet agreement of July 1941) taking charge of the armed forces. Sosnkowski was not only persona non grata to the Soviets but unacceptable to Mikołajczyk as well; yet the new prime minister lacked the stature to overcome Raczkiewicz's insistence on naming the general to the top military post. Mikołajczyk was able, however, to secure the appointment of his Peasant Party associate, Władysław Banaczyk, to succeed him at the Interior Ministry; to retain Kot, who had recently taken over the Information Ministry, in that post; and to replace Raczyński in the Foreign Ministry with the government's last ambassador to the Soviet Union, Tadeusz Romer.[9] This new cabinet might have been on the whole closer to Mikołajczyk politically than the old one, but it was no more acceptable to the Soviets;[10] and its hold over the army and the underground in the occupied homeland was far from firm.[11]

In the formation of the new government explicit consideration appears to have been given to the advisability of appointing a Jew to a top-level post. A report called "The Course of the Government Crisis Following the Death of General Sikorski," prepared for the leadership of the Peasant Party in underground, noted that "[people] will be convinced that the government is democratic only if a Jew receives an important position in the state apparatus."[12] This consideration was taken into account, the report explained, in the naming of Ludwik

Grosfeld, a former director-general of the Ministry of Social Welfare and a member of the Polish Socialist Party, as treasury minister.[13]

As it happened, the government-in-exile had good reason to consider the public relations implications of such an appointment. Jews had figured prominently among the organizers of the Union of Polish Patriots; in fact, nine of ten members of the editorial board of *Wolna Polska* were of Jewish origin.[14] Though this fact might in the first instance merely have reinforced the *Żydokomuna* stereotype within the exile regime, it also made it that much easier for the Soviets to argue that, in contrast to the Poles, they were especially sensitive to Jewish rights and needs. As it turned out, at the time of the Polish cabinet crisis, the Soviets were in the midst of a propaganda campaign aimed at making just that point in Western public opinion.

The Soviets' attempt to link Jewish concerns to their cause was conducted by the prominent Jewish actor Shlomo Mikhoels, director of the Moscow Yiddish Theater, and the Soviet Yiddish poet Itsik Feffer. The two were leaders of the Moscow-based Jewish Antifascist Committee, the successor to the Jewish Anti-Hitlerite Committee that Erlich and Alter had earlier been called upon to form. One of the primary purposes of this committee was to mobilize pro-Soviet sentiments among the Jews of the West.[15] In the wake of the publication of the news of Erlich and Alter's execution and the subsequent severing of Polish-Soviet relations, the Soviet leadership evidently felt that a visit to the West by two such prominent Jewish spokesmen could repair whatever damage Soviet prestige might recently have suffered and solidify the Soviet position in the battle for Western public opinion. Accordingly Mikhoels and Feffer set out from the Russian capital in early May 1943 on a seven-month journey to the major Jewish centers in the United States, Mexico, Canada, and Great Britain.

From the Soviet perspective, the tour was a success.[16] The two Jews spoke to a nationwide U.S. radio audience on 4 July, on a program introduced by the famous American actress Helen Hayes. Four days later they appeared before 50,000 people at a Jewish-sponsored rally at New York's Polo Grounds. In subsequent weeks they visited the largest cities in the United States, making contact with leading figures in American cultural life. In England they spoke at a rally organized by the Jewish section of the Red Cross Fund for Russia under the patronage of Clementine Churchill, and they met with the British Section of the World Jewish Congress and the Board of Deputies of British Jews. Their message was a simple one: the Soviet armed forces, by fighting Hitler, were helping to save European Jewry from death; thus the Soviet Union was the Jewish people's greatest friend. They even intimated that the Soviet government might be favorably inclined toward Zionist aspirations in Palestine. Mikhoels and Feffer encountered a warm reception virtually everywhere, despite some opposition from Bund and Labor Zionist circles in the United States. Indeed, upon their departure from New York the prominent rabbi Israel Goldstein, president of the Synagogue Council of America, told them that they were riding on "the crest of a high tide of goodwill to Soviet Russia."[17]

The Polish government received intelligence concerning the Mikhoels-Feffer mission—the purpose of which it regarded as "winning American Jewish circles over into an anti-Polish direction"[18]— even before the arrival of the two Jewish spokesmen in the United States.[19] From the moment that this information was obtained, the Foreign Ministry and the Ministry of Information jointly resolved to attempt to neutralize in advance whatever damage the mission might potentially inflict upon the Polish cause. However, the only means that they seem to have been prepared to employ in order to accomplish this goal was to circulate a rumor implicating Mikhoels in the arrest and subsequent execution of Erlich and Alter.[20] This idea, moreover, had originated with the Bund, which had been the government's principal informant about the Soviet Jews' visit, and Bund spokesmen realized that "in light of public opinion" this charge could not be proclaimed too loudly.[21] Indeed, it appears that the Poles looked upon this tactic as little more than an act of desperation, and in the wake of the failure of previous efforts to generate an anti-Soviet backlash among American Jews over the Erlich-Alter affair, it is difficult to understand how they might have viewed it otherwise. Thus on 22 July, Ciechanowski reported to Tadeusz Romer that although he had instructed the Polish consuls in the United States to inform Jewish spokesmen of Mikhoels's alleged part in the murder of the two Bund leaders, the organizers of the Mikhoels-Feffer visit had successfully co-opted "the most influential and best-known Jewish scholars, writers, publicists, and community workers" to their cause.[22] Subsequently the Polish Embassy in Washington issued a statement, "The Organization of

Soviet Propaganda in the U.S.A.," noting in a tone of resignation that Mikhoels and Feffer's arrival "demonstrated that Jewish circles, even the wealthy and industrial ones, had become the object of widespread Soviet infiltration" and offering no suggestions as to how this trend might be reversed.[23]

In the same fashion Polish leaders sat by helplessly after Mikhoels and Feffer's departure from the United States as they observed the Soviets making ever stronger inroads into the Jewish community in Great Britain. On 6 October, Olgierd Górka, pondering the question of how Poles ought to respond to the presence of the two Soviet Jewish delegates in the seat of the Polish government, concluded that even a Polish attack on Mikhoels's purported role in the Erlich-Alter affair would not yield the desired result and might even backfire against the Polish interest. His only suggestion was for Polish observers openly to monitor Mikhoels and Feffer's public appearances, in the hope that a visible Polish presence might deter the two speakers from attacking Poland directly.[24] Observers were indeed dispatched to several large meetings in the London area (at which, it turned out, the Polish-Soviet conflict was never specifically mentioned), but their reports could offer nothing more than the consolation that the speeches were banal and the speakers uninspiring.[25] In the meantime the chief rabbi of Great Britain and several other prominent British Jewish figures lent their public sanction to the mission of the two Soviet spokesmen and frequently appeared with them on the same platform.

Soviet propaganda overtures were made at the same time to the Jewish community in Palestine. While Mikhoels and Feffer were in Britain, the Soviet ambassador to the Court of St. James, Ivan Maisky, visited Jerusalem for talks with Zionist leaders.[26] According to Polish diplomatic and military intelligence sources these talks yielded evidence of growing collaboration between the Soviets and the Zionist movement and of Soviet efforts to extract from the Zionists an explicitly pro-Soviet statement on the question of the future border with Poland in return for Russian government assistance to Soviet Jews.[27] One military intelligence official depicted the results of the Soviet ambassador's trip in the blackest of terms from the Polish point of view: "The visit of Maisky, who demonstrated such a lively interest in the rebuilding of Palestine [and dropped] various suggestions from Moscow about [the Soviets'] regard for the theses of Zionism, [together with] the promise to allow Polish Jewish citizens possessing [immigration] certificates [to Palestine] to leave the country . . . , has weakened the opinion that the return of the eastern territories to Poland lies in the Jews' interest."[28]

Indeed, during the months that Mikhoels, Feffer, and Maisky were abroad, Polish officials had been confronted with yet another round of Jewish demands for action and statements of grievances against the exile regime. Labor Minister Stańczyk, for one—who traveled to Palestine in June 1943 on a tour of Polish military installations in the country[29]—found himself set upon by Jewish spokesmen hopeful that his personal intervention might help turn the government's response to Jewish demands in a more favorable direction.[30] Those demands were now reiterated to him in a series of notes and meetings. On 19 June, Abraham Stupp of the Reprezentacja sent him a six-point memorandum calling upon the Polish government to intervene again with the Allies regarding action to rescue the Jews of the occupied homeland; to provide material assistance for the hundreds of thousands of Jews still presumed to be alive in the Polish ghettos;[31] to work more seriously than in the past to improve the attitude of the Polish community at large toward the Jews (an attitude that the Reprezentacja continued to regard as unsatisfactory despite several previous government declarations suggesting that the age of anti-Jewish discrimination in Poland had passed); to permit the Reprezentacja to send delegates to Polish diplomatic posts in neutral countries in order to promote rescue activities from points closer to the area of German control; to provide assistance in relocating Polish Jewish refugees who had managed to escape from the homeland to Hungary, Romania, and other countries;[32] and to make certain that in any future evacuation of Polish citizens from Russia Jews would be proportionately represented, as they had not been in the evacuations of the previous year.[33] Stupp also told Stańczyk in person on 1 July that the government's record to that point in all of these areas was a source of dissatisfaction and pain for Jews and that the grounds for dissatisfaction were "quite serious."[34] On the same occasion Stupp's colleague from the Reprezentacja, Yitshak Lew, complained that "in the matter that is most decisive and of the first order of importance, the matter of resisting the mass slaughter being perpetrated against the Jewish population, the matter of rescue action and assistance, the government took steps too late, when the number of murdered had already reached several hundreds of thousands; and whatever it did do was not consonant with the enormity of the tragedy."[35] Both

Lew and Stupp suggested that the regime's relative inaction on rescue indicated that a large gap still remained between the government's periodic declarations of its commitment to regard Jews on the same basis as all other Polish citizens and its actual attitude. As the latter explained, there was a widespread conviction among Jews that "despite all of the changes that have taken place [in the overall orientation of the Polish government since the outbreak of war], when it comes to its attitude toward Jews, nothing has changed at all."[36]

To all of these charges Stańczyk gave a highly defensive response that, however much he might have wished otherwise, at times actually tended to confirm that the Jews' needs were indeed less important to the government that those of ethnic Poles. After arguing that the possibilities for sending aid to the Jews remaining in the Polish ghettos were limited by the Allied blockade on shipments to Axis-occupied countries, for example, he explained that the government could not request a dispensation from the blockade, "because we are proceeding on the assumption that Poland has enough food, and even if the Germans do not intercept the shipments, their response will be to increase the quotas exacted from the [Polish] peasants."[37] Similarly, he defended the inclusion of but a small number of Jews in the evacuation transports from the Soviet Union on the grounds that Polish military officials had quite naturally "wanted their own people to get out first."[38] Such statements merely heightened the irony in the minister's declaration later that day before a meeting of the executive of the General Federation of Jewish Workers (Histadrut) that "in the Polish people the Jewish population has a genuine ally prepared to cooperate and to assist."[39] Indeed, he gave no indication that the government-in-exile was prepared under any circumstances to meet any of the demands that had been presented to him.[40]

Stańczyk was also called upon unexpectedly to deal with an acute flareup of Polish-Jewish tensions in Palestine occasioned by an incident that occurred during his stay there. On 20 June 1943, less than two weeks prior to Stańczyk's meetings with the Reprezentacja and the Histadrut, the newspaper *Eshnav*, organ of the Palestinian Jewish defense force Haganah, published a Hebrew translation of an order issued by General Anders to his division commanders on 30 November 1941—an order that had explained that although "for now no manifestation of the struggle against the Jews is . . . allowable, . . . when we are masters in our own home after our victorious campaign, we shall dispose of the Jewish question as the greatness and sovereignty of our homeland and ordinary human justice demand."[41] This order had been issued, according to its own testimony, because many Polish soldiers had complained that a previous order stressing the necessity to maintain strict equality between Jews and non-Jews in the ranks was "incomprehensible, historically unjustified, and confusing" because it did not take account of "the disloyal and often hostile behavior of Polish Jews from the eastern territories during the years of our ordeal 1939–40." The publication of the text in Palestine aroused considerable anger among the country's Jews, who saw Anders's words as "possessing a markedly anti-Jewish character, recognizing antisemitic disturbances in the army as 'an expression of fervid patriotism,' and suggesting a settling of accounts with the Jews in the homeland following the attainment of independence."[42]

Stańczyk was confronted with Anders's order (of whose existence he claimed already to have known) by Abraham Stupp on 1 July. Stupp asked the minister, "What meaning can all of the declarations of the government have when taken against this document?" and requested an immediate official government reaction.[43] Stańczyk replied that the general had merely sought to "explain a certain matter that had met with opposition," adding that although he had done so "maladroitly," his clumsiness could be ascribed to the fact that he was "merely a soldier, not a politician."[44] The minister saw no evil motive in Anders's remarks and asked the Jewish representatives not "to make an international incident out of them." Nevertheless, the Reprezentacja decided to issue a formal interpellation concerning the order to the government in London; on 5 July it addressed a letter to the prime minister and the minister of defense inquiring whether they were aware of the order and what they intended to do about it.[45]

This letter was evidently never transmitted to London. Instead, on 12 July, Consul-General Rosmarin in Tel Aviv sent the Reprezentacja a short note stating that Stańczyk had recently met with Anders and that the general had assured him that he had never issued such an order. The note quoted Stańczyk, who earlier had expressed no doubts as to the authenticity of the order,[46] to the effect that he was "personally convinced that we are dealing here with an invention of hostile propaganda aimed at unsettling Polish-Jewish relations."[47] An official of the Polish Consulate-General in Jerusalem similarly told Yitshak Gruenbaum of the Jewish Agency's Rescue Committee that "such an order does not exist and was never issued."[48] The same official also expressed the hope "that the Jewish Agency, recognizing [that] this sort of publication creates misconceptions within the Jewish community and can impair the foundations of Polish-Jewish relations, will use its influence in such a way that public opinion is duly informed of the status of the matter."

The Jewish Agency and the Reprezentacja appear to have been willing to go along with the Polish request, even though they evidently did not accept the contention that the order was a forgery.[49] Polish leaders feared, however, that other Jewish organizations, particularly in the United States, might not be so compliant. On 11 August the Ministry of Information notified Commander-in-Chief Sosnkowski that, according to information received from New York, several Jewish newspapers were planning "a campaign against Gen. Anders and the Polish Army."[50] This plan, the ministry warned, was undoubtedly connected with the Mikhoels-Feffer mission; it indicated that "the forces hostile to us will overlook no opportunity, in this time that is especially difficult for us, to exploit the motif of antisemitism against us."[51] Sosnkowski immediately forwarded the text of the Information Ministry's statement to Anders, "in order to allow him to correct the version of whose maliciousness I have no doubt."[52] It was only in response to this veiled instruction from his commander-in-chief that Anders himself declared the text published in *Eshnav* to be "falsified from A to Z."[53]

The furor over the Anders order died quickly; the general's denial of its existence proved difficult to combat. The fact remained, however, that, as the summer of 1943 turned to fall, Jewish groups were demonstrating greater anger than ever toward the Polish government. The Reprezentacja, in particular, displayed a subtle but nonetheless noticeable change in the manner in which it officially stated its relation toward the London regime during this period. During the meeting with Stańczyk on 1 July, Yitshak Lew had reiterated the terms of a resolution adopted by his organization on 11 February 1942, according to which the Representacja declared its "identification with the political and military actions of the Polish people [aimed at] reestablishing an independent, great, and democratic Poland and [its] willingness to give full support to the government in its activities in the realm of foreign policy."[54] On 4 August 1943, however, a new resolution adopted in conjunction with the convening of the Mikołajczyk cabinet, while continuing to express support for the government's conduct of foreign affairs, called only for the reestablishment of a "free and democratic Poland," pointedly eliminating any reference to the country's territorial extent.⁵⁵ On 16 September the Reprezentacja addressed a lengthy, detailed, and highly contentious memorandum to the government that failed to indicate any support for any aspect of Polish policy, foreign or domestic.⁵⁶ The direction in which the attitudes of this bellweather of organized Jewish opinion was moving—and moving rapidly—was clear.

For the Poles this development may not have been altogether surprising, but only with great difficulty could it be looked upon with equanimity—especially when viewed against the background of the continuing success of the Mikhoels-Feffer mission.⁵⁷ However, observers who gave thought at the time as to whether anything might be done to reverse the trend had on the whole few promising ideas to offer. Kot appointed a Jew, Marceli Dogilewski, to head the Information Ministry's Benelux desk and made Jewish affairs a specific part of his portfolio, with the hope that the information and reports that he would supply to the British and Anglo-Jewish press would "clear the atmosphere on Jewish matters both among British Jews and among the non-Jewish public."⁵⁸ Some other officials suggested that the government gather and publish materials on the condition of Jews in Soviet prison camps (and in the USSR generally) and that it issue a public statement supporting the creation of a Jewish state in Palestine following the war, but at the same time they conceded that the Russians' skill in the propaganda field would make it difficult for the Poles to get their message across to Jewish leaders.⁵⁹ Indeed, it appears that Polish officials who contemplated the problem of Polish-Jewish political relations during this period had resigned themselves merely to hoping that Jews would eventually realize that they were being manipulated by the Soviets and would thus think twice before cooperating with Soviet efforts to blacken the Polish government's good name;⁶⁰ all Poland could do in the meantime was avoid giving Jews any obvious pretext for taking their complaints about the government's attitude toward them before the British and American public.⁶¹ Even if Jews were their enemies, the Poles could not fight them.

The quandary in which the Polish government now found itself vis-à-vis the Jews was thus perhaps even more vexing than any of the difficulties that it had confronted in this regard since the beginning of the war; it seemed as though the Poles were bound to lose no matter what approach to the Jewish situation they tried. Nevertheless, they could not give up the struggle for Jewish opinion entirely, for to do so would have meant—given their view of the importance of the Jewish voice in the formation of Western public opinion overall—the virtual abandonment of much of the propaganda field to the Soviets. With every possible course of action seemingly leading to a blind alley, however, it seemed that they could do no more than wait passively for an opportunity to regain some leverage over the Jews of the West.

Once again an opening presented itself, from a direction that should perhaps have appeared obvious but that was in fact altogether unanticipated.

This new opening resulted from a two-month visit made by Jan Karski to the United States during the summer of 1943. Since his arrival in London in November 1942 the courier from the Polish underground had been meeting with a host of public figures, explaining the Polish situation, the suffering and heroism of the Polish people, and Poland's contribution to the war effort to the shapers and movers of British policy and opinion.[62] He had also met, among others, with the U.S. ambassador to the Polish government-in-exile, Anthony Drexel-Biddle, who, as Karski was to recall later, had been "very much moved" by what the emissary had to report.[63] In June 1943 Biddle had suggested to Sikorski that Karski be sent on a propaganda mission to the United States and had offered to intervene personally with Roosevelt to arrange a private interview with the president.[64] One of Sikorski's final acts had been to consent to this idea.[65]

The object of Karski's mission, as the courier himself summarized it in his final report upon returning to London, was "to inform . . . [certain] people about matters pertaining to the homeland, especially about the vital parts of our work, the structure of the [underground's] liaison with the government, attitudes within the [Polish] community, [and] the results of the underground movement's efforts—naturally on a scale understandable to [my] listeners."[66] In this connection he endeavored to stress the official character of the underground, the interdependence of its civilian and military aspects, the widespread support that it enjoyed among the Polish population, and the danger that it faced from growing Soviet infiltration. His initial meetings were with some of Roosevelt's closest political advisors, including former ambassador to the USSR William Bullitt, Assistant Secretary of State Adolf Berle, and members of Roosevelt's so-called brain trust Ben Cohen, Oscar Cox, and Leon Henderson. Bullitt had reportedly been particularly impressed with Karski's information about the modus operandi of Communist agents inside Poland and had played a key role in getting the president to speak with the emissary. Karski's audience with Roosevelt, which lasted one hour and fifteen minutes, took place on 28 July 1943.[67]

Karski had most emphatically not been dispatched to the United States to speak about the murder of Polish Jewry,[68] and there is no indication that he did so in any of his meetings prior to his audience with Roosevelt. In his discussion with the president, however, he raised the matter on his own initiative.[69] At the time Roosevelt did not appear to Karski to show much interest in this subject.[70] Nevertheless, within several hours of the meeting Ambassador Ciechanowski, who had served as Karski's interpreter, received a hand-delivered message from the White House containing a list of prominent Americans and others whom the president thought Karski should meet. Included in the list were Stephen Wise, Nahum Goldmann, Supreme Court Justice Felix Frankfurter, and other prominent figures on the American Jewish scene.[71] It was at this point, evidently, that a decision was made to incorporate Karski's eyewitness testimony about the Warsaw ghetto and the execution of Jews into his mission and to attempt to reap a reward from it for Polish diplomacy.[72] On 9–10 August, in New York, Karski held seven separate meetings with leaders of Jewish organizations, including the American Branch of the Reprezentacja, the American Jewish Congress, the World Jewish Congress, the American Jewish Committee, the American Jewish Joint Distribution Committee, the American Federation of Polish Jews, and the Bund. He also met with such prominent Jewish figures in the American labor movement as David Dubinsky and Sidney Hillman.[73]

From the reports that he submitted to London during his stay in the United States, Karski appears to have viewed his discussions with Jewish leaders as highly satisfactory. In particular, he noted, "it made a good impression . . . that an 'Aryan [*aryjczyk*]' brought up Jewish matters."[74] He believed that those who had heard him speak had sensed that he was "indeed moved by the fate of the Jews in Poland and wanted to help them somehow, as much as possible." He also indicated that he had tried "to create the impression that sympathy and an understanding of Jewish affairs were to be found among the Polish population." He did this in the first place by stressing that the underground Government Delegacy was involved in extending aid to Jews.[75] In addition he made reference to the fact ("which by the way," he told the government, "is true") that a branch of the Polish

Socialist Party and the Bund were cooperating in conspiratorial work. "This point of my presentation" he reported, "aroused the interest of all of the Jews, no matter what their [ideological] convictions or party affiliation," adding that "being able to refer to this fact makes an excellent impression and helps the Polish cause greatly in American Jewish circles." [76] To be sure, the courier noted, "almost all [of the Jewish leaders] asked me assiduously whether *antisemitism* still existed in Poland," [77] but he felt that he had been able to make them understand "that in the present atmosphere in the country it is simply not possible for any Pole, whatever his political convictions, to declare himself openly to be an antisemite or to express solidarity with German methods." Indeed, he observed that "almost all emphasized that they saw in my good will and sincere desire to come to the aid of the Jews in Poland *proof of a change in the atmosphere toward Jews within the Polish community.*" [78]

Karski suggested further that the positive impression that he had made was likely to redound to Poland's political benefit. He believed that he had been able to refute Soviet propaganda circulating in the United States to the effect that the Polish underground was murdering "leftist patriots" in Poland—propaganda that he felt had previously been taken seriously by most of those with whom he spoke. In fact, he was even able to cite what he took as specific evidence of this ostensible change in the Jewish attitude toward the Polish cause:

> Rather characteristic was the utterance of *Rabbi Wise* (president of the American Jewish World Congress [*sic*]. At the end of our discussion he spoke several words directed, as it were, toward Poland. He said, "Seeing how honestly and wholeheartedly you are working to help our people, how you are taking risks in order to assist the Jewish cause, even though you are not a Jew, I want to stress to you *that my goal and the object of my work is the rebirth of a great and independent Poland in which the Jewish people will be able to live freely on the basis of equal rights with all denizens of the Polish state.* The fact *that you are here and can speak to us shows how strong the Polish underground movement is. Poland shall rise again!*" [79]

Karski's positive evaluation of the results of his meetings with Jewish leaders was seconded by Sylwin Strakacz, Polish consul-general in New York, who had participated as an observer in the various discussions. "In all cases," Strakacz noted in a report to Ciechanowski, "Mr. Karski's remarks made a tremendous impression upon his listeners," commenting further that "the Jewish organizations have high regard [for the fact] that the Polish government is working closely together with them and has dispatched to them on the first occasion one of the highest officials of underground Poland to report on the situation in the homeland."[80] Although he felt that he could not predict "what concrete results Mr. Karski's mission would bring," he professed absolute certainty "that the two days of his [Karski's] presence here galvanized [*wstrząsnęła*] the entire Jewish community and gave us a trump card [*atut*] of the first magnitude in cultivating good relations between the local [Polish] authorities and the Jewish organizations."

Both Karski and Strakacz indicated quite clearly in their reports what they believed that trump card was. "Before I left New York," Karski wrote, "Rabbi Wise, together with Messrs. Goldman and Baldman of the World Jewish Committee [*sic*],[81] invited themselves to me, wishing to find out the most effective way to deliver aid to the Jews in Poland."[82] Elsewhere Karski indicated that the Joint Distribution Committee had decided immediately to send $500,000 in assistance to Polish Jewry, promising that "of course this aid will also encompass 'the most unfortunate from among the Poles,'" and that it had asked Karski how it ought to go about doing so.[83] Strakacz, too, noted this interest, observing that a similar question had been asked by the American Federation of Polish Jews.[84] In response, Karski consistently argued that it was virtually impossible to distribute any funds, supplies, documents, or other items intended for Jews under Nazi occupation in Poland except through the channels maintained by the Polish government-in-exile and the Polish underground. He assured his listeners that "it is absolutely unthinkable [*nieprawdopodobne*] and even technically impossible for aid transmitted to the Jewish population in Poland in any form to be used by any elements other than Jewish ones" and that use of Polish government conduits would "guarantee the greatest efficiency and the fairest distribution" of whatever was sent.[85] Karski felt his argument had won the day: where Wise and Goldmann had initially expressed the hope of establishing "an *immediate* link with the Jewish underground movement in the homeland *independent of and not controlled by the Polish government*," by the conclusion of their meeting they no longer insisted upon this point.[86]

Indeed, in subsequent weeks those with whom Karski had spoken approached Polish authorities with concrete requests for cooperation in rescue and aid activities along the lines that the courier had discussed. In September the Joint Distribution Committee transferred

$100,000 of the $500,000 it had discussed with Karski to the Polish Embassy in Washington with a request that the government state how and to whom those funds would be paid in the occupied homeland.[87] At around the same time the World Jewish Congress and the Jewish Labor Committee arranged for a similar transfer of $45,000, with a promise of an additional $155,000 to follow.[88] The Jewish Agency designated an additional £10,000 for the Polish government to distribute among forty-nine specified communities.[89] Arieh Tartakower sent the government a list of nineteen prominent Jewish activists in occupied Poland, in accordance with what he claimed had been Karski's suggestion that the underground was prepared to help them escape to a neutral country. Tartakower added that Jewish organizations would participate in whatever costs the Polish agencies might incur in carrying out this request.[90]

The importance of these exchanges for the Polish government was patent: the concern of Jewish organizations in the free world for the fate of their brethren under Nazi occupation tied them of necessity to the Polish exile regime. The government might therefore have used that necessary connection—now reinforced by the desire of Jewish organizations to send funds and other forms of assistance to the homeland, against the background of the goodwill that Karski's mission had engendered—to improve its standing in the eyes of world Jewry, in the hope of sealing off the inroads that Soviet propaganda had purportedly made. It does not appear, however, that government policymakers realized the political potential inherent in this situation. On the contrary, no follow-up to Karski's mission was planned, and evidently no efforts were made by the government to develop a regular procedure for transferring funds from Jewish organizations to occupied Poland.[91] The Jewish National Committee and the Bund in underground—the two primary recipients of Jewish aid from abroad—complained of irregularities in the delivery of funds,[92] and Schwarzbart, who attempted to investigate the fate of funds entrusted to the government, seems to have encountered difficulties in obtaining information from official sources on the nature and amount of assistance actually distributed.[93] Moreover, Schwarzbart was unable to extract from the government a commitment to supply substantially increased monies from its own budget for the rescue of Jews.[94] The government, in short, does not appear to have shown much interest at this time in playing the trump card that the Karski mission seemed to have given it.

That lack of interest may have been encouraged by a memorandum from the underground Government Delegacy received in London at around the same time that Karski was conferring with Jewish leaders in New York. The memorandum was written by Roman Knoll, a former Polish envoy in Berlin who was currently serving as head of the delegacy's Commission on Foreign Affairs.[95] In it Knoll noted that although "the mass murder of Jews in Poland by the Germans will reduce the dimensions of the Jewish question in our country, it will not liquidate it entirely"; he contemplated that after liberation Poland might still have to deal with a Jewish population of "one or two million."[96] This fact, he argued, stood to present Polish policymakers with a difficult problem, for, as he viewed the prevailing attitudes among the Polish populace, "the return of masses of Jews would be experienced by the population not as restitution but as an invasion against which they would defend themselves, even with physical means."[97] He thus suggested that the government engage in a diplomatic effort to prevent the repatriation of Jewish survivors to Poland, preferably by creating a separate "national centre for the Jews of Eastern Europe."[98] Such words could only have reminded government leaders once again of the domestic political risks involved in any activity aimed at promoting Jewish welfare[99] and might well have served as a caution against too visible an involvement in transferring relief funds from abroad for Jews under occupation.

On another level, though, the inability of Karski's palpable success with Jewish spokesmen to arouse much excitement among Polish leaders in London represented an additional reflection of the general atmosphere of pessimism and helplessness that seems to have pervaded government thinking about Jewish matters at this time. Evidently most Polish policymakers simply could not believe that there was any real possibility of developing a relationship of active cooperation with Jewish organizations, despite the optimism that not only Karski but also Strakacz had shown. As a result, the Karski mission, for all of the promise that it offered, failed in the long run to bring the government any significant benefit in the Jewish field. Instead, officials in London remained mired in malaise and inaction, in effect leaving the purported power of world Jewry to influence Western public opinion to be exploited at will by the Poles' Soviet adversaries.

The reaction to Karski's discussions with Jewish leaders by Consul-General Strakacz did indicate, however, that not all Polish officials shared the pessimism of the London leadership. There was at least one other group of Poles, in another part of the world altogether, that was evidently not prepared at this time to write off the possibility of harnessing free-world Jewish influence to the Polish cause and that continued during the latter half of 1943 to pursue a Polish-Jewish political alliance. The efforts of this group were to generate a curious sidelight to the story of the wartime interactions between Poles and Jews—a sidelight that, because of one of the personalities involved, has since come to assume a significance far beyond that which it seemed to possess in its immediate context. Nevertheless, it appears that this peripheral episode can throw some important light on another possible reason why the Karski mission remained without long-term effect.

The group in question was comprised of a small number of officers and enlisted men serving with Polish military intelligence in Palestine. Toward the end of 1943 these individuals began to take a renewed look at the possibility of forming an alliance with the one faction of the Zionist camp that throughout the war had consistently maintained a pro-Polish, anti-Soviet position. That faction was the small Revisionist bloc,[100] which had been founded by Ze'ev Jabotinsky in 1925 and seceded from the World Zionist Organization ten years later.[101] Even before the war this breakaway party had sought active cooperation with the Polish government,[102] and in the early stages of the conflict some Polish officials had sought to develop close links with it.[103] However, by mid-1941 the government appears to have come to the conclusion that the Revisionists did not possess enough influence in Jewish circles to make them a valuable ally, and, lest too close an association with them antagonize both the Zionist mainstream and the British government, it resolved to limit its dealings with them to "non-obligating contacts" only.[104] Nevertheless, the Revisionists had continued to believe that the interests of their movement coincided with those of Poland, and on several occasions they had repeated to the government their desire to work with it in order to advance their mutual goals.[105]

Some prominent Revisionists, moreover—especially those from Poland who had been interned in the Soviet Union at the beginning of the war and had joined the Polish exile army under General Anders in 1941—had developed close relationships with certain senior Polish military officials, particularly in the intelligence service, and, through their outspoken anti-Soviet attitude, had gained those officers' confidence.[106] With the establishment of Polish military headquarters in Palestine following the evacuation from the Soviet Union, the significance of these contacts had grown in both Polish and Revisionist eyes;[107] not only did the Revisionists again become prominent in the thinking of some Poles as potential political allies, but the Poles appeared to Revisionist leaders to hold the key to solving what had by late 1943 become for them the central problem of the future of their movement. Since the late 1930s the Revisionists had maintained a close association with an underground Palestinian Jewish military organization known as Irgun Tseva'i Le'umi, which had been built upon the premise that military force would represent a central element in the attainment of Zionist goals in Palestine. Even before the outbreak of the Second World War the Irgun, as it has commonly come to be known, had undertaken—with Revisionist concurrence—small-scale paramilitary actions against the Zionists' two principal antagonists in the country, the local Arabs and the British mandatory authorities.[108] Once Britain entered the battle against Nazi Germany, however, a majority within the Irgun—again in accordance with the Revisionist line—had consented to suspend anti-British military operations for the duration of the war.[109] Nevertheless, by mid-1943, following assimilation by Jews of the news of the Holocaust and in light of the British government's steadfast refusal to open the gates of Palestine to Jewish refugees from Nazi-occupied Europe, Revisionist circles in particular had begun to doubt the wisdom of such a course; within the Irgun calls were heard to reopen the armed struggle against the British mandate in order to make it possible for a Jewish regime in Palestine to rescue the masses of Jews still believed to be alive in Europe.[110]

At the time such calls for an anti-British revolt began to circulate, however, the Irgun was in no position to launch a military uprising. Its commander, David Raziel, had been killed in 1941 while on an undercover mission for the British in Iraq, and his successor, Ya'akov Meridor, had proven unable to build the organization into a serious fighting force. As one of the central figures among the Palestinian Revisionists explained, "The Irgun's strength was limited, both in manpower and in armaments . . . , and greater still was the concern over the lack of popular support and of political and moral leadership."[111] The Revisionists thus realized that unless they could place a strong leader at the head of this organization any talk of ousting the British from Palestine by force would remain idle.

In this context Revisionist leaders appear to have begun to consider inviting a former head of their youth organization in Poland, who had arrived in Palestine in May 1942 with the Polish exile army and was then serving as a translator at Polish military headquarters in Jerusalem, to fill the post of commander of the Irgun. This thirty-year-old corporal named Menahem Begin was widely regarded in Revisionist circles as a fitting heir to the charismatic mantle of Jabotinsky and Raziel. The veteran Revisionist Aryeh ben Eliezer noted that Begin had first come to his attention at the world conference of Betar, the Revisionist youth movement, which had been held in Warsaw in September 1938; there Begin had appeared as "a legendary figure to hundreds and thousands of Jewish young people." Such a person, remarked Ben Eliezer, "revered by thousands of Betar members throughout Europe, was the one who could give us the leadership that we needed in these historic times of trial."[112] Although at first there appear to have been some doubts about Begin's fitness for such a role in view of his lack of a military background,[113] by the fall of 1943 the Revisionist leadership in Palestine had decided to seek his release from the Polish army so that he could take command of the Irgun.[114]

Despite the Revisionists' connections with the Polish army, however, securing Begin's release proved to be a difficult task. Obviously the Revisionists could not reveal to the Poles their plans for a revolt against British rule in Palestine, for the Poles, as Britain's junior allies, would be bound to cut off all contacts with them. Indeed, the same considerations that had earlier led the government-in-exile to reduce the level of its contacts with the Revisionist movement continued to be noted by Polish officials at this time,[115] with the result that initial efforts to have Begin discharged from the Polish forces were unsuccessful.[116] The Poles' reluctance to deal with the Revisionists on this matter was no doubt augmented, moreover, by the fact that they stood to receive no tangible benefit from acquiescence. The Revisionists were aware that their efforts would need to depend on more than the close personal connections of some of their number with top echelons in the army; in the meantime, they began to fear that their designated commander would soon be dispatched with the remainder of the Polish exile army to the Italian front, far from the site of the planned revolt.[117]

Ben Eliezer appears to have provided the key to breaking the impasse. He had spent most of the summer months in the United States, where, with other Revisionist activists, he had taken a leading role in forming the Emergency Committee to Save the Jewish People of Europe, a group dedicated to directing maximum public attention to the dangers facing the Jews under Nazi rule.[118] The Emergency Committee had had a highly visible impact upon the American scene, enlisting the active support of such leading political figures as Harold Ickes and Fiorello la Guardia and journalists and men of letters such as William Randolph Hearst, Max Lerner, Ben Hecht, Pierre van Passen, and William Allen White. According to Ben Eliezer, "Representatives [of the Polish government] in America," recognizing the importance of the connections that the committee had developed, "turned to [it] for assistance in one matter or another."[119] Thus the Revisionist leader suspected that it might be possible to create a similar impression among the Polish military authorities in Palestine and to use that impression as a vehicle for obtaining Begin's release:

> The Polish government in London was concerned not only for American public opinion in general but especially for Jewish opinion in the United States. . . . On the basis of this assumption I decided to approach the representatives of the Polish government in Palestine in the name of the [Emergency] Committee in the United States with the following program and request: With the withdrawal of the Red Army from Poland [following the German invasion of June 1941], many Polish citizens, including Jews, had fled eastward as well. . . . We have found it essential to raise the matter of the Polish Jews in Russia. . . . We wanted to begin [to direct] propaganda and pressure at the Russian government to free the Jews from the [internment] camps and guarantee their right to return to liberated Poland or to immigrate to Palestine after the war. In order to arouse public opinion in America and other countries in favor of these demands, we requested, according to the plan, several individuals who are themselves Polish citizens, who as Jews had experienced all the sufferings of the Russian hell and who could appear as spokesmen for their brothers still in the wastelands of Siberia or in internment camps. And one of those individuals was to be Begin.[120]

After obtaining the consent of the Revisionist leadership in Palestine, Ben Eliezer, together with the titular head of the Palestinian

Revisionists, Aryeh Altmann, placed his proposal for sending a Polish Jewish delegation to the United States formally before the chief of the army's Document Bureau, Capt. Kazimierz Święcicki. He presented the plan as a vehicle for achieving Polish-Jewish cooperation in the United States, through which the Emergency Committee would place its apparatus at the disposal of the Polish government "in certain Polish matters." In particular, he offered to distribute "materials in the possession of the [Document] Bureau depicting the difficult situation of Jewish Polish citizens in Soviet Russia and the negative consequences, from the perspective of Jewish interests, of the communist solution to the Jewish question." In order to make such distribution as effective as possible, he explained, it was "indispensable that the leadership of this action rest in the hands of people who had felt with their own skin what Soviet Russia is." Because the only people meeting that description were those who had been evacuated from the Soviet Union with the Polish army, he continued, the delegation of which he spoke could be constituted only by releasing several Jewish soldiers from active service. He mentioned several names of possible candidates for the delegation, among them that of Begin.[121]

From the Revisionists' perspective, of course, the idea of sending a delegation of Polish Jews from Palestine to the United States to conduct anti-Soviet propaganda was nothing more than a ruse designed to secure the discharge of the Irgun's designated commander from the Polish forces; but they took care not to let on to the Poles their actual intentions. Indeed, as Ben Eliezer explained, "It was decided . . . that I should deal not with Begin's release alone but with that of four others from among our members, so as not to arouse suspicion that we were interested in Begin alone."[122] From the Polish point of view, on the other hand, the Revisionists' proposal could not have come at a more opportune time, especially with the memory of Maisky's recent visit to Palestine and Mikhoels and Feffer's triumphant tour of the United States and Britain still fresh in Polish minds.[123] Moreover, the Revisionists were most likely unaware that the idea of organizing such a Palestinian delegation, under the guise of a fund-raising campaign for the Jews of Russia, had been broached in Polish government circles over a year before, only to be shelved, it appears, because of the belief that Jewish volunteers for such a delegation could not be found.[124] In any event, Polish military intelligence officials who reviewed the proposal, although noting the necessity for "far-reaching caution" in keeping the government from being identified publicly with the activities of the proposed delegation, were evidently sufficiently enthused about it to recommend its implementation to the second-in-command of the Polish forces in Palestine, Gen. Michał Tokarzewski.[125] On 31 December 1943 Tokarzewski signed an order granting leave to six Jewish soldiers, including Menahem Begin, for the purpose of participating in a propaganda mission on behalf of the Polish government in the United States, under the aegis of the Emergency Committee to Save the Jewish People in Europe.[126]

For the Poles nothing ever came of the idea, for the mission never departed. The British mandatory authorities evidently were not eager to see a British ally cooperating officially with a Zionist group, and they would not permit the delegation to leave the country. In the meantime, though, Begin and his fellow dischargees went into hiding underground and one month later raised the Irgun's standard of revolt against British rule in Palestine.

Whatever the long-term significance of this action for the future history of the Middle East, it is clear that in its own right it had no importance for the development of the relations between the Polish government-in-exile and the Jews. However, the considerations that led Polish military officials to fall, as it were, for the Revisionists' ruse were consequential in that regard, for they revealed how painfully oblivious many Poles were to the thoughts and feelings that animated those whom they hoped would be their allies. Those considerations were outlined in a memorandum evidently circulated among top officials of Polish military intelligence in Palestine following the meeting at which Ben Eliezer first broached the plan to Captain Święcicki:

> The publication of materials relating to the situation of the Jews in Soviet Russia will be altogether correctly treated by Soviet officials as anti-Soviet propaganda. The mission of Mikhoels and Feffer to America is indicative of the great weight that Soviet officials place upon American Jewish opinion. Hence the tendency of Soviet propaganda organs to interfere with all propaganda activities by the [Emergency] Committee that run counter to Soviet interests will also be easily understandable. The American [Emergency] Committee is planning to expand its rescue activity to include not only those Jews under Hitlerite occupation but also those who found refuge in Russia. Such action by the Committee is inseparably connected with opposition to all manner of Soviet annexationist tendencies, for recognizing such claims nec-

essarily denies hundreds and thousands of Jews the non-Russian (Polish, Romanian, Lithuanian, Latvian, and Estonian) citizenship by which they are being served today.[127]

Perhaps most striking in this evaluation is its ascription to the Revisionist-led Emergency Committee of a motive that—ironically—carried more weight among the mainstream Zionists represented in the Jewish Agency. These latter circles had shown far greater concern over the preceding two years for the rescue of Jewish refugees in the Soviet Union than had the Revisionists. In fact, it was in large measure precisely that concern that had prompted the mainstream Zionists to engage in those actions of deference toward the Soviet government that many Polish officials appear to have interpreted in the light of the *Żydokomuna* stereotype. Yet for the Polish intelligence officers who prepared this analysis of the Revisionist proposal it appeared axiomatic that concern for the fate of Jews who had been forced by the Nazi onslaught to seek shelter in the USSR would of necessity lead Jewish organizations to oppose Soviet designs for westward territorial expansion at Poland's expense. Thus the Polish officials who advocated the formation of the Revisionist propaganda delegation did not contemplate the possibility that the Revisionists might have had any ulterior motive in making their proposal. For them the Revisionists' offer represented nothing more than a desire for "actual honest cooperation in defense of mutual interests." [128]

This desire, moreover, according to Polish military intelligence officials, was self-generated; they thought it had been aroused not because of any Polish concessions to Jewish interests but, rather, by a Jewish group's own apparent heightened sensitivity to the sufferings of fellow Jews under the Soviet yoke. Polish policymakers might well have taken considerable comfort in this interpretation. In the first place it could be regarded as a demonstration that no matter how great the purported affinity of Jews for Communism, at least some Jews recognized that their interests and those of the Soviets clashed. If so, Polish leaders might have reasoned, then as other Jewish bodies developed the same degree of commitment to rescuing refugees in the USSR as the Revisionists now appeared to be showing, they too might conceivably arrive at the same assessment.

Carried to its logical conclusion, this line of reasoning stood to lead to the inference that world Jewry might not need to be written off as an inveterate enemy after all, and there might still be hope that its power could be harnessed in favor of the Polish cause. Moreover, this interpretation suggested that the Polish government would not need to take any action in order to bring about such a change in Jewish thinking. Specifically, it implied that the Polish response to Jewish demands for rescue action in the occupied homeland stood to influence Jewish attitudes toward the Polish-Soviet dispute far less than did the physical suffering of Jews under Soviet rule. As a result, the Poles' own inability to induce the Jews of the West to behave as the Poles wished and the apparent susceptibility of Jewish organizations to Soviet propaganda did not need to be regarded as quite so worrisome as they had been a few months earlier; indeed, one Polish observer actually noted in November 1943 that, in Palestine at least, "the attitude of local Jewish elements toward the Polish question has undergone improvement during the past year."[129]

Such thinking was apparent most notably in a highly optimistic thirty-five-page memorandum on prospects for future Polish-Jewish cooperation prepared by a staff member of the Document Bureau shortly following Ben Eliezer's meeting with Święcicki.[130] This memorandum, observing that "Jewish opinion . . . is flexible" and that many Jews prominent in the economic and professional life of Palestine were "definite Polish sympathizers" who would "gladly take part in [projects for] Polish-Jewish cooperation," suggested that the Polish government needed to take only minimal steps in order to nurture these positive trends. Such steps included establishing closer personal contacts with Zionist leaders, "showing greater interest in the Jews' work" in Palestine, expressing support for the mass resettlement of Jewish survivors from Nazi-occupied Europe in Palestine following the conclusion of hostilities, encouraging former Polish Jewish refugees in the Soviet Union to speak of their experiences under Soviet rule, and instructing Polish soldiers and officers to demonstrate a friendly attitude toward Jews serving in the Polish armed forces. By taking these steps, the author of the memorandum implied, Poles could increase the already high probability that Jews, and especially Zionists, would eventually come around to support the Polish side in the Polish-Soviet conflict.[131]

This was a remarkable position for a Polish propagandist to assume, considering the inability of the government-in-exile to arouse a significant anti-Soviet backlash among free-world Jewry in the wake of the Erlich-Alter affair and the recent success of the Mikhoels-Feffer mission to North America and Great Britain, both of which had appeared earlier to reinforce the *Żydokomuna* stereotype in the minds of many Polish leaders. Yet the author of this memorandum was not alone in such an optimistic appraisal. In fact, it appears that such optimistic thinking was beginning to permeate the central leadership in London as well. In late October, Marceli Dogilewski, head of the newly created Benelux and Jewish desk in the Polish Ministry of Information, noted dissatisfaction among Jewish circles in Great Britain with certain recent Soviet actions, including the establishment of a military order named for the seventeenth-century Cossack hetman Bogdan Chmielnicki (who, although a national hero to the Ukrainian people, was infamous among Jews as the leader of a wave of massacres in 1648–49 that had destroyed some 300 Jewish communities).[132] According to Dogilewski, not only had the Revisionists in London formally protested this action to the Soviet embassy, but Selig Brodetsky, president of the Board of Deputies of British Jews, who but a short time earlier had welcomed Feffer and Mikhoels to the British capital, had requested the Soviet ambassador to receive a delegation to discuss the matter. In addition Dogilewski indicated that the head of the Jewish Committee for Aid to Soviet Russia had called for that organization to meet, arguing that it could no longer take part in assisting "a country that glorified one of the most abominable figures" in Jewish history.[133] For Dogilewski, as for his superior, Kot, who was presented with his observations, these developments must have seemed parallel to the trend that other observers had noted in the Revisionists' approach to the Polish military authorities in Palestine.

Perhaps the seeming contradiction between the optimistic evaluation of Jews' attitudes toward Poland that prevailed, at least in some Polish circles, toward the end of 1943 and the more pessimistic evaluation that vied with it for dominance in the minds of Polish policymakers indicates just how deeply Polish planners felt the necessity of obtaining world Jewish support in their diplomatic struggle and just how adamantly unwilling they were to face the possibility that that support might never be forthcoming. For people who believed that the Jews of the United States, Great Britain, and Palestine exerted potentially decisive influence over Allied public opinion, the conclusion that the Jews were hopelessly lost to the Polish side suggested that the chances that the Allies would back Poland's territorial claims vis-à-vis the Soviet Union were approaching nil. Following the evacuation of the Polish armed forces from the Soviet Union, the rupture of Polish-Soviet diplomatic relations and the subsequent formation of an alternate Polish military force under Soviet patronage, and the political crisis engendered by the death of Sikorski, Allied support remained the government-in-exile's only hope for achieving its outstanding diplomatic objective. Resigning the hope of ever obtaining such support was thus tantamount to giving up the diplomatic struggle altogether, something that in late 1943 no exile Polish politician was prepared to do. The approach taken in the first instance by the army's Document Bureau and other branches of the Polish government to the problem of promoting Polish-Jewish cooperation, then, appears to have represented in no small measure a comfortable way for Poles to avoid confronting an increasingly bitter reality in areas far transcending the issue of Polish-Jewish relations.

However, the evaluation of Jewish attitudes toward Poland upon which this device for escaping reality depended was itself a fantasy. Polish military officials in Palestine had made the mistake not only of interpreting the Revisionists' scheme for securing Begin's release from the Polish army as a sincere expression of a desire for collaboration but also of reading this purported attitude of a small renegade Zionist faction as indicative of the thinking of much larger and more influential Jewish groups. It was only on the basis of this misinterpretation that they could expect to win Jewish cooperation without making any substantial concessions to Jewish demands in the area of rescue. In maintaining this expectation, however, they appear willfully to have ignored what Jewish leaders had been trying to make clear to the government-in-exile for over a year—that what concerned them most (although, to be sure, not exclusively) with regard to the Polish government was how that government could be of assistance to the Jews in Nazi-occupied Poland. Thus when the Polish consul-general in New York sent what was in the final analysis a no less sanguine message about possibilities for future Polish-Jewish cooperation than those then being issued by Polish military circles in Palestine, the government in London paid little heed. The reason, of course, was that the former had suggested that in order to achieve the desired level of cooperation the government would need to become actively involved in an operation in which, at bottom, it did not wish to take part, whereas the latter had implied that the same cooperation could be had in effect for no price at all.

In this context there does not appear to have been much possibility for Jewish leaders to get their message about the centrality of rescue across. Indeed, by the end of 1943 the sort of dialogue between Polish and Jewish representatives that had been taking place periodically in Palestine since mid-1942 had begun to develop a highly ritualized mien. Such, for example, was certainly the tenor of the meeting between a delegation from the Reprezentacja and Henryk Strassburger, a former treasury minister now serving as minister of state for the Middle East, held at the Polish consulate in Jerusalem on 17 December 1943. At this confrontation Abraham Stupp spelled out once again for the Polish minister the usual range of Jewish complaints and demands, tellingly commenting that "perhaps our biggest complaint is precisely that we must continually complain."[134] Anshel Reiss, too, remonstrated once again that "on our part we are doing everything in order to create a different atmosphere [between us], but we do not see this on the part of the government and its organs."[135] Once again the Polish minister charged Jews with "hypersensitivity [przewrażliwienie]," admonishing the leaders present not to paint such a dark picture of Polish-Jewish relations, insisting that the regime could not fairly be called antisemitic, and reporting that during a visit to the United States he had "encountered complaints [from Polish emigrés] that we [the government-in-exile] talk only about the Jews."[136] When pressed with the question of what the government planned to do in the matter of rescue, Strassburger replied that, although this was, to his mind, an important matter, he could not comment upon it for lack of information.[137] The meeting ended without result.[138]

Another meeting, held in London on 13 January 1944 between Schwarzbart and Tartakower on one side and Mikołajczyk on the other, graphically illustrated both the unwillingness of the government to become involved in rescue activities and the reason why at this time it felt no compulsion to do so. Tartakower, who had only recently come to London in order to strengthen Jewish representation vis-à-vis the Polish authorities, asked the prime minister whether the government would be willing to establish "a special department . . . for matters related to saving the remnants of Polish Jewry."[139] He explained that "not only Polish Jews in America but American Jewry and public opinion in its entirety attach special weight to this subject," adding that "our concern with rescuing the remnants of Polish Jewry is the sole purpose of our lives." He believed, he noted, that "concentrating the resources dispersed among various components of the government apparatus . . . in the form of a special authority would facilitate the intensification of action and would also . . . make the best impression upon public opinion."

According to Schwarzbart's summary of the meeting, Mikołajczyk thought for a while in silence before offering his response. The matter, he began, merited consideration. However, he stated that right away he could foresee administrative and political difficulties in implementing Tartakower's suggestion. If such a department were created for the Jews, he argued, then it would also be necessary to establish a similar department for Ukrainian affairs; but for political reasons it was impossible to do so. Moreover, he maintained, setting up such a department was tantamount organizationally to creating an entire new government ministry, presumably a most complicated procedure. In any case the government was already doing much in the field of rescue, he explained, and the underground in the occupied homeland was assisting Jews despite the mortal danger involved in such action.

Schwarzbart attempted to counter Mikołajczyk's excuses. He pointed out that the situation of the Ukrainians could in no way be likened to that of the Jews, which had by now become a matter of the utmost urgency from a strictly humanitarian point of view. He also explained that it would not be necessary to set up the proposed department as a new ministry; it could, rather, be established with a minimum of administrative difficulty within the framework of the prime minister's own office or of the Ministry of Labor and Social Welfare. With proper leadership, he argued, "all political and organizational complications could easily be overcome."

Mikołajczyk's lack of enthusiasm for the entire idea, however, was patent. The prime minister attempted to counter Schwarzbart's refutation of his initial objections by warning that if a Jewish department were to be established within the Ministry of Labor it was liable to be dominated by influences from the Bund—a development that Zionists such as Schwarzbart and Tartakower were not likely to welcome.[140] Schwarzbart, however, was quick to respond that such an eventuality did not deter him. "Realizing this demand," he stated, "ought to benefit all Jews; we do not make distinctions." Besides, he pointed out, locating the department within the Ministry of Labor represented only one organizational possibility of several; locating it within the prime minister's office was even preferable. That suggestion, of course, put Mikołajczyk on the spot, but he managed to evade the pressure by announcing that he would ponder the matter. His intention, though, was evidently well understood by the Jewish spokesmen, who dropped the issue at this point.[141]

If the Poles had at times shown frustration over their difficulties in dealing with Jews, Jewish leaders must have been no less frustrated over exchanges such as this one. Yet ironically, in the discussion at hand Schwarzbart and Tartakower had from the outset actually given Mikołajczyk the best possible justification for his evasive attitude. Tartakower had opened the meeting by declaring ceremoniously that "Polish Jewry and especially the Reprezentacja fully support the government in its struggle and political efforts" and that "today, when the [Polish] Republic is going through such a tragic period, the government can count on Polish Jewry." This assurance was given unconditionally, before the Jewish representatives had mentioned any demands of their own. They undoubtedly believed that such an approach would make the prime minister more amenable to their suggestions. To Mikołajczyk, though, their seeming readiness to provide gratis what the Poles had long demanded of them must have confirmed the suspicion brewing in some government circles during the previous few months that Jews were beginning to move spontaneously in a pro-Polish direction. Thus, after listening to Tartakower's opening statement, the prime minister must have felt no political incentive to be forthcoming with regard to his demands. Within the guidelines that had long since been set by the Polish government for dealing with Jewish matters, then, his actual response to those demands made eminent good sense.

Three days after this meeting, however, an event took place that was eventually radically to alter the manner in which the government-in-exile viewed Jewish rescue demands.

4

Soldiers

The event that ultimately changed the pattern of relations that had developed during 1943 between the government-in-exile and the Jews was the desertion, on 16 January 1944, of sixty-eight Jewish soldiers serving with Polish military units stationed in Great Britain and their subsequent demand to be transferred to the British armed forces.[1] These soldiers, on a weekend furlough in London from their bases in Scotland, congregated at a shelter in Gower Street maintained by the Federation of Polish Jews in Great Britain and announced publicly that they would not return to their units. This step, they declared, was to be regarded as a protest against the hostility and ill-treatment to which they claimed to have been subjected by their officers and fellow soldiers—hostility and ill-treatment that to their minds they experienced for no other reason than that they were Jews.[2] Following several weeks of negotiations between the soldiers, various Jewish leaders with whom they were in contact, the Polish Defense Ministry, and the British War Office, an agreement was reached providing for the transfer of the deserters, without punishment or prejudice, to the British Pioneer Corps.[3] Even earlier, during the initial stages of the negotiations, the Polish Defense Ministry and commander-in-chief had summoned an investigating commission to determine whether the deserters' complaints had any basis in fact.[4]

The tendency of the Polish authorities appears to have been to do all in their power to keep the incident from gaining widespread public attention, as the complaints of the Jewish soldiers could certainly provide grist for hostile propaganda mills.[5] The British government, too, for reasons of its own, was also interested in disposing of the matter as quickly and as quietly as possible, and after satisfying itself that no insurmountable procedural obstacles existed, it consented to accept the deserters into the ranks of its own armed forces.[6] However, the efforts to liquidate the problem with dispatch were not to bear fruit. On 22 February 1944, even before the Polish military investigating commission had completed its report, a second group of 136 Jewish soldiers absented itself without leave in a fashion similar to the first cohort and demanded identical terms to those that had been granted its predecessors.[7] The same considerations that had shaped the Polish and British attitudes toward the first group appear to have applied in this case as well, and the second group of deserters was quickly transferred. However, this time the British informed the Poles that they would not accept any more Jewish transferees under such circumstances, in effect instructing them both to tighten discipline in their own ranks and to eliminate the ostensible causes of the desertions.[8] Clearly in response to this British stricture, Defense Minister Kukiel issued, on 13 March 1944, an order to all Polish units in Great Britain, informing them that henceforth any soldier found absent from the ranks without leave would be treated as a deserter during time of war and punished with the full severity of Polish military law.[9] One week later, Commander-in-Chief Sosnkowski, adopting a somewhat different approach to the problem, informed the troops that "the [Polish] armed forces must be based upon equality of rights and duties without regard to creed or political convictions, always on condition of absolute loyalty to Poland," and indicated that he would "fight all instances of prejudice and lack of comradeship" among them as detrimental to the Polish interest.[10]

Nevertheless, the desertions continued. On 21 March, the day following the promulgation of Sosnkowski's order, a third group of twenty-four soldiers followed the path of its predecessors.[11] Seven more soldiers joined this group during the ensuing week,[12] bringing the portion of Jews who had left the Polish forces in protest over alleged ill-treatment in the ranks to almost one-third of all the Jewish soldiers serving with Polish units in Great Britain.[13] This time, however, in accordance with the British fiat and Kukiel's admonition, the deserters were taken into custody and tried in a Polish military court, where most were sentenced initially to prison terms of up to two years.[14]

The arrest, trial, and sentencing of the Jewish soldiers, along with similar measures taken against twenty-eight White Russian and Ukrainian deserters who had also left the ranks in March,[15] proved of considerable deterrent value: desertions came to an end.[16] However, as Kukiel noted, these tactics also produced a negative outcome from the Polish point of view: "They let loose a storm throughout the entire world against the Polish authorities and armed forces."[17] Indeed, in the weeks following the arrest of the third group the question of the status of Jews in the Polish army, and with it the overall attitude of the Polish government toward Jewish matters, became once again a matter for widespread public debate in Britain and in the United States in a manner that the Poles found not only embarrassing but invidious.[18] Interpellations on the subject were made in the House of Commons,[19] and the issue was also brought to the attention of the United States House of Representatives.[20] The British press also castigated the Polish government in "righteous indignation" for its alleged failure to put a stop to anti-Jewish discrimination and hostility in its armed forces.[21]

This result of its handling of the desertions stood to be especially deleterious to the regime's efforts in the diplomatic arena, where the cause of the government-in-exile had continued to suffer notable setbacks during the preceding months. In late 1943 and early 1944 it had become clear to the government's leaders that not only the integrity of Poland's prewar boundaries but also the leaders' own survival as the country's recognized spokesmen was increasingly being called into question.[22] Indeed, Churchill, Roosevelt, and Stalin, meeting at Tehran in November 1943, had effectively decided to impose a new border settlement upon Poland, and shortly thereafter the British had begun to press Mikołajczyk and other senior officials to accept territorial changes.[23] Withstanding such pressure had proven difficult enough at the time,[24] but the situation was soon to become complicated even further. On 4 January 1944, Soviet troops had crossed the prewar Polish frontier and had begun to reoccupy territory that had belonged to Poland before 17 September 1939. The government-in-exile had taken cognizance of this new development with a statement demanding the reestablishment of a "Polish sovereign administration in the liberated territories,"[25] a demand that had led Stalin to proclaim that the exile regime was "incorrigible."[26] The Soviets now began openly to demand that the Polish government, which, they claimed, contained "Fascist elements," be reconstituted,[27] and Churchill, for one, realized that, as the Red Army would clearly occupy Warsaw, it would be in an unassailable position "to set up a Polish Government, based on a plebisite [sic], having every aspect of democratic and popular foundation, and in full accord with the Russian view."[28] In fact, the foundations of such a government had already been laid: in December 1943, Communist elements in occupied Poland had proclaimed the establishment of the National Council for the Homeland

(Krajowa Rada Narodowa—KRN) as *"the actual political representation of the Polish people*, empowered to act in the name of the nation and to direct its destiny until Poland is liberated from occupation." [29]

The KRN manifesto had sharply attacked the government-in-exile as a "clique of reactionaries" seeking to reimpose the rule of the "antidemocratic" prewar regime that had been "loathed by the people." The government's policies, the manifesto claimed, had placed Poland "in an ambiguous position between the Allied bloc and the German satellites." [30] In January 1944 this view of the London regime as somehow guided by principles inconsistent with those in whose name the Allies had ostensibly gone to war in the first place had begun to permeate the British press. [31] In such a situation Polish officials could not help but have been aware that the charges brought by the Jewish deserters could easily lend credence to such an image. [32] The government could scarcely have afforded such adverse publicity before, but at a time when it was fighting for its life, the possible impact of such accusations was multiplied sevenfold. As a result, the desertion of the Jewish soldiers was to prove a serious political embarrassment for the exile government, one that led remarkably to the generation of more paper by more government agencies than any other matter concerning Jews with which the government dealt before or since. It aroused sharp controversies among various branches of the regime; it pushed several Jewish organizations—including, perhaps most surprisingly, the Revisionists—over the brink into active public opposition to the government's most fundamental postulates; and in the end it appears ironically to have provided impetus for the government to become, at least on the surface, more actively involved in matters of Jewish rescue than it had ever been previously. Thus a seemingly minor episode at the periphery of the Polish-Jewish arena acquired central significance in the evolution of the relations between the Polish government-in-exile and the Jews.

The soldiers who left their units in Great Britain were not the first Jews to abandon the Polish forces. In 1942–43, officials of the Polish exile army in the Middle East had faced a wave of desertions by Jewish soldiers serving with the army in Palestine. These desertions began shortly after the arrival of the first contingent of military evacuees from the USSR in the British mandatory territory in May 1942. By August of that year 225 defections of Jewish soldiers (of a total of

600 Jewish military personnel who had left the Soviet Union in the first evacuation) had been recorded by the chief of the army's field tribunal.[33] During the following year, as additional troops were transferred to Palestine from Iran and Iraq, the number of desertions climbed: official estimates ranged between 600 and 800 by mid-1943, 800 and 1,000 by November, and even more by the beginning of 1944.[34] In sum, at least one-quarter and perhaps as many as one-half of the total number of Jewish soldiers who came to Palestine with the Polish forces quit the ranks upon arrival in the country.[35]

Obviously these desertions were closely related to the location of the army at the time they occurred; indeed, defections of Jews from the Anders army anywhere else were rare.[36] The connection is not at all surprising. In the first place, as at least two Polish reports on the desertions observed, Jewish soldiers in the Polish forces were increasingly realizing, in the face of accumulating information about the devastation of Polish Jewry, that at the end of the war there would be virtually no one left in Poland to help them rebuild the Jewish communal life that had, more than anything else for many, made that country their home.[37] It evidently appeared to growing numbers that the type of Jewish community that could provide a meaningful framework for their lives was now to be found only in Palestine, and their fortuitous presence in that country at this moment might, for all they knew, represent their only chance to get there.[38] Moreover, in Palestine conditions facilitating desertion were present that were not conceivable anywhere else. Many soldiers had family or friends in the country who could assist them; others could count on the aid of organized bodies, such as Jewish political parties, youth movements, and collective farms (kibbutzim) in establishing themselves in their new environment.[39] Finding employment was not difficult in what was an expanding economy, and the lack of compulsory registration of addresses, combined with the basic physical and cultural resemblance of the soldiers to many others in the local population, made it relatively easy for the deserters simply to dissolve into their new surroundings.[40]

Polish reports emphasize, however, that the positive attraction of Palestine was not the sole motive for the deserters' action. More frequently mentioned as a cause of defection was an attitude of hostility demonstrated by Polish soldiers toward Jews in the ranks.[41] To be sure, Jewish soldiers had complained of such hostility ever since they first arrived in Palestine, and Jewish spokesmen had regularly forwarded their protests to the Polish government.[42] The use of such complaints to legitimize desertion, however—especially in the months following the break in Polish-Soviet relations—presented the Polish authorities with a special problem. As one report explained, any evidence seemingly supporting the notion that "relations between the national groups in the ranks of the Polish army are unbearable . . . will naturally be transmitted to the appropriate elements in the United States, where the activities of . . . Michels and Pepper [sic][43] have created suitable anti-Polish tendencies that bear also upon the problem of our eastern border."[44] The challenge to the Poles was thus not only to put a stop to the desertions but to do so in a fashion that would not play into the hands of hostile propagandists.[45]

The Poles' ability to meet this goal, however, was impaired by two factors. In the first place, Polish observers frequently agreed that a definite undercurrent of antagonism toward Jewish soldiers, and toward Jews in general, did indeed pervade the ranks. As a memorandum prepared on 6 August 1943 described the situation, "although lately [hostility] has weakened to a notable degree [compared with its level during the period of the evacuation from the Soviet Union], great antipathy toward the Jews is still in evidence."[46] Moreover, Polish military authorities in Palestine found themselves under increasing pressure from the British mandatory administration not only to end the mounting disaffection but to seek out the deserters hiding in the kibbutzim and to return them, properly chastised, to their units.[47] This pressure had involved Polish military police in raids on two kibbutzim, Hulda and Ramat HaKovesh, in October and November 1943—raids that had failed to turn up any deserters but had led to a flare-up of tensions between the Poles and the leadership and population of Jewish Palestine.[48]

In this context, the Polish authorities developed a two-pronged approach to dealing with the problem of the desertions. On the one hand, they endeavored to convince the British that further Polish participation in raids on kibbutzim was inadvisable, "for conflicts which are likely to result on such grounds undoubtedly can be made use of in an unfavourable manner towards the Polish army."[49] More importantly, however, they themselves attempted to curb expressions of hostility toward Jews on the part of Polish soldiers. On 28 June 1943 Kukiel announced that "in our present political situation, and in connection with the exploitation by unfriendly or even hostile forces of any real or exaggerated friction and discord against a religious or ethnic background, especially in the army, it becomes necessary energetically to counteract any expressions of this kind . . . , [which] can create conditions making it easier for enemy forces to operate." He thus declared his intention "to set about introducing a planned educational program that will explain the dangers to the interests of the Polish state" that arise from the existence of intergroup hostility in the ranks.[50] In accordance with this intention, on 5 July he instructed Anders to implement a program along these lines,[51] and, indeed, shortly thereafter outlines for such a program were prepared.[52] In addition, on 22 July, Kukiel himself issued an order to all officers in the Polish forces instructing them "to take a stand clearly indicating the equality of all soldiers without regard to creed or origin" and declaring that tolerating any hostile or unfriendly expression toward Jews was a punishable offense.[53]

Whether such measures were successful in changing attitudes in the ranks to a significant degree is impossible to determine. It is certain, however, that they did not noticeably affect the pace of the desertions that they were designed to control. On the other hand, the Poles did succeed, after November 1943, in keeping British pressure at arm's length. In any event, the desertions from the Polish forces in Palestine never mushroomed, as some had feared they might, into a major political problem. In the final analysis, though, the lack of damage that they did to the Polish cause was most likely determined by two conditions that had nothing to do with the Poles' own actions. First, the desertions occurred in a region far from the center of public attention in the West, meaning that those "hostile forces" that the Poles so feared would have had to invest considerable energy in any effort to turn them to their own advantage. Secondly, the deserters themselves had no interest in focusing public awareness upon their situation; they sought to blend into their new surroundings as quietly as possible and in no sense looked upon their action as a protest against the insalubrious treatment that they had purportedly met in the ranks.

When, on the other hand, Jewish soldiers deserted from Polish units stationed in Great Britain, neither of these conditions was present, a fact that complicated the situation for the Polish authorities immeasurably.

When the pace of desertions from the Polish forces in Palestine was at its height, in mid-1943, rumors had begun to circulate among Polish troops in Great Britain that several Jewish soldiers were planning to call attention to the hostility that they and their fellow Jews allegedly experienced in the ranks, first by openly abandoning their units, then by organizing a mass demonstration against the manner in which they claimed their commanders treated them.[54] Indeed, it appears that during this time the relations between Poles and Jews in the units stationed in Britain, which had long been a source of embarrassment to the Polish authorities,[55] had taken a turn for the worse. Jewish soldiers began to complain that Poles who had recently been transferred to Britain from Palestine had brought with them much of the ill feeling that from the Jews' point of view had characterized relations between the two groups in the Anders army.[56] In addition, in mid-1943, following the German surrender in North Africa, a number of ethnic Poles who had previously served in the German army under General Rommel had joined the Polish forces in Great Britain as part of an arrangement that allowed them to avoid being held as prisoners of war. Several Jewish soldiers noted that these former fighters of the Wehrmacht had made an effort to stir up animosity toward Jews in the ranks. Some, according to Jewish testimonies, had even bragged that they had personally had a hand in the Nazis' so-called final solution of the Jewish question.[57] As one Jewish soldier, who eventually deserted with the third group, explained, "Among such people, who did I-don't-know-what things, who served in the German army, who had been in Warsaw, who told about Auschwitz—in such an atmosphere, among people who had been brought up upon hatred of Jews, it was impossible to go on."[58]

Evidently in response to the rumors of impending desertion, as well as to the mounting defections from the troops in the Middle East, the Polish Defense Ministry established a special Desk for Jewish Affairs as part of its Political Division.[59] The head of this desk, Lt. Jerzy Flaum, and his immediate superior, Marian Heitzman, chief of the Political Division, appear to have devoted considerable attention to preventing the threatened protest flight from materializing and to keeping complaints about the treatment of Jewish soldiers in the Polish army out of the public eye. As Heitzman explained in a letter to Kukiel, "I regard the Jewish question as extremely important, not because it has become greatly inflamed, so to speak, in the army, but because even the smallest untoward incidents, even unintentional ones, are immediately exploited and blown up to fantastic proportions by forces hostile to us."[60] Accordingly Flaum began organizing a program to teach Polish soldiers about the culture of Polish Jewry and to instruct them regarding the proper behavior that they were to show their Jewish comrades-in-arms. He also attempted to satisfy what he perceived to be the Jewish soldiers' cultural needs; before the Jewish High Holidays in September 1943 he issued a special newspaper entitled *Żołnierz Polski-Żyd*, containing articles about aspects of the Jewish religion, greetings to Jewish soldiers from various government and military officials, and declarations that in liberated Poland Jews would enjoy complete political and social equality.[61] Heitzman for his part held meetings with the Board of Deputies of British Jews and with representatives of the Anglo-Jewish press in an effort to persuade them to show restraint in reacting to whatever they might hear about the sufferings of Jewish soldiers under Polish command. At these meetings he professed determination to lower intergroup tensions in the ranks—the existence of which he acknowledged quite clearly[62]—but he argued that his chances of doing so depended upon his ability to operate behind the scenes.[63]

Heitzman and Flaum also co-opted Schwarzbart in a direct attempt to dissuade Jewish soldiers from any contemplated defection. Schwarzbart had long preferred to deal with instances of friction between Poles and Jews quietly and away from public scrutiny,[64] and he consented to use his influence to keep the soldiers in the ranks. In September 1943 he visited the bases in Scotland where the Jewish soldiers were stationed, and he outlined the steps that he and other Jewish leaders in Great Britain were taking in order to make conditions better for them. He also expressed his conviction that their situation would soon improve.[65] Schwarzbart's efforts, together with those of Heitzman and Flaum, appear to have convinced most of the Jewish soldiers to delay execution of whatever plans they might have made to desert and to attempt once again to find redress for their grievances through the established military channels.[66] Other soldiers sought the intervention of Jewish organizations or of British political figures on their behalf as an alternative to quitting the ranks.[67] However, as one of the eventual deserters from the first group warned the Jewish representative even before he had made his visit to Scotland, "If the situation of the Jewish soldiers does not change, they will leave."[68]

Evidently, as far as many Jews were concerned, the months following Schwarzbart's visit did not bring any noticeable improvement, and the affected soldiers decided to bring their dissatisfaction to the attention of the British public. The result of this decision was the desertion of the first group of soldiers on 16 January 1944. Polish officials appear to have realized immediately that this action had created a major public relations problem for them. Virtually all of them who considered the situation were of the opinion that the only course open to their government was to seek to satisfy the deserters' demands.[69] It thus took only three days following the defection of the first group for the government officially to announce its policy: it would overlook the act of desertion by any soldier who would report to a specified Polish induction center, and it would support the request of all such soldiers to be transferred to British command.[70]

British military authorities, however, evidently demanded an explanation for the sudden rush of requests for transfer coming, with Polish approval, from Jewish soldiers in the Polish forces, and Polish officials were placed in a difficult position. They could hardly tell their patrons that they were seeking primarily to cover up an indication of ethnic friction in their armed forces; nor could they admit that the deserters' complaints had any foundation—despite the fact that, however much they might have found those complaints exaggerated, they generally acknowledged that the attitudes and behavior of many Polish soldiers toward their Jewish comrades were far from irreproachable.[71] Yet if they denied that the deserters had any cause to be dissatisfied in the ranks, they had to adduce some alternative reason for the defections.

From this situation the standard official public Polish interpretation of the desertions emerged. This interpretation was first adumbrated by Kukiel in a letter to the British liaison officer to the Polish forces, Gen. A. E. Grasett, on 26 January 1944. In this letter Kukiel stated emphatically, in rather stilted English, that "there is no objective explanation of the undertaken action of desertion." He insisted further that "there has been no outspread anti-Semitism in the Polish Army," claiming that "the cases which had been reported to the Authorities have been immediately and effectively dealt with." He claimed that "the Polish Military Authorities have devoted their constant attention to this problem and issued several orders and circular letters with the object of mopping out any traces of anti-Semitism in the Polish Army. The results," he reported, "have been satisfactory." Thus, he suggested, the reasons for the desertions lay elsewhere than in the actual experience of the Jewish soldiers in the ranks. In the first place, he claimed, a number of "agitators" had been active for several months in the units from which most of the deserters fled: "Members of the

Secret Service reported already a few months ago of these agitators' activities and the projected desertion." Hence he concluded that "the whole action characterises an organised plot." Moreover, he hinted that many of the deserters might have been motivated primarily by the fear that they would soon be called upon to take part in the upcoming invasion of France. He explained that he had been moved to think along such lines "in connection with the fact [that] according to reports received from the Polish Army in the Middle East more than 1,500 Jews deserted just before the embarkation of divisions leaving for the front began."[72]

This explanation was, of course, no less self-serving than was the deserters' own justification for their action. By attributing the defection exclusively to a combination of Jewish treachery and cowardice the Polish government absolved itself of all responsibility for what had happened; and by announcing that "the Army Authorities will not take the consequences of desertion, which will be forgotten,"[73] it presented itself to the British authorities and public as extraordinarily forbearing in the face of an act that by right warranted severe punishment. A similar approach to the matter was taken by the special Defense Ministry investigating commission to study the situation of Jewish soldiers in the Polish army, whose formation had been promised the deserters in return for their acquiescence to the government's proposed course of action and which had indeed been ordered into existence by Kukiel on 25 January 1944.[74] Between that date and 23 February—an interval of less than one month—the commission, headed by Gen. Mieczysław Boruta-Spiechowicz, commander of the Polish forces in Great Britain, and consisting of three additional Polish officers and Heitzman, held an indeterminate number of meetings, during which it heard the testimony of deserters, of Jewish soldiers who had not left the ranks, of Polish soldiers who had been accused of hostile behavior toward Jews, and of Polish officers in the field.[75] On 25 February it submitted its report to Kukiel.[76]

Like Kukiel's letter to Grasett, the report vigorously denied that the actual relations between Poles and Jews in the ranks had in any way moved the deserters to take their step. On the contrary, it claimed, "the group desertion . . . was carried out at a time when a relaxation of the atmosphere had set in in the units as a result of orders issued."[77] Moreover, it insisted that "there is an enormous disproportion between the extremely serious step represented by plotting and organizing mass desertion in wartime and the facts about which the deserters complained." Those complaints, according to the report, had centered almost exclusively on verbal jibes that had been made long in the past; the affected soldiers had not seen fit to complain about them when they occurred because then they had not taken them seriously. Only now, it argued, were these isolated minor incidents being used to justify a step that "had nothing to do with antisemitism" but had more likely been aroused by "frustrated ambitions or political motives." Among those motives the report gave prominence to an alleged "lack of emotional bonds with Poland" on the part of Jewish soldiers who, although "formally Polish citizens, had long since left Poland and for all practical purposes tied themselves to other surroundings."[78] Indeed, the report pointed out that a portion of the Jewish soldiers consisted of longtime emigrants from Poland who had been conscripted into the Polish forces against their will or who had volunteered for service solely in the hope that they would be able thereby to remain in Great Britain or the United States.[79] "These [soldiers]," it declared, "demonstrate a highly negative attitude toward the army and toward service in the units." It maintained further that an additional 30 percent of the Jewish soldiers were "minimally patriotic, poor soldiers who sought to evade their duties and constantly called at the sick bays and hospitals."

In an appendix the report also ventured an additional reason why the deserters were complaining so vociferously about a phenomenon—ill-treatment on ethnic or religious grounds—that in the commission's view hardly existed. Jews, the report argued, had become so upset by the news of the murder of their coreligionists in occupied Poland that they were no longer able to judge accurately the nature of others' intentions toward them. Thus, it claimed, any harsh words directed at a Jewish soldier by a non-Jew, even if purely personal in character, even if in the nature of a reproach by a superior for poor performance of an assigned task, were automatically interpreted as expressions of unbridled hostility. The soldiers who complained of such hostility, the report suggested, were actually in an "overwrought emotional state"; they suffered from a "malignant psychosis in which any untoward or truculent behavior by their fellow soldiers was interpreted as an antisemitic reaction."[80] On the other hand, however, the report noted six cases in which charges brought by Jewish soldiers appeared to warrant further investigation. It recommended that such investigation be carried out and that, should the charges prove well founded, those guilty of behavior hostile to Jews as such be held responsible. It also called for an order to be read by all unit commanders stating that they would enforce the principle of absolute equality in the armed forces, as well as for a series of meetings to be held with Polish and Jewish soldiers on the subject of collegiality and coexistence in the ranks. On the whole, though, the report left the impression that whatever problems did exist between Polish and Jewish soldiers in the Polish army, the responsibility lay more on the Jewish than on the Polish side.

In any case, there appears to be reason to question whether the special investigating commission of the Defense Ministry actually delved into the roots of the desertion as deeply as it might have. In the first place, complaints from Jewish soldiers about ill-treatment at the hands of Polish officers and enlisted men had in fact been voiced vigorously and consistently virtually from the outset of the war and had frequently been brought to the attention of Polish military and civilian officials.[81] These complaints had mentioned not only verbal insult but also deliberate interference with mail delivery; discrimination in duty assignments, training, and promotion; unequal punishments for disciplinary infractions; physical abuse; inaction by commanders in response to requests for redress; and even retaliation for bringing such incidents to the attention of superior officers.[82] Although Polish officials had generally dismissed such charges as without foundation, other observers appear to have believed that there was more than a kernel of truth in them. As Denis Allen of the British Foreign Office noted when presented with a set of letters written by several of the deserters and other soldiers to a Jewish organization in London, "These statements . . . seem to me to read convincingly, and they leave a nasty impression."[83] Moreover, one of the deserters, in a description of the manner in which the commission took testimony from him and his fellows, objected that "the general tendency [of the commission] is to shorten the statements on the actual anti-Semitic outbreaks."[84] This soldier felt that he had not been given an opportunity by the investigators to present his grievances fully; in fact, he had not actually been called before the commission to deliver his testimony in person but had merely been asked to present a deposition for later submission to the panel by a delegation of its members. On the other hand, he indicated that this delegation had asked him a number of "objectionable questions . . . [that] have nothing at all to do with the object of the Commission, i.e., fight with anti-Semitism." Among these questions, according to his statement, were "Where and what family did you leave in Poland?"; "What influenced you to go to the Russian-occupied part of Poland?"; "Have you not enough strength for revenge?"; "To what party did you belong before the war?"; and "Do you know how many Poles were killed by Jews in Poland?"

In fact, it seems that even before it ever convened, the commission may well have had an idea of the shape that its conclusions would take. As it happened, when the rumors of impending desertion had first begun to circulate, in mid-1943, Heitzman had conducted an investigation among field commanders to determine the reasons for the ferment. In his summary of his findings he had indicated that, according to the commanders, the primary problem in dealing with Jewish soldiers was a lack of emotional ties to Poland on the part of those who had joined the army abroad. He had also noted the commanders' opinion that the overwhelming majority of conflicts between Jews and non-Jews in the ranks involved precisely these Jewish soldiers and that the problems stemmed less from specifically anti-Jewish feelings on the part of the Poles than from the conviction that those Jews who had not been raised and educated in Poland constituted an "inferior military element." Indeed, as Heitzman represented the commanders' position, many of the Jewish soldiers' complaints about ethnic hostility actually stemmed from incidents in which a non-Jew had rebuked a Jew for poor performance or a breach of discipline. The tendency of many Jewish soldiers to represent every reprimand as being directed against them solely because they were Jews was attributed in turn to four factors: a "mental complex" involving hypersensitivity to any expression that might smack of ethnic prejudice; the difficult psychological situation stemming from worry over the fate of their loved ones in Poland; lack of concrete action by the Allies to put a stop to the Nazi murder campaign, which alienated Jews from the non-Jewish world altogether and weakened their emotional stamina; and the hostile propaganda of Communist elements seeking to incite as much friction as possible between Poles and Jews.[85] In other words, much of the thesis that was eventually embodied in the investigating commission's report had already been voiced almost six months before any Jewish soldier had deserted.[86]

Schwarzbart, who had earlier used his influence to try to prevent the desertion, appears to have been furious over the commission's work. "The Poles," he wrote in his diary, "want to get rid of the Jews [in the army], while at the same time leaving the impression that they do not want to do so."[87] Whatever the case, conditions for those Jews who remained in the ranks after the first group of deserters had departed seem, by their own accounts and those of other observers, to have worsened notably. A number of those who eventually left with the second or third groups later testified that their decisions to defect were taken in light of the heightened friction that they felt at this time; they recalled that Polish soldiers would approach them regularly with the question, "Why are you still here?"[88] Arieh Tartakower, who had undertaken a tour of Polish military installations in Scotland at the request of the Polish Defense Ministry shortly after the desertions, reported that "the condition of the Jewish soldiers in the Polish army . . . is highly abnormal" and that "the primary cause of this condition is rampant antisemitism among the soldiers."[89] Moreover, the British ambassador to the government-in-exile, Sir Owen O'Malley, noted having gained the sense from talks with Polish Foreign Minister Romer that the Poles "would very gladly be rid of . . . [the Jewish soldiers] if any means could be found of achieving this."[90] As if to confirm this impression a Defense Ministry official told Schwarzbart on 1 February that an additional eighty Jewish soldiers were planning to desert their units and that the Polish government was not about to take any steps to prevent such action.[91]

Indeed, on 22 February the second group of deserters departed. In the meantime the procedural obstacles that had prevented placing the first group under British command had been resolved,[92] and within a matter of days the second group was attached, like its predecessor, to the British Pioneer Corps.

Strangely, although the transfer of the soldiers was carried out in accordance with the preference of both the Polish and British governments, it did not reflect the initial desires of those who saw themselves as the responsible representatives of Polish and British Jewry. Schwarzbart, in particular, expressed concern lest the refusal of Jewish soldiers of Polish citizenship to bear arms in defense of Poland's independence create a backlash of intensified hostility among the Poles and frustrate his efforts to insure that the Jews who remained in liberated Poland would live under a regime of complete civic and social equality.[93] Thus, within less than a day of the desertion of the first group he told the soldiers that they must return to their units before any redress of their grievances could be sought, and he opposed their demand to be placed under British command.[94] Schwarzbart's position was seconded by Alexander Easterman and Noah Barou of the British Section of the World Jewish Congress and by Adolf Brotman of the Board of Deputies of British Jews.[95] These leaders of the Jews in Great Britain evidently feared that the defection of the soldiers would be viewed negatively by the British public and would reduce sympathy for the Jewish victims of ill-treatment in the Polish forces.[96]

It appears, however, that within a short time the position of the spokesmen for British Jewry, along with that of Arieh Tartakower, who had also taken part in the initial discussions with the deserters, began to change. The soldiers proved unwilling even to consider the suggestion that they return to their units, and they were prepared even less to hear criticism of their action from those who were supposed, they felt, to represent their interests. Tartakower and the British Jewish leaders thus came to feel that in order to retain the confidence of the deserters (and with it the possibility of influencing their future actions) they would have, while continuing to condemn the act of desertion itself, to support their request for transfer.[97] Schwarzbart, however, remained adamant in his position, and he found new support both from his colleague on the National Council, the Bund representative Emanuel Szerer, and from Anshel Reiss of the Reprezentacja, who had recently been dispatched to London to lobby the Polish government for increased attention to the rescue of Jews.[98] Reiss even went so far as to tell all other Jewish leaders involved in the affair that he would continue to oppose transfer even if the soldiers were to disavow him.[99] The resulting operational split among the Jewish leadership was to influence the direction in which the episode developed further.

At first the Jewish leaders endeavored to settle their differences behind the scenes, so that they might present a united front before the other parties involved. On 19 January, Schwarzbart and Tartakower hammered out a compromise that was embodied in a confidential letter sent in the name of the Reprezentacja to the Polish Defense Ministry the same day.[100] The letter "condemn[ed] this step [of desertion] as contrary to the law and military discipline," while at the same time it "applauded" the ministry's willingness to forgo punishment of the deserters. On the other hand, it suggested that "we have before us a complex set of circumstances that have determined this desperate and unfortunate step of the soldiers" and expressed the hope that "this time the remedies that have already been attempted several times by the high military authorities will succeed in creating conditions of complete and cordial brotherhood-in-arms among the members of our army, so that all of its Jewish members may be happy there as well." This attempt by spokesmen of Polish Jewry to strike a balance between sensitivity to the demands of their constituents and duty to their country of citizenship was most clearly expressed in the letter's operational paragraph:

> We have taken and continue to take the position that a Polish citizen must serve in the Polish army. Obviously we apply this principle to Jewish Polish citizens as well. For this reason we are opposed to the transfer of Polish soldiers to the British army, unless [such transfer] is carried out in the form of a detachment by our own military authorities, in a fashion of which we have many examples. Should there be individuals who nevertheless feel that the proper course for them is to submit individual requests [for transfer], and should their plans meet with the agreement of the military authorities, then we can have no influence.

This position was clearly a defensive one; as Schwarzbart indicated to Easterman, "Our reply . . . may in [the] future serve you to meet eventual charges against our attitude."[101] Nevertheless, the Jewish leaders proved unable to maintain such a united stance amid the conflicting pressures from the soldiers and the government. To be sure, Schwarzbart, Tartakower, and Reiss joined together following the defection of the second group in imploring the Jewish soldiers remaining in the ranks to continue to do their duty no matter how difficult the conditions and to place their confidence in their leaders' efforts to make those conditions more bearable.[102] However, even before this call was issued, Tartakower had begun to disagree openly with his two colleagues before the soldiers, expressing readiness to explore the possibility of negotiating a group transfer to British units.[103] The Polish Jewish representatives also began to meet separately with Polish and British officials and members of Parliament, as did delegates from the Board of Deputies and the British Section of the World Jewish Congress, and to put forth divergent positions.[104] The degree of coordination among the various Jewish leaders of efforts on behalf of the soldiers appears, in fact, to have been so minimal that at one point three different Jewish delegations, unbeknownst to one another, had made appointments to discuss the situation with Mikołajczyk on the same day.[105] Schwarzbart later wondered what the prime minister must have thought of "this Jewish jungle."[106]

Of more immediate importance, however, was the soldiers' reaction to the confusion and disunity shown by their ostensible leaders. In a letter sent on behalf of the second group of deserters to Selig Brodetsky, president of the Board of Deputies, on 13 March, the group's spokesman noted a "complete lack of confidence displayed by the Jewish soldiers towards Dr. Schwarzbart" and asked Brodetsky "to use all [his] authority in persuading him [Schwarzbart] that his position is harmful and undesirable for both Poles and Jews alike."[107] Similarly, in a letter to Tartakower six days later the same spokesman expressed concern lest Schwarzbart and Reiss exert pressure upon "the only man who enjoyed the confidence of the Jewish soldiers" and force him to change his position in favor of transfer.[108] At least some of the soldiers, however, appear to have doubted Tartakower's ability to withstand such pressure and to have come to the conclusion that the official leadership of Polish and British Jewry would not represent their interests satisfactorily. Thus, from a relatively early point in the affair, even before the disposition of the first group of deserters had been determined, the soldiers made efforts to find alternative advocates for their cause.

Their search led in the first place to a body known as the Committee for a Jewish Army, a front organization set up by emissaries of the Revisionist-backed Irgun in Britain and the United States in 1941.[109] The committee's London office, headed by Capt. Jeremiah Helpern, had actually been following the situation of Jewish soldiers in the Polish forces at least since August 1942, when a Jewish private named Jakób Rosenberg had complained to the committee about ill-treatment in the ranks and had asked for its support of his request for transfer to a Jewish battalion.[110] At the time, Helpern, evidently conscious of the Revisionists' efforts to cultivate the goodwill of the Polish government, did not publicize Rosenberg's charges but merely forwarded his communication to Sikorski, stating that the "Committee here and in the United States are fully aware of the attitude of genuine friendliness of your Excellency and your Government towards the Jewish people and consider that the unsatisfactory position disclosed by the enclosed letter and by similar documents in our possession is in no way a result of policy, but rather the inevitable consequence of pre-war conditions in Poland."[111] He had also met with Raczyński and had attempted to persuade him that the only way to avoid re-currence of such complaints was to create "a separate Jewish Unit in the Polish Army, with Jewish officers and non-commissioned officers, under a non-Jewish Polish commander, enjoying popularity among the Jewish soldiers."[112] Since then Helpern had apparently developed contacts with a number of Jews serving in the Polish forces, includ-ing some from among the first group of deserters, and these men had spoken with him following their defection. At first, according to his own testimony, Helpern had refused to involve the committee in negotiations with the Polish and British authorities, "because they [the soldiers] had their official representatives here, Mr. Tartakover [sic], Dr. Schwartzbart [sic] and Mr. Szerer."[113] However, on 4 Febru-ary 1944 a spokesman for the first group, Seweryn Pomeranc, stated that the soldiers' desire was not "to settle our case by getting only [the] negative satisfaction . . . [of] go[ing] out of the Polish Forces and join[ing] the British forces as Polish citizens" but "to see the fruits of our labour in the shape of a Jewish Battalion, formed of us and our friends in the Polish Forces who asked Dr. Tartakover [sic] during his tour, to be transferred to the British forces."[114] At this point the com-mittee agreed to speak on behalf of the deserters, as their demand "fell within the sphere of [its] activities."[115]

Having made this decision, the committee concentrated its efforts, in contrast to the official Jewish leadership, not upon the Polish but upon the British side of the affair. The committee's lay president, Lord Strabolgi, MP, pleaded the case of the deserters for their transfer to Jewish units in meetings with Foreign Minister Eden, War Minister Sir Percy James Grigg, and Deputy Prime Minister Clement Attlee, while Helpern himself circulated among cabinet ministers a set of testimonies by Jews in the Polish forces illustrating how they viewed their situation in the Polish ranks.[116] The thrust of these contacts was that the soldiers, as Helpern explained in a letter to Grigg, "do not want to be accused that they are trying to escape the Second Front by being put in the Pioneers, and while their comrades will fight, they will be relegated to peeling potatoes or with a pick and shovel [sic]." Instead, according to Helpern, they wanted to be placed in com-bat units. However, he noted, "they understand perfectly well that if they were spread throughout the British Army without a sufficient command of the English language, and not being familiar with the British military traditions, they might create disharmony in the units, which might cause unnecessary bitterness." Thus, Helpern argued, "the only way is for them to join the separate Jewish units which are to-day fighting in Italy, or those who are stationed in the Middle East, as they feel themselves that they are Jews and want to fight as such."[117]

Helpern later claimed that "as a result of the negotiations conducted by Lord Strabolgi . . . the 200 soldiers were being transferred, partly to British units, the rest to the Pioneer Corps, with the promise that after a certain amount of training they would be able to join any British units, among them the Jewish Battalions in Palestine."[118] Such a claim, however, is without foundation. In the first place, the committee's contacts with British officials began only on 7 February, whereas by that time the British government had already consented in principle to the transfer to the Pioneer Corps. Moreover, there is no indication that the Pioneer Corps—to which the committee specifically opposed transferring the soldiers—was ever intended to serve merely as a training base for soldiers who would eventually be reassigned to other units. Indeed, it appears that the ineffectiveness of the committee's interventions was apparent to the deserters themselves; they evidently cut off contact with the Revisionist agency shortly after the desertion of the second group.[119]

Clearly disillusioned by the ineffectiveness of Jewish organizations in advancing their cause, the deserters seem to have decided to approach potentially sympathetic members of Parliament on their own. Beginning in February they made contact with several well-known figures of the British left, including Thomas Driberg, D. N. Pritt, and G. R. Strauss, who had participated actively in earlier public discussions about the situation of Jews in the Polish army.[120] Driberg and Pritt, in particular, were generally regarded as favoring the Soviet position in the Polish-Soviet conflict; in fact, Polish intelligence believed that Pritt was a paid Soviet agent.[121] These parliamentarians thus did not feel the same impulse to keep the matter of the desertions quiet as did the official British, Polish, and Jewish representatives.[122] As a result Driberg made it known that he intended to raise the matter publicly in the context of a parliamentary interpellation.[123]

His announcement was greeted with consternation by all those who had been trying to dispose of the situation behind the scenes;[124] Schwarzbart, in particular, was adamant in trying to dissuade Driberg from his proposed question in the Commons.[125] For a while such efforts succeeded, but following the arrest of the third group Driberg determined to proceed. On 3 April he circulated a letter to fellow parliamentarians asking for their support in a matter that he "expect[ed] to have to raise in the House this week."[126] For a man of Driberg's known pro-Soviet proclivities, the tone of the letter was surprisingly mild. In it he indicated that "the courts are competent to pronounce sentence of death" upon the deserters of the third group who were to be brought to trial and argued that "we cannot . . . concur with equanimity in the severe punishment, possibly the death, of a handful of men whose crime is that they sought by the only means known to them—means already twice implicitly endorsed by the British Government—to escape from racial prejudice and persecution on British soil." He was careful to stress that he did not regard the affair as having political ramifications. "These Jews," he explained, "form a clearly definable, limited group; no frontier or other political problems can arise in their case." He also made it clear that although, to his mind, there was "overwhelming evidence of the persistence of virulent Anti-Semitism within the Polish Forces in this country"—evidence that he sought to provide by attaching excerpts from soldiers' testimonies to his letter—he appreciated that the Polish government and military authorities had made serious, though ultimately unsuccessful, efforts to bring the phenomenon under control. Finally, he asked that the contents of his letter be kept confidential and not released to the press. As he explained, "There is still a slight chance that the matter may be arranged satisfactorily without its being raised in Parliament; for obvious reasons it might be better to settle it without a great deal of public discussion." He stated that he wished merely that the British government "reopen negotiations at once with the Polish authorities, in order to secure the transfer to the British Forces of . . . the 30 or so Jews who were arrested last week . . . and . . . such of the remaining 570 or so Jews in the Polish Forces who wish to apply for transfer."

Reaction to Driberg's letter came, among others, from his colleague in the House of Commons, Eleanor Rathbone. On 5 April she forwarded a copy of the letter to Raczyński, indicating that although she believed that "publicity at this stage might do harm to the cause both of Poland and of the Polish Jews," she was convinced that Driberg was "determined to proceed, unless he can get some assurance, both that the latest group of deserters will not be court martialled and that the whole matter of their transfer to the British Army will be reconsidered."[127] The warning to the Polish government was patent. Nevertheless, Raczyński did not show much urgency about avoiding a parliamentary interpellation. He replied that he had indeed "had some information about recent instances of desertion of groups of Polish soldiers of Jewish extraction," which "came at a particularly awkward moment just when our troops . . . are seriously preparing for an early emergency."[128] He stated that although "the previous incidents have been settled somehow thanks to the willing cooperation of our military authorities with the British military authorities," the former settlement "has been considered by both these authorities as an unfortunate precedent which cannot be . . . repeated." For his part, he declared, he was "under the painful impression that this 'technical' desertion has been organised by agencies ill disposed towards the Polish Government and towards the friendly relationship between Poles and Jews." He gave no indication that the Polish government was considering any measures other than placing the deserters on trial.

Whether a more conciliatory response by Raczyński or other Polish officials would have dissuaded Driberg from bringing the matter of the Jewish soldiers to public attention is a moot point. It is certain, however, that the Polish authorities did not give him any sense that there was room for negotiation. As a result, despite continued pressure from Schwarzbart and other Jewish leaders not to do so—pressure that he later described as "lachrymose pleading"[129]—Driberg rose in the House of Commons during the session of 5 April to inquire why the British government was not prepared to accept any Jewish soldier serving with the Polish forces into the ranks of the British army.[130] His action broke the barrier of official silence that had surrounded the affair since its inception and laid the foundation for a groundswell of public anger toward the Polish government, not only in Britain but in the United States and other countries as well.

Shortly following Driberg's interpellation, major newspapers in Britain and the United States began to publish articles and editorials on the situation of Jews in the Polish army—articles that did not present the Polish authorities in a favorable light.[131] Similarly, protests about conditions for Jewish soldiers were received from Jewish communities throughout the world and from most major Jewish organizations in the United States.[132] Emphasis in these statements was placed on the possible fate of the third group of deserters, about which rumors abounded. Indeed, at the time that Driberg raised the matter in the Commons, and for some time thereafter, no one other than the Polish military authorities had any idea what was to be done with these soldiers. Even the British government appears to have been left somewhat in the dark; on 13 April, Frank Savery of the British Embassy to Poland complained to the Polish Foreign Ministry that his government had not been kept fully abreast of the situation regarding this group and stressed that it was necessary for the two governments "to work in closest collaboration" on the matter.[133] Only the next day did the British government learn that the trial of the deserters was set to begin four days hence.[134] In the meantime word seems to have circulated among the British public that some of the soldiers of the third group had committed suicide.[135]

The mounting atmosphere of ostensibly humanitarian worldwide public concern for the fate of the deserters and apprehension concerning the intentions of the Polish government toward them worried Polish officials outside of the Ministry of Defense considerably. On 24 April, following the conclusion of the trial but prior to the promulgation of the verdicts and sentences, Olgierd Górka wrote to Interior Minister Banaczyk that the British public's ideas about Poland's future eastern border were being strongly influenced by the belief that members of minority groups serving in the Polish army were being mistreated—a belief that had been strengthened recently as a result of the publicity surrounding the deserters.[136] Górka urged that the government reconsider its entire approach to the desertion affair. Similar sentiments had been brewing in the Foreign Ministry ever since Driberg's interpellation. Although that intervention had been directed exclusively toward the British government and had been careful to stress that the Polish authorities had done all in their power to prevent expressions of hostility toward Jews in the ranks,[137] Foreign Ministry officials were convinced that the actual purpose of the interpellation was to embarrass the government-in-exile and to weaken the extent of its public support.[138] A report on the parliamentary debate prepared by the Polish Embassy in London argued that "despite the outward appearances that Driberg maintained in the form of his interpellation, it can be assumed that he operated under the influence of inspirations hostile to us, emanating 'from the outside.'"[139] The reference was undoubtedly to Soviet and other Communist elements; indeed, the report pointed out that among those who had taken Driberg's side in the debate, many were "known for their Soviet sympathies."[140] Thus the feeling began to permeate the Polish government that the desertion episode had been provoked and orchestrated from the outset by elements interested in strengthening the Soviet position in the Polish-Soviet dispute.[141]

This feeling evidently led Foreign Minister Romer to take a more active interest in the affair. Although the handling of the situation had previously been left to the Defense Ministry, Romer and his subordinates believed that the possibility that Soviet influences underlay the desertions lent the matter a political character with which the military authorities were not competent to deal.[142] On 14 April he asked Kukiel to postpone the opening of the deserters' trial "in order to permit the government to consider properly all of the ramifications and possible repercussions of the situation, which we ought, in my opinion, to discuss in advance with the British government."[143] In addition he spoke of the need to neutralize attacks upon the Polish government in the British press by bringing to trial alongside the Jewish deserters Polish soldiers who had been named by Jews as having mistreated them.[144] The defense minister's responses to these requests, however, do not appear to have been to Romer's liking; Kukiel did not consent to put off the trial and stated that there was no possibility of instituting proceedings against Poles accused of misconduct at least until the end of the coming month.[145] He did, however, indicate his willingness to reduce the charges against the Jewish soldiers from "desertion," which carried a maximum penalty of fifteen years' imprisonment, to "absence without leave [*samowolne opuszczenie szeregów*]," a far less serious offense, for which it was likely that suspended sentences could be imposed.[146] Still, this concession was not enough for Romer; on 24 April a member of his staff wrote to Mikołajczyk that "in order to erase and correct the negative image [that has been made on the British and American public] . . . it is necessary to overcome the approach of the Polish military elements . . . , who regard the problem purely from a military standpoint without taking into account that it came into being upon the territory of a foreign country and not within the realm of exclusive and unlimited Polish sovereignty."[147] The same official added that "it is impossible to deny the existence of antisemitism" in the armed forces and warned that the government must take action on this matter "over the heads and in spite of the military elements."

Discontent with the manner in which the military authorities were handling the situation was also expressed in the Polish National Council. On 25 April eleven members submitted an interpellation aimed at forcing Kukiel to acknowledge the existence of discrimination against

Jewish soldiers in the Polish forces.[148] The interpellation was based upon Commander-in-Chief Sosnkowski's order of 20 March, in which he had complained that the call he had issued upon assuming command of the Polish forces for all soldiers to work together "regardless of differences in outlook or origin" had not been heeded.[149] The members of the National Council called upon the defense minister to explain why such a situation should exist and to inform the council what steps he had taken to rectify it. The next day ten members introduced an urgent motion asking Kukiel to discuss all aspects of the desertion situation with the council "at the earliest possible moment," and Schwarzbart, together with eleven others, called for the council to establish its own special investigating commission to determine why so many Jewish soldiers had sought to leave the ranks of the Polish army.[150] Both motions were adopted unanimously at the council's plenary session on 2 May.[151]

In spite of the expressions of dissatisfaction with the manner in which he had managed the desertion affair until that point, Kukiel remained adamant in denying the existence of any serious Polish-Jewish tension in the ranks. In responding to the National Council's interpellation on 10 May, he claimed that outbursts of hostility toward Jews had been only "sporadic" and had involved only "a few dozen individuals."[152] According to him, such incidents had been thoroughly investigated and those responsible for them punished. He even went so far as to maintain that some Jewish soldiers who had been cited for disciplinary infractions had received lighter than normal punishments precisely because they were Jews. By this time, however, Kukiel's biases, and those of the Polish military establishment as a whole, were well known to others in the government. On 27 April, Marceli Dogilewski, head of the Jewish desk in the Ministry of Information, prepared a report for the minister on the trial of the third group of deserters (at which he had been present as an observer); in it he indicated that the court had not permitted the accused to bring witnesses who would testify about expressions of hostility toward the Jewish soldiers.[153] In addition he appended a list of twenty-five Polish soldiers whom the deserters had named in their trial as having abused or discriminated against them. He urged that these cases be investigated as soon as possible, because he was "convinced that in the event of a slow inquiry all evidence of violations will vanish."

Pressure from all sides, however, did not move the Defense Ministry, and the trial of the deserters proceeded apace. After three days of hearings, twenty-one soldiers were convicted of absence without leave with intent to avoid military service and sentenced to prison terms of one to two years.[154] Unofficial word of the verdicts and sentences evidently reached circles outside of the Polish government by 26 April, prompting a significant public outcry. Driberg raised the issue in Parliament once again. This time, however, in contrast to his interpellation of three weeks previous, he directed his fire less against the British than against the Poles. He argued that the Allied Forces Bill that had been enacted by Parliament in 1941 [155] placed the ultimate responsibility for the welfare of all soldiers serving in any of the armies stationed on British soil upon the British government and demanded that in fulfillment of this responsibility toward Jews serving in the Polish forces the government impose checks upon the autonomy of the Polish command. Also in contrast to the previous parliamentary debate, front-benchers, including Aneurin Bevan, rose in support of Driberg.[156] The situation of Jews in the Polish army was also brought to the attention of the U.S. House of Representatives by Congressmen Emanuel Cellar and Samuel Dickstein, with the latter mentioning names of Polish soldiers who had been charged with untoward behavior against their Jewish comrades-in-arms.[157] On 27 April, Ciechanowski cabled Romer from Washington, mentioning a mounting wave of hostility toward Poland that was beginning to appear in the U.S. press.[158] On 2 May he followed with a second telegram indicating that American public opinion demanded full amnesty for the deserters, their transfer to British units, and the filing of charges against those accused of mistreating Jewish soldiers.[159]

In light of these developments the Foreign Ministry formulated a plan calling for delay in carrying out the sentences against the deserters pending their successful reassignment as a group to a single Polish unit, announcement of concrete measures to be taken against those guilty of abusing Jewish soldiers, immediate creation of an investigating commission by the National Council, and a renewed declaration that all Polish citizens must fulfill their military obligations in the ranks of the Polish army.[160] However, the plan does not appear to have been acceptable to the Defense Ministry; nine soldiers were sent immediately to a military prison, eleven were offered suspended sentences if they would return to their former units, and one case was referred for final decision to the commander-in-chief.[161] At the same time, though, the Defense Ministry began negotiations with Selig Brodetsky of the Board of Deputies, suggesting that if the Jewish leader could convince all of the soldiers to return to the ranks, suspended sentences for all of them would follow.[162] On the other hand, with regard to punishment of Polish soldiers for their behavior toward Jews, the ministry adamantly refused to take any action.[163]

As it happened, the Defense Ministry's attitude at this point was irrelevant, for the deserters made it known that they preferred to serve their prison terms rather than return to the Polish army. In fact, even those who had been offered suspended sentences insisted upon being incarcerated with their fellow deserters.[164] Meanwhile, though, the Polish cabinet had come to the conclusion that the best way to counteract the mounting wave of protests against the government was to announce that the deserters had been formally pardoned.[165] Accordingly, on 12 May, President Raczkiewicz issued a decree of amnesty covering a range of military transgressions including desertion, thereby allowing the soldiers of the third group to be set free. In announcing the amnesty, the government mentioned that the National Council's special investigating commission was about to begin its work and expressed sympathy for the sufferings of Jews under Nazi rule in Poland. It also declared categorically that "the Polish government and commander-in-chief will not tolerate any expression of uncollegial behavior or discrimination on racial or religious grounds in the ranks of the Polish armed forces."[166]

As a public relations gesture, however, the amnesty and its accompanying statement by the government proved unsuccessful; the British government still refused to accept the soldiers into the British army, and the soldiers continued to refuse to serve anywhere else.[167] As a result public protests on behalf of the deserters continued. On 14 May the National Council for Civil Liberties organized a mass rally at the Stoll Theatre, at which Driberg, Strauss, and Michael Foot spoke out against the manner in which both the Polish and the British governments had handled the affair. The participants declared themselves "shocked by the anti-Semitism from which Jews in the Polish Forces are suffering"; they "protest[ed] against this racial discrimination on British soil" and "call[ed] upon His Majesty's Government to take immediate steps to arrange for all those Jews in the Polish Forces who so desire to transfer to the British Forces."[168] In conjunction with this rally Driberg circulated a leaflet entitled "Absentees for Freedom: The Case of the Jews in the Polish Forces," in which he referred to the deserters as "refugees" from an intolerable atmosphere of hatred to which they were subject in the Polish ranks.[169] During subsequent weeks, additional public protests were held throughout Great Britain, to the point where Raczyński complained of a "witch-hunt against Polish anti-Semitism."[170]

Among those who protested most vigorously in the wake of the trial of the third group of deserters were the Zionist Revisionists, who until that time had been among the most active organized Jewish advocates of cooperation with the Polish government. On 19 May the Committee for a Jewish Army issued a "last appeal" to the British and Polish governments "to avert a major catastrophe which would arouse the indignation of the democratic world," a catastrophe that would result if Jews were forced to continue to serve with the allegedly "great number of Polish soldiers [who] have threatened . . . that when the Second Front is opened they will take advantage of the battle conditions to shoot as many Jews as possible in the back."[171] This appeal was followed shortly thereafter by an even stronger statement, according to which "Jewish soldiers serving in the Polish Army stationed in this country and in the Middle East are being subjected to the same kind of treatment as in Nazi Concentration Camps, except for the physical torture and physical extermination."[172] The latter statement, signed by Helpern, also drew some radical political conclusions from the affair:

If there is reason to change the Vichy Government in North Africa, to withdraw support from the Royal Yugoslav Govt., and to change the Badoglio Govt., there is as much or more reason to force the Polish Govt. to go, and to bring the present Polish Army staff to trial in the same way as the Vichyites. . . . This Government cannot be trusted with the restoration of Polish liberty, for unlimited liberty for such a Government must mean unlimited persecution and misery for all the minorities in Poland. I am no Communist, and I always believed that the Polish Government was right in demanding that the integrity of her territory should be restored. . . . But I must confess that the Polish Army leaders, who are supposed to be fighting for the liberation of Poland, and are instead fighting the Jews, have convinced me that the Russian attitude towards the minorities is the right one. I can see no reason for forcing the minorities liberated by the Russians back into the Polish grip unless a real democratic Poland is created.

Such a call from quarters that had always been counted as firmly anti-Soviet must have shaken the Polish authorities greatly.[173] However, to their good fortune, public attention to the matter subsided in June, no doubt due to the capture of the front pages by news of the invasion of Normandy and the progress of Allied forces on the continent. The National Council's investigating commission began to take testimony from the soldiers of the third group in July, but it appears to have quickly come to the conclusion that its work was not vital. Between 8 August and 30 December the council held no meetings. In January 1945 it convened four times to hear the testimonies of Heitzmann and Flaum; subsequently it did not reconvene, and apparently it never submitted a final report.[174]

Nevertheless, although the large majority of deserters were never deposed by the commission, the testimonies taken from the soldiers of the third group do shed some light on the factors that might have motivated so many to leave the ranks. Of the twenty-two soldiers interviewed, fifteen had resided continuously in Poland until the outbreak of war, and two others had left the country only in 1938. Moreover, of thirteen soldiers who responded to a question asking why they had initially joined the Polish forces, nine specifically stated that they had volunteered either from a sense of duty to fight for Poland or in direct response to Polish recruiting efforts. The third group of deserters, then, may not have been composed, as the Defense Ministry's investigating commission charged with regard to the first group, largely of "formally Polish citizens [who] had long since left Poland and for all practical purposes tied themselves to other surroundings."[175] The primary reason given for leaving was a general sense that their presence in the ranks was not desired by the Polish soldiers, who constantly taunted them, reviled them, and threatened them with physical violence because of their Jewish origin. All of them, however, were able to cite a large number of specific instances of such behavior. Together they named twenty-two different Polish soldiers, including three officers, who, they claimed, had exhibited such behavior or had discriminated against them in duty assignments, promotions, or furloughs. Most complainants indicated that they had previously attempted to obtain redress for their grievances through appeal to their commanding officers but had found this procedure to no avail; some even charged that they had been ostracized by their units after having done so. They represented seven different divisions, including the navy. In short, it appears that the comments made by the Defense Ministry's investigators about the soldiers of the first group of deserters did not apply to the third group; among these soldiers, the perception of widespread ill will toward them in the ranks, from which they might eventually suffer physically, was real and seems to have been sufficiently powerful, especially in light of the success of the first two groups in escaping from it, to impel them to desert.

During the course of the National Council's investigations, some soldiers reported that if they could not be reassigned to British military units they would accept hazardous labor duty in its place. None expressed any willingness, on the other hand, to return to the Polish army under any circumstances. Evidently the suggestion of assignment to labor service was seized upon by the Polish and British authorities as a way out of an unpalatable situation. On 17 July, O'Malley asked Romer whether the Polish government would permit the soldiers to serve as miners in British coal fields, promising to keep the arrangement secret.[176] Three days later Romer contacted Kukiel and urged him to accept the British proposal. On 27 July, Kukiel indicated his acceptance to Romer, and two days later the Polish and British governments concluded a formal agreement along these lines.[177] Technical difficulties delayed the implementation of the agreement for three months, but on 24 October over twenty Jews who had formerly served in the Polish army took up new positions as colliers.[178]

The deserters, then, appear to have been the principal victors in the entire affair; the Polish government, the principal loser. The government-in-exile realized that, in Raczyński's words, it had "handled the matter clumsily and played into the hands of [its] enemies." [179] Once the affair became public knowledge, on 5 April, the government was thus faced with the problem of repairing the public relations damage that it had, to an extent, brought upon itself.

This situation provided the matrix for what on the surface appeared to be a significant change in the government's approach to Jewish matters. Since late 1942 Jewish organizations had stressed that what was most important to them in their dealings with the Polish government was serious action with respect to the rescue of Jews from the occupied homeland. Previously the government, not considering accession to Jewish demands to be politically advantageous, had taken only circumscribed steps in this regard. Now, however, with the government's back seemingly pressed against the wall, its leaders evidently began to perceive that the rescue issue might offer it a final chance to rehabilitate its public image. The second half of 1944 was thus to be characterized by a highly visible Polish attempt to portray the exile regime as an enthusiastic protector of threatened Jews.

5

Rescue

The vehicle for the government's formal entry into the rescue field was the Council for Matters Relating to the Rescue of the Jewish Population in Poland (Rada do Spraw Ratowania Ludności Żydowskiej w Polsce), called into being by vote of the Polish cabinet on 20 April 1944.[1] The creation of the Rescue Council made the Polish government the second Allied regime—following the United States, where an executive order had created the War Refugee Board on 22 January 1944—to establish an official body dedicated to assisting the remaining Jews of Nazi-occupied Europe avoid the sentence of death that had been imposed upon them, and the Polish government was the first to state unambiguously that the objects of its rescue agency's efforts were to be Jews.[2] In fact, the Rescue Council was mandated not only "to work together with Polish government agencies and private organizations in action to save the Jewish population in Poland" but also "to maintain contact, through the mediation of the Polish authorities, with foreign organizations whose goal is to render aid to Jews and to cooperate in the rescue of both Jewish citizens of Poland and foreign and stateless Jews who have been deported to Polish territory."[3] The council was also presented with a more specific set of instructions:

> [The Council for Matters Relating to the Rescue of the Jewish Population in Poland has as its function] the formulation of ongoing plans . . . to provide food for the Jewish population in the homeland, to provide arms to that portion of the Jewish population that is suited to do battle with the Germans, to hide the Jewish population in the cities and villages, to provide the Jewish population with documents that might shield it from deportations and murder, to transmit funds to the homeland for the purpose of covering expenditures connected with on-site action, to organize the passage of a certain portion of the Jewish popu-

lation to neighboring countries, to insure the maintenance of those Polish Jews who make it across the border, to organize assistance for Jewish Polish citizens located upon occupied territory or threatened by the enemy beyond the borders of the homeland, to undertake any other steps aimed at improving the situation of the Jewish population in Poland, and to carry out these plans by using any means attainable through government activity.[4]

Thus with a single stroke of the pen, as it were, the Polish government-in-exile placed itself in the forefront of the struggle to foil the design of the Nazis to kill every Jew within their reach.

Such action by the Polish government must have come as a profound surprise to those who had followed its response to the various Jewish demands for rescue action that had been placed before it repeatedly since late 1942. In particular, Polish officials had hitherto steadfastly refused to consider creating the very sort of agency that the Rescue Council represented.[5] Yet the government now sought to portray itself as having been the world's foremost champion of the Jewish cause all along. On 11 May 1944 an official Polish press communiqué announcing the creation of the new council presented the body as an extension of the "Welfare Committee for the Jewish Population of Poland," which had purportedly been operating in the occupied homeland under government sponsorship during the previous two years.[6] By establishing the new Rescue Council, the communiqué explained, the government had made it possible for "Polish and Jewish communal workers and organizations from abroad" to become involved in the enterprise of assisting Jews.

In a later paragraph, though, the government's statement noted that the council had been set up in response to a request by the Reprezentacja following extensive Polish-Jewish negotiations. This indication that the Rescue Council was more the result of Jewish than of Polish initiative appears closer to the truth. In actuality, the Polish-Jewish negotiations that had led proximately to the creation of the council had been proceeding for some three months, and the Poles hardly appear to have pursued them with great enthusiasm.

The catalyst for these discussions had been the arrival in London in early January 1944 of two leading spokesmen for Polish Jewry, Arieh Tartakower and Anshel Reiss. Tartakower had been dispatched by the World Jewish Congress in New York to negotiate with the various exile governments in London about their involvement in the rescue of Jews;[7] Reiss had come to the British capital on behalf of the Palestinian Reprezentacja to assist in organizing activities to aid the Jews of Poland.[8] At the time the men arrived, there did not appear to be much possibility that their talks with Polish officials would yield significant results; Tartakower, in fact, had encountered Mikołajczyk's lack of interest in the idea of establishing a special rescue agency within a week of the beginning of his mission.[9] Nevertheless, Olgierd Górka had evidently believed it advisable for the government-in-exile to keep open channels to the organizations that these two men represented, on the prospect that such contacts might contribute to improving Polish-Jewish relations.[10] His Nationalities Division had thus organized a series of meetings for the two Jews (and for Schwarzbart, who maintained close, if not always friendly, working ties with them) with staff members of the Polish Foreign and Interior ministries to discuss a variety of issues on the minds of both sides.

The first such meeting was held on 27 January 1944. Five items were listed on the agenda, which had most likely been prepared by Górka alone: "a Congress of Polish Jews in the United States . . . ; Polish propaganda in the United States from the Jewish point of view . . . ; a special department within the Ministry of the Interior for saving the Jews of Poland . . . ; aid to the Jewish population . . . ; [and] rebuilding Jewish life in the homeland."[11] However, only the first item was discussed at this opening session, and the results were inconclusive.[12]

It was not until the second meeting, on 7 February, that the idea of a special rescue department was raised, and it was raised then because during the intervening period the Jewish delegates had on their own initiative drafted a detailed plan for such a body.[13] Tartakower presented the written plan to the Polish delegates at the outset of the second meeting, thereby preempting the discussion and forcing the Polish representatives to deal with a subject that, as the ensuing conversation was to demonstrate, they had not initially been prepared to discuss.[14] Tartakower's document began by warning of the possibility that "by the time the homeland is liberated the Jewish population will have been murdered in its entirety."[15] It then went on to criticize previous efforts by the Polish government to confront this situation. However well intentioned those efforts might have been, the proposal declared, they had been conducted in the past only by individual ministries or sections of ministries, and in consequence they had never been able to achieve the degree of interagency coordination necessary for rescue measures to be effective. The results of prior measures had thus been, in Tartakower's words, "often incommensurate not only with the enormity of the task but also with the actual outlay of energy and means" that had accompanied them. Organizing a special rescue department, the draft implied, would overcome this difficulty. Moreover, as the document explained, the establishment of such a department "would . . . have substantial propaganda importance, directing the attention of the world toward the problem of saving Polish Jews as well as documenting the good will and vigor behind the government's initiative in this area."

For all of these reasons, the plan called for the creation of a distinct department for rescuing Polish Jews, to be connected organizationally with the office of the prime minister and to work in close cooperation with the Interior, Foreign, Social Welfare, and Defense ministries. The department was to be headed by a director holding the rank of an undersecretary of state (*podsekretarz stanu*), with a commensurate staff to be placed at his disposal. The plan further suggested that the new department should have a parallel branch (*ekspozytura*) within the underground organization in the occupied homeland similar to the branches already maintained by other government ministries. Finally, it recommended the summoning of an associated advisory council, to be composed of government-appointed experts in the field of rescue together with Jewish representatives. The prime minister's office and the Interior, Foreign, Social Welfare, and Defense ministries were called upon to provide special allocations from their own budgets to finance the activities of the rescue department in part, with remaining funds to come from contributions made by other public and private bodies.[16]

The response of the Polish officials who read Tartakower's proposal was far from encouraging. Karol Kraczkiewicz of the Foreign Ministry stated that a body such as the one Tartakower had outlined ought to be concerned with reconstructing Jewish life in postwar Poland, together with "certain problems of current policy in whose sphere this kind of an organization could become an advisory organ to the government."[17] Antoni Serafiński of the Interior Ministry took Kraczkiewicz's suggestion one step further, recommending that the immediate problem of rescue be dealt with within the already existing framework of activities on behalf of the overall population of the homeland and suggesting that a separate department under the auspices of the prime minister's office confine its attention to postwar reconstruction alone. Górka, though praising Tartakower's plan for "skillfully getting around the tactical political difficulties that have arisen until now in projects to create an undersecretariat of state for minority affairs" and declaring that he supported the fundamental idea that the government should organize rescue activities for Jews,[18] cautioned that any public announcement of the establishment of a special body for that purpose might result in "a new case of repression for the Jewish population [in Poland]." Kraczkiewicz then used Górka's reservation in order to turn the discussion back to the question of postwar reconstruction, declaring that if a distinct body dealing with Jewish affairs were to place the major focus of its activities upon this matter and to "conceal externally the question of immediate rescue," the "practical difficulties" associated with the proposal could be avoided.

The Jewish representatives were palpably angered both by the attempt to divert the discussion to another issue and by the suggestion that whatever the government might do in response to Tartakower's proposal ought to be done secretly—a suggestion that clearly appeared to them as an excuse for avoiding consideration of the entire matter. Schwarzbart pointed out with an evident tone of desperation that unless efforts were directed toward saving the remnants of Polish Jewry at once, there would be no Jews left to benefit from plans for rebuilding Jewish life in liberated Poland. Regarding Górka's strictures about the risks inherent in any open efforts on behalf of the Jews during wartime, he declared that Roosevelt's announcement of the creation of the War Refugee Board less than three weeks earlier did not appear to him to present any danger to those whom the new American agency was intended to save. In any case, he argued that an announcement could not be avoided.

Reiss expressed Schwarzbart's exasperation even more vividly:

Only one question stands before the Jewish representation at present: What can be done *now* to save what remains of the Polish Jews? All other questions are of secondary significance. The Reprezentacja raised this question in its memorandum to the government in July 1941,[19] and the majority of its discussions with Prof. Kot in Palestine were devoted to questions of rescue.[20] Nevertheless, to this point no results have been obtained. Today Polish Jewry finds itself in a situation in which it has nothing to lose; it can only win. For this reason the fear about the danger [involved in] conducting activity openly does not appear to be material.

Tartakower, too, underscored the points made by his colleagues. He charged further that a public announcement of the creation of a rescue agency, far from placing Jews under Nazi rule in additional danger, would likely have an important psychological effect upon the German bureaucracy and especially upon the satellites of the Third Reich. These countries, he claimed, needed to see that the fate of the Jews was a matter of importance to all of the Allies; if they did so, then they would have an incentive to improve their own records with regard to the treatment of Jews once they realized that Germany would eventually lose the war. Moreover, he suggested (obviously searching for a more effective if less pertinent way to overcome the objections his plan had encountered), failure to call public attention to organized Polish efforts in the rescue field would deprive the Polish government of whatever propaganda benefit it might derive from such activity.

The arguments of the Jewish spokesmen, however, do not appear to have made much of an impression on their Polish counterparts. Immediately after all three had finished delivering what appear from the minutes to have been their long and rather impassioned speeches, Kraczkiewicz attempted to divert the discussion back to the issue of postwar reconstruction and to some of the technical details of the proposed agency's operations. He agreed that if the representatives of the Jews did not perceive any danger in conducting rescue activity openly he would not press his objection further, but he warned that Jews must be prepared to take full responsibility for the eventual consequences of this attitude. Reiss interjected once again that the primary question to be discussed was not whether to announce the taking of any particular action but the action itself. Nevertheless, the Jewish delegates were instructed to rework their proposal, taking into account all of the suggestions that had emanated from the discussion, and to submit it for reconsideration at a later date.

That instruction, however, was not followed. Instead, on 11 February, Tartakower and Schwarzbart sent a copy of the unaltered proposal directly to Mikołajczyk, with the request that the prime minister look upon the matter benevolently and treat it with the appropriate urgency.[21] It is difficult to fathom why the Jewish leaders should have taken such a course, given the prime minister's reluctance to discuss the subject directly at his meeting with them only a month earlier.[22] But whatever the case, this action appears to have worried Górka precisely because he feared that the Jews would meet with another rejection. As he explained in a letter to Interior Minister Banaczyk on 17 February, although he realized that "the demand for an under-secretariat of state for Jewish affairs . . . cannot be dealt with quickly and positively even in part, this sort of matter needs to be worked over slowly, without giving any outward sign of opposition."[23] If, he explained, "nothing comes of all these negotiations, conferences, and visits [with Jewish leaders] . . . , then instead of an improvement in Polish-Jewish relations in America, attitudes will turn in a frankly opposite direction, [leading] eventually to Jewish attacks upon the present Polish government as such."[24] He indicated that his strategy in responding to the principal Jewish demand had thus been to buy time by giving the appearance of negotiating. Now, however, presumably because of Schwarzbart and Tartakower's renewed contact with Mikołajczyk, he requested "as forcefully as possible, in the interest of the entire political situation, independently of and notwithstanding current problems of the greatest weight," that the government take some action that would "make it possible [for the Jewish spokesmen] to appear legitimate in the eyes of their own community by obtaining definite results." Specifically, he urged the government to vote a large appropriation to underground organizations for the purpose of rescuing Polish Jews, to instruct the government delegate in underground to provide as many arms as possible to Jewish military groups, and to reiterate that hiding Jews in the towns and villages was "a political and human duty." Such steps, he hoped, would satisfy at least some of the Jewish leaders and enable them to claim that through their efforts "they had brought about a strengthening of activities to save the Jews in Poland."[25]

Górka's apprehensions about Mikołajczyk's response might have been exaggerated, for the prime minister appears to have ignored Tartakower's proposal altogether.[26] Banaczyk, on the other hand, most likely accepted the argument that it was necessary for the Jewish leaders to be able to show some results from their negotiations with the Poles, for on 21 February the Interior Ministry dispatched two instructions to the government delegate along the lines Górka had recommended. The first explained that "a visible increase in aid for the Jews, as well as an order and appeal to the Polish community, will have great political significance in the present situation and will make it possible to obtain notable monies,"[27] while the second instructed the delegate "independently of [regular] monthly contributions to make without delay a one-time payment of 3 million zł. to the Council for Aid to Jews, for the purpose of [bringing about] a quick visible increase in rescue action."[28] The latter cable also asked for more arms to be provided to Jewish organizations and repeated the instruction that the Polish population be called upon to aid Jews and hide them in the cities and villages.

No doubt Górka believed that such actions would satisfy the Jewish delegates and permit him to steer the discussions with them back toward the question of how Jews might assist Polish propaganda efforts in the United States. If so, however, he was to be disappointed. When he opened his fourth meeting with the Jewish leaders on 25 February with an announcement that the Interior Ministry had recently instructed the homeland to intensify rescue efforts, Reiss replied that he "did not regard such orders as something that would solve the present problem."[29] Górka riposted that although he realized that the extent of aid provided by the government-in-exile represented but "a drop in the ocean of needs," it was necessary to emphasize that Polish actions were of far greater practical significance for Jews than anything that the British or U.S. governments had ever done in this regard. The principal Allies, he claimed, had satisfied themselves with "summoning committees that deliberate and issue pompous declarations, while the Jews of the occupied countries, who need real assistance, actually get nothing at all out of this . . . enterprise." Clearly he intended to denigrate the significance of the newly established War Refugee Board and to dissuade his Jewish adversaries from pressing further their demand to create a Polish government rescue agency, but the Jewish representatives refused to yield. During the remainder of the meeting on 25 February, Tartakower, Reiss, and Schwarzbart made it clear that their primary concern continued to be the establishment of a formal structure that would guarantee application of substantial government resources to the rescue of Polish Jews in accordance with the desires of their own spokesmen in the free world. The inability or unwillingness of the regime to do so, they implied, would indicate that the government was not serious about responding to the Jews' dire needs.

The failure of Górka's stratagem became apparent at an especially difficult time for the Poles. Friction between the government-in-exile and the Jews was mounting as a result of the recent desertions of the first two groups of Jewish soldiers from the Polish army, and the government was clearly worried about the damage to its public image that the desertions might cause.[30] Moreover, discussion in Parliament over the outcome of the Tehran conference had recently come to a close, and the debate had given the appearance that support for the exile regime's territorial claims was continuing to wane.[31] In fact, in the course of that discussion the very right of the government-in-exile to continued recognition as the legitimate authority in Poland had been called into question largely because of what one speaker called the "very considerable racial discrimination" alleged to exist in the Polish armed forces.[32] In such a situation it was hardly in the interest of the government to give Jewish spokesmen yet another reason to cast doubt upon its commitment to the values in whose name the war was ostensibly being fought. A way needed to be found to convince the Jews that the exile leadership was sincerely interested in promoting the cause of rescue to the maximum extent possible.

In line with this thinking Górka, at his next meeting with the Jewish leaders on 3 March, proposed a compromise.[33] He told the Jewish representatives frankly that "in the present political situation the government cannot undertake any action that would result in a reconstruction of the cabinet"[34] and explained that "the creation of a special department with an undersecretary of state . . . is tantamount to establishing a new ministry." However, he also indicated that "because the government appreciates the import of the dangers threatening the remainder of the Jewish population in Poland, it is determined to undertake action through an organ that it wishes to establish within the Ministry of the Interior." This proposal fell short of Tartakower's call for a high-ranking, interministerial department, but it did represent the first time any Polish official had met the Jewish demand with anything other than a wall of objections.

The Jewish response to Górka's compromise proposal was divided. Reiss declared flatly that "the project that has been presented to us today . . . does not create the possibilities for which we have been waiting in the matter of rescue action" and charged that "the government does not display a [proper] attitude toward the Jewish problem."[35] Evidently he reasoned that the desk that Górka had offered to establish in the Interior Ministry would not have sufficient decision-making power and would not control whatever funds the government might devote to rescue operations.[36] Tartakower, in contrast, was somewhat more sanguine. "If," he suggested, "the organ that the government plans to call into being could be developed further, this might to a certain extent satisfy the demand we have set down." On the other hand, he indicated that he did not believe "that one little desk [*stolik*] in the Interior Ministry would be able to solve and manage tasks that require large-scale initiative." If indeed a single desk was all that the government intended to create to deal with the rescue problem, he stated, then he regarded Górka's proposal as tantamount to a "first-class burial" of his plan.

Górka and Kraczkiewicz must have found some encouragement in Tartakower's response, for they ignored Reiss and directed their further comments to him alone. Both hinted that the suggested compromise was intended to overcome objections that the government was likely to present to Tartakower's original proposal; it was not, however, meant to constitute the government's final action on rescue. They also assured him that the proposed organ would not be merely another cog in the government bureaucracy but would rest upon the work of a public council broadly representative of the Jewish and Polish communities. "The clerical apparatus within the Interior Ministry," Górka explained, "is only the executive agency for the resolutions and plans of the commission."

Evidently during the next few days the Jewish leaders gave serious thought to Górka's suggestion, for on 8 March they returned with a united positive—although qualified—reply.[37] They had no objection, they stated, to the creation of a council of Polish and Jewish public representatives with an executive director to be appointed by the Interior Ministry, assuming that the details of the council's composition and the selection of the executive director were acceptable to the Jewish side.[38] However, they stressed most forcefully that they did not view the establishment of such a council as a satisfactory response to Tartakower's original proposal, declaring that they would continue to struggle for the creation of a cabinet-level body to take charge of rescue matters. The Poles do not seem to have anticipated this position; indeed, the thought that Górka's suggested compromise would not obviate Jewish complaints about the government-in-exile appears to have distressed them greatly. They thus endeavored to persuade the Jewish spokesmen that, in effect, there was no difference between the two plans, emphasizing again that, in contrast to the governments of Britain and the United States, the Polish government would make certain that whatever form the rescue agency to be established under its auspices took, it would undertake serious steps to provide the Jews of the homeland with practical assistance. It was unfair, Górka claimed, that Jews abroad continued to view Britain and the United States as more "liberal" than Poland with regard to the rescue issue when the Polish government had taken far greater risks to extend succor to their coreligionists under the Nazi yoke.

The Jews, however, appear to have remained unconvinced of the exile regime's good intentions.[39] In such a situation Górka could either abandon his attempt at compromise or continue to develop his idea, hoping that involving the Jewish spokesmen in ongoing negotiations would eventually lead them to commit themselves to support whatever agency finally emerged from the talks. Evidently he chose the latter course. Over the next five days he prepared a detailed proposal of his own for establishing an "organ for matters pertaining to the rescue of the Jewish population in Poland," submitting it to the Jewish leaders on 13 March.[40] He also endeavored to enlist the support of other Jews, in addition to the three with whom he had been meeting regularly for almost two months, for his plan. In this regard he seems to have been successful; as he informed Schwarzbart, Reiss, and Tartakower, Emanuel Szerer, the Bund representative on the National Council, not only had no objection to establishing a rescue agency under the auspices of the Interior Ministry but actually preferred this idea to creating "yet another government [department] at the level of an undersecretariat of state."[41] Moreover, after examining Górka's proposal the three Jewish spokesmen chose not to restate their insistence upon a cabinet-level agency but actually began to negotiate over the specifics of the plan on the table.[42] Their primary objection was that the proposal did not address the question of funding. Górka noted that he had originally felt it better to obtain the consent of the government to the idea of a rescue agency before approaching it with a concrete funding request, but he agreed to look into the possibilities of obtaining a budgetary commitment from the government in advance. The next day he informed the Jews that the question of funding for the proposed commission, together with the matters of its structure and scope of activities, would be placed on the agenda of the government's Political Committee for consideration.

With this announcement Górka's negotiations with Schwarzbart, Reiss, and Tartakower came to an end. Górka could well be satisfied with the outcome of the talks. They had forestalled, at least for the time being, the likelihood of Jewish leaders renewing their attacks upon the Polish government, and as long as negotiations continued, the Poles could feel reasonably secure that Jews would avoid taking a public stand against their cause. The government thus had a political interest in prolonging those negotiations as long as it could without giving the Jews the sense that it was stalling, and indeed, there are some indications that it did intend at first to do precisely that. In any event, for two weeks following the conclusion of the Jewish representatives' meetings with Górka little action appears to have been taken on the matter by the government. On 28 March, Schwarzbart asked Banaczyk whether any progress had been made and was informed that at least three procedural hurdles had to be cleared before the envisioned council could formally come into being: Górka's proposal had to be redrafted by the government's legal counsel, "for in its present form it is not suitable" for presentation as a bill before the cabinet; the revised bill then had to be brought to the cabinet's Committee on Homeland Affairs for deliberation; and the funding request had to be considered by the Political Committee.[43] Only after approval by those two committees could the plan be brought before the government as a whole for acceptance, rejection, or modification. That route to enactment of the proposal was considerably more involved than Górka had indicated two weeks earlier,[44] and even though review by the legal counsel may in fact already have been completed at the time Schwarzbart met with Banaczyk, the process did not appear to be susceptible to rapid conclusion.[45]

As it happened, however, the entire process was completed during the ensuing three weeks, culminating in the government's enabling resolution of 20 April summoning the Rescue Council. The impetus for such rapid movement by the Polish government was undoubtedly provided in the first instance by the gathering public storm over the desertions of the Jewish soldiers. That storm had been touched off by the government's decision to try the thirty-one Jews who had left the ranks of the Polish army between 21 and 30 March; on 5–6 April the disposition of the deserters had become a subject for discussion in the British Parliament, and subsequently the extent of Poland's adherence to the values for which the Allies purportedly stood had been called into question by significant segments of the British and American publics.[46] The government-in-exile, now fighting for its life against the increasing tendency of the two principal Western Allies to accept many of the Soviet demands regarding the postwar territorial settlement and the reorganization of the Polish regime, thus found itself in immediate need of an antidote to the public relations damage that the desertion affair was causing. By presenting itself as the champion of the mortally threatened Jews of the occupied homeland, including those Jewish citizens of other countries who had been deported to Poland, the government could at once demonstrate its dedication to the anti-Nazi cause and deflect the spotlight from the friction between Jews and non-Jews in its armed forces.

The connection between the soldier scandal and the decision to establish the Rescue Council was reflected in several documents dating from around the time of the official adoption of Górka's proposal on 20 April. On 8 April, Sylwin Strakacz in New York, commenting on the public relations implications of the desertions, warned that "the Jewish masses, incited against Poland by any incident, even the smallest, bearing a greater or lesser trace of antisemitism, are prepared to pay Russia their dues at Poland's expense."[47] In this context, he suggested, "a decision by the government to create a Department for the Rescue of Jews in the Ministry of the Interior . . . will be especially important and beneficial."[48] Similarly, Karol Kraczkiewicz pointed out that "the adoption of a resolution by the cabinet calling into being a Council for Matters Relating to the Rescue of Polish Jews will provide a splendid opportunity . . . for making a broad constructive pronouncement about the policy of the Polish government with regard to the Jews"—a pronouncement that must include an explicit response to adverse charges about the situation of Jewish soldiers in the Polish army.[49] In the same fashion Górka chided Schwarzbart for not forestalling Driberg's interpellation about the desertions in the House of Commons after the government had "proven its good will" by considering the plan for the Rescue Council.[50]

Thus it appears doubtful that without the serious damage to its public standing that the government-in-exile had absorbed in Britain and the United States—damage whose extent was made manifest by the reaction to the government's decision to try the third group of deserters—the Rescue Council would ever have been established.[51]

———

More than a month elapsed between the passage of the enabling resolution establishing the Rescue Council and its opening meeting, which was held on 25 May. In the interval the extent of the public relations damage that the trial of the deserters had caused the government-in-exile had become increasingly obvious and alarming—a new interpellation about the situation of Jews in the Polish armed forces had been presented in Parliament; the matter had been brought to the attention of the U.S. Congress; and even the president's amnesty decree had failed to assuage public anger.[52] Hence the Rescue Council came to appear, perhaps more than ever before, as a vital element in Poland's ever more desperate battle for the hearts and minds of its principal allies and their citizens.

That the newly established body was intended by its creators largely to serve a public relations purpose was indicated by the Interior Ministry's decision to open the council's first meeting to British and foreign dignitaries as well as to the local and international press.[53] In fact, the six members appointed to the council by the Interior Ministry[54] were instructed on 19 May to submit their speeches for the opening session in advance, for translation and distribution to the news services.[55] At the meeting itself, moreover, Banaczyk made certain that the principal conclusions that the Poles wished to see drawn from the creation of the new rescue agency would not be lost on those in attendance:

> The Council for the Rescue of the Jews in Poland . . . is one of the numerous and various efforts of the Polish Government and Polish people towards helping the Jews in occupied Poland, doomed by Hitler. . . . Without underestimating the efforts and achievements of Jewish organisations it may be stated that it was the Polish Government who first organised active help and relief for the Jews in Poland. In this task they were fully supported by the Polish people in occupied Poland, whose fate is hardly less cruel than that of the Jews. To those who try to besmirch the name of Poland by accusing Poles wholesale of intolerance as well as to those who are inclined to charge the Jews with illoyalty [sic] on the strength of a few desertions we may . . . say: Look at the reality as it exists in occupied Poland; there you will see a different picture. . . . Co-operation is not possible when on account of a few isolated incidents a whole nation with one of the finest records of religious and racial tolerance is violently accused. Such unjustified accusations could be hardly regarded as a stimulant to our people in Poland to risk their lives every day by sheltering hundreds and thousands of Jews. Fortunately they do it as a duty towards humanity and towards Poland and do not care particularly for appreciation. . . . All attempts at arousing the opinion of the world and of Jewry against us will not and cannot distract us from the path . . . to help and rescue as many Jews in Poland as it is possible.[56]

The three Jewish members of the council, however, made it quite obvious in their statements that they were not about to permit the new body to become a forum for the blanket praise of the Polish government and people.[57] Reiss was most explicit in this regard, declaring that "it does not become . . . this moment to discuss in this Council the situation of the Jewish soldiers in our army" and urging that the recently summoned investigating commission of the National Council be permitted to gather its findings before judgment was pronounced in that matter.[58] Abraham Babad, representing the orthodox Agudas Yisroel, agreed with Banaczyk that it was wrong to condemn all Poles for the misdeeds of a few but added that nevertheless "we must not ignore the symptoms of anti-Semitism wherever they may appear . . . , especially . . . if they concern the Armies of Poland in which all must fight the common enemy."[59] Emanuel Szerer, while stating explicitly that the Poles were thus far the only people who had taken meaningful action to assist Jews, still insisted that "we must create in Poland such an atmosphere of tolerance as to make all our compatriots realize the necessity of increasing their efforts at rescue work."[60] Both Szerer and Reiss, moreover, criticized previous government and underground action for assistance: Szerer charged that financial support for rescue work had hitherto been inadequate, and Reiss argued subtly that "the help extended to Jews in Poland by their Christian compatriots out of their sense of duty as fellow-citizens and fellow-men . . . [constitutes] the best proof of what could be done if such action were organised on a larger scale and formed part of the duties of the clandestine state administration in occupied Poland."

These minor tones notwithstanding, the general atmosphere at the meeting appears to have been festive and optimistic, with the Polish delegates committing themselves publicly to their "Christian obligation to save Jews, both as human beings and as Polish citizens."[61] The Poles' expectation that such solemn declarations would substantially improve their government's public image, however, does not seem to have been fulfilled. The focus of public attention upon Polish-Jewish relations was not removed from the desertion affair; on the contrary, both Jewish and general newspapers remained far more concerned with reporting the ongoing story of Jewish soldiers in the Polish army than with the government's involvement in rescue.[62] In fact, the obviously self-serving nature of Banaczyk's speech may, ironically, even have alienated some Jewish spokesmen. When word of the interior minister's remarks reached Palestine, in the form of a press release by the Polish Telegraphic Agency that did not include the responses by Reiss, Babad, and Szerer, Yitshak Gruenbaum and members of the Reprezentacja were quick to express bitterness at what they took to be a denigration of their own rescue efforts.[63]

Perhaps, then, it was to be expected that, under such conditions, the government would lose enthusiasm for the Rescue Council rather quickly. In any event, it does not seem to have given much of a push to the newly formed committee to set to work. The council did not meet again until 12 June, when it heard the report of a courier from underground Poland who had already been debriefed by the National Council six weeks earlier.[64] Not until 20 June, almost four weeks after the ceremonial opening session, did the council take its first official action.

The primary measure taken at the meeting of 20 June was made necessary by the fact that the Polish government, although it had established the Rescue Council, had not appropriated any funds for its operation.[65] The council thus called upon the government to place £80,000 at its disposal immediately for forwarding to the underground Council for Aid to Jews in the occupied homeland.[66] The request appears to have been rather modest, both in relation to the amounts the government was already spending on relief for Poles in the occupied homeland and abroad and in relation to the amounts that the council itself deemed necessary in order for it to fulfill its assigned task. The 1944 budget of the Ministry of Labor and Social Welfare, which was the body primarily responsible for transferring funds for assistance to the Polish civilian population to the underground, called for an expenditure of £473,000 for "aid to the homeland," which consisted of shipments of food, clothing, and medicines to Poles living under German occupation.[67] During the year, however, government appropriations to the homeland increased substantially, reaching a total of some £3 million.[68] Moreover, the Rescue Council estimated, on the basis of information provided by Jewish underground groups and by the Council for Aid to Jews, that the cost of maintaining 100,000 Jews in hiding or assisting them to escape across the Polish border reached over £1.2 million *per month*.[69] The sum of £80,000 was thus obviously intended merely as a means of priming the Rescue Council's pump. Indeed, on 30 June the council asked the government to seek loans that would cover two-thirds of its estimated monthly cost of operation, with the remaining funds to be contributed by Jewish organizations.[70]

For all of its professed commitment to the work of rescue, however, the government was not quick to respond to the council's monetary entreaties. Although it agreed to supply the requested £80,000, in fact it remitted only $50,000 (£12,500).[71] Moreover, it does not appear to have made any immediate effort to obtain the loans for continued financing that the council had requested.[72] Such dilatoriness proved profoundly distressing to Jewish leaders. Reiss, Szerer, and Babad issued a joint statement declaring that "any delay [by the government] in carrying out its resolutions makes it difficult for the Council to continue to function and negates its right of existence."[73] In addition, Schwarzbart protested to Mikołajczyk that "this state of affairs must arouse deep dissatisfaction, for the Rescue Council, on which so many hopes rode, is proving itself, in the area of the government's material assistance, a veritable fiction."[74] Reiss later indicated that he had considered resigning from the council in protest over the government's lack of support; in the end he remained only at the insistence of colleagues, who urged him not to relinquish "the last thread to the Jews of Poland."[75]

Such dissatisfaction was reinforced by what Jews regarded as government recalcitrance on another issue as well. On 1 August 1944 Reiss and Szerer, together with Adam Ciołkosz, the Polish Socialist Party (PPS) delegate who had been elected chairman of the Rescue Council, approached Banaczyk about the government's delay in providing the promised £80,000. In the course of the meeting they also requested that a special radio program be broadcast to the homeland containing speeches by the interior minister, representatives of Polish political parties, and members of the council calling upon Poles to come to the aid of their Jewish neighbors, to be followed by an ongoing series of shorter reminders on the same subject.[76] The nature of Banaczyk's response is unclear: according to an account of the conversation written by Reiss the following day, he stated that there was "no room" for such a program in the schedule of broadcasts to the homeland,[77] whereas in a second account prepared five days later, Reiss indicated that the interior minister had agreed to the idea.[78] What is clear, however, is that authorization for such broadcasts was never given, and Jewish spokesmen who attempted to pursue the issue felt that they were being run through a bureaucratic labyrinth.[79] Polish leaders finally explained that the crisis in the homeland resulting from the beginning of the uprising against the Germans in Warsaw on 1 August made it difficult to devote a broadcast to the plight of the Jews; although Jewish representatives then confined their request to a brief appeal for aid by the prime minister or minister of the interior during one of their speeches to the country, it does not appear that such an appeal was made.[80] In this context Schwarzbart explained to Mikołajczyk at the end of August that "Jewish public opinion interprets the government's silence as proof of [its] lack of interest [in the Jews' plight]; any other interpretation is impossible."[81] Indeed, it seems that whatever possibility that the formation of the Rescue Council might redound to the benefit of the exile regime's public image had disappeared altogether within three months of the council's widely publicized opening meeting.

Nevertheless, the very existence of the council does appear to have provided Jewish leaders from various parties and organizations in the free world with an important focus through which they could coordinate their own efforts at assistance, as well as with a conduit for transferring the funds that they raised to occupied Poland. Jewish bodies in the United States and Palestine substantially increased their fund-raising activities on behalf of Polish Jewry during 1944, to the point where between April and December of that year they sent the Polish government over $1.7 million for distribution to the Council for Aid to Jews, the Jewish National Committee, the Bund, and other underground Jewish groups.[82] Doubtless the establishment of the Rescue Council encouraged this increase in aid, as previous attempts to establish a regular mechanism for transmitting funds through the government-in-exile had met with little interest from the Polish side.[83]

These transfers of funds, though—no matter how much the council's creation might have served as a catalyst for them—did not involve the rescue body directly; they were administered by the government apparatus and monitored by the two Jewish representatives on the National Council, who gave instructions regarding their destinations and endeavored to make certain that they reached them (as, it appears, they frequently did not).[84] As a result, the Rescue Council spent most of its time dealing with matters other than direct assistance to Jews in the occupied homeland. It happened, for example, that the council had come into being precisely as Germany was beginning the mass deportation of Jews from Hungary to the death camp at Auschwitz.[85] The council's mandate specifically included concern for "foreign . . . Jews who have been deported to Polish territory";[86] it was thus to play a role in efforts to save this latest Jewish community to fall victim to the Nazi murder program.

Speculation that the more than 760,000 Jews under Hungarian jurisdiction[87] would likely be shipped to Poland for killing abounded following the occupation of Hungary by German forces on 19 March 1944.[88] Jewish spokesmen immediately advised British and U.S. leaders of this prospect, calling upon them to admonish the Hungarian people "not to admit application of [the] policy of extermination of Jews by German butchers or Hungarian Quislings."[89] The leaders responded promptly: at a press conference on 24 March, Roosevelt, noting that "hundreds and thousands of Jews . . . in Hungary . . . are now threatened with annihilation," cautioned that those who abetted "the deportation of Jews to their death in Poland" would be regarded as "equally guilty with the executioner himself";[90] Eden issued a similar warning in the House of Commons six days later.[91] The principal Western Allies evidently did not doubt, moreover, that the threat of deportation was real: as early as 5 April the U.S. Office of Strategic Services was reporting that the Germans intended to liquidate the Jews of Hungary in "the most efficient pogrom of them all."[92]

Polish officials, too, speculated whether their country would become the place where Hungarian Jews, like Jews of so many other European lands, would meet their deaths. In some cases, however, the Polish leaders' evaluations differed from those of their British and American counterparts. Banaczyk told Schwarzbart on 28 March that he knew nothing about what was happening to the Jews in Hungary; he stated only that efforts to help Polish Jews escape to that country, which had increased of late, would now cease.[93] In addition, on 3 April the Polish consul-general in Istanbul, Zdzisław Szczerbiński, sent an urgent memorandum to his Foreign Ministry regarding "the forecasts [of local observers] . . . as to the extent to which the policy of extermination will be applied to the Jews of Hungary . . . and the possibilities of effective aid from the outside."[94] This memorandum dealt, however, only with the issue of extermination, for its author saw no need for considering outside assistance. After examining the nature of Hungarian-Jewish relations, Germany's military and economic situation, and the character of the new Hungarian government that the Germans had just installed, Szczerbiński came to the conclusion that "physical extermination according to the model carried out in Poland appears altogether improbable."[95] This observation led him to a remarkable operative suggestion: "If the Polish government is planning . . . one more time to condemn Nazi atrocities against the Jewish community, it ought to set about formulating a suitable declaration without delay, for at a later time, should the reining in of the extermination policy become a matter of common knowledge, the most appropriate tactical moment for our statement might have passed by." That was Szczerbiński's only comment regarding how his government should respond to the inauguration of what he himself termed "a period of persecution and broad exclusion of Jews from political, economic, and cultural life," including compulsory wearing of the yellow star, confiscation of property, and large-scale arrests. Although at the outset of his memorandum he stated that his evaluation of the situation could serve "to guide the government of Poland . . . with regard to our role in the defense of human rights being carried on by the United Nations," evidently he regarded that role as nil.

Nonetheless, if Szczerbiński saw Poland's interest in the situation of the Jews in Hungary as lying solely in the propaganda field, the Polish Foreign Ministry, to whom his observations were addressed, viewed matters differently. On the eve of the German occupation there were some 11,000 Polish citizens in Hungary, of whom 2,000 to 3,000 were Jews.[96] This latter figure appears to have represented mainly refugees who had arrived in the country since May 1943.[97] Such a large influx created difficulties for the local Polish Civic Committee (Komitet Społeczny), which had been established with official sanction after Hungary's June 1941 entry into the war on Germany's side had forced the Polish legation in Budapest to close.[98] The head of that committee, Henryk Sławik, reportedly explained to Polish Jews who applied to him for assistance that he did not possess funds to take care of all of their needs sufficiently,[99] a statement that left him open to charges of anti-Jewish discrimination.[100] In this situation the Foreign Ministry evidently came to the conclusion, with the encouragement of the Interior Ministry and the Ministry of Social Welfare, that the most effective way to ease pressure on the relief apparatus, as well as to obviate claims that Polish Jewish refugees in Hungary were being treated inequitably by an agency of the Polish government, was to endeavor to resettle the refugees in other countries.[101]

This idea, moreover, must have seemed like a fruitful course to pursue not only because of its inherent logic but also because Jewish groups in Allied and neutral countries had for several months been imploring the Polish government to act in precisely that fashion.[102] Such entreaties appear to have been prompted, at least in part, by a sense that conditions for Jews in Hungary were not quite as secure as they seemed on the surface.[103] This sense grew stronger in the months leading up to the German occupation, evidently on the basis of public threats by Hungarian officials that Jewish refugees in the country would soon be sent back to their countries of origin.[104] Polish officials were aware of these Jewish apprehensions,[105] and on the eve of occupation they put serious requests to British and American officials to provide their Jewish charges with entry visas for new havens.[106]

The German invasion on 19 March 1944 did not change the Foreign Ministry's approach. On the contrary, with Germany now dominating all aspects of Hungarian politics, the ministry reasoned that non-Jewish Polish refugees might also find themselves in danger and that success in extricating Jews from the country could perhaps open exit channels that might need some day to be employed by others as well.[107] As a result, despite a rather lukewarm initial British response,[108] the ministry continued to press the two Western Allies for action on the visa proposal.[109] Hence the Polish Foreign Ministry became involved in ongoing discussions with the Allied governments that had of necessity to take note of the situation of Jews in Hungary in general. It also had an interest in monitoring that situation closely. In this regard it depended to a considerable extent on information from Jewish sources, obtained largely by the Polish diplomatic posts in Bern and Istanbul.[110]

Thus, by pursuing efforts to have Polish Jewish refugees in Hungary relocated in other countries, the Polish Foreign Ministry unintentionally found itself in the position of an intermediary between Hungarian Jewry and the Western Allies. In this capacity it was able to transmit to the West some of the first accurate information about the deportation of Hungarian Jews to Poland, a process that began on 15 May. Although rumors that the Jews of Hungary were slated for killing had been circulating among the Allies ever since the German takeover of the country, the beginning of the deportations was not immediately known outside the Nazi realm.[111] On 3 June, however, Ciechanowski sent the U.S. State Department a memorandum reporting that 310,000 Jews had been confined to ghettos in all parts of the country in order "to break them before they are exterminated" and that "ruthless deportations" had already begun in Kassa, Munkács, and Nyíregyháza.[112] The Polish ambassador concluded with the exhortation that the report on which his memorandum was based "ends with an appeal to the Jewish organizations and communities in the USA for immediate help," stressing "that many people can still be rescued if adequate funds are provided immediately."

Sometime following the transmission of this memorandum, however, the Polish government was made privy to the gist of contacts that British and American representatives had been holding with Joel Brand, a member of the clandestine Assistance and Rescue Committee (Va'adat Ezra veHatsalah) in Budapest. Brand had turned up mysteriously in Istanbul on 19 May in the company of one Andor (Bandi) Grosz, a known smuggler and spy who worked simultaneously for German, Hungarian, British, and American intelligence units. Claiming to represent the Jews of Hungary, Brand had brought with him, in the words of the British ambassador in Ankara, "a proposal formally addressed to him by [the] Gestapo for exchanging [the] remaining Jews in Axis occupied territory against either commodities or foreign currency." [113]

For a variety of reasons neither the British nor the U.S. government was prepared to pursue the reported German offer. [114] On 26 June, Eden circulated a note among the Cabinet Refugee Committee stating that "to start talking about material recompense [for threatened Jews] . . . would open an unending series of blackmail, and must be firmly refused." [115] Evidently he also approached the Polish government to associate itself with this position, [116] for the next day, at Romer's instigation, the Polish cabinet authorized its foreign minister "to join the Polish government's name to the protest being prepared by the Allied governments against the German blackmail attempt in the matter of the Jews in Hungary." [117] The Poles, however, do not appear to have felt entirely comfortable about taking this step; indeed, such an action clearly ran counter to their desire to appear as a leading promoter of rescue efforts as well as to their previous role as an advocate for threatened Jews in Hungary. Moreover, they seem to have been concerned that the Western Allies' negative response to the Brand proposal might lead Britain and the United States to abjure involvement in the fate of the civilian population in Hungary altogether—a most unwelcome development in Polish eyes, as the government-in-exile was also anxious over the fate of non-Jewish Poles in Hungary and might have hoped that the Allies would intervene on their behalf should such intervention ever become necessary. [118] As a result, while calling upon the government to dissociate itself from the German scheme, Romer also recommended an approach to the British and Americans aimed at inducing them to issue a public statement warning that all who took part in any German crimes would be held accountable for them, as well as to appeal to Sweden, Switzerland, and the Vatican to endeavor to dissuade the Hungarian government from continuing cooperation with the German program of deportation.[119] Moreover, together with the Interior Ministry, the Foreign Ministry developed a stratagem that it evidently thought would lend the Polish approach greater weight in American and British eyes. That stratagem involved the Rescue Council.

The plan was outlined in a memorandum from Górka to Banaczyk on 27 June.[120] According to it, the Nationalities Division of the Interior Ministry would transmit to the Rescue Council "information coming from the Homeland about the killing in Auschwitz of 100,000 Jews transported from Hungary," with a request that the council adopt appropriate resolutions.[121] The council was also to be instructed to appeal formally to the Polish government to address a note to the Allied regimes, calling upon them to take precisely the steps that Romer had earlier suggested to the Polish cabinet. "This sort of a resolution by the Council for Matters Relating to the Rescue of the Jewish Population in Poland," explained Górka, "would be made public, while independently the Foreign Ministry, in consultation with the Interior Ministry, would set about preparing the aforementioned note to the government without delay, so that the entire apparatus could begin to function following the adoption of the initial resolution by the Council." In other words, the Polish government planned to use the Rescue Council as a vehicle for lending moral force to its own entreaties to the British and American authorities.

Thus the situation of the Jews in Hungary proved a convenient field for cooperation between the government-in-exile and the Rescue Council.[122] On 30 June the council adopted two resolutions on the matter, calling not only for the steps that the government had suggested but also for Polish officials themselves to arouse public opinion in the Allied and neutral countries and to request the assistance of the principal Western Allies in several concrete proposals.[123] The government, for its part, did not hesitate to oblige. On 3 July, Romer addressed a note to the British and U.S. embassies to the government-in-exile expressing "the conviction [of the Polish government] that it is a matter of the utmost urgency that the United Nations reconsider the possibility of finding the means to save the Jewish population, which is threatened with total extermination."[124] Five days later Polish diplomatic representatives in Ankara, Bern, Lisbon, Stockholm, and the Vatican were instructed to entreat the governments to which they were accredited "to undertake in their own names an intervention with the Hungarian government aimed at restraining it from participating in this crime [of deporting Jews—a crime] that cannot go unpunished following the victory of the Allies and whose effects may impinge upon the fate of Hungary."[125] Moreover, during the next two weeks the Foreign Ministry followed up on these steps, stressing that action on its requests would not admit delay.[126]

Jewish spokesmen expressed satisfaction over the government's steps on behalf of the Jews of Hungary. Alexander Easterman of the World Jewish Congress, for example, wrote to Romer thanking Polish officials for bringing to light facts about the murder of Hungarian Jews in Auschwitz.[127] Reiss was especially encouraged with the role that he believed the Rescue Council had played in motivating the government to action. As he remarked to Schwarzbart, "I have the impression that . . . for the first time we [on the council] have achieved something concrete, and it also seems to me that the action carried out by the government has had a certain effect."[128] Unfortunately he was correct on neither count. Far from serving as a stimulus to government action, the Rescue Council had actually addressed the situation of Hungarian Jewry at the government's behest. The government, in turn, appears to have become involved in this situation more out of concern for the welfare of non-Jewish Polish refugees in Hungary than as a result of pressure directed at it by Jewish organizations in the West. Moreover, the regime's interventions with the Allied and neutral governments do not appear to have had any appreciable impact. Portugal and Turkey responded negatively to the government's entreaties.[129] Britain replied to the concrete proposals for action that had originated in the Rescue Council in a fashion suggesting that no action would be taken.[130] Although Sweden, Switzerland, and the Vatican all indicated that they would intervene with the Hungarian government, they had in fact already done so prior to being approached by the Poles.[131]

In fact, before the Rescue Council's resolutions of 30 June had a chance to have any effect, the Hungarian authorities, suddenly reasserting their own sovereignty against a Germany whose rapidly deteriorating military situation now prevented it from insisting that its will be done unconditionally, ordered that all deportations of Jews to Poland be stopped as of 8 July.[132] This development appears to have made the entire subject of the Polish government's concern for the fate of its citizens in Hungary, and in particular the matter of rescuing Jews from that country, seem less pressing.[133] In response, the government adopted a policy of watchful waiting, freezing all of its initiatives as long as the deportations remained suspended but retaining the option of renewing them should the transports ever begin to roll anew. In the meantime, too, the Rescue Council had begun to take up yet another matter.

▬▬▬▬▬▬

That problem involved the fate of close to 4,000 Jews, most of them Polish citizens, who had managed during the war to acquire passports or other official documents identifying them as citizens of a country of Latin America.[134] Such documents—generally issued by consular officials in Europe without instruction from their governments, whether for humanitarian reasons or for personal gain—had been distributed through various channels, including sale by Gestapo agents to Jews hiding in Warsaw following the liquidation of the ghetto in that city in May 1943.[135] Their value lay in the fact that Germany had made a practice of holding Allied nationals, including Jews, for eventual exchange for German civilians interned abroad, meaning that Jews who could demonstrate that a country that had entered the war against Germany owed them protection stood a chance of avoiding deportation to the death camps.[136] Indeed, beginning in mid-1942, several groups of Jews holding Allied citizenship documents were separated from the masses slated for killing and interned in special exchange camps, such as Tittmoning and Bergen-Belsen in Germany and Vittel in France.[137] The Polish government—in particular Poland's legate in Bern, Aleksander Ładoś—fully supported the efforts of free-world Jewish organizations to obtain such passports and to transmit them to Jews in the occupied homeland, and the Bern Legation became a center for communications about such endeavors.[138]

In December 1943, however, the government-in-exile received word that the situation of Polish Jews possessing Latin American passports was not as secure as their bearers had initially thought. Evidently a representative of the Spanish government, which represented the interests of the Latin American countries in Berlin, informed German officials that the states that had provided passports to the several hundred Jews being held at the camp at Vittel—especially Paraguay, whose consuls had given out perhaps 250 such documents[139]—no longer recognized them as valid.[140] In response to this information the camp authorities were reported to have confiscated the Jewish inmates' identity documents, thus raising the fear that the internees were no longer regarded as suitable for exchange and that they would soon be shipped to Poland for death.

For reasons that are not altogether clear,[141] the Polish government decided to urge at least some of the Latin American states involved to affirm the validity of the papers that their own consular officials had issued.[142] Their interventions had mixed success: Paraguay agreed, responding to entreaties not only from the Poles but from the United States and the Netherlands;[143] but Venezuela and Haiti temporized, while Peru and Ecuador flatly denied responsibility for Polish Jews who happened to possess their citizenship papers.[144] Whether the Germans were aware of the expressed positions of the issuing countries is uncertain; but whatever the case, on 20 March they removed 240 Jews from the Vittel camp and detained them in a nearby hotel, informing them that unless the validity of their documents was confirmed shortly, they would be treated as stateless persons and dispatched to Poland.[145] In fact, on 18 April, 163 of these detainees were shipped first to the concentration camp at Drancy, near Paris, then to the death camp at Auschwitz. A second transport followed on 16 May, after which only 12 Jews bearing Latin American passports remained at Vittel.[146]

The Polish government did not possess an accurate picture of these developments as they happened, any more than did any other agency outside the Nazi orbit. On 5 April the Foreign Ministry heard that the authorities at Vittel had ordered the deportation of all internees with South American passports unless there were an immediate possibility to exchange them for German citizens.[147] Two days later Kraczkiewicz explained to Schwarzbart that "only an official declaration of the South American governments . . . that such an exchange is possible can save these people's lives," adding that the U.S. government and the Vatican had both been approached about intervening with the governments in question.[148] On 26 April the government received (inaccurate) word that "all internees in Vittel have been deported" to Drancy;[149] that was the last information it was to obtain for the next three months.[150] The government's actions during subsequent weeks were thus predicated on the false assumption that the Jews from Vittel had been removed to a concentration camp, where they were being held for immediate exchange.

Those actions were aimed at creating the impression that the exchange sought by the Germans was imminent. On 10 April the Foreign Ministry instructed its diplomatic missions to investigate the possibilities of opening indirect discussions with the German regime about such a transfer of German citizens in Latin American countries for Jews holding Latin American passports, even if in fact there was no realistic possibility for bringing the desired exchange about.[151] It also endeavored to coordinate action on this matter with the United States.[152] As before, however, the results of these interventions were meager: Peru once again abjured any involvement,[153] while Paraguay and Haiti, although expressing agreement in principle with the goal of discussing an exchange with Germany, indicated that they would be able to take practical steps in this direction only at some future date.[154] Even the U.S. State Department was hesitant about discussing an exchange that might not ever come about.[155]

Once the Rescue Council was established, it took over coordination of Polish efforts on behalf of the Vittel internees. Toward the end of July, Manfred Lachs, the council's executive director, met with Sidney Brown of the U.S. War Refugee Board in an effort to develop a plan of action that would benefit the Jews in question.[156] However, at precisely that time a report was finally received in London indicating that the large majority of the Jews in Vittel had been sent to "an unknown destination" and were "probably in some Jewish Camp in Upper Silesia."[157] The report, prepared by a British woman who had been interned at Vittel, together with over 400 other Britons, for over four years, suggested that "it is . . . most urgent now to find those people . . . and to . . . demand them by name for an exchange against Germans." Although the report stressed that "the gravity of the situation cannot be exaggerated . . . , [nor can] the need for immediate action," the Rescue Council found that there was little that it could do. In mid-August it attempted to have the subject discussed at the plenary meeting of the Intergovernmental Committee on Refugees, but the committee's director, Sir Herbert Emerson, indicated merely that his organization had "met with difficulties" when it had tried to intervene on behalf of the threatened Jews.[158] Shortly thereafter word was obtained that all but twelve Jews from Vittel had been deported to Poland, a fact that made the matter disappear from the council's agenda.[159]

Thus, as in the case of its involvement in the situation of the Jews in Hungary, no sooner had the Rescue Council begun to take up the problems of Jews possessing Latin American passports than external developments obviated the need for action—although, to be sure, under far less optimistic circumstances than in the former case. As it happened, the council's brief intervention in this matter marked its last attempt to mobilize action on behalf of Polish Jews beyond the borders of the homeland. Developments on the eastern front soon forced its attention back to the situation in Poland proper.

While attempting to plead the case of the former Vittel internees, the Rescue Council began to receive disquieting reports from territories recently liberated by the advancing Red Army. These reports indicated that prior to their retreat German forces in Lithuania had killed the few Jews still alive in their custody and suggested that they were likely to do the same to the Łódź ghetto and the camps in which Jews were still alive.[160] The Rescue Committee of the Jewish Agency in Jerusalem, which had transmitted this information, asked that the Polish government instruct its underground forces to move against the camps and to extricate Jewish inmates from them.[161] Schwarzbart passed this request on to Mikołajczyk on 18 August, pleading that "it may soon be too late" to save anyone.[162] However, since 1 August the Home Army had been pouring all of its resources into an armed uprising to liberate Warsaw, and action along the lines desired by Jewish spokesmen was hardly likely to be considered. As a result, after waiting in vain for a favorable response, the council decided, on 28 September, to issue its own plaintive public appeal:

> From reliable sources news has reached the Polish Government that the Germans intend to liquidate and annihilate all those kept by them in various camps in Poland.
>
> A desperate appeal was sent out from Poland imploring help and indicating the immediate danger facing those in Oświęcim and other camps. SS detachments and planes are supposed to be used to this aim.
>
> This means nothing else but the murder of those who, having survived years of trial and persecution, will not live to see the day of victory dawn.
>
> Among those threatened with annihilation are the remnants of the Jewish population in Poland.
>
> The Council for Rescue of the Jewish Population in Poland issue hereby this appeal to all those in whose hands are vital de-

cisions and who are the great leaders in this war—to make an attempt to rescue those doomed fighters and victims.

Before the eyes of humanity scores of thousands are being murdered most brutally, and no help is being given to them.

We appeal on behalf of those who fought on the ruins of the Ghetto of Warsaw, those who take now part in the fight for Warsaw's liberation. We feel that we are entitled to put forward this demand for full help.

Immediate help is imperative. Tomorrow it may be too late.[163]

The council, however, was unable even to make certain that the appeal was seen by those "great leaders" to whom it was addressed. Lachs had to ask Raczyński to forward copies to the British Foreign Office and to the U.S. Embassy in London.[164] On 4 October the Polish leader complied with this request.[165] Whether the Foreign Office took any notice of the document is not known; however, the U.S. ambassador, John Winant, informed Raczyński that the council's appeal would be delivered to the State Department, which would in turn direct the attention of the War Refugee Board to its contents.[166] By that time, however, another two weeks had passed; only then could the matter begin to be discussed by the U.S. administration. Such was the urgency with which the council's cry for help was regarded by all concerned.[167]

Within a few months of its inception, then, the Rescue Council found itself reduced to insignificance. As 1944 gave way to 1945, and the Allied forces closed in on Germany from east and west, the council necessarily found its attention taken up more and more by the problems of those Jews who could now be called survivors of the Nazi horrors. In early 1945 a council delegation, together with Schwarzbart, visited liberated France and Belgium to locate Jewish Polish citizens who had lived through the war in those countries and to finds ways of assisting them to rebuild their lives.[168] However, even this mission proved of no consequence, as the Polish government proved dilatory about supplying funds to underwrite its efforts.[169]

The irrelevance of the Rescue Council was not lost on the council's members themselves, nor on those who had labored most for its establishment. On 8 February 1945 Schwarzbart told a Foreign Ministry official that, in his opinion, "the Rescue Council is a fiction; it has done practically nothing."[170] Nor was he alone in his view. At its final meeting, on 20 June 1945, precisely one year after it had held its first working session and requested an allocation of £80,000 that was never appropriated in full, the council passed its concluding resolution:

> The Council contends that from its inception, in the decision of the Council of Ministers of 20 April 1944, until today the Polish government has not discharged its tasks in the area of financing activities aimed at assisting and protecting the Jewish population, to which it was bound by the contents of the aforementioned decision.[171]

The grievances that Jewish leaders had expressed toward the Polish government-in-exile throughout the war had not been resolved as the war came to a close.

Envoi

While the Rescue Council was struggling in vain to find an area of endeavor in which it could be effective, the government-in-exile's diplomatic position continued to deteriorate. On 22 July 1944, with the Red Army having crossed into Polish territory to which the Soviets did not lay claim, the new Polish Committee of National Liberation (Polski Komitet Wyzwolenia Narodowego—PKWN) met in Moscow, intending, as Stalin explained to Churchill, to "constitute the core of a Provisional Polish Government made up of democratic forces."[1] Quickly this committee established itself in Lublin, which had just been freed from German occupation. On 1 August the Home Army launched an armed uprising in Warsaw with the aim of forcing the already weakened Germans from the Polish capital and establishing a Polish authority in the country loyal to the exile regime. The uprising, however, proved a dismal failure, resulting merely, following a two-month siege, in the decimation of the Home Army and the effective termination of its ability to offer any meaningful resistance to the imposition of a new Soviet-backed government in the liberated homeland.[2] In October, Mikołajczyk, under pressure from Britain and the United States, consented to a Polish-Soviet border that would leave virtually all of the territories annexed by the USSR in 1939, with the exception of Lwów, in Soviet hands; but even this offer would not satisfy Stalin, whose forces had already advanced to the Wisła and would clearly occupy the entire country sooner or later.[3] Mikołajczyk, attempting to salvage some measure of influence for his government over the course of events, urged his cabinet to agree to all Soviet territorial demands and to the formation of a new government including elements from PKWN, but three of the four parties in his coalition demurred.[4] In response, on 24 November, Mikołajczyk resigned the premiership, taking Romer and Raczyński with him.[5] He was replaced by Tomasz Arciszewski, a veteran socialist who only recently had escaped from the occupied homeland. Britain recognized this government as a matter of course, but Churchill assured Stalin that it would be treated coldly.[6] On 31 December, the Soviets formally recognized PKWN as the provisional government of Poland, and by 1 February 1945 Britain and the United States had effectively jettisoned the exile regime forever.[7] From that moment, the Polish government-in-exile survived as little more than a pretender to legitimacy.

These months of decline and virtual disappearance witnessed few developments of note in the government-in-exile's thinking about Jewish matters. Some government leaders continued to strive to present an image of being seriously concerned over the fate of Poland's Jews, and indeed of Jews throughout the world, as part of an ongoing effort to make the government appear a staunch defender of the principles in whose name the Allies purported to have gone to war. On 4 October, for example, Romer urged Mikołajczyk to endorse a call by Jewish groups in the United States for an international bill of rights, guaranteeing, among other things, "the inalienable right of all religious, ethnic and cultural groups to maintain and foster their respective group identities on the basis of equality," as part of the new world order to be established at the end of the war.[8] In response a proposal was drafted for a presidential decree "on combating the propagation of hatred toward a person on the basis of his origin, religion, or ethnic identity," which declared such hatred to be "contrary to the principles of democracy upon which Poland bases its existence" and promised to make any public expression of it punishable by three years' imprisonment.[9] This decree, however, was not immediately signed,[10] a fact that evidently worried those who were convinced of its public relations importance. On 17 November, Górka wired the Interior Ministry from New York, urging the government to take immediate action:

> Signs of the government's positive legislative action are necessary in general, and especially for the Jews, if only as a counterweight to such propaganda coming from Lublin. I ask for great pressure and haste. Cable me news about the status of the law regarding racial hatred. . . . Please intervene with the prime minister and place pressure upon the cabinet, for a propaganda effect will be possible if the law about antisemitism is announced around the 23rd or the 24th of this month.[11]

Górka's timetable, which had been suggested by the upcoming War Emergency Conference of the World Jewish Congress, set for 26 November at Atlantic City (at which Secretary of State Edward

Stettinius was slated to deliver an address), would in any case have been foiled by Mikołajczyk's resignation. Nonetheless, the government appears to have continued to believe it important to cultivate a favorable public image on Jewish matters. Arciszewski's first speech to the National Council contained a passage that stood to be helpful in this regard:

> I wish to emphasize that the national minorities in Poland will enjoy complete equality. They will have not only duties but also rights on an equal basis with the Polish population. The government devotes special attention to citizens of Jewish nationality [*narodowości żydowskiej*], who bore the greatest and most painful losses in the struggle against the occupiers and who showed an ability not only to suffer but also to fight against the Germans, as the defense of the Warsaw ghetto in 1943 demonstrated. Renewing its expressions of sympathy for the persecuted and its words of condemnation of the executioners, the government declares that, in accordance with its oft-repeated statements, all German decrees directed against the Jews in Poland are without legal force and carry no obligation to obey. The government will make every effort to right the wrong inflicted by the German barbarians and to return the situation to one that accords with the best traditions of Polish tolerance.[12]

The text of Arciszewski's statement was sent, among other places, to the Polish Consulate-General in Tel Aviv with a request to bring it to the attention of the editors of the country's Jewish newspapers.[13] But the government could hardly have expected that now, when it was on the verge of final abandonment by the Western Allies, Jews would suddenly rally to its side. Indeed, most government observers appear to have been finally convinced, if they had not been earlier, that world Jewry was solidly pro-Soviet.[14] Górka reported that the War Emergency Conference had struck a "decidedly pessimistic" tone with regard to Polish affairs and to Polish-Jewish relations and noted that the speeches of Stephen Wise and (especially) Nahum Goldmann had affirmed that the Soviet Union should have a decisive say in the future organization of Eastern Europe.[15] No doubt reacting to the desperate nature of his government's situation, Górka sharply criticized the lack of attention that the government had, to his mind, demonstrated toward Jewish affairs throughout the war and charged that government spokesmen had failed to represent the Polish case properly to

Jewish audiences. He also railed severely against the Polish community in America, which, he charged, had "done nothing to induce Jews to work with it rather than against it."[16] He urged immediate action to improve this situation.

But what sort of action could the government take? Prior to Mikołajczyk's resignation Stanisław Kot had endeavored to find a new lever with which to cajole Jews into doing what the government desired. In a conversation with Schwarzbart on 25 October, in which he indicated that the cabinet would have to make significant concessions on the border issue in order to have any chance of surviving as the recognized government of Poland, Kot warned that Polish Jews now living in areas likely to remain under Soviet control who preferred to live under Polish rule might well find themselves unwelcome by the Polish people and were liable to encounter difficulties from the Polish side.[17] "For this reason," he advised, "it is essential that the Jews in America actively adopt a positive stance toward Poland's demands," including "complete independence [and possession of] Lwów and Drohobycz. This," he promised, "would facilitate the admission of Jews into Poland." But even this potential bargaining chip was effectively eliminated once Mikołajczyk gave up the last of Poland's eastern territorial demands and the exile regime appeared less and less capable of holding up its end of any bargain that it might make.

Indeed, the government-in-exile and individuals in the homeland associated with it were already beginning to appear inconsequential in Jewish eyes. In fact, when a courier arrived from the homeland in August 1944, Schwarzbart actually professed no interest in speaking with him:

> Meetings with people from the homeland always interested me from the point of view of the possibilities of rendering assistance [to Jews]. The disappearance of the Jews has lessened my interest in meeting with emissaries from the homeland. Moreover, I have lost confidence in what they have to say, for in none of them, even in Karski, did I feel a heart for the Jews. For these reasons all of these conversations have at bottom no meaning at all.[18]

As a result, following the Soviet offensive of the summer of 1944 and the establishment of PKWN on Polish soil, Jewish organizations began to forge direct contacts with the newly created agencies of administration in the liberated homeland. Beginning in September 1944, Emil Sommerstein, a veteran Zionist leader and former Sejm deputy from Lwów who had spent much of the war in Soviet prisons only to be co-opted to PKWN, addressed appeals for aid to Jewish leaders throughout the world, and Jewish leaders responded.[19] In January 1945 Sommerstein was appointed head of the newly created Central Committee of Jews in Poland in newly liberated Warsaw; on 2 February he spoke to the remnants of Polish Jewry: "We have great duties in regard to the Polish State as citizens. The first democratic government of Poland is now building a new, just and people's Poland, assuring full actual and formal equality for us."[20]

As Jews throughout the world turned their attention from rescuing those condemned to death to helping those who had survived the Nazi horror rebuild their lives, it was clear that they would work through the governments and institutions that were being established in the territories just freed from German rule—especially if it appeared that those governments and institutions enjoyed the survivors' confidence. The Polish government-in-exile had ceased to play a role in Jewish life.

Did anything of significance change in the relationship between the Polish government-in-exile and the Jews as a result of the news that the German occupiers of the homeland were carrying on a systematic campaign to kill every Jew within their reach? For the Jewish organizations in the free world that maintained contact with the government-in-exile and represented the needs of the threatened Jews before it, a distinct change was indeed noticeable from the end of 1942. Whereas prior to that time those organizations had been most concerned, in their dealings with the government, with guaranteeing the civic equality of the Jews in the future liberated Poland and with preventing discrimination against Jewish refugees from the homeland by official Polish agencies, the eyewitness reports of mass killings that reached the West as the war approached its fortieth month, and their subsequent confirmation by the British and U.S. governments, caused these Jewish groups to focus their attentions primarily upon ways in which the Polish exile authorities could help rescue Jews from the Nazi abyss. Not only could this new focus of interest be inferred from the demands that Jewish groups set before the Polish government beginning in December 1942; it was also stated explicitly by Jewish leaders to Polish representatives on several different occasions.[21]

In addition, Jewish spokesmen demonstrated an occasional willingness, which they had not shown during the first part of the war, to moderate the intensity of their public criticism of the Polish regime in matters related to the treatment of Polish Jews outside of the homeland. They were prepared, for example, not to challenge General Anders's assertion that his notorious order of 30 November 1941 was a forgery, even though they did not believe him. They also cooperated with the government's efforts to keep the matter of the desertion of Jewish soldiers from the Polish army in Great Britain out of the public eye, even to the point of endeavoring actively to dissuade a member of Parliament from raising the issue in the House of Commons. In fact, until the desertion story caught the attention of the Western public—a development attributable directly to the decision of the Polish Defense Ministry to try the soldiers of the third group and not to any plan by Jewish organizations to create a public scandal in service of their interests—the treatment of the government-in-exile in the Jewish press in Britain, the United States, and even Palestine appears on the whole to have been considerably milder during the interval from December 1942 to April 1944 than it was prior to that time.[22]

This temporary toning down, as it were, of the public edge of the confrontation between the exile government and the Jews—a development that does not appear to have resulted from any conscious decision on the part of Jewish organizations—is difficult to explain. Certainly Jewish leaders were no happier with the Polish regime after December 1942 than they had been before; on the contrary, the tenor of their private exchanges with government representatives appears to have grown progressively more hostile as their dissatisfaction with the government's response to their rescue demands mounted. Perhaps, then, Jewish leaders realized, even intuitively, that if they hoped ever to change the government's attitude toward those demands, they ought not to give the government any objective reason to be angry with them. Indeed, it was unlikely that the Poles could be shamed into carrying out the Jews' rescue program, as they had essentially been shamed earlier into issuing declarations about Jewish rights and were later to be shamed into granting amnesty to the third group of Jewish deserters.[23] For reasons that have yet to be fathomed, it proved much easier to exercise British and American public opinion about allegations that several hundred Jewish soldiers were being taunted and abused in the Polish army than about reports that German forces were systematically murdering millions of Jewish civilians in centers especially designed for that purpose. The campaign to gain Polish government assistance in helping Jews stay out of those centers could not be fought in the pages of the press, something that Jewish leaders evidently grasped.

To be sure, cessation of public attacks upon their government was something that Polish leaders had long demanded from their Jewish counterparts; Kot had even explicitly made such action a precondition for positive government response to Jewish rescue postulates. Yet the Poles also wanted more: they wanted open Jewish support for their political demands vis-à-vis the Soviet Union. Ironically, though, the news of the murder of Polish Jewry actually appears to have made many Jewish spokesmen—especially those connected with the Zionist movement, which during the war had become increasingly dominant on the world Jewish political scene [24]—even more reluctant to consider giving such support. By the end of 1942 it was clear that the Jews under Soviet rule represented the largest reservoir of potential citizens for the Jewish commonwealth in Palestine that the Zionists had just then undertaken officially to create. One of the greatest challenges facing the Zionist leadership, then, was to find a way to tap that reservoir, to convince the Soviet authorities that those Jews be allowed to settle in their historic homeland. The Soviet Union also stood to play a central role in deliberations over the political future of Palestine, and the Zionists hoped that that influence would be exerted to their benefit. Accomplishing these goals depended entirely upon Soviet goodwill; Jews had no means to bring any significant pressure to bear upon Stalin's regime, and they had no cause to suspect that the regime would find it in its interest to underwrite the Zionist enterprise by granting millions of its citizens the exceptional privilege of emigration. Antagonizing the Soviet Union, then, was something that Zionist policymakers assiduously wished to avoid, especially as that country was bearing the brunt of the war against Germany and was fighting to liberate territories where the bulk of the threatened Jews resided. From this perspective, siding with Poland against the USSR appeared foolhardy.

Having abjured such a move, however, all that Jews could do to gain Polish acceptance of their rescue demands, besides muting their public criticism of the exile regime, was to appeal either to the government's humanitarian sensibilities or to its sense of obligation for the welfare of Jewish citizens of Poland. They had to hope that the realization that, as Raczyński himself had declared in his seminal declaration of 10 December 1942, "the German plans for the extermination of the Jews of Europe were being fulfilled by wholesale massacres of Jews in the Polish ghetto area"[25] would bring such sentiments, which had on the whole not guided Polish policy toward the Jews during the first part of the war, to the fore. However, that realization does not seem to have done so. After December 1942, just as before, the Polish government-in-exile appears to have approached matters of concern to Jews from the perspective of what it deemed to be its own best interests, the best interests of the Polish state, and those of the Polish community (for whom that state had principally been created), and not of the expressed needs of its Jewish citizens.[26] In most instances Polish officials who considered how the immediate sentence of death that had been imposed upon their country's Jews ought to influence official actions did so in response to a direct Jewish demand; on the few occasions when they initiated such consideration without being prompted by Jewish spokesmen, as with regard to the deportation of Polish Jews from Vichy France in 1942 or from Hungary in 1944, they appear to have acted either because they perceived a threat to Poles in the same situation that was imperiling Jews or as an outgrowth of actions in which they had been engaged before Jewish lives had been in jeopardy.[27] Moreover, in responding to Jewish demands for rescue action Polish officials seem always to have weighed the costs and benefits of the requested action to their government, state, and community before taking into account the unique nature of the danger facing those needing to be rescued.

Sometimes that cost-benefit analysis dictated acceptance of a Jewish proposal. Hence, for example, the government's general willingness to serve as an advocate for rescue demands aimed primarily at the major Western Allies; such actions called for a minimal expenditure of its own resources and did not require it to appear before the Polish population of the occupied homeland as especially solicitous of Jewish welfare—an impression that it had been advised on numerous occasions to avoid creating. In other situations, however, the same analysis yielded opposite results, as with the government's consistent reluctance to earmark funds from its own budget specifically for assisting Jews in the homeland or to deliver funds once they had been earmarked. With regard to the two demands that Jewish spokesmen appear to have regarded as most important—an instruction to the people of the homeland actively to aid their threatened Jewish neighbors and the establishment of an official government agency to promote and coordinate rescue work—the outcome of the

analysis changed over time, leading initially to refusal, later to qualified agreement.

The primary factor influencing both of these changes appears to
have been the changing context of Polish-Soviet relations. Indeed, it
hardly seems a coincidence that both took place close on the heels of
a major crisis in the government-in-exile's diplomatic situation. Sikorski's request of 4 May 1943 to Poles under occupation "to offer all
succour and protection to the threatened [Jewish] victims . . . of a bar-
barism the like of which has never been known in history"—an action
that Sikorski's government had pointedly refused to take throughout
the previous six months—came but nine days following the Soviets'
break with the London regime over Katyn, when the government-
in-exile found itself under heavy criticism and its commitment to
the ostensible values of the anti-German alliance was being vigorously called into question. Similarly, the establishment of the Rescue
Council in April 1944, following months of resistance to the idea,
was undertaken in the context of Britain's public announcement of
consent to the substantial modifications of the Polish-Soviet border
discussed at the Tehran conference, when the government's ability to
withstand the pressure being placed upon it for territorial compromise had been markedly weakened by the scandal over the trial of
Jewish deserters from the Polish army. In fact, even the last major
crisis in the government-in-exile's life, leading up to and following
Mikołajczyk's resignation in November 1944, was also accompanied by
steps toward fulfilling earlier Jewish postulates regarding the status
of Jews in liberated Poland—rescue demands having become by that
time of little practical consequence.

It is significant, though, that even in these times of crisis the government's action on Jewish matters always fell short of what Jewish
spokesmen had actually demanded. Sikorski's request, buried incon-
spicuously in a speech about another matter altogether, surely was
not the instruction or even the vigorous appeal that Jewish leaders
had in mind when they broached the idea. Nor was the Rescue Council that was eventually created the sort of body envisioned in Arieh
Tartakower's original plan. Indeed, these steps do not appear to have
been aimed primarily at currying Jewish favor; government officials—
with some exceptions, notably Górka—seem to have been convinced
throughout the latter years of the war that most Jewish organizations in the free world were incurably anti-Polish and pro-Soviet and
that the Polish government could do nothing to change their orien-

tation. Rather, government actions appear to have been essentially defensive measures, aimed at avoiding giving the Jews an easy excuse for attacking the government and, even more, at providing the Poles with ammunition to parry attacks when launched by the Jews or the Soviets. For these purposes the measures in question were sufficient even though they did not satisfy Jewish desires fully. In fact, it may even be that in these cases the concept of a cost-benefit analysis does not reflect the thinking of Polish policymakers accurately. More likely their decision to reverse their previous inclination and to take the steps that they took was rooted in a sense that, in the diplomatic context of May 1943 and April 1944, the cost of action would probably be less than the cost of inaction.

To be sure, throughout the final years of the war Jewish spokesmen, albeit without necessarily intending to do so, provided the government-in-exile with many good reasons for believing that they would never give the Poles what they wanted. In particular, the failure of the murder of Erlich and Alter to dissuade Jews from the warm expressions of support for the Soviet war effort that they offered during the tour of Mikhoels and Feffer made the government believe that there was virtually nothing that it could do to enlist their aid in the Polish cause. Moreover, even though for much of the period in question the regime did not suffer terribly from public attacks by Jewish organizations, privately Jewish leaders, in the course of their efforts to arouse the government's humanitarian concern or sense of obligation for their threatened coreligionists, repeatedly made clear to government representatives their ever-growing displeasure with the government's response to their demands. When these facts were combined with the *Żydokomuna* stereotype, the historic perception of Jews as in general ineluctably hostile to Poland, and the apparent reinforcement of that perception during the first three years of the war, most Polish policymakers found it difficult to believe that free-world Jewry might ever be anything but an enemy.[28] Toward an enemy in time of war, few are likely to act primarily from a sense of human or even legal obligation.

The only way that Jewish spokesmen might have received a more satisfactory response to their rescue demands from their point of view, then, was to convince the Polish government that the major Jewish organizations of the free world would be prepared, in return for favorable Polish action on those demands, to assume an unambiguous, vocal pro-Polish stance in the Polish-Soviet dispute. To be sure, there is no guarantee that the government would have been prepared to deal with the Jews on such a basis; although some in the regime, especially Kot, favored a quid pro quo arrangement along these lines, others appear to have felt that even in such a situation the costs of promoting the most important of the Jewish rescue postulates still outweighed the potential benefits of doing so. Without being able to see such a prospect, however, the Polish government could find few benefits even to consider. Jewish leaders, on the other hand, calculated that their own long-term collective interests, and those of the Jewish people as a whole, demanded that they maintain good relations with the Soviet Union, and as a result, no matter how horrible the fate of their brethren under Nazi occupation, they did not make any serious sustained effort to pursue this one chance of getting the government-in-exile to do what they demanded of it.

In the end, then, it appears that the approach of free-world Jewish organizations to the plight of the Jews of occupied Poland also was not rooted entirely in humanitarian concerns or a sense of obligation. Precisely because an assessment of interests also played a role in their approach, they had ironically to appeal to the Polish government entirely on the basis of duties and values. The Polish government, though, was hardly more likely to act on this basis toward its Jewish citizens than were those who claimed to be the principal advocates for those citizens' needs. As a result, the response of the government-in-exile to Jewish rescue demands was bound not to satisfy those who made them.

Appendix: Who Was Who

ADLER-RUDEL, SOLOMON (1894–1975), Zionist communal and social worker. Originally from Austrian Bukovina, he held positions in various Jewish social and political organizations in Vienna and Berlin before fleeing to Britain in 1936. While in London he engaged in organizing assistance for Jewish war refugees. In 1949 he migrated to Israel, where he served as head of the Leo Baeck Institute in Jerusalem.

ALTER, WIKTOR (1890–1941), Jewish socialist leader. An engineer by training, he first became involved with the Bund before the First World War. He spent the war years in England, having escaped from exile in Siberia; he returned to Poland in 1917 and became a member of the Warsaw city council, a post he held until 1936. He was also a member of the Bund Central Committee during the entire interwar period. Arrested by the Soviets in 1939, he was released following the restoration of Polish-Soviet relations in 1941, only to be executed later that year.

ANDERS, WŁADYSŁAW (1892–1970), Polish general. Anders served in the Russian army during the First World War and fought with the Poles against the Red Army during the Polish-Soviet War of 1919–20. During the September 1939 campaign he was captured by the Soviets. Following the restoration of Polish-Soviet relations in July 1941 he was chosen to command the Polish exile army to be established on Soviet territory in accordance with the Polish-Soviet agreement. He remained commander of this force throughout the war, migrating with it from the Soviet Union to the Middle East and eventually to Italy. Following the war he settled in Great Britain, where he became one of the principal leaders of the Polish exile community.

ARCISZEWSKI, TOMASZ (1877–1955), prime minister of the Polish government-in-exile, 20 November 1944–5 July 1945. A veteran PPS activist, he was a member of the Sejm from 1919 to 1935 and served as minister of labor and social welfare and as minister of posts in two early Polish governments (1918–19). From 1939 to 1944 he was one of the leaders of the socialist underground organization WRN. He arrived in London in the fall of 1944 and was named prime minister upon Mikołajczyk's resignation shortly thereafter.

BEN ELIEZER, ARYEH (1913–1970), Revisionist Zionist activist. Born in Lithuania, he settled in Palestine in 1920. He joined the Irgun Tseva'i Le'umi in the late 1930s and quickly became an important figure in its ranks. During the war he was part of an Irgun delegation to the United States that sought to promote the rescue of European Jewry. Following the establishment of the

State of Israel he became chairman of the Executive Committee of the Herut Party and served as deputy speaker of the Knesset.

CIECHANOWSKI, JAN (1888–1973), Polish ambassador to the United States, 1941–45. After graduating from the Universities of Karlsruhe and Birmingham he began his career as a professional diplomat, serving variously as head of the British section of the Polish Foreign Ministry (1918), chief secretary of the Polish delegation to the Versailles Conference (1919), counselor to the Polish Legation in London (1920–25), Polish minister to the United States (1925–29), and secretary-general of the Polish Foreign Ministry (1939–41).

DRIBERG, TOM (1905–1976), British journalist and member of Parliament. From 1928 to 1943 he was on the editorial staff of the London *Daily Express* and wrote a regular personal affairs column. In 1942 he was elected to Parliament as an independent for Maldon; from 1945 to 1955 he represented the same constituency as a member of Labour. From 1959 to 1974 he was Labour MP for Barking. He was a major figure in Labour's left wing during the 1940s and 1950s, but he frequently followed an independent course that placed him in conflict with the party's top leadership. Shortly before his death he accepted a peerage as Baron Bradwell and entered the House of Lords.

ERLICH, HENRYK (1882–1941), Jewish socialist activist and journalist. A native of Lublin, he studied at the Universities of Warsaw and St. Petersburg. He became a member of the Bund Central Committee prior to the Russian Revolution. In the months following the revolution he played a central role in the Petrograd soviet, where he advocated, among other causes, independence for Poland. In October 1918 he settled in Warsaw, where he became editor of the Bund's daily newspaper, *Folkstsaytung*. He also served as a member of the Warsaw city council. Like Wiktor Alter, Erlich was arrested by the Soviets in September 1939, released in August 1941, and executed in December 1941.

FEFFER, ITSIK (1900–1952), Soviet Yiddish poet. A member of the Communist Party since 1920, he wrote poetry extolling the virtues of Stalin's regime. During the Second World War he became a lieutenant colonel in the Red Army and was later co-opted as one of the leaders of the Jewish Antifascist Committee. Nevertheless, he was ultimately a victim of the postwar Stalinist anti-Jewish campaign and was arrested in 1948 and executed in 1952.

GOLDMANN, NAHUM (1895–1982), Zionist leader. An important Zionist publicist in Germany during the First World War and the 1920s, Goldmann became a member of the Zionist Actions Committee in 1926. In 1935 he was appointed the Jewish Agency for Palestine's representative to the League of Nations, and in 1936 he was one of the organizers of the World Jewish Congress. During the Second World War he lived in New York, where, as head of the Zionist Emergency Council, he played a central role in negotiations aimed at rescuing Jews from Nazi occupation. Following the war he occupied a number of important positions in organized Jewish life, including president of the World Zionist Organization (1956–68).

GÓRKA, OLGIERD (1887–1955), Polish historian and government official. In the former capacity he exercised considerable influence through his revision of a number of central myths concerning the history of Poland in the seventeenth century. He also took an interest in the relation between the Polish state and the various ethnic groups that comprised its population and was regarded as favorably disposed toward the concerns of the national minorities, especially the Jews. After taking part in the September campaign in 1939, he made his way to France, where he became head of the Division of National Minorities in the government-in-exile's Information Ministry. He held this post throughout the war. In 1945 he returned to Poland, serving as director of the Foreign Ministry's Bureau of Jewish Affairs from 1946 to 1947 and as Polish consul in Jerusalem from 1947 to 1952.

GROT-ROWECKI, STEFAN (1895–1944), Polish general and underground leader. During his early military career he was primarily an education officer, serving as director of the Polish army's Educational Division from 1923 to 1926. From 1926 to 1930 he was an officer on the inspector general's staff, and from 1930 to 1939 he was a field commander at the regimental and division level. Refusing to surrender to the German forces in the September campaign of 1939, he became chief of staff to Gen. Michał Tokarzewski, who headed the first Polish underground military force. In June 1940 he was named commander of the Polish theater by Gen. Kazimierz Sosnkowski, and in February 1942 he became commander of the newly formed Home Army (Armia Krajowa). He was arrested by the Germans in Warsaw on 30 June 1943 and was transferred to the concentration camp at Sachsenhausen, where he was put to death in August 1944.

GRUENBAUM, YITSHAK (1879–1970), Polish Zionist leader. A lawyer by profession, he became active in Zionist circles in the Russian Empire in the early years of the twentieth century and from 1905 was regularly chosen a delegate to the World Zionist Congress. He was a deputy to the Sejm from 1919 to 1932, where he advocated cooperation between the Jewish parties and the representatives of the other national minorities in opposition to the government. In 1933 he settled in Palestine and became a member of the Jewish Agency Executive, heading the Labor Department from 1935 to 1948. During the Second World War he was in charge of the Jewish Agency's Rescue Committee. In 1948 he became the first interior minister of the State of Israel, but in 1949 he failed to win election to the Knesset and retired from politics.

HELPERN, JEREMIAH (1901–1962), Revisionist Zionist leader. Immigrating to Palestine from Russia at the age of twelve, he became active in the

Revisionist Betar youth movement and helped organize the group that eventually developed into the Irgun Tseva'i Le'umi. He also served as commander of Berit HaHayal, a Revisionist-led organization of Jewish veterans. During the Second World War he headed the office of the Committee for a Jewish Army in London.

KARSKI, JAN (1914–), Polish courier. After training for a career in diplomatic service, Karski (born Jan Kozielewski) served as a lieutenant during the September campaign. He was captured by the Red Army and was subsequently exchanged to the German side, where he enlisted in the Polish underground. Entrusted with a secret mission to the government-in-exile in early 1940, he delivered the first detailed report about the situation of Polish Jews under German and Soviet occupation. In 1942, incidental to another mission to the West, he carried eyewitness testimony about the Warsaw ghetto and German mass killings of Jews. Toward the end of the war he settled in the United States, becoming professor of government at Georgetown University in Washington, D.C. In 1982 his activities on behalf of Polish Jewry were recognized by Yad Vashem, the official Holocaust Memorial Authority of the State of Israel.

KNOLL, ROMAN (1888–1946), Polish diplomat. From 1918 to 1920 he headed the Eastern Division of the Polish Foreign Ministry; from 1920 to 1921 he was general secretary of the Polish delegation to the Polish-Soviet negotiations at Riga. Following the conclusion of these negotiations he represented Poland in Moscow, first as chargé d'affaires, later (until 1923) as legate. He later served as Poland's legate in Ankara (1924–25), Rome (1926–28), and Berlin (1928–31). During the war he was active in the underground, serving as director of the Central European Division of the Government Delegacy's Foreign Affairs Department.

KORBOŃSKI, STEFAN (1903–1989), Polish underground leader. A soldier in the Polish army from 1918 to 1921, he became active in the Polish Peasant Party during the 1920s, becoming chairman of the party's Białystok region in 1936. He fought in the September campaign in 1939 and was captured by the Soviets, only to escape and to join the Polish underground organization in Warsaw. In 1941 he was appointed to head the Directorate of Civil Resistance (Kierownictwo Walki Cywilnej), and in March 1945 he became the government-in-exile's last delegate in underground. In June 1945 he was arrested by the Soviets but was released shortly thereafter and was elected chairman of the Warsaw district of the Peasant Party. In January 1947 he was elected to the Sejm, but later that year, fearing rearrest, he fled Poland. From November 1947 until his death he resided in the United States. In 1980 he was recognized by Yad Vashem for activities on behalf of Jews during World War II.

KOT, STANISŁAW (1885–1976), Polish historian and political leader. From 1920 to 1933 he served as professor of history at the University of Kraków, publishing works on Polish cultural and intellectual history during the sixteenth and seventeenth centuries and on the history of education. In 1933 he was stripped of his professorship, largely for political reasons; in the same year he joined the Peasant Party. In 1939 he became interior minister in the government-in-exile, holding that post until 1941, when he became Poland's ambassador to the Soviet Union. From 1942 to 1943 he was Polish minister of state in the Middle East; in July 1943 he assumed the portfolio of minister of information. In 1945 he returned to Poland, serving the new government as ambassador to Italy until 1947. In that year he left government service and returned to London, where he remained a leading figure in Polish emigré circles.

KUKIEL, MARIAN (1885–1971), Polish general and historian. During the 1920s he headed the Historical Bureau of the Polish army and taught history at the University of Kraków; from 1930 to 1939 he was director of Kraków's Czartoryski Museum. Escaping to the West following the German invasion in 1939, he served as commander of the First Polish Army Corps in Great Britain from 1940 to 1942 and as minister of defense from 1943 to 1944. Following the war he became director of the General Sikorski Historical Institute (today the Polish Institute and Sikorski Museum) in London.

MAISKY, IVAN (1884–1975), Soviet diplomat. Educated at the Universities of St. Petersburg and Munich, he served as Soviet minister to Finland from 1929 to 1932, Soviet ambassador to Great Britain from 1932 to 1943, and assistant commissar for foreign affairs from 1943 to 1946. He was instrumental in negotiating treaties establishing diplomatic relations between the Soviet Union and several other countries, including South Africa, Canada, the Netherlands, Ethiopia, and Egypt. He was also the principal Soviet negotiator in the talks that led to the Polish-Soviet agreement of July 1941.

MIKHOELS, SHLOMO (1890–1948), Soviet Yiddish actor. Born Shlomo Vovsi, Mikhoels initially studied law but joined the Moscow State Jewish Theatre in 1918. He became director of the theater in 1928. In August 1941, following the German invasion of the Soviet Union, he was named chairman of the Jewish Antifascist Committee. In January 1948 he was assassinated by the Soviet secret police in what was to become recognized as the first step in Stalin's postwar anti-Jewish campaign.

MIKOŁAJCZYK, STANISŁAW (1901–1966), Polish political leader. During the interwar period Mikołajczyk distinguished himself as one of the leaders of the Polish Peasant Party, representing the party in the Sejm. In September 1939 he fled Poland and was named minister of the interior and deputy prime minister in the government-in-exile. Following Prime Minister Sikorski's death in July 1943 Mikołajczyk succeeded to the premiership, but he resigned in November 1944 in a controversy over Polish concessions to Soviet political and territorial demands. In June 1945 he returned to Poland as second deputy prime minister and minister of agriculture in the new Polish provisional government. He tried to organize the non-Communist forces in Poland under his leadership, only to abandon the struggle and leave Poland following Communist manipulation of the election of 1947. He eventually settled in Britain and later in the United States.

PRITT, DENIS NOEL (1888–1972), British attorney and member of Parliament. Originally elected to the House of Commons as a Labour member in 1935, he was expelled from the party in 1940 after he defended the Soviet invasion of Finland; from 1940 to 1950 he retained his seat as an independent. Pritt was strongly identified with left-wing causes, and although he was never a member of the Communist party, he was a vocal admirer of the USSR and was awarded the Stalin Prize in 1954. As an attorney he showed special interest in cases possessing political implications; he made headlines by representing such controversial political figures as Jomo Kenyatta of Kenya, Julius Nyerere of Tanzania, and Ho Chi Minh of Vietnam.

RACZKIEWICZ, WŁADYSŁAW (1885–1947), Polish president-in-exile, 1939–47. Raczkiewicz served three terms as interior minister in 1921, 1925–26, and 1936; he was also governor of several Polish provinces. From 1930 to 1935 he was speaker of the Polish Senat. On 29 September 1939 Polish President Ignacy Mościcki, having fled Poland for Romania, invoked the provision of the 1935 Polish constitution permitting the president to appoint a successor and named Raczkiewicz the new president of the Polish Republic.

RACZYŃSKI, EDWARD (1891–1989), Polish diplomat. From 1932 to 1934 he served as Poland's delegate to the League of Nations; in 1934 he became ambassador to Great Britain, a post he held until the withdrawal of British recognition from the Polish government-in-exile in 1945. From 1941 to 43 he also served de facto as Poland's foreign minister. Following the war he remained in London and held high positions in the exile government, eventually becoming Polish president-in-exile.

RATHBONE, ELEANOR (1872–1946), British social critic and member of Parliament. Rathbone was active in causes of special interest to women, heading the constitutional wing of the women's suffrage movement, working to improve the position of widows under the Poor Law, and pressing for changes in the status of women in India and other parts of the British Empire. She was especially known for her advocacy of welfare allowances for families. In 1929 she was elected to Parliament as independent member for the Combined English Universities, retaining her seat until her death. During the war she became increasingly concerned with Jewish affairs and came to advocate the Zionist cause in Palestine.

REISS, ANSHEL (1886–1984), Labor Zionist leader. Born in Galicia, Reiss migrated to Palestine in 1925. He returned to Poland during the late 1930s to head the Jewish Agency office in Warsaw, managing to escape shortly after the beginning of the Nazi occupation. Following his return to Palestine in

1940 he became one of the principal figures in the Representation of Polish Jewry. In 1944 he was sent to London, where he was co-opted into the Polish government-sponsored Rescue Council. Following the war he served in various capacities in the World Zionist Organization and in the Labor movement in Israel, and in his later years he was president of the World Federation of Polish Jews.

ROMER, ADAM (1892–1965), Polish journalist and diplomat. Following several years as an intelligence officer in the Polish army, Romer became head of the Press Division in the Office of the Polish Prime Minister in 1924. Less than a year later he left government service and turned to journalism, writing extensively on foreign and economic affairs for conservative and Catholic publications and sharply criticizing the policies of Foreign Minister Józef Beck. A close associate of Sikorski since 1929, he kept the general informed about the political situation in Poland while Sikorski was abroad. In 1939 he escaped from Warsaw, and upon his arrival in France Sikorski appointed him to direct the Prime Minister's Office. In this capacity he was entrusted with several delicate missions on Sikorski's behalf, with regard both to foreign affairs and to internal government politics.

ROMER, TADEUSZ (1894–1978), Polish diplomat. While a student in Lausanne he met Polish nationalist leader Roman Dmowski; in 1917 he became Dmowski's personal secretary and eventually was appointed secretary of the Polish National Committee. From 1919 to 1921 he served as first secretary of the Polish Embassy in Paris; in 1921 he returned to Warsaw, where until 1927 he held various posts in the Polish Foreign Ministry. From 1927 to 1935 he was counselor at the Polish Legation (later Embassy) in Rome; from 1935 to 1937, plenipotentiary in Lisbon; and from 1937 to 1942, plenipotentiary in Tokyo. In 1942 he was appointed Poland's ambassador to the Soviet Union, a post he held until the rupture in Polish-Soviet relations in April 1943. In the reorganization of the Polish cabinet that followed Sikorski's death in July 1943 he was named foreign minister. Following the war he migrated to Canada, where he became professor of romance languages at McGill University in Montreal.

SCHWARZBART, IGNACY (1888–1961), Jewish activist. A native of Chrzanów, Schwarzbart practiced law in Kraków before becoming involved in Zionist politics. For several years he served on the Kraków city council, and in 1938 he was elected to the Sejm. Following the German invasion he fled Poland via Romania to France, where he was appointed to the Polish National Council. He served on the council throughout its existence. From 1940 to 1946 he also maintained an office dedicated to gathering and disseminating information about the condition of Polish Jewry. After the war Schwarzbart migrated to the United States, where he served as director of the Organization Department of the World Jewish Congress.

SHERTOK, MOSHE (1894–1965), Zionist leader. Born in the Ukraine, Shertok was brought to Palestine at the age of twelve. He studied at the University of Constantinople before the First World War and from 1920 to 1925 at the London School of Economics. In 1925 he became deputy editor of *Davar*, the influential daily newspaper of the Palestinian Jewish labor movement. In 1931 he was appointed secretary of the Political Department of the Jewish Agency, and in 1933 he became head of the department. In this position he was responsible for maintaining contacts between the Jewish Agency and the British Mandatory authorities; essentially he was the chief diplomatic officer of the Zionist movement. With the establishment of the State of Israel he became the country's first foreign minister (after Hebraizing his surname to Sharett), a post he held until 1956. From 1954 to 1955 he simultaneously held the position of prime minister.

SIKORSKI, WŁADYSŁAW (1881–1943), Polish prime minister in exile. Sikorski grew up in Galicia and served in the Austrian army, but in 1908 he founded a clandestine Polish military organization. During the First World War he was one of the leaders of the Polish Legion, and he became a high-ranking officer in the Polish army after Poland became independent. In 1921 he was appointed chief of staff. Following the assassination of President Gabriel Narutowicz in 1922, Sikorski was named prime minister, but he served in this post for less than six months. He also served as minister of military affairs from 1924 to 1925. An opponent of the Piłsudski regime, he was stripped of his military command in 1928, after which he spent much time in exile in France. When the formation of a Polish government-in-exile was contemplated following the German invasion, Sikorski was chosen by President Raczkiewicz to head it. In July 1941 he signed the treaty restoring diplomatic relations between Poland and the Soviet Union, but in April 1943, after confronting the Soviets over the Katyn affair, he witnessed the severing of those relations. Shortly thereafter he was killed in an airplane crash near Gibraltar.

SOSNKOWSKI, KAZIMIERZ (1885–1969), Polish general. Sosnkowski began his career in the military organization of PPS, where he became a close associate of Józef Piłsudski. During the final year of the First World War he served as chief of staff of the First Brigade of the Polish Legion. In 1921 he was appointed minister of military affairs, retaining this post until 1924. From 1927 until the outbreak of the Second World War he held the position of inspector of the Polish army. After the war began, he joined the government-in-exile as minister without portfolio and as the designated successor to the president. He resigned from the government in 1941 in protest over the terms of the restoration of diplomatic relations between Poland and the Soviet Union. Upon Sikorski's death in 1943 he was named commander-in-chief of the Polish armed forces. After the war he migrated to Canada.

STAŃCZYK, JAN (1886–1953), Polish labor leader and politician. From 1919 to 1939 he was a member of the governing council of PPS, and from 1925 to 1939 he served as general secretary of the Central Union of Miners. He also represented PPS in the Sejm from 1922 to 1935. In the Sikorski and Mikołajczyk cabinets of the government-in-exile he served as minister of labor and social welfare. Following Mikołajczyk's resignation he returned to Poland, where he was also named to head the labor ministry. He resigned this post in 1946.

STRASSBURGER, HENRYK (1887–1951), Polish economist and politician. He was deputy minister of industry and commerce in 1918 and later director-general of the ministry. From 1923 to 1924 he served as deputy foreign minister and from 1924 to 1932 as Polish general commissioner in Danzig. In the exile government he served variously as treasury minister and minister of state in the Middle East. Following the war he served the new Polish government as ambassador to Great Britain, but he broke with the government in 1949 and remained in Britain until his death.

STROŃSKI, STANISŁAW (1882–1954), Polish politician and scholar. He served as professor of romance languages at the University of Kraków from 1909 to 1927 and at the Catholic University of Lublin from 1927 to 1939. From 1922 to 1935 he was a deputy to the Sejm. Politically he was associated with the Front Morges movement, of which Sikorski was one of the leaders. From 1939 to 1943 he served as minister of information in the government-in-exile.

STUPP, ABRAHAM (1897–), Polish Zionist leader. He served for many years as a member of the General Council of the World Zionist Organization. During the war he was secretary of the Representation of Polish Jewry. Later he served a term in the Israeli Knesset, from 1951 to 1955.

SZERER, EMANUEL (1902–1977), Jewish socialist activist. He began his public career as editor of several Polish-language publications for the Bund in Warsaw. In 1930 Szerer became the youngest person ever elected to the Bund Central Committee. He fled to the United States following the German invasion of Poland in 1939; there he joined the Bund leadership in exile. In 1943 he was chosen to replace Szmul Zygielbojm as the Bund's representative on the Polish National Council. In 1946 he returned to the United States, where he served as editor of the Bund organ *Unzer Tsayt*.

TARTAKOWER, ARIEH (1897–1982), Jewish sociologist and activist. A prominent figure in Labor Zionist circles in Poland, he was elected to the Łódź city council in 1938. In 1939 he fled to the United States, where he headed the Polish department of the World Jewish Congress and served as deputy director of the Congress's Institute of Jewish Affairs. He held various posts with the World Jewish Congress until his death. In 1946 he was appointed lecturer in Jewish sociology at the Hebrew University of Jerusalem; his writings about the sociology and demography of the Jews remain of central importance for students of these subjects.

WEIZMANN, CHAIM (1874–1952), Zionist leader. Weizmann was born in the village of Motol, near Pińsk, and earned a doctorate in chemistry from Fribourg University in Switzerland. He was a delegate to the Second Zionist Congress in 1898 and quickly rose to prominence in the movement. He was a central figure in the negotiations with the British government that led to the issue of the Balfour Declaration in 1917. From 1920 to 1931, and again from 1935 to 1946, he served as president of the World Zionist Organization. In February 1949 he was chosen to be the first president of the State of Israel.

WISE, STEPHEN S. (1874–1949), U.S. Jewish religious and civic leader and prominent figure in the Zionist movement. His close personal ties with President Franklin Roosevelt made him a particularly important figure in American Jewish diplomatic activities. He was a guiding force behind the formation of both the American Jewish Congress (established 1920) and the World Jewish Congress (established 1936), serving as president or honorary president of the former organization from 1925 to 1949 and as president of the latter organization from 1936 to 1949.

ZYGIELBOJM, SZMUL (1895–1943), leading figure in the Jewish socialist Bund in interwar Poland. Born in a village near Lublin, he was a member of the Bund Central Committee from 1924. He also served terms as a member of the municipal councils of Warsaw and Łódź. Following the German invasion of Poland in 1939 he was co-opted onto the Warsaw Judenrat. In January 1940 he escaped from occupied Poland, eventually making his way to the United States. In February 1942 he traveled to London to assume the position of Bund representative in the second Polish National Council. On 12 May 1943 he committed suicide as an act of protest against the failure of the Allied governments to take significant action to rescue the Jews of Nazi-occupied Europe.

Notes

ABBREVIATIONS USED IN THE NOTES

AH	Histadrut Archives
AIP	Archiwum Instytutu Polskiego
AKD	*Armia Krajowa w Dokumentach*
CZA	Central Zionist Archives
DPSR	*Documents on Polish-Soviet Relations*
DRI	Diaspora Research Institute
FRUS	*Foreign Relations of the United States*
HIA	Hoover Institution Archives
-MSW	Ministerstwo Spraw Wewnętrznych
-PG	Polish Government*
(MID)	Ministerstwo Informacji i Dokumentacji
(MSZ)	Ministerstwo Spraw Zagranicznych
-RN	Poland. Rada Narodowa
-US	Poland. Ambasada US
HL	Hoover Library
JI	Jabotinsky Institute
JLBA	Jewish Labor Bund Archives
JTA	Jewish Telegraphic Agency
PC	Private Collections
PRO	Public Record Office
SPP	Studium Polski Podziemnej
WL	Wiener Library
YVA	Yad Vashem Archives

INTRODUCTION

1. It was a bit distressing, for example, to read in an otherwise compli-
mentary review of *In the Shadow of Auschwitz* that the reviewer believed that
book to have been deliberately constructed in order to present the case of

*The Polish Government Collection at Hoover Institution Archives has recently been bro-
ken into several smaller collections, according to the original provenance of the documents.
Materials cited in this book come from two of these new collections: Poland. Ministerstwo
Spraw Zagranicznych; and Poland. Ministerstwo Informacji i Dokumentacji. In order to
facilitate location of these materials, the original provenance of each cited file is given
together with the original file number and title. This information should permit the archive
staff to identify the new collection and box in which any cited document has been placed.

"the Jews, trapped in the maw of the beast and lacking a natural protector." Pease, "New Books," p. 350. If indeed that was the book's purpose, then the effort seems to have failed, for by far the angriest review was written by a Jewish historian, who called it "an interpretive apologia for the indifference of the Polish Government-in-Exile" and claimed that it "argues that in spite of a carefully documented and detailed description of pervasive pre-war anti-Semitism on the part of Poles and of the various Polish governments, responsibility for the indifference of the Government-in-Exile lay not with the anti-Semitism of that government but with the Jews, who were intolerant of Polish anti-Semitism." Lerner review, p. 36.

2. Neither of the reviewers cited in the previous note perceived the intention of the book accurately; nor was either able to present convincing evidence for his reading. Lerner, in fact, offered no evidence at all; he simply mistook one of the book's concluding factual statements—that Jewish spokesmen consistently refused to take certain steps demanded of them by the Polish government as an essential concomitant of any favorable Polish action on Jewish demands—for a condemnation of that refusal. In reality, the book ventured no opinion about whether the Jewish spokesmen's reasons for their behavior, which were also analyzed in the text, were valid or not. Moreover, although the book did suggest that Jewish behavior adversely affected Jews' ability to obtain what they wanted from the Polish government, it made no comment as to whether that same behavior might have advanced other, perhaps more fundamental, Jewish interests and thus been practically valid as well. See Engel, *In the Shadow of Auschwitz*, pp. 206–11. Such statements about the moral or practical validity of Jewish behavior would of necessity be propositions of value rather than of fact and would thus not be susceptible to argument based upon the tools of the historical discipline.

Pease, in contrast, found evidence of the book's alleged "scholarly and emotional . . . obligation" toward Jews in four places. First, he argued that "to say that Polish-Jewish relations operated on a 'virtual war footing' [a phrase taken from *In the Shadow of Auschwitz*, p. 207] is to exaggerate," implying, via the context in which this objection was raised, that that exaggeration renders an "unduly harsh or suspicious judgment of the Poles." Secondly, he stated his opinion that the book, although "properly businesslike in pursuing evidence of callousness or anti-Jewish bias in wartime Polish society or its military and political elites, . . . tiptoes somewhat more gingerly in the vicinity of details that embittered Polish opinion toward Jews, such as significant Jewish desertions from the Polish armed forces or the favorable response of much of eastern Polish Jewry to the Soviet invasion of 1939." Third, he contended that the book's use (on pp. 190–91) of the mention by "a Polish emigré journal . . . of the execution of a Polish physician discovered while treating a Jewish patient" in the context of a story about deportations of Jews from the Warsaw ghetto as evidence of "a Polish intent to dilute the impression of Jewish agony" is in fact an example of "an author trying too hard to make the data fit his thesis." Finally, he objected that the book's contention "that in 1942 the London government for some months deliberately hushed up its knowledge that the *Endlösung* had commenced for fear that the news would distract attention from the sufferings of Poles at German hands, only deciding to release the information once it became impossible to keep hidden" is no more probable than "the interpretation that the Poles— preoccupied with other matters, dealing with fragmentary intelligence, and slow to realize that murderous brutality had escalated to systematic eradica- tion—acted with relative dispatch upon drawing the correct conclusion" and therefore that if the book preferred the former argument over the latter, this preference indicated too great a readiness "to render unduly harsh or suspicious judgment of the Poles." Pease, "New Books," pp. 349–50.

To be sure, some of these objections refer to substantive issues that are debatable. For example, it is certainly not only reasonable but even advisable to ask whether the evidence presented in *In the Shadow of Auschwitz* for the argument that the Polish government did not wish the suffering of Poles to be overshadowed by that of Jews is sufficient to demonstrate the argument's truth. Indeed, during the period examined by the book, no Polish official ever stated such a concern in as many words (although at least two officials, one central to the government's decision-making apparatus, the other on the periphery of it, *did* do so during the period examined by the present vol- ume; see below, Chapters 1 and 2). The fact that the book did represent the considerable inferential and circumstantial evidence—including, inter alia, the relatively small amount of attention devoted in Polish government pub- lications and news releases to the Jewish as opposed to the Polish plight throughout the period in question, Sikorski's explicit refusal to include men- tion of Jews in the St. James's Palace declaration of 13 January 1942, ŚWIT's explicit eschewing of broadcasts describing Nazi actions against Jews, the ton- ing down of information received in the May 1942 Bund report in Sikorski's broadcast to the homeland of 9 June 1942, and the deliberate elimination by the National Council of a reference in a proposed resolution to "the complete physical extermination" of the Jews on 7 July 1942—as sufficient to war- rant such a conclusion, however, does not necessarily prove anti-Polish bias, let alone an intention to plead the Jewish cause, even when taken together with all of Pease's other putative proofs of an approach that is "not quite evenhanded." For the record, the characterization of Polish-Jewish relations during the interwar years as having been on a "virtual war footing" echoed the evaluations of contemporary Polish and Jewish observers cited earlier and was certainly not intended pejoratively toward the Poles; Jewish deser- tions from the Polish army were not discussed because they became an issue in Polish-Jewish relations only after the book's closing date (they are dis- cussed in some detail in the present volume; see below, Chapter 4); Jewish behavior toward the Soviet invaders in 1939 and Polish perceptions of that behavior were in fact treated (pp. 59–62), and if the text pointed out that Polish perceptions were generally inaccurate, it also pointed to instances in which Jewish perceptions of Polish behavior were false and rooted in intolerance or prejudice (for example, pp. 99, 127–29, 130–31, 206, 241–42 n. 108, 243 n. 127); and the discussion of a "Polish emigré journal's" handling of the news of the onset of deportations from the Warsaw ghetto (the "emigré journal" was in fact the regime's official organ, *Dziennik Polski*, printing a story transmitted by the official Polish Telegraphic Agency) was undertaken to show that all treatments of the story demonstrably stemming from an official Polish source differed in consistent fashion from treatments that cannot be unquestionably attributed to an official Polish source. This point was made, in turn, to buttress the contention (derived from considerably more evidence than this one fact) that the Polish government-in-exile was not directly responsible as a body for the publication of the first news of the deportations in the West.

More to the point, however, Pease assumed that an argument that the Polish government preferred to accentuate the suffering of Poles at the expense of Jews necessarily represents "harsh . . . judgment of the Poles." Here he read a moral evaluation into the text that was not present on the face of things. For a more extensive discussion of this point, see below.

3. This study, then, was conceived without any prior reference to the public issues discussed below. It was rather, in the first instance, the result of the need of a young academician (who himself had no personal recollection of the period being explored) to publish lest he perish, coupled with the altogether fortuitous proximity of a mass of previously unexamined documents relating to the subject in question.

4. Cf. the conclusion of one such work: "The achievements of the Poles lie . . . in the field of political culture and moral civilisation, and the mission they have fulfilled has been an ethical one. [The Polish poet Adam] Mickiewicz did not pull his messianic vision out of a hat: at some level it corresponded to the historical truth that the Poles were playing the part of moral guinea-pigs subjected to a series of political experiments. . . . The Poles themselves have emerged from the experiments . . . remarkably unscathed, and if they have lost their political freedom and sovereignty, they have abandoned none of their moral positions." Zamoyski, *The Polish Way*, pp. 395–96.

5. Notable among such works is Steven's *The Poles*, commissioned during the "high summer of Solidarity's existence," whose stated aim was "to explain the Poles and their country to a world that, throughout history, periodically woke up to their existence and then shamefully forgot them once their immediate crisis was over" (p. ix).

6. It will be instructive to see how the success of the opposition movement in Poland will affect this perception. Andrzej Bryk, for one, has suggested that the "hidden complex of the Polish mind" that causes Poles to "find themselves in the dock together with the Germans" stems from the sense that "modern Polish history has been a story of nearly consistent defeat and internal failure" and that "many contemporary Poles need a glorious yesterday as a dependable justification for a grey today." Andrzej Bryk, "The Hidden Complex of the Polish Mind: Polish-Jewish Relations during the Holocaust,"

in Polonsky, *"My Brother's Keeper?,"* pp. 161, 172. If so, then the opposition's victories of 1989–90 and the collapse of the Communist regime can be expected to mitigate the feeling of threat.

7. Jan Błoński, "The Poor Poles Look at the Ghetto," in ibid., pp. 34–48.

8. Władysław Siła-Nowicki, "A Reply to Jan Błoński," in ibid., p. 59. He also termed Błoński's article "a very dangerous propagandistic enunciation."

9. Witold Rymanowski, "The Disseminator of Anti-Semitism? A Rejoinder to Jan Błoński," in ibid., p. 155.

10. Korboński, *The Jews and the Poles*, p. vii. He referred again to "the campaign of slander against the Poles" on the following page.

11. Ibid., p. 89.

12. "Today" in this case can be taken as meaning approximately the end of 1989. It is still too early at the time of this writing to determine what effects developments in Poland after that time will have upon these attitudes. See above, n. 6.

13. Cf. Siła-Nowicki, in Polonsky, *"My Brother's Keeper?,"* p. 62: "[Błoński speaks] in a language which in its contents is the language of its [the Polish people's] *deadly* enemies and slanderers" (emphasis added).

14. The final sentence of this characterization is inferred from passages in Korboński, *The Jews and the Poles*, pp. vii, viii, 84, 86, 89–90, and 93, as well as from the fact that an entire chapter of the book, ostensibly about the period of the Second World War, was devoted to documenting what Korboński termed "ten years of Jewish rule" in postwar Communist Poland. All other sentences are echoed, inter alia, in ibid., pp. vii–viii, 22–26, 29–35, 45–70, and, more concisely and directly, in the essays by Siła-Nowicki and Rymanowski in Polonsky, *"My Brother's Keeper?,"* pp. 65, 67–68, 159.

15. See, for example, Dawidowicz, "The Curious Case," pp. 68–69, and Dawidowicz letter, pp. 11–12.

16. Cienciała review. The term *universe of obligation* has been most prominently employed in analyzing the responses of bystanders to the Holocaust by Helen Fein, who defined it as "that circle of persons toward whom obligations are owed, to whom the rules apply, and whose injuries call for expiation by the community." Fein, *Accounting for Genocide*, p. 33.

17. "Negative evaluation" is taken from the review under discussion.

18. Engel, *In the Shadow of Auschwitz*, p. 203.

19. Ibid., pp. 180–85.

20. The phrase is from Avital, "The Polish Government in Exile and the Jewish Question," p. 43.

21. Pease, "New Books," p. 351.

22. See below, Chapter 2.

23. See Engel, "The Polish Government-in-Exile and the Erlich-Alter Affair," esp. n. 1.

24. On the problems associated with the use of this word in describing Polish-Jewish relations, see Engel, *Semantikah uFolitikah*, pp. 11–14.

25. One reviewer criticized *In the Shadow of Auschwitz* for mentioning

the violence inflicted by Poles upon Jews in 1918–19 and the dispatch of American, British, and French observers to investigate these incidents while "fail[ing] to add that these observers, upon reflection, refused to characterize as 'pogroms' these disorders." Pease, "New Books," p. 351. Obviously the use of the word was a matter of some importance to the reviewer, as indeed it was to the Polish government at the time of the disorders themselves. In fact, the Polish Foreign Ministry conducted a campaign to dissuade foreign investigators from employing the term, although in its own internal memoranda it used it freely. See Engel, *Semantikah uFolitikah*, p. 9; Tomaszewski, "Lwów," pp. 281–85. What was at stake in this campaign was essentially the moral stigma attached to the word. For historians, however, the essential problem in discussing the events in question is less what to call them than to determine and to describe as accurately as possible what precisely happened between Poles and Jews in Lwów on 22 November 1918, in Pińsk on 5 April 1919, or in other places where multiple Jewish losses of life took place at Polish hands. That goal, like the goal of describing Polish-Jewish relations during the Second World War, is ill-served by reopening the political controversies of yesterday in order to take sides in them today.

26. Pease, "New Books," p. 349.

27. See below, Chapter 2.

28. See below, Chapter 4.

29. Readers who do wish to draw value-laden inferences from the text should, moreover, not expect to find their positive and negative evaluations of both sides balancing each other in the end. Just as this volume has not sought to place the preponderance of praise or blame on one side or the other, it has also not made any effort to apportion praise and blame more or less equally between the two parties or to split their conflicting claims, as it were, down the middle. Thus partisans of a particular side are liable to come away either mostly encouraged or mostly distressed by what they have read and to conclude that the book aimed consciously at fostering such a balance. In truth, however, this text has simply not concerned itself with praise and blame at all, and if readers find that on the whole it arouses in them a predominantly positive or negative view of Poles or Jews, they should not assume that it had such a view in mind from the start.

30. When this scope is properly understood, the criticism that *In the Shadow of Auschwitz* did not mention the order by the governor general of occupied Poland, Hans Frank, of 15 October 1941, which provided that Poles who sheltered or assisted Jews would be punished by death, seems off the mark. Cienciała review, p. 487. It may be surprising that this order was not invoked in Polish government documents as a factor influencing the government's actions with regard to Jews, but such is in fact the case. Yet even so the fact that "in Poland . . . assistance to Jews was, at least from 1941, a capital offense" was noted on the book's very first page. The reviewer observed that such an order would have been "quite unnecessary if Poles were not helping Jews." That interpretation may be open to dispute, but in reality the book

did not venture any overall determination of the extent to which Poles in the occupied homeland helped Jews, making the statement in the review irrelevant. Similar considerations apply to the criticism in the same review that *In the Shadow of Auschwitz* did not mention that "a special organization to help Jews . . . was set up by the underground in the fall of 1942." In reality, the Polish government did not know of the existence of this organization until the very end of the period treated in *In the Shadow of Auschwitz*, and nothing that the government did during that period was influenced by this body. During the period treated in the present volume, in contrast, this organization did impinge upon government thinking, and it is discussed in this context. See below, Chapters 1, 2, and 5.

CHAPTER ONE

1. Actually the period of bereavement, as it were, began during the final week of November. On 24 November 1942 the major Jewish dailies in Palestine printed a statement issued the previous day by the Jerusalem Executive of the Jewish Agency, indicating that "following the visit of Gestapo chief Himmler to Warsaw in June of this year the Nazi authorities in Poland opened systematic action toward annihilation [*hashmadah*] of the Jewish population in the cities and towns of Poland." The statement also mentioned that "mass deportations of Jews from the cities of Central and Western Europe are continuing apace." During the following week these newspapers appeared with black borders surrounding either the entire front page or individual headlines relating further news on the situation of European Jewry. In the United States the first to follow this pattern was the Labor Zionist monthly, *Jewish Frontier*, in its issue of November 1942. Most of the Yiddish-language dailies published in New York appeared with black-bordered front pages on 2 December, and over the ensuing month the major national English-language weeklies and monthlies followed suit. In Britain the weekly *Jewish Chronicle* reported the days of mourning in Palestine in its issue of 4 December and printed its own black-bordered edition, bearing the headline "Two Million Jews Slaughtered," a week later. *Zionist Review* also published a black-bordered edition the same day, 11 December, after having headed its issue of a week previous with the baleful announcement, "Five Million People Sentenced to Death: Two Million Jews Have Already Perished." For more on the Jewish press's treatment of the news of the Holocaust during this period, see, among others, Porat, *Hanhagah beMilkud*, pp. 59–67, 76; Beit-Tsvi, *HaTsiyonut haPost-Ugandit*, pp. 68–73; Wyman, *Abandonment of the Jews*, pp. 48–52; Lookstein, *Were We Our Brothers' Keepers?*, pp. 108–28.

2. For a description of the events of these three days, see Porat, *Hanhagah beMilkud*, pp. 76–78; Penkower, *The Jews Were Expendable*, p. 83.

3. Wyman, *Abandonment of the Jews*, p. 71; Penkower, *The Jews Were Expendable*, p. 83.

4. *Jewish Chronicle*, 11 December 1942; see also Penkower, *The Jews Were Expendable*, p. 83.

5. *Reconstructionist*, 11 December 1942; facsimile plate in Lookstein, *Were We Our Brothers' Keepers?*

6. *Congress Weekly*, 4 December 1942; facsimile plate in Lookstein, *Were We Our Brothers' Keepers?*

7. See Gilbert, *Auschwitz and the Allies*, pp. 42–54; Lipstadt, *Beyond Belief*, pp. 162–76; Wyman, *Abandonment of the Jews*, p. 22; Beit-Tsvi, *HaTsiyonut haPost-Ugandit*, esp. pp. 37–67.

8. Several mass protest rallies were sponsored by American and British Jewish organizations during the second half of 1942, most notably at Madison Square Garden in New York on 21 July and at Royal Albert Hall in London on 29 October. But even among the Jewish leadership the fact that all of European Jewry had been marked for total physical extirpation does not appear to have been fully assimilated at this time. In its description of the situation of Polish Jewry during 1942, for example, the *American Jewish Year Book*, a publication of the American Jewish Committee, described Nazi policy in Poland as consisting of "expropriation of Jews and their elimination from the economic and social life of the country, their segregation from the general population through yellow badges and ghettos, their subjection to forced labor, and similar measures." The aim of these measures, the almanac reported, was "the ultimate destruction of the Jewish population." However, the publication evidently understood something different by this phrase than what the Germans in fact intended, for it subsequently declared that "whereas the Nazis may ultimately succeed in physically destroying the Jewish population in Poland, they will never succeed in breaking their spirit of resistance against their despised oppressors." *American Jewish Year Book*, 44 (1942–43): 243–44. This statement was prepared following the release of information from the letter transmitted from Poland by the Jewish socialist Bund in June 1942; see Engel, *In the Shadow of Auschwitz*, pp. 175–76, 180, 183–84. Similarly, only two weeks following a press conference sponsored by the British Ministry of Information on 9 July 1942, at which Polish and Polish Jewish representatives reported the death of 700,000 Jews as part of a Nazi campaign to eliminate all of Polish Jewry, Selig Brodetsky, president of the Board of Deputies of British Jews, gave a public speech on "The Jewish People at the Coming Peace Conference," stressing the importance of Palestine as a target for postwar Jewish emigration, which would be "very much greater than after the last war." *Jewish Chronicle*, 24 July 1942 ("Post-War Problem: Reconstruction of the Jewish People"). Jewish leaders often expressed considerable skepticism over the veracity of reports emanating from Europe and were on the whole reluctant to regard such reports as a guide for action. On various aspects of the response of free-world Jewry to news of the Holocaust prior to the end of 1942, see Porat, *Hanhagah beMilkud*, pp. 44–59; Beit-Tsvi, *HaTsiyonut haPost-Ugandit*, pp. 68–105; Laqueur, *The Terrible Secret*, pp. 162–90; Penkower, *The Jews Were Expendable*, pp. 59–80; Bauer, *The Holo-*

caust in Historical Perspective, pp. 19–25; Wyman, *Abandonment of the Jews*, pp. 24–27; Sompolinsky, "HaHanhagah haAnglo-Yehudit," pp. 65–82.

Nor was this phenomenon confined to the leaders of Western Jewry. On 19 November 1942, the very eve of the breakthrough in understanding the news of the Holocaust, Ignacy Schwarzbart, a veteran Zionist leader from Kraków, former deputy of the Polish Sejm, and member of the Polish National Council in London, prepared a five-page, typewritten, single-spaced memorandum for Prime Minister Sikorski on problems of organizing aid for the postwar reconstruction of the Polish Jewish community. Although Schwarzbart acknowledged in this document that German "methods of extermination" had markedly reduced the Jewish population and that news from Poland indicated that "the process of biological, systematic, mass, and intentional destruction of Jewry by the occupier is proceeding rapidly apace," he stated at the same time that "at the moment when the German army leaves Poland there will be perhaps millions of Polish Jews and Jews deported to Poland from the other countries of Europe on its territory." Hundreds and thousands of Polish Jews, he observed, had been deprived of their livelihoods by the occupiers, and Jewish property had been expropriated. Now was the time, according to Schwarzbart, for the government to begin planning to arrange for restitution to be made to Polish Jewry after the war. Schwarzbart to Sikorski, 19 November 1942, YVA—M2/78.

9. Eyewitness confirmation had come to Palestinian Jewry with the arrival of sixty-nine exchangees from Europe on 16 November; see, among others, Laqueur, *The Terrible Secret*, p. 190; Porat, *Hanhagah beMilkud*, pp. 62–63. In Britain a similar role had been played by Jan Karski, the emissary from the Polish underground who arrived in London on 15 November; see, among others, Laqueur, *The Terrible Secret*, pp. 119–20. On confirmation of the news by the American government and on the British government's somewhat more hesitant affirmation, see, among others, Penkower, *The Jews Were Expendable*, pp. 78–92; Wyman, *Abandonment of the Jews*, pp. 42–55; Wasserstein, *Britain and the Jews of Europe*, pp. 169–72.

10. *Zionist Review*, 27 November 1942 ("Am I my brother's keeper?").

11. *Jewish Chronicle*, 11 December 1942 ("The Slaughter of European Jewry").

12. On various aspects of these matters, see Feingold, *Politics of Rescue*, pp. 174–77; Wyman, *Abandonment of the Jews*, esp. pp. 67–73, 86–103; Porat, *Hanhagah beMilkud*, esp. pp. 264–308; Sompolinsky, "HaHanhagah haAnglo-Yehudit," pp. 83–121.

13. The feeling appears to have been current even at the time that the killing centers had been established in Poland because the Germans believed that they could count upon the identification of the Polish people with the aims of the murder program. See Engel, "The Polish Government-in-Exile and the Holocaust," document 8, p. 304. However, no evidence has been adduced from German sources indicating that such a consideration was ever raised by the architects of the final solution. The more likely explanation

seems to be a simple logistical one: locating the killing centers in the country with the largest Jewish population meant that fewer Jews would have to be transported over long distances in order to bring them to the murder sites.

14. At times the government had transmitted information received in a timely fashion; at other times it had not, according to conjunctural considerations. See Engel, *In the Shadow of Auschwitz*, pp. 170–202.

15. The confirmation took the form of a diplomatic note addressed to the Allied governments. Republic of Poland, Ministry of Foreign Affairs, *The Mass Extermination of Jews in German Occupied Poland.*

16. Wasserstein, *Britain and the Jews of Europe*, p. 173; Gilbert, *Auschwitz and the Allies*, p. 103.

17. Cf. Schwarzbart's comment in his diary entry for 12 December 1942: "Since allied governments are reluctant to do anything, help can practically come only from the Gentile population in Poland by taking out the Jews from the ghettos and hiding them. Small trickles may escape through the South[ern] borders." Schwarzbart Diary, 12 December 1942, YVA—M2/770. The most likely destinations for escape were the German client states of Slovakia and Hungary. Deportations from Slovakia, which had begun in March 1942, had been suspended the following October, and in Hungary deportations were not begun until 1944. There were some organized efforts, most notably by a Zionist youth movement in the Zagłębie region, to help Jews escape from Poland to these countries. See Gorodenchik, "Berihat Tenu'ot haNo'ar miZaglembie."

18. A thorough investigation of the agenda of Jewish organizations in the free world with regard to European Jewry during World War II is still to be undertaken. In the meantime, see the remarks in Engel, *In the Shadow of Auschwitz*, pp. 169–70, and above, n. 8.

19. For a capsule description of these parties, see Engel, *In the Shadow of Auschwitz*, p. 220 n. 48, with accompanying references.

20. The reference is probably to the sixty-nine exchangees from occupied Europe who arrived in Palestine on 16 November; see n. 9 above. Although the Reprezentacja as a body did not have immediate contact with the exchangees until 25 November, the broad outlines of the exchangees' stories had most likely been made known to them earlier. The group had been interrogated on 18–19 November by Eliyahu Dobkin and Moshe Szapiro, members of the Committee on Poland of the Jewish Agency Executive and members of the Reprezentacja ex officio. On the Reprezentacja's meeting with the exchangees, see Reprezentacja, *Sprawozdanie*, pp. 46–51.

21. The Polish government-in-exile had no Ministry of Propaganda. The reference is probably to the Ministry of Information and Documentation.

22. Reprezentacja, *Sprawozdanie*, pp. 45–46. Rosmarin dispatched the telegram three days later; cable, Rosmarin to Polish Foreign Ministry, 22 November 1942 (no. 78), HIA-PG, Box 700 (MSZ), File 851/e, Subfile: "Ratowanie Żydów." There are some minor discrepancies between the text that was given to Rosmarin and the text of the cable that was actually received in London.

23. Technically, Raczyński's title was not Foreign Minister but Director of the Ministry of Foreign Affairs (Kierownik Ministerstwa Spraw Zagranicznych). According to his own testimony he eschewed the ministerial title upon assuming control of Poland's foreign affairs in August 1941 because at the same time he continued to serve as Poland's ambassador to the Court of St. James. He did not feel it proper, he claimed, for an ambassador to be a government minister. See Raczyński interview and Raczyński, *In Allied London*, p. 98. Republic of Poland, *List of Members of the Government*, refers to Raczyński as Minister of State and Acting Minister of Foreign Affairs. In practice, however, he was known as the Polish foreign minister.

24. See Raczyński to Mikołajczyk, 27 November 1942 (Nr. 245/IV.Z/42), HIA-PG, Box 700 (MSZ), File 851/e, Subfile: "Ratowanie Żydów."

25. Schwarzbart Diary, 12 December 1942, YVA—M2/770.

26. "Rozmowa z Prezydentem Raczkiewiczem," 15 December 1942, YVA—M2/77.

27. Kraczkiewicz to Schwarzbart, 5 February 1943, HIA-PG, Box 700 (MSZ), File 851/e, Subfile: "Ratowanie Żydów"; Schwarzbart Diary, 6 February 1943, YVA—M2/771; Schwarzbart to Mikołajczyk, 17 February 1943, YVA—O55/3.

28. Cable, Korsak to Polish Foreign Ministry, 3 January 1943 (no. 5), HIA-PG, Box 700 (MSZ), File 851/e, Subfile: "Ratowanie Żydów."

29. Engel, "The Polish Government-in-Exile and the Holocaust," document 5, p. 289.

30. Ibid., pp. 296–97. The quoted words are Ben Gurion's.

31. Cable, Reprezentacja to Sikorski, 7 December 1942, CZA—J25/2. The Reprezentacja also sent similar wires to Polish President Raczkiewicz and to the Polish government as a whole; see Reprezentacja, *Sprawozdanie*, pp. 58–59.

32. See, for example, Yitshak ben Tsvi, chairman, General Council of the Jewish Community of Palestine, to Korsak, 27 December 1942, with attached "Appeal to the United Nations," 23 December 1942; cable, Raczyński to Ciechanowski, 20 January 1943 (no. 31); and A. L. Easterman, World Jewish Congress, European Division, to Charles [*sic*] Kraczkiewicz, Polish Foreign Ministry, 21 January 1943, with attached "Draft Memorandum on Measures for the Rescue of European Jewry," HIA-PG, Box 700 (MSZ), File 851/e, Subfile: "Ratowanie Żydów." See also Engel, "The Polish Government-in-Exile and the Holocaust," document 1, p. 274; document 6, p. 293; document 7, p. 298.

33. Engel, "The Polish Government-in-Exile and the Holocaust," document 6, p. 293; document 8, p. 305; Stupp to Kot, 26 January 1943, CZA—J25/2; cable, Kot to Polish Foreign Ministry, 9 February 1943 (no. 76), YVA—O55/3.

34. Olgierd Górka, "Pro memoria dla Pana Ministra Strońskiego," 30 December 1942, HIA-PG, Box 700 (MSZ), File 851/e, Subfile: "Ratowanie Żydów."

35. Engel, "The Polish Government-in-Exile and the Holocaust," document 1, p. 274; document 5, pp. 289–90; document 6, p. 293; document 7, pp. 296–97; Stupp to Kot, 26 January 1943, CZA—J25/2.

36. Engel, "The Polish Government-in-Exile and the Holocaust," document 1, p. 274; document 5, p. 289.

37. Szmul Zygielbojm, "Notatka dla Pana Ministra Spraw Zagranicznych E. Raczyńskiego," 15 January 1943, HIA-PG, Box 700 (MSZ), File 851/e, Subfile: "Ratowanie Żydów." Zygielbojm first raised this demand at a meeting of the Polish National Council on 27 November 1942. See the text of his remarks in Gutman and Krakowski, *Unequal Victims*, pp. 93–94. See also Fiszman-Kamińska, "Zachód, Emigracyjny Rząd Polski oraz Delegatura," p. 48.

38. Engel, "The Polish Government-in-Exile and the Holocaust," document 1, p. 274.

39. Stupp to Kot, 26 January 1943, CZA—J25/2.

40. Engel, "The Polish Government-in-Exile and the Holocaust," document 2, p. 276.

41. Ibid., p. 296.

42. Ibid., p. 307.

43. Karski, *Story of a Secret State*, p. 328. Karski's transmission of the messages of the Jewish leaders was actually incidental to his official mission, which was conducted on behalf of the underground Government Delegacy (Delegatura Rządu w Kraju) and the Home Army (Armia Krajowa) and had been set in September, before contact with the Jewish leaders had been established. See "Notatka dla Rządu Polskiego dotycząca misji Jana Karskiego w Londynie," 30 November 1942, HIA-Karski, Box 2, File 8-4. The Jewish leaders learned of Karski's mission and asked the government delegate for permission to take advantage of his departure in order to pass on a message of their own. Karski, *Story of a Secret State*, pp. 309, 320; also Karski interview. When Karski arrived in London, he presented a lengthy written report to Sikorski that made no mention of the Jewish situation at all; the report is located in HIA-Karski, Box 1. Evidently Karski presented his material on Jews orally, as he did materials on other subjects as well. He recorded the content of his messages on Jewish matters from memory in 1979; see Laqueur, *The Terrible Secret*, p. 232. In 1987 he claimed that he had carried a written report, prepared by three underground officials, about the Jewish situation and that he presented this report in microfilm to "the commander of the Polish underground in France, Aleksander Kawalkowski." Maciej Kozlowski, "The Mission That Failed," in Polonsky, *"My Brother's Keeper?,"* p. 91. Karski never mentioned such a microfilm report previously, and it has not yet been found.

44. Quoted in Laqueur, *The Terrible Secret*, pp. 232–33. Emphasis in original.

45. Karski, *Story of a Secret State*, pp. 326–28.

46. Laqueur, *The Terrible Secret*, pp. 233–34.

47. Ibid., p. 234. Karski's statement that "many Polish criminals" black-

mailed Jews in hiding is extremely difficult to evaluate. Lukas, in *The Forgotten Holocaust*, pp. 117, 250–51, contends that blackmailers "probably did not number more than 1,000 people in Warsaw." He bases this figure on an unspecified number of interviews and correspondence conducted during the 1980s, especially upon a letter to him from a Home Army officer "who had visited the Warsaw Ghetto regularly," written in 1984. The source of his informant's figure, however, is not indicated. There does not appear to be any numerical estimate available from the period itself. Contemporary qualitative statements from Polish sources, however, suggest that the dimensions of the phenomenon may have been larger than Lukas suggests. See, for example, a letter from the Council for Aid to the Jews to the government delegate from April 1943, quoted in Ringelblum, *Polish-Jewish Relations*, p. 123n: "This phenomenon [of blackmail] is on the increase at an appalling rate. . . . This increasingly widespread type of crime haunting our streets day by day cancels out the Council's attempts at assistance, in fact renders them impossible, and is also evidence of the proliferating gangrene of demoralization." On the government delegate and the Council for Aid to the Jews, see below, nn. 50, 51. Similarly, the leadership of a faction of the Polish Socialist Party in underground noted in a memorandum of 5 January 1943 that "incidents of exploitation by dishonest elements of Polish society of the tragic situation in which the Jews of Poland currently find themselves, and particularly instances of . . . material exploitation, blackmail, and even denunciation to the German authorities, are repeating themselves ever more frequently." Quoted in Prekerowa, *Konspiracyjna Rada Pomocy Żydom*, p. 277. Other contemporary sources spoke of blackmail as a "mass phenomenon." See Council for Aid to the Jews to government delegate, [1943], YVA—O6.48/10a. Jewish testimonies are even more emphatic in this regard. For example, Michał Borwicz, a Jewish historian who escaped from the Janowska Road camp in Lwów and eventually took command of a unit of the Polish Home Army, maintained in his postwar survey of Jews posing as non-Jews that "to speak of 'Aryan papers' without mentioning the blackmailers is almost the same as . . . writing about flying through the stratosphere while neglecting to mention the difference in air pressure." Borwicz, *Arishe Papirn*, 1:144. Sociologist Nehama Tec, who interviewed 308 Jewish survivors from Poland during the 1970s—people "representing by definition success in averting disaster"—found that "71 percent reported having experienced blackmail," while "the remaining 29 percent spoke of it in relation to others." Tec, *When Light Pierced the Darkness*, p. 47. Of course, such perceptions may have been skewed somewhat by the realization that—as Ludwik Hirszfeld, an eminent Jewish-born Christian physician who had been forced by Nazi racial legislation to reside in the Warsaw ghetto, put it—"one evil blackmailer or denouncer could destroy thousands." Hirszfeld, *Historia jednego życia*, p. 407. Whatever the case, the significant fact for the present discussion is that the threat of blackmail represented a constant danger for virtually every Jew living in hiding or trying to pass as a Pole, and Jewish leaders hoped that the government-in-exile and the underground leadership would take steps to mitigate it. For an analysis of various cases in which Poles, whether as individuals or as members of a group, are reported to have "blackmail[ed], denounce[d], or even murder[ed] Jews in hiding," see Gutman and Krakowski, *Unequal Victims*, pp. 208–25. For additional primary accounts of the phenomenon, see Ringelblum, *Polish-Jewish Relations*, pp. 119–33; Borwicz, *Arishe Papirn*, 1:144–90; [Meed], *Fun Beyde Zaytn Geto-Moyer*, pp. 113–19; Goldstein, *Finf Yor in Varshever Geto*, pp. 369–73; Lubetkin, *BiY'mei Kilayon uMered*, pp. 180–83. For secondary discussions, see Prekerowa, *Konspiracyjna Rada Pomocy Żydom*, pp. 265–95; Berenstein and Rutkowski, "Vegn Rateven Yidn," p. 97.

48. Laqueur, *The Terrible Secret*, p. 234. The reference is to the Jewish Fighting Organization (Żydowska Organizacja Bojowa—ŻOB), which had been established at the end of July 1942 in response to the beginning of the mass deportation of Jews from the Polish capital to the death camp at Treblinka. See Gutman, *Yehudei Varshah*, pp. 248–67. Underground Jewish military organizations and partisan units had been formed earlier during 1942 in various locations, most notably in Wilno. See Arad, *Vilna haYehudit*, pp. 198–201; Korczak, *Lehavot baEfer*, pp. 46–71; Krakowski, *Lehimah Yehudit*. At the time the Jewish leaders met with Karski in October 1942, ŻOB had requested arms from the Home Army, but these had not been given. See, inter alia, Bartoszewski and Lewin, *Righteous among Nations*, pp. xxxvii, liv; Iranek-Osmecki, *Kto ratuje jedno życie*, pp. 147–48. Tadeusz Bór-Komorowski, at the time deputy commander (later commander) of the Home Army, wrote in his memoirs that earlier, in July 1942, immediately following the onset of the deportations from Warsaw, Home Army Commander Stefan Grot-Rowecki had initiated a meeting with Jewish leaders and offered to supply them with "arms and ammunition and to co-ordinate their attacks outside with Jewish resistance from within." Bór-Komorowski, *The Secret Army*, pp. 99–100. Aside from the message brought by Karski (which, he claimed, he had cleared with Grot-Rowecki prior to his departure), substantial evidence has been adduced to cast strong doubt on this version of events. See Gutman, *Yehudei Varshah*, pp. 272–75. For an argument that Bór-Komorowski's testimony "cannot be entirely ignored," based on limited documentary support, see Lukas, *The Forgotten Holocaust*, p. 173.

49. Laqueur, *The Terrible Secret*, p. 235.

50. The office of the government delegate in the homeland served as the principal vehicle through which the government-in-exile sought to exercise civil authority in the occupied homeland. For details on the manner in which this office functioned and on its relations with the exile regime, see Korboński, *The Polish Underground State*, pp. 34–39; Duraczyński, *Kontrowersje i konflikty*.

51. The Civic Committee for Aiding the Jewish Population (Społeczny Komitet Pomocy Ludności Żydowskiej), also known as the Commission for Social Assistance for the Jewish Population (Komisja Pomocy Społecznej dla Ludności Żydowskiej) and in later sources as the Provisional Committee

for Aid to Jews (Tymczasowy Komitet Pomocy Żydom), was established on 27 September 1942, mainly upon the initiative of individuals affiliated with the Democratic Party (Stronnictwo Demokratyczne), the Union of Polish Syndicalists (Związek Syndykalistów Polskich), the Catholic Front for the Rebirth of Poland (Front Odrodzenia Polski), and the faction of the Polish Socialist Party known as Freedom-Equality-Independence (Wolność-Równość-Niepodległość—WRN). The motivation for the creation of this organization appears to have been humanitarian. During the two months of its existence the committee, by its own estimate, extended assistance to more than 180 Jews (of whom half lived in Warsaw and 70 percent were children), mainly by locating living quarters for Jews who had escaped from the ghetto and providing them with false identity papers and funds. In December 1942 the committee was reorganized and reconstituted as the Council for Aid to Jews (Rada Pomocy Żydom). Both the committee and the council were commonly known by the code name Żegota. On the activities of the committee, see Prekerowa, *Konspiracyjna Rada Pomocy Żydom*, pp. 51–57; Arczyński and Balcerak, *Kryptonim "Żegota,"* pp. 75–79; Gutman and Krakowski, *Unequal Victims*, pp. 252–61.

52. "Radiogram," 31 October 1942, in Bartoszewski and Lewin, *Righteous among Nations*, p. 690. Cf. Polish text, quoted in Prekerowa, *Konspiracyjna Rada Pomocy Żydom*, p. 55.

53. Quoted in Arczyński and Balcerak, *Kryptonim "Żegota,"* pp. 80–81.

54. Quoted in Prekerowa, *Konspiracyjna Rada Pomocy Żydom*, p. 300. Cf. the archival copy of the same document, cable to Mikołajczyk, 8 January 1943, received 29 January 1943 (No. 10, L. dz. 431/43), AIP—[EP], "Sprawy Żydowskie."

55. Message signed by "Trojan," "Mikołaj," and "Borowski," January 1943, YVA—O6/48b.10b. It is possible that the petitioners inflated their request; they referred to their intention to assist "the 10,000 children remaining in the Warsaw ghetto," but that many children were no longer alive at the time. In fact, it is unlikely that during its entire existence the council extended aid to even half this number of Jews, adults and children alike. See Gutman and Krakowski, *Unequal Victims*, pp. 264–65.

56. The demands included a government declaration on the responsibility of all those who took part in the murder campaign, exercise of pressure upon the Allies and neutral countries for reprisals and asylum, an instruction to the Polish population to render assistance to Jews, and a protest by the Polish clergy. See Engel, "The Polish Government-in-Exile and the Holocaust," document 1, p. 274.

57. Ibid., pp. 274–75. Moshe Kleinbaum of the Reprezentacja concluded the discussion with a rejoinder: "It seems to me that the Government overestimates our capabilities. You may believe that the Jews can do everything, but to us it seems that the Government can do much more than we can. The Jews are constrained by the policies of the governments of the various countries; nevertheless the Jews in America have organized a great protest demonstration to which both Roosevelt and Churchill sent their messages." Ibid.

58. See the minutes and summaries of the various meetings in ibid.

59. Stupp to Kot, 26 January 1943, CZA—J25/2.

60. Cable, Raczyński to Ciechanowski, 20 January 1943 (no. 31), HIA-PG, Box 700 (MSZ), File 851/e. Cf. A. L. Easterman, World Jewish Congress, to Kraczkiewicz, 21 January 1943, ibid.

61. Schwarzbart Diary, 12 December 1942, YVA—M2/770.

62. Ibid., 14 December 1942. Schwarzbart did not indicate whether Serafiński offered any explanation.

63. "Rozmowa z Prezydentem Raczkiewiczem," 15 December 1942, YVA—M2/77.

64. Cable, Schwarzbart to Reprezentacja, 12 February 1943, YVA—M2/602; cf. Schwarzbart Diary, 6 February 1943, YVA—M2/771.

65. For the derivation of this conclusion, see Engel, *In the Shadow of Auschwitz*.

66. Olgierd Górka, "O Dziale Narodowości Min. Spraw Wewnętrznych," n.d., YVA–O55/3. Cf. the joint declaration of principles by the Polish Socialist, Peasant, and Labor parties, July 1941: "The government is the instrument of the authority and will of the entire body of citizens of the Polish Commonwealth and must serve its well-being." Quoted in Kwiatkowski, *Rząd i Rada Narodowa*, p. 104.

67. Retinger, *All about Poland*, pp. 65–67.

68. On these matters, see Engel, *In the Shadow of Auschwitz*, pp. 88–90, 97–98, 125–29, 133–43.

69. See ibid., pp. 17–21.

70. See ibid., pp. 59–64. For a discussion of how Polish Jews perceived the Soviets at the time of the Red Army's invasion, see Levin, "The Response of the Jews," pp. 87–102; Gross, *Revolution from Abroad*, pp. 31–33.

71. See, for example, Mersin, "Sytuacja w Warszawie i w Generalnym Gubernatorstwie," 30 September 1940, HIA-Komorowski, Box 3; Sztab Naczelnego Wodza, Oddział VI, "Narodowościowe Sprawy," 16 April 1941, HIA-PG, Box 920 (MID), File N/18; "Sprawy narodowościowe," 15 July–15 September 1942, SPP—56/120. See also Gross, *Polish Society*, pp. 185–86.

72. See Engel, *In the Shadow of Auschwitz*, pp. 72, 242. See also Iranek-Osmecki, *Kto ratuje jedno życie*, p. 69.

73. See Engel, *In the Shadow of Auschwitz*.

74. In February 1942 the government had even provided itself with a theoretical loophole through which it could, if necessary, evade the practical implications of its professed nondiscriminatory orientation. In his declaration of principles presented in the name of the government at the opening session of the Second National Council, Sikorski stated that "to the national minorities that fulfill their civic obligations to the state, Poland guarantees equal rights for equal duties." Quoted in Kwiatkowski, *Rząd i Rada Narodowa*, p. 107. By mid-1942 some Polish officials had begun to intimate openly that Jews had on the whole not satisfactorily fulfilled their civic obligations. See Engel, *In the Shadow of Auschwitz*, pp. 149, 151.

75. Such thinking was often noticeable in the distribution of assistance to Jewish refugees who were Polish citizens. Polish representatives in Palestine, Portugal, and unoccupied France who were charged with administering welfare activities for Polish citizens in these countries tended to exclude Jewish Polish citizens from their purview on the grounds that Jewish charitable organizations would take care of Polish Jews. See Engel, *In the Shadow of Auschwitz*, pp. 97–98. Szmul Zygielbojm fought against this practice in the National Council on the grounds that it "creates the impression that Poles benefit from the protection of the state, whereas Jews are sentenced to be protected by philanthropic institutions (Żydzi skazani są na opiekę instytucji filantropijnych)." "Wniosek S. Zygielbojma w sprawie ujednolicenia form opieki nad wszystkimi uchodźcami z Polski," 20 February 1943, YVA—M2/33.

76. At issue was the future of over half of Poland's prewar area. The government-in-exile viewed the return of these territories as its paramount war aim. See, inter alia, Zabiełło, *O rząd i granice*, pp. 30–32.

77. "Uwagi kierownika Biura Studiów," [handwritten date: 1943], AIP—A.XII.1/65. For similar comments by a member of the National Council, see T. Kiersnowski, "Pro memoria," 7 October 1942 (No. 4985/Ia/42), AIP—PRM. 88/2.

78. For extended discussion of this process, see Engel, "HaSichsuch ha-Polani-haSovieti," pp. 26–28.

79. On 4 January 1941 the Polish general staff had approached British military officials with a request to launch an airborne attack upon the concentration camp at Auschwitz, which at the time housed mainly Polish political prisoners, not Jews (Poles and other non-Jews continued to be incarcerated there throughout the war). The request was denied on the grounds of impracticality. Richard Peirse to Polish chief of staff, 15 January 1941 (Nr. RECP/DO/56), HIA-Komorowski, Box 2. In January 1942 the Polish government had convened an Inter-Allied Conference on German Atrocities, whose declaration promised reprisals against Germans for their country's "regime of terror" in occupied lands. Britain and the United States, however, had not signed this declaration. See Inter-Allied Information Committee, *Punishment for War Crimes*. In March 1942 Sikorski had presented the U.S. State Department with a formal demand for "immediate measures of retaliation applied to German nationals." "Memorandum of Conversation by the Acting Secretary of State [Sumner Welles]," 25 March 1942, in *FRUS*, 1942, 3/2:131. No response was given by the Americans. In April the Polish Foreign Ministry had again requested the British government to bomb German positions inside Poland in response to German atrocities against Poles, and again the request was denied. "MSZ do Szefa Sztabu N. W. . . . ," 22 April 1942, in *AKD*, 2:220–22. The request had been repeated to both Roosevelt and Churchill by Sikorski in June 1942, in a letter in which he declared that the German regime in Poland "obviously aims at the extermination of the Polish nation." Sikorski to Roosevelt, Sikorski to Churchill, 22 June 1942, HIA-US, Box 11, File 1.

80. See "Opening Remarks," n.d., attached to letter from Polish minister of information to Polish prime minister and others, 11 March 1941, HIA-PG, Box 455 (MSZ), File 851/e, Subfile: "Żydzi w W. Brytanii"; "Rozmowa z panem Weitzmanem," 25 September 1941 (Nr. 2454/VIII/41), YVA—O25/79.

81. "Uwagi ogólne," n.d. (L. dz. K.2385/42) HIA-Mikołajczyk, Box 9, File: "Committee on Occupied Poland: Correspondence, 1942–43." A variant of this statement was later incorporated into a Polish Interior Ministry report on conditions in the homeland. See Laqueur, *The Terrible Secret*, p. 112.

82. See Engel, *In the Shadow of Auschwitz*, pp. 170–71, 180–85. Lukas, in *The Forgotten Holocaust*, p. 153, states that "in March 1942, Sikorski especially emphasized the plight of the Jews and urged the United States to warn Hitler of reprisals if he continued his policy of exterminating entire groups of the Polish population." The text of the memorandum cited in support of this statement, however, speaks of "terrorist acts and crimes committed against the Polish and Jewish populations," referring subsequently exclusively to the suffering of the "Polish Nation" and demanding retaliation for the "inhuman extermination of the Polish people." "Memorandum of Conversation . . . ," 25 March 1942, in *FRUS*, 1942, 3/2:131. This language does not seem to demonstrate any special emphasis upon the Jewish situation. It appears, rather, that the Polish government's general practice was to mention the Jewish situation in passing within the context of discussions about the persecution of Poles, using the mention of Jews as a highlighting device. For examples of documents from the latter half of 1942 that seem to have been formulated in accordance with this principle, see "Depesza z Londynu," 23 September 1942, HIA-US, Box 11, File 2; *Biuletyn Polski*, 24 September 1942, ("Wilenszczyzna"); Ciechanowski to Cordell Hull, 2 October 1942, HIA-US, Box 11, File 2.

83. On the beginnings of deportations from the occupied zone, see Marrus and Paxton, *Vichy France and the Jews*, pp. 255–62; Klarsfeld, *Vichy-Auschwitz*, pp. 135–60.

84. About half a million non-Jewish Poles had emigrated to France during the 1920s and 1930s. See Janowska, *Polska emigracja zarobkowa*, p. 106. Others had made their way to the country following the outbreak of war in September 1939; of these, many had fought in the exile Polish army but had not been evacuated to Britain following France's fall. On the community of Poles in France during the war years, see Kalinowski, *Emigracja polska we Francji*, esp. pp. 29–40.

85. Sikorski to Raczyński, 5 September 1942 (L. dz. 2441/VIIa/42), HIA-PG, Box 587 (MSZ), File 738/Z. Facsimile in Engel, "The Polish Government-in-Exile and the Deportations of Polish Jews from France," pp. 108–9.

86. Stańczyk to Raczyński, 12 September 1942 (L. dz. 7496/42), HIA-PG, Box 587 (MSZ), File 738/Z. Facsimile in Engel, "The Polish Government-in-Exile and the Deportations of Polish Jews from France," pp. 110–12.

87. Stańczyk was referring to a cable from Stanisław Zabiełło, director-

general of the Polish Offices in France, in which the Polish official had indicated that although he had been assured by the French authorities that the deportation of Polish workers from France to Germany was not under discussion, "we must count in theory on the possibility of such a danger in the future, given the . . . complete failure to recruit French volunteer workers." Cable, Zabiełło to Polish Foreign Ministry, 15 August 1942 (no. 80), HIA-PG, Box 587 (MSZ), File 738/Z. See also Engel, "The Polish Government-in-Exile and the Deportations of Polish Jews from France," pp. 102–3. Raczyński had also received a report from the Polish general staff indicating that according to French informants the same measures being applied to Jews were to be enforced against Poles as well beginning on 15 September. Col. Sulisławski to Raczyński, 11 September 1942, HIA-PG, Box 587 (MSZ), File 738/Z.

88. Engel, "The Polish Government-in-Exile and the Deportations of Polish Jews from France," pp. 114–15.

89. Ibid., pp. 115–19.

90. The first official Jewish representation calling for Polish government action on behalf of Polish Jews in occupied France was made by Zygielbojm to Raczyński in person on 12 September. Schwarzbart followed with a memorandum to the foreign minister three days later. Raczyński's subsequent actions went beyond the steps called for by the Jewish leaders. For citations, see Engel, "The Polish Government-in-Exile and the Deportations of Polish Jews from France," p. 116n. Curiously, Zygielbojm had mentioned to Raczyński that Polish Jews in France were faced with "deportation to the ghettos in Poland, where they will perish," as early as 27 August, but at the time he had asked only that insofar as the Polish government was able to reunite soldiers serving in the Polish army in Britain with their families who had been forced to remain in France in June 1940, the families of Jewish soldiers be given preference in this regard. Zygielbojm to Raczyński, 27 August 1942, HIA-PG, Box 587 (MSZ), File 738/Z.

91. Engel, "The Polish Government-in-Exile and the Deportations of Polish Jews from France," pp. 117–21.

92. This army, under the command of Lt. Gen. Władysław Anders, had been created in accordance with the Polish-Soviet agreement of 30 July 1941. The Poles had hoped that this force would fight alongside the Red Army against Germany on the eastern front and would be in a position to prevent the Soviets from taking military control of the disputed territories after liberation. The army had been evacuated following the failure of Polish efforts to come to terms with the Soviet authorities over such fundamental issues as recruitment, supply, training, and deployment of the Polish forces. The evacuation represented a major defeat for Prime Minister Sikorski's strategy vis-à-vis the Soviet Union. See Terry, *Poland's Place in Europe*, pp. 199–244.

93. See Babiński, *Przyczynki historyczne*, pp. 126–27; Kacewicz, *Great Britain*, p. 141; Polonsky, *The Great Powers and the Polish Question*, pp. 23, 111–12.

94. Polonsky, *The Great Powers and the Polish Question*, p. 23; Terry, *Poland's Place in Europe*, p. 299.

95. See Izek, "Roosevelt and the Polish Question," pp. 71–153.

96. See Terry, *Poland's Place in Europe*, pp. 309–11. Indeed, it appears that the U.S. State Department may already have concluded that the 1939 boundary between the two countries should not be reestablished. See Polonsky, *The Great Powers and the Polish Question*, p. 114; Izek, "Roosevelt and the Polish Question," pp. 124–25.

97. Kacewicz, *Great Britain*, pp. 149–50.

98. "Note from the People's Commissariat for Foreign Affairs to the Polish Embassy in the U.S.S.R. . . . ," 16 January 1943, in *DPSR*, 1:473. Earlier the Soviet government, although claiming all residents of the annexed territories as Soviet citizens, had, as an ostensible gesture of "good will and readiness to compromise," treated ethnic Poles as citizens of Poland. "Note from the People's Commissariat for Foreign Affairs in reply to the note of the Polish Embassy . . . ," 1 December 1941, in *DPSR*, 1:227–28.

99. Eden to Sir Cecil Dormer, 22 January 1943, in Polonsky, *The Great Powers and the Polish Question*, pp. 115–16.

100. See Eden to Churchill, 16 March 1943, in ibid., p. 118: "The President, somewhat to my surprise . . . thought that . . . Poland . . . would gain rather than lose by agreeing to the Curzon line. In any event we, the United States, and Russia should decide at the appropriate time what was a just and reasonable solution, and if we agreed, Poland would have to accept."

101. See Ciechanowski, *The Warsaw Rising*, pp. 87–90; cf. "Gen. Rowecki do Centrali . . . ," 19 May 1942, in *AKD*, 2:265.

102. Ciechanowski, *The Warsaw Rising*, p. 90. Government officials also expressed concern over what seemed to them the increasing effectiveness of pro-Soviet propaganda in the West. See, for example, the memorandum of the Polish Foreign Ministry of 18 January 1943 headed "Buenos Aires Nr. 13," with handwritten annotation, "Do rozmowy z min. Strońskim," HIA-Mikołajczyk, Box 35, File: "'Polish Patriots Union' and other pro-Soviet groups, 1943."

103. "Gen. Rowecki do Centrali . . . ," 22 June 1942, in *AKD*, 2:273–75.

104. "N. W. do Gen. Roweckiego . . . ," 28 November 1942, in *AKD*, 2:369–71.

105. The likelihood of this scenario appears to have been understood by at least some who were well beyond the highest levels of the Polish leadership. See, for example, the remarks of Tadeusz Kiełpiński, a representative of the right-of-center Labor Party (Stronnictwo Pracy) on the National Council at a meeting of the council's Military Committee in January 1943: "In all of the discussions I have held so frequently with the [General] Staff, one refrain kept turning up: '1918 . . . is bound to repeat itself. . . . The Germans will finish off Russia, the English will defeat the Germans, and everything will be all right.' . . . Well, 1918 may repeat itself, but it may also not repeat itself. . . . We have to reckon with the conquest of Poland by the Russian armies." "Posiedzenie Komisji Wojskowej Rady Narodowej," 14 January 1943, HIA-RN, Box 8, p. 13.

106. "Gen. Rowecki do Gen. Sikorskiego . . . ," 12 January 1943, in *AKD*, 2:403.

107. See "N. W. do Gen. Roweckiego . . . ," 6 February 1943, in *AKD*, 2:412–13.

108. See Lukas, *The Forgotten Holocaust*, pp. 163–65.

109. "Report on Conditions in Poland," HIA-US, Box 29, File 2. The courier was most likely Jerzy Salski, who had been sent from London to Poland in November 1941 and remained in the country until the beginning of October 1942. See "Protokół spisany dnia 18 kwietnia 1943 . . . ," YVA—M2/261. Salski also brought reports about the murder of Jews in gas chambers at Auschwitz. See Engel, *In the Shadow of Auschwitz*, p. 201.

110. "Gen. Rowecki do N. W. . . . ," 23 December 1942, in *AKD*, 2:393–94.

111. "Kierownictwo Walki Cywilnej do Min. Mikołajczyka . . . ," 23 December 1942, in *AKD*, 2:394. See also Garliński, *Poland in the Second World War*, p. 182.

112. Quoted in Szarota, *Rowecki*, p. 204. Szarota erroneously gives the date of the document as 10 October 1942. Cf. the archival copy, "Rozkaz Nr. 71," 10 November 1942, Centralne Archiwum Komitetu Centralnego Polskiej Zjednoczonej Partii Robotniczej, Akta Armii Krajowej, 203/I-2/6. Thanks are due Paweł Korzec for a photocopy of this document.

113. See above, n. 111.

114. See above, n. 109. Additional expressions of this fear are quoted in Gutman and Krakowski, *Unequal Victims*, pp. 70–73. Jan Karski's report to Sikorski, on the other hand, spoke only of "the German intention of annihilating the Polish intelligentsia, the Polish political, social, cultural, and economic leadership . . . ," not of a plan to murder every Pole. Typescript in HIA-Karski, Box 1. Several months later Karski indicated that neither he nor the underground leadership could state positively that the entire Polish population was threatened with mass murder. Karski to Tadeusz Romer, Polish foreign minister, HIA-Karski, Box 2, File 8. Similarly, on 10 November 1942, Grot-Rowecki wrote that "the chief German objective in regard to us can be described as the absorption of our nation" and called for "counter-balancing the apprehensions [among the Poles that the fate of the Jews might soon be visited upon them] with reassuring persuasions." See above, n. 112. The exact nature of the Germans' ultimate designs upon the Polish population remains a subject for systematic research. For some preliminary observations, see Tal, "On the Study of the Holocaust and Genocide," pp. 38–41.

115. See above, nn. 110, 111.

116. See above, n. 111.

117. See above, n. 109.

118. See, for example, "Sprawozdanie Komisji Spraw Zagranicznych [Rady Narodowej], 2–4 January 1943, YVA—M2/8, in which the Foreign Affairs Committee of the Polish National Council recommended that the council adopt a resolution stating, among other things, that "world opinion is not sufficiently prepared to accept our war aims" and that "the organization of

propaganda on behalf of the interests of Polish policy must be recognized at this moment as a leading issue that will not suffer delay." The resolution called upon the Ministries of Foreign Affairs, Information, and War Aims to develop appropriate programs for swaying "specific political, social, academic, and financial circles, primarily in Great Britain, the United States, and the countries of Latin America," to the Polish cause. Another resolution whose adoption was recommended in the same report claimed that "German plans to annihilate all classes of Polish society are already striking at the very biological existence of the nation" and stressed that "immediate Allied aid for Poland must be regarded as one of the points in a general plan for prosecuting the war."

119. There is no indication that Kot received any instructions from London to offer such a bargain, although Raczyński had suggested "a discrete raising of the possibilities of a further exchange of opinions with the leaders of the Jewish circles regarding cooperation both in the area of foreign policy and with regard to solving the Jewish question in Poland." Cable, Raczyński to Polish Consulate, Jerusalem, [20 November 1942] (Nr. 462), HIA-PG, Box 459 (MSZ), File: "Mniejszości Żydzi." See also Engel, "HaSichsuch haPolani-haSovieti," p. 34. A similar strategy seems to have been employed by a prominent member of the National Council, Władysław Banaczyk, at a meeting with Polish Jews in Great Britain in January 1943. See Schwarzbart Diary, 18 January 1943, YVA—M2/771.

120. Engel, "The Polish Government-in-Exile and the Holocaust," document 4, p. 285. See also Engel, *In the Shadow of Auschwitz*, pp. 139–55; Engel, "HaSichsuch haPolani-haSovieti," pp. 26–38.

121. Engel, "The Polish Government-in-Exile and the Holocaust," document 9, pp. 306–7.

122. See Engel, "HaSichsuch haPolani-haSovieti," p. 38.

123. Mokrzycki to chief of Military Intelligence (Oddział II), 9 December 1942, AIP—KOL. 11/24.

124. Korsak to Polish foreign minister, 5 January 1943 (Nr. 851/Pl/5), HIA-PG, Box 700 (MSZ), File: "Żydzi—prześladowania niemieckie." See also Korsak to Polish Foreign Ministry, 20 January 1943 (Nr. 851e/Pl/11), ibid., File: "Mniejszości Żydzi."

125. Korsak to Raczyński, 12 January 1943, HIA-PG, Box 700, File: "Mniejszości Żydzi"; Hebrew translation in Engel, "HaYishuv," p. 418. On the other hand, the Polish consul-general in Tel Aviv, Henryk Rosmarin, offered a much more optimistic appraisal of Jewish readiness to cooperate with the government. See cable, Rosmarin to Raczyński, 23 December 1942 (Nr. 80), HIA-PG, Box 700 (MSZ), File: "Żydzi—Prześladowania niemieckie," Subfile: "Ratowania Żydów."

126. On Soviet efforts in this direction, see Redlich, *Propaganda and Nationalism*, pp. 135–44. For Polish comments on these efforts, see "K," Teheran, to Polish Foreign Ministry, 29 September 1942, YVA—O55/2; "Notatka

o sowieckiej propagandzie i akcjach politycznych w Palestynie," January 1943, HIA-Anders, Box 72, doc. 342; "Nastroje Sowieckie i Komunistyczne w Palestynie," HIA-Anders, Box 72, doc. 343.

127. Korsak to Raczyński, 12 January 1943 (Nr. 233/Pl), HIA-PG, Box 700, File: "Mniejszości Żydzi"; Hebrew translation in Engel, "HaYishuv," p. 418. On the Soviet delegation, see Redlich, *Propaganda and Nationalism*, pp. 141–42.

128. Engel, "HaYishuv," p. 418. Korsak seems to have moved away from the position he had held two months earlier, when he had stated that he saw no possibility of active collaboration between the Jewish Agency and the Soviet Union, mainly because of Soviet lack of interest in such collaboration. See ibid., p. 409.

129. Cable, Kot to Polish Foreign Ministry, 2 February 1943 (Nr. 76), HIA-PG, Box 700 (MSZ), File 851/e. Cf. Polish Foreign Ministry to distribution list, 9 February 1943, YVA—O55/3.

130. See previous note. It is not certain which "previous declarations" Kot had in mind; the government had never before stated that Jewish refugees in neutral countries would be readmitted to Poland after the war. Perhaps he was referring to two earlier statements made by Labor Minister Stańczyk on the status of Jews in postwar Poland. For references, see Engel, "HaSichsuch haPolani-haSovieti," pp. 28, 39.

131. A month earlier Olgierd Górka had made a similar suggestion to his superior, Information Minister Stroński, and had even recommended offering financial support to Polish Jewish refugees in neutral countries. In practice, he pointed out, such a gesture would cost the Polish government nothing, both because the government in any case provided subsidies to its refugee citizens and because "the number of eventual refugees will be negligible." Nevertheless, he stressed that "from the propaganda standpoint this project is *extremely important and extremely urgent*" (emphasis in original). "Pro memoria dla P. Ministra Strońskiego," 30 December 1942, HIA-PG, Box 700 (MSZ), File 851/e, Subfile: "Ratowanie Żydów."

132. Kurcjusz's official title was chief of the Division of Continental Operations (Dział Akcji Kontynentalnej) of the Interior Ministry in Turkey. This was a division that conducted covert "special operations connected with the war effort on the continent." See "Sprawozdanie w przedmiocie budżetu Ministerstwa Spraw Wewnętrznych na r. 1943," YVA—M2/33. On Kurcjusz's title and his appointment by Kot, see Kurcjusz to Kot, 18 November 1940, in Tendyra, "Archiwum Kota," p. 149. Part of Kurcjusz's function was evidently to keep watch over the activities of some of the key figures of the prewar Polish regime who had taken up refuge in the countries of the eastern Mediterranean and were suspected of plotting against the government-in-exile. Kot's visit to Palestine was also apparently prompted by concern that rebellion might be growing in the upper ranks of the army. See [Drohojowski], *Wspomnienia dyplomatyczne*, pp. 214–20; "Rozmowa z Min. Prof. Kotem," 13 January

1943, CZA—J25/2; Wilk to Mikołajczyk, 30 January 1943 (L. dz. K.506/43), HIA-Mikołajczyk, Box 25, File: "Deputy Prime Minister's Correspondence, January–June 1943."

133. "Uwagi na marginesie przemówienia p. Min. Kota w dniu 19 stycznia 1943 w Tel Aviv na przyjęciu Reprezentacji Żydów Polskich," signed by Jerzy Kurcjusz, hand dated 4 February 1943, stamped "Najścislej tajne," AIP—KOL. 25/24. For the text of Kot's remarks at the banquet, see Reprezentacja, *Sprawozdanie*, pp. 92–95.

134. Kurcjusz, who had been associated with the extreme right-wing political faction ONR-ABC, known for its vociferous advocacy of forced Jewish emigration from Poland, seems to have been aware that his comments might be taken as an expression of hope that the Nazis would continue their systematic slaughter of Jews. Thus he took pains to prevent such a reading. He called antisemitism "not only the inspiration of Hitlerite Germany . . . [but] dangerous nonsense" and stated that "the fact that the Jews of Poland are being murdered by the German butchers is shocking, hideous, and worthy of the most severe condemnation." On the other hand, though, he claimed that "from antisemitism so conceived . . . it is necessary to distinguish the reasonably understood sense of the existence in Poland of a Jewish question and its dangers."

135. "Raport sytuacyjny," 15 November 1941–1 June 1942, HIA-Karski, Box 1, File 1.

136. "Prasa Tajna," HIA-Karski, Box 1, File 6, pp. 16, 20, 22–35.

137. For references and quotations from sources, see Engel, *In the Shadow of Auschwitz*, pp. 62–63, 80, 93–94, 297; Gutman and Krakowski, *Unequal Victims*, pp. 52–53, 79, 86; Gross, *Polish Society*, pp. 184–85.

138. From a report by the underground government delegate, 15 August–15 November 1941, quoted in Gutman and Krakowski, *Unequal Victims*, p. 51.

139. "Ryszard" to minister for home affairs, 8 November 1941 (L. dz. K.3708/41), YVA—O25/89. See also Gutman and Krakowski, *Unequal Victims*, pp. 52–53; Engel, *In the Shadow of Auschwitz*, p. 297.

140. See, for example, the complaints by Anders, as recorded in Hulls to British minister of state, Cairo, 18 March 1943 (Most Secret Memorandum No. PL 9), and in "Record of Meeting between Minister of State, General Anders, General Beaumont-Nesbitt and Mr. Hopkinson," 1 April 1943, PRO—FO 921/54.

141. See Engel, *In the Shadow of Auschwitz*, pp. 171–72, 177–83.

142. Ciechanowski to Polish Foreign Ministry, 30 December 1942, HIA-PG, Box 700 (MSZ), File 851/e.

143. See, for example, minute by D. W. Allen, [January 1943], PRO—FO 371/34549.C1071; "Gen. Sikorski do Prez. Roosevelta . . . ," 22 December 1942, in *AKD*, 2:391–92; "Szef Sztabu Amerykańskiego do Gen. Sikorskiego . . . ," 7 April 1943, in *AKD*, 2:490. See also Lukas, *The Forgotten Holocaust*, pp. 163–64. Lukas discusses the Polish approaches to the Allied governments outlined on these pages in the context of government efforts to

draw attention to the murder of Jews, but in fact his own text indicates that the exchanges cited related not to Jews but to Poles.

144. Eden to Bracken, 15 December 1942, PRO—FO 371/30924.C12490.

145. Cable, Raczyński to Weizmann, 3 December 1942, HIA-PG, Box 700 (MSZ), File 851/e. Cf. Gutman and Krakowski, *Unequal Victims*, p. 97.

146. A similar course had been taken a week earlier by Mikołajczyk in a speech to the National Council. In that speech the deputy prime minister declared that Poland was "powerless . . . to stop the German killings"; Poles, in his words, could only "protest from the depth of [their] compassionate, indignant and horror-stricken hearts." Nevertheless, he expressed the hope that such protest would "lead to the resolve of all the Allies to punish these crimes." Quoted in Gutman and Krakowski, *Unequal Victims*, p. 92.

147. See Frank Savery to F. K. Roberts, 3 December 1942, PRO—FO 371/30924.C12221; Breitman, "Auschwitz and the Archives," p. 370. These notes, however, did not contain all of the most recent information then in the Polish government's possession.

148. O. Harvey to Central Dept., 1 December 1942, PRO—FO 954/19b/465. See also memo by F. K. Roberts, 9 December 1942, PRO—FO 371/30924.C12490. The original conference had taken no notice of the plight of the Jews under Nazi occupation and had specifically refused to include mention of the Jewish situation in the declaration that it issued. See Engel, *In the Shadow of Auschwitz*, p. 178.

149. Memo by F. K. Roberts, 9 December 1942, PRO—FO 371/30924.C12490; Roberts to Raczyński, 16 December 1942, HIA-PG, Box 700 (MSZ), File 851/e. On the Polish negotiations with the Allied governments leading to the issuance of this declaration, see Gilbert, *Auschwitz and the Allies*, pp. 96–104; Wasserstein, *Britain and the Jews of Europe*, pp. 170–73; Wyman, *Abandonment of the Jews*, pp. 73–75.

150. Eden to Brendan Bracken, 15 December 1942, PRO—FO 371/30924.C12490. See also Gilbert, *Auschwitz and the Allies*, p. 104; Wasserstein, *Britain and the Jews of Europe*, p. 174.

151. Quoted in Gutman and Krakowski, *Unequal Victims*, p. 98.

152. See above, n. 15.

153. J. Morawski, Polish Foreign Ministry, to distribution list, 4 January 1943, HIA-US, Box 64, File 5.

154. "Notatka z dyskusji na zebraniu Ministrów Spraw Zagranicznych sojuszniczych krajów europejskich . . . ," 18 January 1943, HIA-PG, Box 700 (MSZ), File: "Żydzi—Prześladowania niemieckie."

155. Cable, Raczyński to Ciechanowski, 20 January 1943 (Nr. 31), HIA-PG, Box 700 (MSZ), File 851/e.

156. Cable, Ciechanowski to Raczyński, 1 February 1943 (Nr. 52), ibid.

157. Ibid. The same undersecretary indicated that he had discussed the matter of assistance to Jewish refugees in neutral European countries with Stephen S. Wise, president of the American Jewish Congress. On behalf of his government Eden told Raczyński that Britain was "prepared to concern

itself with the fate of refugees . . . in the neutral countries, especially in Spain, *treating all refugees equally*," and "supported taking up the problem of Jewish refugees through international action" (emphasis in original). See above, n. 153.

158. See above, n. 155. This comment was written on the draft of the cable but was not transmitted.

159. See above.

160. "Uchwała Rady Ministrów," 12 February 1943, YVA—M2/62.

161. See above.

162. *News Bulletin on Eastern European Affairs* (Yiddish), 1 January 1943 ("Naye khvalie fun shreklikhen teror in Poylen").

163. See, for example, *Dziennik Polski*, 5 January 1943 ("Masowa deportacja Polaków," "W Kraju"); 8 January 1943 ("Wszelkie protesty i ostrzeżenia nie odnoszą dotychczas skutku"); 9 January 1943 ("W Turcji o eksterminacji narodu polskiego"); 11 January 1943 ("Dramatyczna samoobrona ludności," "Polacy w Kraju, karząca ręka sprawiedliwości dosięgnie Niemców za teror i mord, za rabunek i głód"); 12 January 1943 ("Teror i opór," "W Kraju"); 13 January 1943 ("W Kraju"); 16 January 1943 ("Tysiące osób aresztowano podczas nowej obławy w Warszawie," "20,000 Polaków z Bośni—w obozie pod Łodzią," "Smutne życie w zburzonej Warszawie"); 18 January 1943 ("Nowe zbrodnie bandytów niemieckich"); 19 January 1943 ("Już trzy dni masowych aresztowań w Warszawie"); 20 January 1943 ("W zaplombowanych wagonach na Wschód Niemcy wywożą tysiące Polaków—do nowych obozów koncentracyjnych"). During the same interval the situation of the Jews was mentioned more than in passing only three times—on 11 January ("W Kraju: Los Żydów w Polsce"), 16 January ("Smutne życie . . ."), and 20 January ("W Kraju: 55 żydowskich obozów udręczeń w Polsce"). The article of 16 January devoted approximately 20 percent (38 of 189 lines) to the Jewish plight; the article of 20 January, about 42 percent (59 of 139 lines).

164. *Dziennik Polski*, 18 January 1943 ("Nowe zbrodnie bandytów niemieckich przedmiotem konferencji dla prasy brytyjskiej, zwołanej przez min. Mikołajczyka").

165. *Manchester Guardian*, 28 January 1943 ("The Nazi Terror: General Sikorski's Appeal").

166. Quoted in Gutman and Krakowski, *Unequal Victims*, p. 98.

167. "Uchwała Rady Narodowej . . . ," and "Tajna Uchwała Rady Narodowej . . . ," 7 January 1943, YVA—M2/8. The secret resolution called specifically for retaliatory bombing in Germany, the issuance of warnings to the German people that the entire German nation would be held responsible "for the monstrous crimes being perpetrated by the Germans in Poland," "immediate publication . . . of a brochure containing exact descriptions . . . of the methods by which the monstrous German plans against the Polish population are being executed," and the submission of a separate note to the Allied and neutral governments concerning the deportations of Poles from the Lublin and Zamość regions.

168. See "WRN do Min. Jana Kwapińskiego," *AKD*, 2:397–99.

169. *Biuletyn sprawozdawczy Rady Narodowej R. P.*, 3 December 1942–1 February 1943 ("Exposé Prezesa Rady Ministrów"), p. 17; message from Polish underground forwarded by Sikorski to British Foreign Office, [January 1943], PRO—FO 371/34549.C1071.

170. Lukas, *The Forgotten Holocaust*, pp. 163–65. See also minute by D. W. Allen, [January 1943], PRO—FO 371/34549.C1071.

171. J. Morawski, Polish Foreign Ministry, to distribution list, 4 January 1943 (No. 851-e/43), HIA-US, Box 64, File 5. The same note indicated that the Soviets had refused to associate themselves with Raczyński's declaration on the grounds that it referred to locations within the provinces annexed to the Soviet Union in 1939 as Polish territory. "In this connection," Morawski wrote, "placing the text of the Polish government's note of 10 December in our official publication together with the text of the [Allied] declaration of 17 December, as well as officially bringing this document to the attention of the governments of the Allied and neutral countries, has its special resonance [*ma swoją specjalną wymowę*]."

172. See Engel, *In the Shadow of Auschwitz*, p. 201. A favorable response to the demand for an instruction to the homeland came only in May 1943, following the collapse of the uprising in the Warsaw ghetto. See below, Chapter 2.

173. Draft by Romer, 14 December 1942, HIA-PG, Box 700 (MSZ), File 851/e.

174. Cable, Raczyński to Rosmarin for Reprezentacja, 21 December 1942, ibid.

175. See, for example, Schwarzbart Diary, 6 February 1943, YVA—M2/771; cable, Schwarzbart to Reprezentacja, 12 February 1943, YVA—M2/602; Schwarzbart to Mikołajczyk, 17 February 1943, YVA—M2/72. In contrast, the underground government delegate was quite blunt in stating to the Council for Aid to Jews that "because of the impossibility of separating the Jewish sector from the general exterminatory action, which affects all citizens of the Republic, a special proclamation to the Polish community regarding assistance to the Jews will not be issued." "Jan" to Rada Pomocy Żydom, 4 March 1943, YVA—O6/48.10a.

176. In April 1944 the government set up the Council for Matters Relating to the Rescue of the Jewish Population in Poland (Rada do Spraw Ratowania Ludności Żydowskiej w Polsce) and allocated £80,000 for the underground Council for Aid to Jews. However, even this sum was not transmitted in full. See below, Chapter 5. The Government Delegacy did make a regular allocation to the council out of its general funds, but it did not receive funds from the government designated explicitly for the council.

177. Some such funds appear to have been transferred in this fashion as early as May or June 1943, although there are signs that the government did not fulfill its role as a transmitting agent enthusiastically. In August the Jewish National Committee in Warsaw cabled the Interior Ministry acknowl-

edging receipt of "the dispatches from May and June" containing "$10,000 for the General Zionists and Right Po'alei Tsiyon party and the first installment of $10,000 toward the £10,000 from the Jewish Agency." Siudak to Schwarzbart, 19 August 1943 (L. dz. 4379/43), YVA—M2/265. The former payment has not yet been corroborated on the basis of the available documentation. The latter evidently refers to a sum of £10,000 transferred to the Interior Ministry by the Jewish Agency in Jerusalem "for assistance to the Jews in Poland." Siudak to Schwarzbart, 12 June 1943 (L. dz. 2989/43), ibid. On 21 June, Mikołajczyk reportedly told Schwarzbart and Berl Locker of the Jewish Agency office in London that he had given the order to disburse the funds. In his memorandum of the conversation Schwarzbart commented, "If I were a judge, I would not believe him." Locker also spoke of an additional £30,000 that had been collected by Jewish workers in Palestine for aid to Polish Jewry, but, according to Schwarzbart, "Mikołajczyk listened without any special interest." "Rozmowa z Mikołajczykiem," 21 June 1943, ibid. On the Jewish National Committee, see below, n. 181; also Chapter 2, n. 107. For more on the transfer of funds to Jews in occupied Poland, see below, Chapters 3 and 5.

178. See "Jan" to Rada Pomocy Żydom, 3 March 1943, YVA—O6/48.10a; "Zestawienie wypłat dla Żegoty," August 1932–March 1934 [sic], YVA—O6/48c.10b. For more on the funding of the council, see Iranek-Osmecki, *Kto ratuje jedno życie*, pp. 234–38; Gutman and Krakowski, *Unequal Victims*, pp. 267–71. On government support for civilian underground activities in general, see Gross, *Polish Society*, pp. 242–46.

179. "Rozmowa z Mikołajczykiem," 21 June 1943, YVA—M2/265. See also Reiss, *BeSa'arot haTekufah*, p. 228; Porat, *Hanhagah beMilkud*, pp. 405–6.

180. See Reiss, *BeSa'arot haTekufah*, pp. 228–29.

181. The Jewish National Committee (Żydowski Komitet Narodowy), the political representation of various Zionist parties in underground, sent five cables through the government delegate's office to Jewish representatives in the West (via Mikołajczyk) before receiving a reply. "Delegat Rządu do Centrali: Depesza Żydowskiego Komitetu Narodowego do Dr. Szwarcbarta," 1 May 1943, in *AKD*, 3:2–3. The first cable was dispatched on 21 January; Żydowski Komitet Narodowy to Wise, Goldmann, et al., 21 January 1943 (L. dz. K. 679/43), YVA—O55/3. See also Iranek-Osmecki, *Kto ratuje jedno życie*, pp. 168–69, and below, Chapter 3.

182. Dział Polityczny [MSW], "Notatka," 4 February 1943, AIP—[EP]. Reiss did not actually obtain a visa until November 1943. Reiss, *BeSa'arot haTekufah*, p. 239.

183. "Uchwały Rady Ministrów," 11 February 1943, AIP—[EP], "Sprawy Żydowskie."

184. Cable, Reprezentacja to Schwarzbart, 4 March 1943, YVA—M2/602. In fact, the creation of the division probably had nothing to do with the demand from Palestine but was, rather, a response to a proposal submitted by Agudas Yisroel to the government even before the issue of rescue had

become central. See A. Serafiński, "Notatka," 17 November 1942, YVA—055/2.

185. "Uchwały Reprezentacji Żydostwa Polskiego," 8 March 1943, CZA—J25/2; cable, Reprezentacja to Schwarzbart, 19 March 1943, YVA—M2/602. See also Reprezentacja, *Sprawozdanie*, p. 101.

186. See below, Chapters 3 and 5.

187. See Reiss, *BeSa'arot haTekufah*, pp. 235–36.

188. See, for example, Schwarzbart Diary, 19 January 1943, YVA—M2/771: "The Poles want to have the Jews working for Poland [and] not complaining about anti-Semitism and they do not want to do anything for the Jews. Every inch must be fought through by me." See also Reprezentacja, *Sprawozdanie*, pp. 98–117.

CHAPTER TWO

1. Terry, *Poland's Place in Europe*, pp. 309–11. See also Babiński, *Przyczynki historyczne*, p. 129; above, Chapter 1, n. 96.

2. Babiński, *Przyczynki historyczne*, pp. 129–30.

3. Ibid., p. 130.

4. "Wyjątek z protokołu LIX posiedzenia plenarnego Rady Narodowej...," 1 February 1943, YVA—M2/8.

5. Sikorski was evidently referring to widespread Jewish complaints over the treatment of Jewish soldiers in the Polish army in the Soviet Union. On these complaints, see Engel, *In the Shadow of Auschwitz*, pp. 132–47. The subject of intergroup relations in the Polish armed forces had long been a bone of Polish-Jewish contention. See ibid., pp. 54, 71–73, 87–88, 96–97, 100–101.

6. The reference was undoubtedly to the Soviet policy of refusing to recognize the Polish citizenship of non-ethnic Poles who had fallen under Soviet rule as a result of the Red Army's occupation of Poland's eastern territories in September 1939. On this policy, see Engel, *In the Shadow of Auschwitz*, pp. 129–30.

7. See, for example, Olgierd Górka, "Rozmowa z panem Weitzmanem," 25 September 1941 (Nr. 2454/VIII/41), YVA—O25/79; Engel, *In the Shadow of Auschwitz*, pp. 94–95.

8. The reference is curious, for Gruenbaum himself was a Zionist rather than a member of the Bund.

9. Sikorski had evidently not waited for a confidential session of the National Council in order to vent his frustration with the Jews. He had made similar remarks to Morris Waldman and Max Gottschalk of the American Jewish Committee at a meeting held with them in New York on 10 January 1943. See Litvak, *Pelitim Yehudim*, p. 262. After leaving the United States he visited Mexico, mainly in order to secure visas for 10,000 Poles who had been evacuated from the Soviet Union and were presently stranded in Iran. While

in the country both he and Retinger held press conferences with local Jewish leaders. At one such conference he reportedly berated Mexican Jews for their "bad behavior" and for conducting "shady deals." When asked how many of the 10,000 visas would be allocated to Polish Jewish refugees in Iran, he is said to have replied, "What do you want? After all, the merchants and diamond polishers of Amsterdam have already saved themselves." At an interview with an American correspondent Retinger allegedly praised his chief for reproaching the Jews of Mexico over their improper conduct. Polish spokesmen later charged that the two leaders had been quoted in "non-rigorous fashion [*w niewybrednej formie*]" by the American Jewish newspapers in which articles about the press conferences had appeared, as part of a "sharp campaign against the commander-in-chief." Gano, head of Intelligence Division, Polish General Staff, to head of Commander-in-Chief's Office, 1 March 1943 (L. dz. 953/tj./Wyw./43), with attachments, PC—Okręt (OF-19).

10. For details, see Golczewski, *Polnisch-jüdische Beziehungen*, pp. 233–40; Korzec, *Juifs en Pologne*, pp. 110–12.

11. In January 1923, upon assuming the premiership in the crisis precipitated by the assassination of Polish President Gabriel Narutowicz, Sikorski had told a plenary session of the Sejm that among Poland's national minorities were those "who listened to voices from abroad" and had specifically criticized Polish Jewry for causing the international press to misrepresent the rights enjoyed by non-ethnic Poles in the Polish state. See Landau, *Mi'ut Le'umi Lohem*, p. 158. Even earlier, in 1920, Sikorski reportedly charged Jews with spreading demoralization in the military, an accusation often accompanied by the invocation of the *Żydokomuna* image. See Golczewski, *Polnisch-jüdische Beziehungen*, pp. 244–45.

12. See Engel, *In the Shadow of Auschwitz*, pp. 147–56.

13. See above, Chapter 1, n. 92. Rudnicki himself had been among the 300 Jewish civilians to accompany the Anders army during the first evacuation from the USSR in April 1942. Together with a handful of other evacuees and local Jews from Tehran, he had helped to set up an aid committee for Jewish refugees in Iran. One of this committee's self-proclaimed tasks had been to assist Jewish evacuees and refugees to make their way to Palestine. In this capacity Rudnicki had established contact with the Jewish Agency, and after April 1942 he had been sending regular reports to Jerusalem. The connection with the Jewish Agency gradually became more formalized, and the aid committee came to be known as Palästina-Amt (the name by which Jewish Agency offices in various European countries had been known before the war). See Kless, *Gevulot, Mahteret uVerihah*, pp. 160–61.

14. For details, see Engel, "HaSichsuch haPolani-haSovieti," pp. 29–30.

15. Ibid., pp. 30–32. Polish spokesmen had indicated to Jewish leaders that publicizing the charges would serve to advance Soviet interests against the Poles. See, for example, the memorandum by Karol Kraczkiewicz, secretary-general, Polish Foreign Ministry, 8 July 1942, YVA—O55/2.

16. Polish circles in Tehran had learned of the report as early as November

1942, but its text does not appear to have been known by Polish leaders in London until January 1943. See Kless, *Gevulot, Mahteret uVerihah*, p. 168.

17. Rudnicki to Jewish Agency for Palestine, 8 September 1942, HIA-US, Box 64, File 6.

18. According to official Polish sources, Jews made up between one-quarter and one-third of the total number of Polish refugees in the Soviet Union. For references, see Engel, *In the Shadow of Auschwitz*, p. 268, n. 60. In his report Rudnicki claimed that the proportion amounted to 40 percent. Moreover, whereas the number of Polish evacuees comprised some 10.5 percent of the total number of Poles in the USSR, Jews who were evacuated made up only 1.5 percent of the total number of Jewish Polish citizens in the country. Engel, *In the Shadow of Auschwitz*, p. 140.

19. On the Soviet citizenship policy, see Engel, *In the Shadow of Auschwitz*, pp. 129–30, with attached references.

20. See ibid., p. 141.

21. In one of these instances, according to Rudnicki, an NKVD captain had even threatened to remove one Pole from the evacuating transports for each Jew denied permission to depart by Polish officials.

22. He even went so far as to suggest that the Soviet government might be induced, upon intervention from Britain and the United States, to give "its consent to conducting a recruiting campaign among the Jewish Polish refugees on Soviet soil for a Jewish legion in Palestine, as well as to the evacuation of the families of these recruits."

23. This mode of operation proved disconcerting to the Poles, who occasionally demanded that the Jews turn over to them whatever solid information they possessed upon the manner in which the evacuation from the Soviet Union had been conducted. See, for example, Engel, "The Polish Government-in-Exile and the Holocaust," document 5, p. 292.

24. W. Arlet, Polish Embassy, Washington, to Polish Foreign Ministry, 11 January 1943 (No. 851-e/SZ-t/1), HIA-PG, Box 129 (MID), File S/9: "Ewakuacja obywateli polskich z ZSRR"; Sylwin Strakacz, Polish Consulate-General, New York, to Polish Foreign Ministry, 18 January 1943, HIA-PG, Box 585 (MSZ), File 738/Z: "Uchodźcy Żydzi w Sowietach—Pretensje Żydowskie (Ewakuacja z ZSRR)."

25. Arlet to Polish Foreign Ministry, 11 January 1943 (see previous note).

26. Polish Foreign Ministry to Polish Legate, Tehran, 8 February 1943, HIA-PG, Box 585 (MSZ), File 738/Z.

27. J. Morawski, Polish Foreign Ministry, to Polish Minister of National Defense, 8 February 1943, HIA-PG, Box 129 (MID), File S/9: "Ewakuacja obywateli polskich z ZSRR."

28. The evidence that the Poles were able to adduce with regard to the charges tended on the whole to be more incriminating than exculpatory. See Engel, *In the Shadow of Auschwitz*, pp. 140–47.

29. See, for example, Arlet to Polish Foreign Ministry, 11 January 1943 (see above, n. 24).

30. Gruenbaum to Kot, 7 March 1943, CZA—S26/1134. This claim had been made before the Polish government was made aware of the Rudnicki report. See, for example, Korsak to Polish foreign minister, 3 November 1942 (Nr. 851-e-Pl/59), HIA-PG, Box 700 (MSZ), File: "Mniejszości Żydzi" (Hebrew translation in Engel, "HaYishuv," p. 411).

31. "Notatka o sowieckiej propagandzie i akcjach politycznych w Palestynie," January 1943, HIA-Anders, Box 72, document 342; "Nastroje sowieckie i komunistyczne w Palestynie," January 1943, ibid., document 343.

32. "Nastroje sowieckie" (see previous note).

33. "Notatka o sowieckich akcjach w Palestynie," January 1943, HIA-Anders, Box 70, document 129.

34. "K" to Polish Foreign Ministry and others, 29 November 1942, YVA—O55/2. For an additional statement that Rudnicki had made his charges against the Poles without foundation, see "Notatka dla P. Adama Głogowskiego . . . ," n.d., AIP—KOL. 25/24.

35. See above, n. 33.

36. Text of the declaration adopted at the meeting in *New Palestine*, 11 May 1942, p. 6.

37. See Halpern, *The Idea of a Jewish State*, pp. 39–40.

38. On the development of this attitude among the Zionist leadership, see Porat, *Hanhagah beMilkud*, pp. 483–85.

39. Palestinian Jewish leaders appear to have believed during the summer of 1942 that as many as 1 million Polish Jews may have found refuge in Russia. Porat, *Hanhagah beMilkud*, pp. 50–53. On the actual number of Polish Jewish refugees in the country, see Litvak, *Pelitim Yehudim*, p. 18; Nussbaum, *VeHafach lahem leRo'ets*, p. 28.

40. David Remez, general secretary of the General Federation of Jewish Workers in Palestine, reported two days following Rudnicki's return from Tehran that he and other Jewish leaders had discussed this issue with the two Soviet diplomats from Ankara who had recently visited the country: "We raised before them as one of our most ardent desires and postulates [the request] to help us strengthen our front here immediately, to allow us actually to double and triple our war effort by adding several tens of thousands of Jewish immigrants from among the Polish deportees." "Protokol miYeshivat haMo'etsah ha-47 shel HaHistadrut," 7 September 1942, AH—Minute Books, Council. On the visit of the Soviet diplomats from Ankara to Palestine, see above, Chapter 1.

41. Rudnicki wrote that "the condition of the Jewish refugees in Russia is horrible. At least 30 percent have died of hunger, typhus, dysentery, and other illnesses. There are about 300,000–400,000 Jewish refugees in Russia, concentrated mainly in the cities, without work. They have only one hope—that we will save them." In such circumstances the leaders of Palestinian Jewry evidently viewed the extrication of these refugees from the Soviet Union as an act of rescue equal in importance to any action that might be taken on behalf of Jews in Nazi-occupied Europe. Thus, for example, in

their discussions with Stanisław Kot in late 1942 and early 1943 they raised the matter of the government-in-exile's treatment of Polish Jews in Russia together with their demands for government action on behalf of the Jews of the occupied homeland. See Engel, *In the Shadow of Auschwitz*, pp. 150–51. In fact, it may well be that these leaders were inclined to devote even more attention to the former category of Jews than to the latter, because their chances of decisively helping the former appeared significantly greater. For more on the conditions of refugee life in the Soviet Union during 1942, see Litvak, *Pelitim Yehudim*, pp. 187–91.

42. This tactic actually appears to have brought at least one immediate dividend: it induced the Polish military authorities to permit their facilities to be used, in cooperation with the Jewish Agency, for the surreptitious transfer of Jewish civilian refugees from Iran to Palestine. On this matter, see Gen. Wiatr to Kot, 19 January 1943 (L. dz. 176/Tjn/43/Of. Łączn. Pal.), AIP—KOL. 25/24. This action represented a reversal of a previous Polish position; earlier the Poles had balked at a suggestion that the army provide uniforms to 1,000 Polish Jewish children in Tehran so as to allow them to pass through Iraqi territory on the way to Palestine without having to obtain transit visas (which the Iraqi government refused to grant). As Kot had explained to David ben Gurion, "Uniforms should not be used for purposes of disguise." Engel, "The Polish Government-in-Exile and the Holocaust," document 2, p. 277. By providing cover for civilians making their way to Palestine, the Poles injected a complication into their relations with the British mandatory regime, from which they sought to extricate themselves by referring to those who had entered the country under their auspices as deserters from the Polish forces. On this subject, see below, Chapter 4.

43. In the final analysis it appears quite certain, on the basis of Polish documentary evidence, that the Polish military authorities did indeed, for a variety of reasons, seek to limit the number of Jews in the evacuating transports. See Engel, *In the Shadow of Auschwitz*, pp. 139–47; Nussbaum, *VeHafach lahem leRo'ets*, pp. 64–69.

44. See, for example, Gruenbaum's explanation of how he had sought to verify one of the key items in the Rudnicki report and why, as a result of this verification, he believed the report to be accurate. Gruenbaum to Kot, 15 March 1943, YVA—O55/3. See also Gruenbaum to Kot, 7 March 1943, CZA—S26/1134

45. See above, n. 33.

46. The Soviet government claimed many of the Polish Jewish refugees as Soviet citizens and sought to enforce upon them the same rules that applied to all other Soviet citizens, including a prohibition upon emigration. Nevertheless, they were willing in practice to permit a small number of Jews to be evacuated with the Polish troops, knowing that the Poles themselves would try to keep this number to a minimum. Thus the Soviet government was able to create a situation in which the Poles could be made to appear solely responsible for the small percentage of Jews among the evacuees. For an expli-

cation of this strategy, see Engel, *In the Shadow of Auschwitz*, pp. 129–30, 146. Tadeusz Romer, who replaced Kot as ambassador to the Soviet Union in late 1942, appears to have understood the Soviet design and to have attempted—albeit unsuccessfully—to dissuade Soviet Foreign Minister Vyacheslav Molotov from persisting in it. See "Rozmowa amb. Romera z Mołotowem o żydach polskich: Sprawa obywatelstwa," 3 November 1942, AIP—KOL. 25/24.

47. In the course of a seven-hour discussion held on 23 December 1942, Yitshak Gruenbaum remarked to Kot that he had often wondered "why the centuries-long historical conflict between Poland and Russia over Poland's border . . . reverberates to the detriment of the Jews. Why have the Jews been selected by the Soviets as casualties [of this conflict] . . . ? This conflict has cost the Jews much blood through the centuries, and today the Jews are paying once again. . . . Perhaps this is a provocation by the Soviet authorities aimed at making the Polish authorities do something to force the Jews into a struggle with the Poles. Perhaps they are trying to show that the Polish authorities have learned nothing, that they are continuing the antisemitic policy of the final years before the war." "Protokół z rozmowy z p. Grünbaumem," 23 December 1942, YVA—055/2.

48. In December 1942, Jewish leaders received an abrupt reminder of this fact. Evidently in mid-November several high-ranking Soviet officials, including the ambassadors in Washington (Maxim Litvinov) and London (Ivan Maisky), had told representatives of the World Jewish Congress that the Soviet government was about to grant 3,000 exit visas for Polish Jewish refugees, of which 700 were to be reserved for rabbis and rabbinical students. Two of these representatives, Stephen Wise and Nahum Goldmann, had even been informed by U.S. Undersecretary of State Sumner Welles that Stalin had assured Franklin Roosevelt in writing that the Soviet government would "open its borders to all foreign citizens who wished to leave." However, shortly after receiving this news the American Jewish Congress was told by Litvinov that the Soviet government had not consented to grant the visas. Evidently the Soviets had decided that the Jews in question were to be treated as Soviet citizens. In this instance Polish Ambassador Romer protested and pressed for the visas to be issued. See Sylwin Strakacz, Polish Consulate-General, New York, to Polish Foreign Ministry, 6 January 1943, and Polish Foreign Ministry to Polish Ministry of Labor, 27 January 1943, HIA-PG, Box 585 (MSZ), File 738/Z: "Uchodźcy Żydzi w Sowietach—Pretensje żydowskie (ewakuacja z ZSRR)"; "Rozmowa telefoniczna z radcą Kraczkiewiczem: Sprawa wypuszczenia obywateli polskich Żydów z ZSRR," 27 January 1943, YVA—M2/62.

49. Such appears to have been the thinking embodied in a memorandum prepared by Yitshak Rabinowicz, himself a former Zionist political prisoner in the USSR and now a member of the Jewish Agency's Committee on Russian Jewry, for Moshe Shertok, head of the agency's Political Department, on 20 November 1942. Rabinowicz indicated that following the war "Soviet Russia . . . will have decisive influence over the question of the Jews con-

centrated in . . . the areas of Russian rule or occupation." "Many signs," he declared, "point to a definite movement in the direction of understanding for us [Zionists]." Thus, he concluded, "through a sensible, careful, and systematic policy we shall be able to build a bridge between us and Russian Jewry and to tear down the wall that has been built up on both sides during the last twenty years." To his mind that policy required that the Jewish Agency place itself firmly on the Soviet side in the Polish-Soviet dispute. In return for such a stance, he suggested, the agency would be in a strong position to demand and to receive official recognition by the Soviet government as the sole body responsible for the welfare of all Jewish refugees in the USSR. This step, in turn, would give the agency a strong foothold within the Soviet Union, a foothold that could presumably be expanded eventually to encompass Soviet Jewry proper as well. Rabinowicz to Shertok, 20 November 1942, CZA—S25/5182.

50. See, for example, Korsak to Polish foreign minister, 3 November 1942 (Nr. 851-e-Pl/59), and Korsak to Raczyński, 12 January 1943 (Nr. 233/Pl), HIA-PG, Box 700 (MSZ), File: "Mniejszości Żydzi." Hebrew translations in Engel, "HaYishuv," pp. 409–13, 417–20.

51. Schwarzbart Diary, 4 February 1943, YVA—M2/771. Schwarzbart claimed that he had actually already prepared such a statement but that the Polish authorities had suppressed it, "probably in order not to irritate Stalin." No such statement has been found in Schwarzbart's extensive files, and the claim sounds highly improbable.

52. Ibid., 6 February 1943. In his report of this conversation he even claimed that the public declaration that he had already made included a pledge of "Jewish loyalty to undiminished frontiers [for Poland] in the East."

53. Ibid.

54. Litvinov to Green, 23 February 1943, HIA-PG, Box 585 (MSZ), File 851/e: "Żydzi w Sowietach," Subfile: "Noty."

55. Cable, Green, Albert Einstein, Henry Smith Leiper (Universal Christian Council), David Dubinsky (International Ladies Garment Workers Union), et al., to Molotov, 27 January 1943, ibid.

56. On the public campaign, see Redlich, *Propaganda and Nationalism*, pp. 30–33.

57. In his letter to Green, Litvinov stated that the two had been executed in December 1942. This was evidently the official Soviet version of events; see, for example, cable, Polish Embassy, Kuibyshev, to Polish Foreign Ministry, 15 April 1943 (no. 173), HIA-PG, Box 585 (MSZ), File 738/Z, Subfile: "Alter i Erlich." In a subsequent communication to Green, however, Litvinov, perhaps inadvertently, placed the execution in December 1941. It appears more likely that Erlich and Alter were put to death at this time rather than a year later, especially in light of the fact that a member of the Bund who had been evacuated with the Polish forces to Tehran in August 1942 reported at that time that Alter was already dead. See Korzec, "Hidat Retsihatam shel Erlich veAlter," pp. 281, 310.

58. Initially, at least, their hope was fulfilled. Redlich, *Propaganda and Nationalism*, p. 33.

59. On 6 September 1939 the Central Committee of the Bund, like the Polish government and other organizations in Poland, had instructed its members, in response to an order by the Polish military authorities, to quit the Polish capital so that they could regroup in territories farther from the front lines. They were, of course, unaware that those territories would soon be occupied by the Red Army.

60. On the orientation of the Bund vis-à-vis the Soviet Union, see Johnpoll, *The Politics of Futility*, pp. 176–78.

61. For details of their initial arrests, see Redlich, *Propaganda and Nationalism*, p. 16; Korzec, "Hidat Retsihatam shel Erlich veAlter," p. 285.

62. In each case the sentence had been commuted to ten years' imprisonment ten days after the conclusion of the trial.

63. Among others, both the Polish and the British governments demanded their release. See cable, Kot to Polish Foreign Ministry, 17 September 1941 (no. 17), HIA-PG, Box 585 (MSZ), File 738/Z, Subfile: "Alter i Erlich"; also Korzec, "Hidat Retsihatam shel Erlich veAlter," pp. 285–86; Redlich, *Propaganda and Nationalism*, pp. 16–18.

64. Redlich, *Propaganda and Nationalism*, p. 17.

65. On the role that the Jewish committee was to play in the overall Soviet wartime propaganda effort, see Redlich, *Propaganda and Nationalism*, pp. 6–13, 19.

66. Among the immediate reasons was evidently the desire to secure the release of other prominent Bund members from prison. See the report by Kot, 3 October 1941, in Korzec, "Hidat Retsihatam shel Erlich veAlter," p. 299 (original Polish text reprinted); Redlich, *Propaganda and Nationalism*, p. 20. Erlich and Alter also apparently believed that their participation in the committee would help socialist circles increase their international influence at the expense of Soviet-dominated Communist groups. See Redlich, *Propaganda and Nationalism*, p. 23.

67. Korzec, "Hidat Retsihatam shel Erlich veAlter," p. 286. The contents of the memorandum are summarized in Redlich, *Propaganda and Nationalism*, pp. 21–22.

68. See Erlich's comments to fellow Bund leader Emanuel Nowogrodzki in New York, quoted in Korzec, "Hidat Retsihatam shel Erlich veAlter," p. 285: "The pleasant manner in which they are treating us now is unbelievable. They are ever trying to convince us that we were released . . . because the authorities came to believe that our sentences were unjust, and they now want to rectify the injustice that they did us." In Moscow Erlich and Alter were given rooms at the Metropol Hotel; in Kuibyshev, at the Grand Hotel.

69. For an eyewitness description of the circumstances of their disappearance, see Lucjan Blit and Leon Oler to Polish Embassy, Kuibyshev, 4 December 1941, HIA-Poland. Konsulat Generalny New York, Box 1.

70. Kot, *Rozmowy z Kremlem*, p. 176. See also the memoranda by Maciej

Załęski, First Secretary, Polish Embassy, Kuibyshev, 4 and 5 December 1941, HIA-Poland. Konsulat Generalny New York, Box 1.

71. Cable, Kot to Polish Foreign Ministry, 13 December 1941 (no. 108), HIA-PG, Box 585 (MSZ), File 738/Z, Subfile: "Alter i Erlich."

72. Most likely Soviet censors had intercepted several letters that Alter had written to colleagues abroad in which he had sharply criticized the mass arrests carried out by the NKVD during the late 1930s and had urged the British Labour Party, the Trade Union Congress, the Polish Socialist Party, and the Bund, among others, publicly to pressure the Soviet regime to grant amnesty to all political prisoners still in custody. The letters have been published (in the original languages) in Korzec, "Hidat Retsihatam shel Erlich veAlter," pp. 291–300. In one of the letters Alter noted, "I am risking my head should my part in this become known; but I shall take that risk, for it is worth it."

73. Erlich had been considered for appointment as the representative of the Bund in the new Polish National Council slated to convene in London, and Alter had been offered a position as a Polish Embassy delegate to the various relief institutions then being created for Polish refugees and deportees in the Soviet interior. See Korzec, "Hidat Retsihatam shel Erlich veAlter," pp. 288, 300–303.

74. For further details, see Engel, "The Polish Government-in-Exile and the Erlich-Alter Affair," pp. 174–75.

75. The government also appears to have felt it more urgent to protest the Soviet claim that Erlich and Alter were Soviet rather than Polish citizens and that the Polish Embassy therefore lacked standing to concern itself with their case. For an explanation of this thinking, see ibid., pp. 175–76.

76. Ibid., pp. 176–77. See also "Oświadczenie Min. Raczyńskiego w Kom. Spr. Zagr.," 5 April 1943, HIA-PG, Box 585 (MSZ), File 738/Z. An indication of British concern for the possible effect of the Erlich-Alter affair on inter-Allied relations is found in a "most secret" memorandum, "U.S.S.R.-Polish Relations," [probably March 1943], PRO—FO 921/54.

77. The government was also bound to respond energetically to the execution because of the Soviets' claim upon Erlich and Alter's citizenship. Even tacit acquiescence to this claim by the Polish government would have been tantamount to an acknowledgment of the legitimacy of Soviet jurisdiction in territories that the Poles claimed as their own. Throughout the affair the Soviets attempted to inveigle such acknowledgment from the Polish authorities. In fact, as late as 15 April 1943, almost two months following the announcement of Erlich and Alter's execution and less than two weeks before the severing of Polish-Soviet diplomatic relations, the Soviet state-operated travel bureau Inturist presented the Polish Embassy in Kuibyshev with a bill for 2,577 rub. to cover the period of the two Jews' stay at the Metropol Hotel in Moscow from 13 September–15 October 1941. The embassy paid the bill in full, indicating in an accompanying wire that "the *Polish citizens* in question are not at present in a position to pay their obligations personally." The

emphasis upon the words *Polish citizens* was, of course, present in the source. Cable, Zawadowski, Polish Embassy, Kuibyshev, to Polish Foreign Ministry, 15 April 1943 (no. 173), HIA-PG, Box 585 (MSZ), File 738/Z.

78. Ciechanowski further observed that "the press has kept silent on the Erlich-Alter affair despite having obtained all information." Cable, Ciechanowski to Polish Foreign Ministry, 5 March 1943 (Nr. 116), AIP—PRM. 98/2.

79. Cable, Raczyński to Polish Embassy, Washington, 8 March 1943 (no. 147), HIA-PG, Box 585 (MSZ), File 738/Z, Subfile: "Alter i Erlich." The claim of "incessant and vigorous" intervention was not altogether an exaggeration. See the collection of documents entitled "Sprawa Altera i Ehrlicha [*sic*]," 4 December 1941–2 June 1942, HIA-Poland. Konsulat Generalny New York, Box 1.

80. On the contrary, it had several indications to the opposite effect. See Engel, "The Polish Government-in-Exile and the Erlich-Alter Affair," p. 178.

81. See above, Chapter 1.

82. "Zebranie protestacyjne amerykańskich sfer robotniczych w Nowym Yorku, w sprawie stracenia Henryka Erlicha i Wiktora Altera," 1 April 1943, HIA-PG, Box 585 (MSZ), File 738/Z. See also Redlich, *Propaganda and Nationalism*, p. 34.

83. Ciechanowski to Raczyński, 8 April 1943 (Nr. 851-e/SZ-t/101), HIA-PG, Box 585 (MSZ), File 738/Z.

84. Redlich, *Propaganda and Nationalism*, pp. 33–35.

85. Ibid.

86. Łunkiewicz, Polish Defense Ministry, Political Department, to Polish Foreign and Information Ministries, 19 April 1943, HIA-PG, Box 700 (MSZ), File 851/e. An indication of where the Jewish Agency stood was contained in the political column of the weekly *HaOlam*, the organ of the World Zionist Organization, on 18 March 1943: "The question of Poland's future borders is certainly a difficult one that will not be settled except by agreement and compromise between Poland and Russia. The only way to a true compromise is for Poland to relinquish [the] Ukrainian, White Russian, and Lithuanian areas and to receive East Prussia [as compensation]. . . . In any event, this is not a simple or an easy question, and precisely for that reason this is not the time [for us] to deal with it." *HaOlam*, 18 March 1943 ("Reshimot Mediniyot").

87. "Drogi propagandy sowieckiej w Palestynie," 17 March 1943, HIA-Anders, Box 72, Document 340.

88. See, for example, Gruenbaum to Kot, 15 March 1943, YVA—O55/3; Kraczkiewicz to Col. Wiśniowski, 30 March 1943, HIA-PG, Box 585 (MSZ), File 738/Z, Subfile: "Pretensje żydowskie (ewakuacja z ZSRR)."

89. For details, see below.

90. In late March, for example, a group of Jewish leaders belonging to the American Jewish Congress, the American Federation of Polish Jews, Agudas Yisroel, and various Zionist parties drafted a memorandum for the Polish government pointing to eight areas in which, in their opinion, government actions on matters of Jewish concern had been unsatisfactory. In particu-

lar, the Jewish representatives complained that "the Polish government has not taken any serious action aimed at coming to the aid of Polish Jewry." Ciechanowski to Raczyński, 20 April 1943 (Nr. 851-e/SZ-t/94), and appendix, HIA-US, Box 64, File 5.

91. Stanley to Schonfeld, 23 February 1943, HIA-PG, Box 223 (MSZ), File 851/e, Subfile: "Rabini w Polsce."

92. Schonfeld to Polish foreign minister, 7 March, 17 March 1943, ibid.

93. J. Marlewski, "Uwagi do pisma Rabina S. Schonfelda z 7-go marca 1943r," 16 March 1943, ibid. Marlewski explained: "Action by the Polish government concerning the departure of several or several tens of rabbis from Poland has great significance in principle, whether or not their departure is at all realistic in view of the probable refusal of the German authorities. Until now we have taken a negative attitude toward requests from individuals to leave the country. Efforts concerning certain groups would undoubtedly provoke a negative reaction of the people of the country. The stance of the government in such matters must be uniform. The Ministry of the Interior is charged with formulating an opinion whether the government in London should undertake any efforts at all concerning the departure of individuals from the country, especially where one or another specific racial group is involved."

94. Memorandum by Kraczkiewicz, 17 March 1943, ibid.

95. See above, n. 93. This thought was expressed even more explicitly in a draft memorandum by Kraczkiewicz intended for Mikołajczyk but never sent: "Efforts made on behalf of a few specific individuals would render them privileged in relation to others. Attempts to extricate certain groups selected according to religious or racial criteria could arouse a negative reaction in the homeland." Draft, Kraczkiewicz to Polish Interior Ministry, 20 March 1943, ibid.

96. This was undoubtedly the import of Kraczkiewicz's twin observations that the Jews would be responsible for making the necessary overtures to the German side and that any such overtures were bound to be rejected; the chances that anyone in Poland would ever see the seven rabbis leave the country and know that the government-in-exile had played a role in securing their release were nil. Indeed, Schonfeld had informed the Poles that once visas for a British colony were obtained, he would approach the Turkish Red Cross [sic] about acting as intermediary in the negotiations with the German side. Kraczkiewicz to Polish Embassy, London, 3 April 1943, ibid.

97. Kraczkiewicz to Polish Interior Ministry, 20 March 1943, ibid. Kraczkiewicz had at first thought to send Mikołajczyk a digest of arguments for and against the proposal, but in the end he did not do so. Instead, Mikołajczyk appears to have received Kraczkiewicz's opinion only; see below.

98. Note by Mikołajczyk, 26 March 1943, ibid.

99. Kraczkiewicz to Schonfeld, 3 April 1943, ibid.

100. On 18 June 1943, Colonial Secretary Oliver Stanley indicated to Chief Rabbi Hertz that the British government was prepared to grant the rabbis

in question visas to the island of Mauritius, on condition that they reside in the detention camp that had been erected on the island to hold Jewish refugees who had tried to run the British blockade against immigrant ships to Palestine. Hertz agreed to this condition, and one week later Stanley passed a request for visas to the Foreign Office. The Foreign Office, however, did not issue the visas immediately but took the entire case under examination. The matter was still under consideration as late as October 1944. See the relevant correspondence in ibid. and in HIA-PG, Box 219 (MSZ), File 851/e, Subfile: "Wyjazd Żydów na Mauritius."

101. Although the Polish documents speak only of a "significant number" of children, it is known that the actual number under discussion was 20,000. Not all of these, however, were to be Polish Jewish children. Adler-Rudel, "Chronicle of Rescue Efforts," pp. 220–28.

102. Schwarzbart to Raczyński, 22 March 1943, YVA—M2/62.

103. As the official who formulated the section's position, most likely Antoni Serafiński, explained, "I am of the opinion that in both matters there should be no objection on the part of the Polish government, first of all for the reason that, as it seems to me, both actions have a rather theoretical character. Should they succeed, they will encompass only a small number of people. A refusal to help by the Polish government would necessarily arouse unpleasant repercussions at a time when all of the governments of the Allied nations are thinking up ways to rescue the Jews." "Notatka," 26 March 1943, YVA—O55/3.

104. T[adeusz] Ullmann, director, Political Department, Polish Interior Ministry, to Polish Foreign Ministry, 1 April 1943 (L. dz. 1141/43), HIA-PG, Box 700 (MSZ), File 851/e, Subfile: "Ratowanie Żydów."

105. Cable, Polish Foreign Ministry to Polish Legation, Stockholm, 2 April 1943, ibid.

106. Squabbling between the principal Western Allies and the Swedish government over technical details might well have defeated the plan even had the Germans been more forthcoming. See Porat, *Hanhagah beMilkud*, pp. 211–13.

107. The Jewish National Committee was formed in late October 1942 in order to provide political supervision for the activities of the underground Jewish Fighting Organization, which had been established in the Warsaw ghetto the previous July. The Bund did not join the National Committee but cooperated with it (in Warsaw but not elsewhere) through a joint Jewish Coordinating Committee. See Perlis, *Tenu'ot haNo'ar*, pp. 385–89; Gutman, *Yehudei Varshah*, pp. 306–8; Dawidowicz, *The War Against the Jews*, pp. 316–17.

108. Cable, Żydowski Komitet Narodowy w Polsce to Mikołajczyk, 21 January 1943 (L. dz. 679/43, no. 15), YVA—O55/3. Blumenthal and Kermisz, in *HaMeri vehaMered*, p. 102, have published a Hebrew translation of this text based on a second copy obtained from SPP. However, Mark, in *Oyfshtand*, p. 201, basing himself on a copy of the dispatch ostensibly taken from the archives of the Government Delegacy (located, at the time of his research,

at Centralne Archiwum Polskiej Zjednoczonej Partii Robotniczej in Warsaw), has offered a Yiddish translation that appears to point to the existence of two distinct versions of the ŻKN communication. In the first place, Mark's document was dated 13 January rather than 21 January. Where his document listed the intended recipients as Stephen Wise and (Nahum) Goldmann (of the World Jewish Congress), the American Jewish Joint Distribution Committee (JDC), and Arbeter Ring (a mutual aid organization for Jewish workers, affiliated with the Bund-oriented Jewish Labor Committee), the text dated 21 January replaced Arbeter Ring with the letters "av Baterring" and added the name of Backer (perhaps George Backer, a prominent journalist and public figure involved in several American Jewish organizations, including JDC and the Jewish Telegraphic Agency). The version of 13 January mentioned that more than 3 million Jews in Poland had been murdered and that 400,000 remained alive, whereas the version of 21 January spoke only of "millions" of victims and did not estimate the number of survivors. Where the later version called upon the addressees to wage "a struggle for our lives and our honor," the earlier one demanded "arms for the struggle for our lives and our honor." And where the later text requested funds "for purposes of aid," the earlier one made the same request "for purposes of self-defense and aid."

How can these discrepancies be explained, and do they have any significance? A plausible assumption is that the text of 13 January represents the dispatch as it was given by ŻKN to the government delegate's office, whereas the text of 21 January represents the dispatch as it was received in London (no evidence has been adduced to suggest that the text of 13 January was ever known to the government-in-exile). The differences between the two versions, then, could have stemmed either from disturbances in the wireless transmission, resulting in an inaccurate deciphering of the message, or from deliberate editing by the Polish underground authorities. With regard to the latter possibility, it certainly seems curious that the earlier text's references to arms and self-defense did not reach London. However, if the dispatch was indeed held up by the government delegate until 21 January, it was then sent under the influence of the first armed ghetto uprising, which began three days earlier. This uprising appears to have resulted in a greater willingness on the part of the Home Army to supply the Jewish Fighting Organization with weapons. See Gutman, *Yehudei Varshah*, pp. 339–41. In this context it would have been strange for the political branch of the underground to suppress a Jewish request for arms. On the basis of currently available evidence, then, there do not appear to be sufficient grounds for concluding that the discrepancies between the two versions of the ŻKN dispatch were anything but accidental; therefore they cannot be regarded as a significant indicator of the thinking of either Polish government or underground leaders about Jewish matters.

109. Mikołajczyk to Raczyński, 27 February 1943 (L. dz. 155 tj/43), HIA-PG, Box 700 (MSZ), File 851/e, Subfile: "Pieniądze dla Żydów w Kraju."

110. Obviously the American Jewish leaders to whom the cable was ultimately addressed were in no position to arrange for population exchanges or reprisals against German civilians on their own. ŻKN clearly meant for these leaders to exert pressure upon the Allied governments to these ends. The Polish government might have been of assistance in this regard, but because the demands had been transmitted not to it but merely through it, it evidently felt free to ignore them.

111. Mikołajczyk indicated that the two Jewish representatives were unaware of the content of the message and stated that he would make them aware of it after it had been delivered to the addressees. According to Schwarzbart, he did so on 8 March. Schwarzbart Diary, 8 March 1943, YVA—M2/771.

112. The January cable was evidently the first effort made by ŻKN to establish contact with Jewish leaders abroad. See Gutman, *Yehudei Varshah*, p. 374.

113. Cable, Polish Foreign Ministry to Polish Embassy, Washington, 15 March 1943 (no. 144), HIA-PG, Box 700 (MSZ), File 851/e, Subfile: "Pieniądze dla Żydów w Kraju."

114. Cable, Ciechanowski to Polish Foreign Ministry, 23 March 1943 (no. 152), ibid. See also cables, Ciechanowski to Raczyński, 3 May 1943 (no. 238), and Ciechanowski to Raczyński, 12 May 1943 (no. 257), ibid. There is also some doubt as to when he presented the full contents of the message to JDC. In his cable to Raczyński of 23 March he implied that he had discussed the matter of fund raising with that organization and indicated that JDC wished to obtain the permission of the U.S. State Department before sending funds to Poland. Mikołajczyk was prepared for JDC to do so; cable, Polish Foreign Ministry to Ciechanowski, 1 April 1943 (no. 209), ibid. On the other hand, a document in the JDC archives indicates that the actual dispatch was not received by the organization until 20 April. Bauer, *American Jewry and the Holocaust*, p. 489 n. 30.

115. See above, n. 109. Mikołajczyk also told Schwarzbart that the ŻKN cable had come from the council. Schwarzbart Diary, 8 March 1943, YVA—M2/771.

116. "Notatka," 15 March 1943, AIP-[EP], III/9.

117. Mikołajczyk to Raczyński, 19 April 1943, HIA-PG, Box 700 (MSZ), File 851/e, Subfile: "Pieniądze dla Żydów w Kraju."

118. Raczyński included this instruction in a confidential information bulletin on 22 April, in ibid.

119. Or, according to the text of 13 January, "for purposes of self-defense and aid." See above, n. 108.

120. On the Bermuda conference, see, among others, Penkower, *The Jews Were Expendable*, pp. 98–121; Friedman, *No Haven for the Oppressed*, pp. 158–79; Feingold, *Politics of Rescue*, pp. 190–202; Wasserstein, *Britain and the Jews of Europe*, pp. 183–202; Wyman, *Abandonment of the Jews*, pp. 104–23. Although the British government insisted that the conference deliberations were "not [to be] confined to persons of any particular race or faith," it was

clear to all concerned that the conference was being called in response to public concern over the Jewish situation. To be sure, the two governments did take up problems of other refugee groups, but by far the most attention was given to Jews. See Wasserstein, *Britain and the Jews of Europe*, pp. 190–98.

121. Gilbert, *Auschwitz and the Allies*, p. 125.

122. See above. In March and April these efforts appear to have become even more pronounced than they had been in January and February. Examples of this intensification can be found in the pages of official Polish publications. During March and April articles regularly appeared in Polish newspapers and press bulletins devoted to illustrating the proposition that since the beginning of 1943 the German occupiers had actually begun to implement their plan to bring about the biological obliteration of the entire Polish people. See, in particular, *Dziennik Polski*, 2 March 1943 (Stanisław Mikołajczyk, "To w Polsce, gdzie uczymy się poznawać Niemcy"—an article initially published in the London-based Free French publication *La France Libre*); 4 March 1943 ("Apel do sumień Narodów Sprzymierzonych o natychmiastowe rozpoczęcie narad nad wynalezieniem środków dla zahamowania zbrodni niemieckich"); 8 March 1943 ("Masowe zwożenie Polaków do Oświęcimia i nieustanne mordowanie ich" and "Wobec zbrodni niemieckich w Polsce"); 20 March 1943 ("Trzydniowy strajk w Radomiu: Masowe egzekucje robotników na placach radomskich"); 23 March 1943 ("Ostatnie wiadomości z Kraju: 80 tysięcy Polaków w obozie śmierci w Majdanku"); *Polish Fortnightly Review*, 1 March 1943 ("The Work of Germanization in the Generalgouvernement"); 1 April 1943 ("Helots of the Herrenvolk"). In contrast, mention in these publications, and in the Yiddish-language *News Bulletin on East European Affairs*, of what was happening to Jews in Poland during the same period tended to be minimal and to be based on outdated information. See *Dziennik Polski*, 2 March 1943 ("Zupełna likwidacja ghetta Lubelskiego"— a report taken from the Nazi *Krakauer Zeitung* of 8 January 1943 about events that had occurred the previous September); 19 March 1943 ("Masakra Żydów w ghecie Warszawskiem"—concerning the ghetto revolt of 18 January 1943 and consisting entirely of the text of a dispatch from the Bund in underground that had recently been received by Zygielbojm). Cf. *News Bulletin on East European Affairs*, 19 March 1943. The item of Jewish concern that received the most attention in these publications during this time was, not surprisingly, the murder of Erlich and Alter.

This is not to say that the Polish government was not at this time in possession of previously unreported information about the situation of Polish Jewry that might have been regarded as newsworthy. A dispatch from the underground Directorate of Civilian Resistance of 23 March reported "tests of the sterilization of women in Auschwitz, [along with] a new crematorium for 3,000 persons daily, mainly Jews." Cable from N. [Stefan Korboński], 23 March 1943, HIA-Mikołajczyk, Box 11, File: "Radio Station ŚWIT—Dispatches from Occupied Poland, March–November 1943." One week later the same source cabled the news that "on the 13, 14, and 15 of this month [March] trucks loaded with Jews were taken from the Kraków ghetto to Auschwitz" and that "Jews are being taken from Łódź in the direction of Ozorków, where they perish." Cable, 30 March 1943 (L. dz. K.1517/43, no. 41), HIA-Mikołajczyk, Box 10, File: "Radio Station ŚWIT—Correspondence, January–March 1943."

123. At least one Polish observer had predicted such a development two months before the conference. See "Reakcja opinji państw aljanckich na wiadomości o terrorze antyżydowskim w Polsce," [February 1943], YVA—O55/3.

124. See above, n. 116.

125. Probably Antoni Serafiński, who headed the Nationalities and Religions Desk of the Political Department, which is given as the memorandum's source.

126. The uprising and the Bermuda conference actually began on the same day, 19 April 1943.

127. See, for example, New York Times, 23 April 1943 ("Warsaw's Ghetto Fights Deportation"). The article, which appeared on p. 9, carried the dateline London and included a statement that "the battle was still raging when the Polish exile government in London received its latest news last night." It is not clear what news that might have been. Two dispatches were sent to London about the ghetto uprising on 20 April, one by Leon Feiner (Berezowski) of the Bund and Adolf Berman (Borowski) of ŻKN to Zygielbojm and Schwarzbart, the other by Stefan Korboński, director of civilian resistance in underground Poland, to the government-in-exile. It is not known when the former message was received; the latter arrived on 21 April. "Funk-Depeshe kayn London vegn Oysbrukh funem Geto-Oyfshtand," in Mark, Oyfshtand, pp. 241–42; Korboński, The Polish Underground State, p. 134; cable headed "otrzymano 21 kwietnia 43," HIA-Mikołajczyk, Box 10, File: "Radio Station ŚWIT, Correspondence, April–May 1943." Korboński also sent a one-sentence message indicating that "in the ghetto resistance is going on" on 21 April. The date of arrival of this message is not indicated. Cable from "N" (Korboński), 21 April 1943, HIA-Mikołajczyk, Box 11, File: "Radio Station ŚWIT, London, Dispatches from Occupied Poland, March–November 1943." On the same day the underground government delegate and commander of the Home Army informed Sikorski and Mikołajczyk that a battle between German troops and the Jewish Fighting Organization had been going on for three days. However, this message was received only on 26 April. "Delegat Rządu i DCA AK do N.W. i Wicepremiera . . . ," 21 April 1943, in AKD, 2:500. The article in the New York Times contained statements supported by none of these reports, in particular one asserting that "the Polish underground has supplied arms and sent trained commanders for a last stand which is said to be costing the Germans many lives."

128. In his message of 20 April, Korboński had asked the government to "speak to the ghetto today" and had insisted that "the broadcast must bear

the mark of great urgency." This suggestion was evidently not heeded. Cable headed "otrzymano 21 kwietnia 43," HIA-Mikołajczyk, Box 10, File: "Radio Station ŚWIT, Correspondence, April–May 1943." On the other hand, an Interior Ministry publication issued on 30 April, which contained a detailed and extensive description of the mass deportations from the ghetto that had taken place during July–September 1942 and a shorter account of the resistance of 18 January 1943, did not mention the events of the previous ten days at all. "Sprawozdanie Krajowe Nr. 1/43," HIA-MSW, Box 2.

129. As printed in *Dziennik Polski*, 5 May 1943 ("Raport złożony krajowi: Przemówienie radjowe Gen. Sikorskiego w dniu 4 maja 1943"). The same issue of the newspaper contained a seventy-nine-line summary of the speech ("Raport Gen. Sikorskiego do Kraju") that made no mention of Sikorski's instruction about assisting Jews.

130. This authorized English text was published in *Polish Fortnightly Review*, 15 May 1943, p. 5.

131. For the text of the broadcast, see *The Crime of Katyn*, pp. 101–2.

132. "Communiqué issued by the Soviet Information Bureau . . . ," 15 April 1943, in *DPSR*, 1:524–25.

133. "Communiqué issued by the Polish Minister of National Defence . . . ," 16 April 1943, in ibid., 1:525–27.

134. "Statement of the Polish Government concerning the discovery of the graves of Polish officers near Smoleńsk," 17 April 1943, in ibid., 1:527–28.

135. Raczyński to Bogomolov, 20 April 1943, in ibid., 1:528–30.

136. See Zawodny, *Zum Beispiel Katyn*, pp. 69–134. For eyewitness testimony on the events immediately surrounding the shooting by one of the few surviving officers (a Jew), see Slowes, *Ya'ar Katyn*, pp. 77–92.

137. Stalin to Churchill, 21 April 1943, in Polonsky, *The Great Powers and the Polish Question*, pp. 124–25.

138. Molotov to Romer, 25 April 1943, in ibid., pp. 126–27.

139. See Babiński, *Przyczynki historyczne*, p. 140.

140. See, for example, *The Times*, 28 April 1943 ("Russia and Poland"), 29 April 1943 ("'No Support from Polish People:' A Moscow Attack"), 1 May 1943 ("Russians and Poles"); also *New York Herald Tribune*, 29 April 1943 (Oscar Lange, "To Blame for Polish Break"). See also Babiński, *Przyczynki historyczne*, p. 141. On the other hand, there were some expressions of dissatisfaction with the Soviet side. See, for example, *Manchester Guardian*, 1 May 1943 ("Poland's Request for Inquiry"); also Nicholas, *Washington Despatches*, p. 184.

141. See, for example, cable, Eden to A. Clark-Kerr, 11 May 1943, in Polonsky, *The Great Powers and the Polish Question*, pp. 130–31; Churchill to Stalin, 12 May 1943, in ibid., pp. 131–32; [Cadogan], *Diaries*, pp. 523–29; Babiński, *Przyczynki historyczne*, p. 144; Kacewicz, *Great Britain*, pp. 158–63; Terry, *Poland's Place in Europe*, p. 340; Lukas, *Strange Allies*, pp. 38–39; Karski, *The Great Powers and Poland*, pp. 461–62.

142. See Engel, *In the Shadow of Auschwitz*, pp. 69–82, 114–18, 147–56.

143. See "Notatka," 11 May 1943, HIA-US, Box 81, File 11. See also Raczyński, *In Allied London*, pp. 144–45.

144. The British Foreign Office had strongly suggested to the Poles that their response to the German revelations about the discovery of the officers' graves contain a condemnation of German propaganda methods. Raczyński, *In Allied London*, p. 142. As it turned out, the Polish statement of 17 April went even further. See below.

145. See above, n. 134.

146. On 28 April, for example, the Polish government issued another statement, this one intended primarily toward affirming "that their policy aiming at a friendly understanding between Poland and Soviet Russia . . . continues to be fully supported by the Polish nation." The statement also contained a paragraph and a half stressing how "the Polish people, making the extreme sacrifice, fight implacably in Poland and outside the frontiers of their country against the German invader." Again, no mention was made of the Jewish situation; most pointedly, the uprising in the Warsaw ghetto, which had then been going on for nine days, was not invoked as an example of resistance being offered to the Nazis in Poland. *Polish Fortnightly Review*, 15 May 1943 ("Polish Government's Statement Issued on April 28th, 1943").

147. Following is the text of the broadcast prior to the mention of the uprising in the Warsaw ghetto:

"For three and a-half years the world has been looking on with horror, but at the same time with the highest admiration, at the happenings in Poland. In was Mr. Winston Churchill who said in one of his inspiring speeches that 'Every week Hitler's firing squads and his gangs are active in many countries. But while every country appears on the list of executions one day in the week, the Poles appear on it always every day of the week.'

"To-day, in the face of the bloody events of the last few years, one could only add: 'every hour.'

"We know why it is so; but the Germans, too, know it well.

"It is because in our country underground organizations are active which direct the self-defence of the nation in accordance with the principle, 'We are laying down our lives on the field of battle so that a great nation may rise like a Phoenix from the ashes.' From the eyes of every Pole looks hard and deadly hatred. Every Polish fist is being clenched at sight of the German murderers. Even their revelations concerning the sinister tragedy of our colleagues at Smolensk has failed to influence the implacable stand of the nation. Nor will it be altered as a result of the cunning and perfidious wooing with which the Germans suddenly appeal to us, hypocritically offering us a relaxation of the yoke into which they have forced you.

"A few days ago I received a report that the Germans had burned down ten villages recently in the Lublin district; most of them with all the inhabitants; they have first seized all those physically fit and deported them for forced labour in the Reich. This was done by way of a reprisal for an act of armed self-defence against German terrorism in that part of the country.

"Led by merry-making German officers, the soldiers competed in their cruelties, outraging many women and throwing children into the fires. This was one more act of bestiality which has placed an unbridgeable abyss between the Germans and the Poles. And the number of villages in Poland which have been destroyed thus must be counted in thousands. The Germans are mass-cremating corpses in their numerous concentration camps, so as to wipe out every trace of their crimes which cry for punishment."

The passage about the Warsaw ghetto was inserted at this point, continuing the same paragraph. Following the conclusion of this passage and the attached appeal to the Polish population to assist the Jews (which came about one-third of the way through the speech), the statement continued (again, without a paragraph break): "All persecution has failed to break the Poles so far. Everywhere, wherever they are, they hate the enemy and fight him. . . . The nation has suffered in this war up to 15 per cent casualties. . . . In face of such facts, not words, is not the accusation of passivity, or worse still, of sympathy with the Germans, an obvious denial of facts?" These themes were repeated throughout the remainder of the speech. The appeal to the Polish population, then, far from being highlighted, appears to have been an insertion en passant into a speech dealing primarily with other themes. The text quoted is the English translation published in *Polish Fortnightly Review*, 15 May 1943, pp. 4–6.

148. Not only was the appeal surrounded with statements on other matters, but two summaries of Sikorski's speech in official or semiofficial Polish publications failed to mention it. *Dziennik Polski*, 5 May 1943 ("Raport Gen. Sikorskiego do Kraju"); *Free Europe*, 21 May 1943 ("Allied Gazette").

149. "Wizyta u min. Raczyńskiego," 5 May 1943, YVA—M2/62.

150. See *News Bulletin on East European Affairs*, 7, 14, 21 May 1943. The Yiddish-language series ceased publication altogether with the issue of 21 May.

151. The Palestinian newspapers all highlighted Sikorski's mention of "heroic armed resistance" by Jews in the Warsaw ghetto, relegating his appeal to the Poles to the final sentences. See, for example, *Davar*, 6 May 1943 ("General Sikorski al Milhemet haGevurah shel Yehudei Varshah"); *HaBoker*, 6 May 1943 ("Sikorski al Hitnagdut haGevurah shel Geto Varshah"); *HaTsofeh*, 6 May 1943 ("Milhemet haGevurah shel Yehudei Varshah"); *HaArets*, 6 May 1943 ("Sikorski al haHitgonenut beGeto Varshah"); *Palestine Post*, 6 May 1943 ("Jewish Defence in Warsaw Ghetto"). The same approach was taken by the London *Jewish Chronicle* on 7 May 1943 ("General Sikorski Hails Ghetto Heroes") and by the New York Yiddish-language daily *Der Tog* in its issue of 6 May 1943 ("Sikorski loybt Heldishkayt fun Iden in Varshever Geto"). *Der Tog*'s leading competitor, *Forverts*, did not report anything about Sikorski's speech.

152. See above, n. 149.

153. Ibid.

154. See Reprezentacja, *Sprawozdanie*, pp. 104–15. In particular, at a meeting with Labor Minister Stańczyk on 1 July 1943, Avraham Stupp complained that "for weeks and months Dr. Schwarzbart had to make efforts to bring about a government appeal to the Polish population in the homeland concerning giving aid to the Jews," adding that "on another occasion, when the prime minister finally spoke a few sentences about the Jews' sufferings, the next day these sentences were erased from the press bulletin and radio [news] broadcasts." Ibid., p. 111.

155. Cf. the remark made at the meeting of the Secretariat of the General Federation of Jewish Workers in Palestine on 13 May 1943: "I am convinced that the connections established by our members [i.e., the members of Labor Zionist parties] in Poland are not with the official underground, because it [the Polish underground] continues to publish defamatory statements against the Jews. . . . I must warn not to be led astray by the propaganda now being conducted by Poland with the clear intention of demonstrating Polish-Jewish cooperation." "Protokol miYeshivat Mazkirut haVa'ad haPo'el," 13 May 1943, HA—Minute Books, Secretariat.

156. "Pegishat haPolanim im haItona'im haYehudim biYrushalayim beYom Nittuk haYehasim bein Rusiyah leFolin," n.d., CZA—S25/6661. Emphasis in original.

157. "Stanowisko żydów w konflikcie polsko-sowieckim," 28 May 1943 (L. dz. 2511/Wyw/43), AIP—A.XII. 3/40a.

158. "Wpływ opinii żydowskiej na przemiany poglądów społeczeństwa amerykańskiego w stosunku do Rosji," [mid-1943], HIA-US, Box 65, File 2. The Bund and Trotsky had in fact been historic antagonists. See, for example, Gelbard, *BeSa'arat HaYamim*, pp. 252–56; Nedava, *Trotsky and the Jews*, pp. 84–99.

159. "Wpływ opinii żydowskiej" (see previous note); T. Ullmann, Political Department, Polish Interior Ministry, to Polish Defense Ministry, 25 May 1943 (L. dz. 1148/43), YVA—O55/3.

160. "Gezegenung mit Chaverim un Fraynd," in [Zygielbojm], *Zygielbojm-Bukh*, p. 366.

161. Zygielbojm to Leon [Oler] and Lucjan [Blit], in ibid., p. 367.

162. "Letster gezegenungs-Briv," in ibid., pp. 364–65.

163. Schwarzbart to Raczyński, 17 May 1943, YVA—M2/62.

164. Schwarzbart to Raczyński, 7 June 1943, ibid. On 16 June, Raczyński termed the idea "not serious," although he told Schwarzbart that he would fervently pursue the matter of "doing something again" with regard to the Jewish situation. "Rozmowa z Ministrem Edwardem Raczyńskim," 16 June 1943, ibid.

165. Thus, for example, when on 8 June the Reprezentacja called upon the government once again to demand that the Allies take "firm action to force the Germans to stop the killing," the Polish Foreign Ministry waited over two

months to respond. By that time a new foreign minister, Tadeusz Romer, had taken over. On 16 August he informed the Reprezentacja that "during the past few days the Polish government has presented the British and American governments with new materials relating to German exterminatory actions in Poland together with concrete suggestions as to steps that the Allies might take." No record of such an intervention has as yet been found. Cable, Rosmarin to Polish Foreign Ministry, 8 June 1943 (no. 38), and cable, Romer to Polish Consulate, Tel Aviv, 16 August 1943 (n.n.), HIA-PG, Box 700, File: "Żydzi—Prześladowania niemieckie."

166. Quoted in Churchill, *Second World War*, 3:443.

CHAPTER THREE

1. Quoted in Kumoś, *Związek Patriotów Polskich*, p. 9.

2. See ibid., pp. 53–56. There is evidence that at least some members of the group looked for it to prepare the groundwork for the formation of a government that would eventually supplant the exile regime in liberated Poland. Ibid., p. 9.

3. See *Publicystyka Związku Patriotów Polskich*, esp. pp. 35–40. See also Nussbaum, *VeHafach lahem leRo'ets*, p. 84.

4. See, for example, *Wolna Polska*, 16 April 1943 (Andrzej Marek, "Miejsce Polski w Europie"). See also Kumoś, *Związek Patriotów Polskich*, p. 58.

5. Polonsky and Drukier, *The Beginnings of Communist Rule*, pp. 8–10.

6. On Berling, see Nussbaum, *VeHafach lahem leRo'ets*, pp. 82–83, 98.

7. See Kumoś, *Związek Patriotów Polskich*, pp. 58–59; Nussbaum, *VeHafach lahem leRo'ets*, p. 86.

8. Stalin to Churchill, 4 May 1943, in Polonsky, *The Great Powers and the Polish Question*, p. 128. See also cables, Sir Archibald Clark-Kerr to Eden, 8 May 1943, and Eden to Clark-Kerr, 11 May 1943, in ibid., pp. 129–31.

9. On the struggle over the appointment of Sosnkowski and the filling of posts in the new cabinet, from different political perspectives, see "Przebieg kryzysu rządowego po śmierci Gen. Sikorskiego," 22 June [*sic*] 1943, in Duraczyński, *Między Londynem i Warszawą*, pp. 185–202 (also Duraczyński's own text, pp. 59–68), and "Streszczenie rozmowy z Prezydentem Raczkiewiczem . . . ," 5 July 1943, in Babiński, *Przyczynki historyczne*, pp. 619–21 (also Babiński's own text, pp. 189–202).

10. The Soviets objected to Kot and to Defense Minister Kukiel (both of whom had assumed their positions prior to Sikorski's death and who had retained their seats in the Mikołajczyk government), and they had not wished to see Raczyński replaced. Polonsky, *The Great Powers and the Polish Question*, p. 128.

11. See Ciechanowski, *The Warsaw Rising*, pp. 120–21.

12. "Przebieg kryzysu rządowego" (see above, n. 9).

13. Grosfeld was not the first Jew to hold a portfolio in the government-in-

exile. Herman Lieberman had served as minister of justice for several weeks prior to his death in 1941.

14. Litvak, *Pelitim Yehudim*, p. 273.

15. See Redlich, *Propaganda and Nationalism*; Schapiro, "The Jewish Anti-Fascist Committee," pp. 286–88.

16. Redlich, *Propaganda and Nationalism*, p. 124.

17. All of these events are detailed in ibid., pp. 118–24. The tour is also reported to have raised some $3 million in relief funds for the Soviet Union. Schapiro, "The Jewish Anti-Fascist Committee," p. 288.

18. Cable, Polish Consulate, Beirut, to Mikołajczyk [received 28 June 1943] (no. 66), HIA-PG, Box 700 (MSZ), File 851/e.

19. Ibid.; see also cable, Polish Consulate, Jerusalem, to Polish Foreign Ministry, 17 June 1943 (no. 297), ibid.

20. Kot, Polish Information Ministry, to Polish Foreign Ministry, 28 June 1943, and cable, Raczyński to Polish Embassy, Washington, 15 July 1943 (no. 460), ibid. The Polish government had circulated rumors accusing Mikhoels of being an agent provocateur against Erlich and Alter as early as October 1942. See Litvak, *Pelitim Yehudim*, pp. 259–61.

21. Cables, Polish Consulate, Jerusalem, to Polish Foreign Ministry, 17 June 1943 (no. 298), and Polish Consulate, New York, to Polish Foreign Ministry, 31 July 1943 (no. 112), HIA-PG, Box 700 (MSZ), File 851/e.

22. Ciechanowski to Polish Foreign Minister, 22 July 1943, ibid.

23. "The Organization of Soviet Propaganda in the U.S.A.," HIA-US, Box 34, File 1. The report went on to note that "this [Soviet] infiltration has a decidedly political character and is related to . . . Zionist conceptions. A certain crisis in Zionist ideology, combined with a complete silence and indifference to Zionism on the part of British and American circles, were skillfully taken advantage of by the Soviets." The conclusion that by the summer of 1943 the Polish government had come to discount the possibility of countering Soviet propaganda among Jews is suggested also by a memorandum of 22 July 1943 from Mikołajczyk to Retinger suggesting the formation of a special cabinet committee for counterpropaganda. The memorandum, in contrast to many previous documents on the same subject, made no mention of the need for work in the Jewish sector. HIA-Mikołajczyk, Box 35, File: "'Polish Patriots Union' and other pro-Soviet groups, 1943."

24. "Notatka dla Pana Ministra Sp. Wewnętrznych," 6 October 1943, YVA —O25/79. A week later Górka, along with Karol Kraczkiewicz of the Foreign Ministry and Antoni Serafiński of the Interior Ministry, met with Selig Brodetsky and A. G. Brotman of the Board of Deputies of British Jews. The Poles asked the Jewish representatives directly about organized British Jewry's stand on the Polish-Soviet dispute. Brodetsky reportedly responded that British Jewry maintained a neutral position, with the qualification that although Jews had nothing against the Poles, they felt that they needed to reckon with Soviet influence after the war. Górka to Polish Interior Minister, 14 October 1943, AIP—[EP], "Sprawy Żydowskie."

25. See, for example, "Notatka," 11 October 1943; "Notatka informacyjna," 17 October 1943; and "Sprawozdanie z zebrania żydowskiego w 'Stoll Theatre,'" 21 November 1943, HIA-Mikołajczyk, Box 35, File: "'Polish Patriots Union' and other pro-Soviet groups, 1943."

26. Some thought had been given to having Mikhoels and Feffer visit Palestine, and they were invited to do so several times by representatives of Palestinian Jewry; but such a visit never took place. See Redlich, *Propaganda and Nationalism*, pp. 145–47. On Maisky's visit, see ibid., p. 138.

27. See, for example, cables, Zażuliński, Polish Consulate, Cairo, to Polish Foreign Ministry, 26 August 1943 (no. 197), and Tabaczyński, Polish Consulate, Jerusalem, to Polish Foreign Ministry and Kot, 16 October 1943, HIA-PG, Box 700 (MSZ), File 851/e; Gano, Polish General Staff, to Polish Defense Ministry, 18 October 1943 (L. dz. 5985/Wyw. Wsch./tj.), YVA—O25/73; Gano to Polish Defense Ministry, 28 October 1943 (L. dz. 6218/Wyw. KW. tj.), AIP—A.XII.3/40a. The second of these reports indicated that Maisky had asked the head of the Financial Department of the Jewish Agency, Eliezer Kaplan, how Palestinian Jewry stood on the question of the Polish-Soviet border and that Kaplan had given an "evasive answer." The last of them reported that Golda Myerson, then a high-ranking official of Histadrut, had told Maisky (in response to his remark that the Jews of Palestine seem friendly toward Poland) that although the Palestinian Jewish community regarded all of the Allies in the same light, it gave many gifts to Russia but none to Poland.

28. T. Lipkowska, "Współpraca polsko-żydowska na terenie Palestyny," 7 November 1943, HIA-Anders, Box 70, Doc. 149.

29. General Anders's headquarters had been reestablished in the Palestinian town of Rehovot following the evacuation from the Soviet Union and the removal of the military evacuees from Iran. ·

30. Stańczyk, a member of the Polish Socialist Party, was generally regarded among Jews as the member of the government-in-exile most sympathetic to their cause. On two occasions, in November 1940 and in December 1941, he had issued proclamations in the name of the government assuring that "future relations between Jews and Gentiles in Liberated Poland will be built on entirely new foundations" and that "Poland will guarantee all her citizens, including the Jews, full legal equality." See Olszer, *For Your Freedom and Ours*, pp. 267–69; Engel, *In the Shadow of Auschwitz*, pp. 79–80.

31. Palestinian Jewish leaders, like virtually everyone else beyond the orbit of the Third Reich, did not realize how far the Nazi murder program had already progressed. At the time that Stupp presented his memorandum to Stańczyk, the largest ghettos in prewar Polish territory that had not already been entirely liquidated were those in Białystok, Lwów, Łódź, Wilno, and the Zagłębie region. In all of these ghettos combined, perhaps 150,000 Jews remained alive.

32. On such refugees, see below, Chapter 5.

33. Stupp to Stańczyk, 19 June 1943, CZA—J25/2.

34. Reprezentacja, *Sprawozdanie*, p. 110.

35. Ibid., p. 109.

36. Ibid., p. 113.

37. Ibid. He added that the Polish government had also opposed food shipments to Belgium for the same reason. Two weeks earlier, however, Stańczyk had allegedly told a group of reporters that at one time the government had tried to send a limited number of food packages from Lisbon to the Warsaw ghetto via the Polish underground, but few of the packages had reached their destinations. The government had thus decided to put an end to this undertaking. Shertok to Klinov, 17 June 1943, CZA—S25/6661.

38. Reprezentacja, *Sprawozdanie*, p. 115.

39. "Przemówienie Min. Stańczyka . . . w Waad Hapoel shel Hahistadrut," 1 July 1943, CZA—J25/2.

40. On the contrary, he pleaded that the government was altogether powerless. "The government is in exile, without any power," he told the Histadrut; "it is a supplicant itself." To illustrate this argument he claimed that the Poles had been forced to remain silent over Katyn, "when they should have screamed." Ibid. It is difficult to see how the Polish government's response to the discovery of the graves at Katyn could have been termed one of silence or how the magnitude of that response could have been compared to the reaction of the government to the news of the Holocaust.

41. *Eshnav*, 20 June 1943 ("Hasatah Anti-Yehudit Rishmit baTsava haPolani: LiDemuto shel haGeneral Anders . . ."). For a full English translation of the order, made from a Polish archival copy, see Engel, *In the Shadow of Auschwitz*, pp. 135–36.

42. Reprezentacja, *Sprawozdanie*, p. 119.

43. Ibid., p. 112.

44. Ibid., p. 116.

45. Ibid., p. 120. The Reprezentacja was not aware at the time that Sikorski had already been killed.

46. Indeed, it appears that the existence of the order was already quite well known beyond military circles. In Stanisław Kot's final summary of his mission to Moscow, presented to Sikorski on 13 July 1942, the former ambassador to the Soviet Union had reported that Anders had "issued a follow-up order [to the order insisting upon maintaining equality in the ranks] containing several paragraphs that are politically touchy. His declaration about 'reckoning' with the Jews in the homeland immediately became widely known in the free countries and the commander of the Polish armed forces came to be regarded as an enemy of the Jews." Quoted in Gutman and Krakowski, *Unequal Victims*, p. 332. Jewish circles in Palestine had evidently known of the order at least since December 1942. See A. Wdziękoński, Polish Consulate-General, Jerusalem, to Polish Foreign Ministry, 10 July 1943 (Nr. 329-b/Pl/6), AIP—A.12/755/2. According to this document, the Jewish Agency, which controlled the newspaper *Eshnav*, had deliberately released the order to coincide with Sikorski's visit to the Middle East.

No evidence has been adduced beyond Anders's own testimony to substantiate his claim that the order had never been issued. Anders evidently first made this assertion orally in a meeting with Tadeusz Romer in Cairo shortly after publication of the order. See A. Wdzięgkoński, Polish Consulate-General, Jerusalem, to Polish Foreign Ministry, ibid. He later made the claim in writing in a telegram to Commander-in-Chief Sosnkowski. Cable, Anders to Polish Commander-in-Chief, 16 August 1943 (Nr. 6010), AIP—A.12/755/2. The Polish Defense Ministry claimed to have ordered an investigation of the matter by the chief of military intelligence for the Eastern sector, Wincenty Bąkiewicz. Bąkiewicz was reported to have failed to turn up an incriminating copy of the order. Cable, Kukiel to Strakacz, 31 August 1943 (L. dz. 1145/WPol/43), ibid. However, at least two Polish archival copies of the order have since been found. For their location, see Engel, *In the Shadow of Auschwitz*, p. 275 n. 136; Gutman, "Jews in General Anders' Army," p. 272. Further confirmation of the order's genuineness was offered by Anders's chief of staff, Gen. Zygmunt Bohusz-Szyszko, in a postwar testimony. See Nussbaum, *VeHafach lahem leRo'ets*, p. 72.

47. Reprezentacja, *Sprawozdanie*, p. 120.

48. A. Wdzięgkoński to Gruenbaum, 10 July 1943, AIP—A.12/755/2.

49. Gruenbaum expressed such willingness to Polish Vice-Consul Jan Weber in return for a statement by the consulate that such an order was never given. The result was evidently Wdzięgkoński's note of 10 July (see n. 48, above). Similarly, in a meeting with Anders on 19 September 1943, Anshel Reiss of the Reprezentacja told the general that "as far as I am concerned the matter of the order has been eliminated by the general's statement." Reprezentacja, *Sprawozdanie*, p. 137. The reference was undoubtedly to Anders's statement to Sosnkowski of 16 August; see below, n. 53. This attitude was, however, clearly tactical; several months later Schwarzbart told Mikołajczyk, "I have no objection against making such a claim for external consumption, but on the inside no one should expect me to believe that it [the order] was a forgery." Quoted in Gutman, "Jews in General Anders' Army," p. 280.

50. Quoted in cable, Sosnkowski to Anders, 11 August 1943, AIP—A.XII. 1/65.

51. The ministry in London may have been overreacting to the information received from the United States. On 26 August, Sylwin Strakacz, Polish consul-general in New York, prepared a summary of his efforts to contain possible damage that the Anders order might cause. He indicated that on 4 August he had spoken with Nahum Goldmann of the World Jewish Congress and with Jacob Landau of the Jewish Telegraphic Agency, informing them that Rosmarin had sent each of them a telegram stating on his word that the alleged order was a forgery. According to Strakacz, Goldmann had not reacted at all to this information. Landau, on the other hand, had reportedly contacted the consul-general several days later, stating that on the basis of further information received from Palestine (including, it appears, a copy of the text of the order), "he had to question Rosmarin's caveat, for . . . it is not supported by a statement from Gen. Anders himself that the incriminat-

ing order has been falsified." Landau had indicated further, Strakacz noted, that "in order to banish all doubt" he had sent Anders a telegram asking him directly for a denial of the authenticity of the alleged order. Ten days after the dispatch of this telegram, Landau was said to have contacted Strakacz again and to have told him that, in the absence of any response from Anders, he felt "compelled to take up the matter in his Agency." Strakacz, however, reported that he had been able to prevail upon Landau to wait a while longer. In the meantime the consul-general declared that he had spoken with Arieh Tartakower of the World Jewish Congress and had prevailed upon him to use his influence to keep Landau from printing a story about the order for as long as possible. In other words, when the Information Ministry told Sosnkowski about a planned press campaign against Anders, it does not appear to have been given any concrete indication that such a campaign was in fact imminent. Strakacz to Polish Foreign Ministry, 26 August 1943 (Nr. 851-SS/T), AIP—A.12/755/2.

52. See above, n. 50.

53. Anders stated further that "during the entire time that I have been in command of the army, no written or oral order against the Jews has been given. On the contrary, very many of my orders have been aimed at normalizing the Jewish question in the army, with the result that antisemitic disturbances in the army do not take place. The Jewish question as such does not exist in the army." Cable, Anders to Commander-in-Chief, 16 August 1943 (Nr. 3478), AIP—A.12/755/2. The claim that "very many . . . orders have been aimed at normalizing the Jewish question in the army" does not appear to be supported by any available archival evidence.

54. Reprezentacja, *Sprawozdanie*, p. 108. The words quoted are from Lew's paraphrase of the resolution, which he mistakenly stated had been adopted on 11 January 1942. For the text of the original resolution, see ibid., pp. 27–28. The term "great Poland [*wielka Polska*]" can most likely be taken in this context as referring to Poland within the boundaries of 1 September 1939.

55. Ibid., p. 123. The text read as follows: "The Representation of Polish Jewry will support the government in its foreign policy and military actions [aimed] at the reestablishment of a free and democratic Poland."

56. Ibid., pp. 126–33.

57. A military intelligence report on the Mikhoels-Feffer visit to Canada, for example, noted that the two Soviets' appearances in that country had aroused considerable sympathy for the Russians in general and specifically with the Russian war aim of taking over all of the Ukraine from Poland. Gano to Polish Defense Ministry, 30 September 1943 (L. dz. 5370/wyw. tj. 43), AIP—A.XII.3/40a.

58. "Okólnik Organizacyjny Ministerstwa Informacji No. 1/43," 27 August 1943, and "Program Pracy Referatu," 4 September 1943, HIA-PG, Box 801 (MID), File: "Referat Belgia, Holandia, Luxemburg, oraz Sprawy Żydowskie."

59. Gano to Polish Defense Ministry, 30 September 1943 (L. dz. 5370/wyw.

tj. 43), AIP—A.XII.3/40a.; also "Sprawy żydowskie," 25 August 1943, AIP—A.48/10a.

60. "Sprawy żydowskie," 25 August 1943, AIP—A.48/10a. This document hinted that a breach in Jewish affinity for the Soviets might open once Jews understood that the Russians, who sought to undermine British imperial power in the Middle East, had a vested interest in promoting Arab nationalism.

61. See, for example, "Sprawy żydowskie w Palestynie," n.d., AIP—A.XII. 3/40a.

62. "O rozmowach Jana Karskiego z politykami i publicystami angielskimi," n.d., HIA-Karski, Box 1, File 7. See also Karski, *Story of a Secret State*, pp. 383–85.

63. Karski interview.

64. Ibid.

65. Karski, *Story of a Secret State*, pp. 385–86.

66. "Raport Znamirowskiego-Karskiego z jego podróży do Stanów Zjednoczonych A.P.," 5 October 1943, HIA-Karski, Box 1, File 7.

67. "Notatka z rozmowy z Prezydentem F. D. Roosevelt'em . . . ," 28 July 1943, ibid.

68. In 1985 Karski wrote, "In August 1943 [*sic*] a courier from the Polish Underground, Jan Karski, was dispatched to Washington with a mission to report on the situation in Poland and on the Nazi extermination of the Jews." Karski, *The Great Powers and Poland*, p. 461. The inaccuracy of the date should serve as an indication that Karski did not check the relevant documents—which do not mention any assignment to report on the Jewish situation—before writing this sentence. Moreover, in 1982, when asked specifically whether he had been encouraged by his government to meet with Jewish leaders in the United States, he replied that he "did not receive any instructions or any mission" regarding the Jews from any government figure or Jewish leader in London. Karski interview. His subsequent meetings with Jewish leaders in New York had not been contemplated prior to his audience with Roosevelt. See below.

In preparation for the meeting with Roosevelt, Ambassador Ciechanowski reportedly gave Karski a list of subjects that he was to emphasize: "the attitude of the Poles toward the person of the president; the disloyal and destructive activity of Communist agents; the extent and official character of the underground authorities; the efficiently functioning liaison [of the underground] with the government; the general attitude of the country toward the government; the preparatory work for the period of revolt; underground contacts with the Czechs, Slovaks, and Lithuanians; the attitude toward the concept of [an East Central European] federation; the existence and extent of German terror and Polish losses; the extermination of the Jews." "Notatka z rozmowy" (see previous note). This final phrase constitutes the only indication that a Polish official other than Karski himself ever expressed a desire to see the courier speak about Jewish matters. For additional details on the context and content of Karski's visit to the United States, see Engel, "Jan Karski's Mission," pp. 367–70.

69. According to Karski's own report of the conversation, Roosevelt had asked Karski how German terror in Poland was expressed. The courier began by describing atrocities committed against Poles, stressing the German application of the principle of collective responsibility. Roosevelt then questioned the death statistics being promulgated by the Polish government. Karski argued that casualty figures do not always convey an accurate picture of reality. In this context he noted that 80,000 to 100,000 Poles had already lost their lives in Auschwitz, "indeed the most horrible concentration camp," but he added that there were many other "concentration camps for Poles" both in Poland and in Germany—including Majdanek, Treblinka, Bełżec, Stanisławów, Dachau, Oranienburg, Mauthausen, and Ravensbrück—with which people were less familiar. It was at this point that Karski observed that "many people are also not aware to what a horrible fate the Jewish population is subject." He mentioned that 1.8 million Jews had already been murdered in Poland and explained that whereas the Germans sought to obliterate the Polish nation as a nation (while leaving the Polish masses, bereft of their leaders, in place), they strove to kill each and every individual Jew. "Notatka z rozmowy" (see above, n. 67).

There is an additional account of Karski's meeting with Roosevelt, written four years after the event by Ambassador Ciechanowski, who served as Karski's interpreter during the meeting. Although Ciechanowski appears to have embellished many details of the conversation (he wrote, for example, that Karski had told Roosevelt that he had been "to the two murder camps, Treblinka and Belzec," whereas in fact Karski had been at most to the latter only and had never claimed to have been in Treblinka), his account bears out that Karski raised the Jewish issue on his own initiative as an addendum to a discussion of German terror against Poles. Ciechanowski, *Defeat in Victory*, pp. 180–90, esp. p. 182.

70. In his account of the conversation, written immediately upon its conclusion, Karski noted that Roosevelt interrupted his recitation on the Jewish situation only once, to ask whether the Poles were cooperating with the Jews. "Notatka z rozmowy" (see above, n. 67). Karski later noted that he was "disappointed that the president did not say anything specific on this subject" and characterized his response as "rather noncommittal." Karski interview. For additional details on the audience, see Engel, "Jan Karski's Mission," p. 370.

71. Karski interview.

72. Karski, in *Story of a Secret State*, p. 387, claimed that he met with Goldmann, Wise, and others before meeting with Roosevelt. This statement is contradicted by his own contemporary reports, which date all of his meetings with Jewish leaders on 9–10 August. "II. Raport," n.d., HIA-Karski, Box 1, File 7.

73. "II. Raport" (see previous note). See also "Raport Znamirowskiego-Karskiego" (see above, n. 66).

74. "Raport Nr. 3 J. Karskiego z pobytu w U.S.A.: Sprawy żydowskie," n.d., HIA-Karski, Box 1, File 7.

75. Ibid. Presumably he was referring to the Committee for Aid to Jews, which operated under the auspices of the Government Delegacy. Later in the same report he spoke of "the cell in the Government Delegacy charged with organizing aid for the Jews."

76. Ibid. The Polish text is as follows: "Ten punkt mojego referatu budził zainteresowanie u wszystkich Żydów bez względu na ich przekonania i przynależność partyjną. Muszę podkreślić, iż fakt, że nie mogłem się na to powołać, robi tu doskonałe wrażenie i dużo pomaga sprawie polskiej w żydowskich środowiskach amerykańskich." The latter sentence appears senseless unless the negative "nie" is removed; it is thus assumed that the appearance of the word in the text is an error. The fact that the text is in general marked by numerous typographical errors makes this assumption plausible.

77. Ibid. Emphasis in original. In another section of his report Karski noted that both Jewish and non-Jewish leaders had frequently expressed concern about the role played by General Sosnkowski in Polish politics. These people, according to Karski, "regarded Gen. Sosnkowski as a nationalist and antisemite harboring programs [reflecting] a negative attitude toward Russia." Karski responded that Sosnkowski was looked upon as a military rather than a political figure and that "public opinion in the homeland . . . does not regard him either as an antisemite or as a programmatic foe of Russia." "Raport Nr. 3 J. Karskiego . . . : Reakcje kluczowych osobistości amerykańskich na mój referat," HIA-Karski, Box 1, File 7.

78. "Raport Nr. 3" (see above, n. 74). Emphasis in original.

79. Ibid. Emphasis in original.

80. "Konferencja z prezesami American Jewish Congress i World Jewish Congress, Dr. Stephen Wise i Dr. Nahum Goldman," n.d., YVA—M2/62. Despite its title, the report in fact considered the full range of Karski's meetings with all of the various Jewish organizations.

81. Karski made several mistakes here. "Goldman" refers to Nahum Goldmann, who at the time was chairman of the executive board of the World Jewish Congress. "Baldman" is undoubtedly Morris Waldman, executive vice-president and executive secretary of the American Jewish Committee. There was no such organization as the "World Jewish Committee."

82. The quotation is from a fragment (labeled section 8, pp. 20–22) of an unidentified document, obviously written by Karski, located in HIA-Karski, Box 1, File 8.

83. "Raport Nr. 3" (see above, n. 74).

84. "Konferencja z prezesami" (see above, n. 80).

85. "Raport Nr. 3" (see above, n. 74).

86. Ibid. Emphasis in original.

87. Cable, Ciechanowski to Polish Foreign Ministry, 23 September 1943 (Nr. 508), HIA-PG, Box 700, File 851/e, Subfile: "Pieniądze dla Żydów w Kraju."

88. Strakacz to Polish Foreign Ministry, 21 September 1943, HIA-PG, Box 700, File 851/e, Subfile: "Żydzi—prześladowania niemieckie."

89. Cable, Emil Schmorak, Jewish Agency, to Schwarzbart, 30 September 1943, ibid. See also Schwarzbart to Banaczyk, 26 October 1943, YVA—M2/265.

90. See above, n. 88. According to Tartakower, Karski had told him that the underground had already taken steps aimed at getting Jewish leaders out of the country.

91. Each shipment of funds appears to have been handled on an ad hoc basis. See, for example, the discussion over how to deal with the first installment of monies received from the Joint Distribution Committee, in cable, Ciechanowski to Polish Foreign Ministry, 23 September 1943 (Nr. 508); Banaczyk to Romer, 4 October 1943; and cable, Ciechanowski to Polish Foreign Ministry, 12 October 1943, HIA-PG, Box 700, File 851/e, Subfile: "Pieniądze dla Żydów w Kraju." See also Schwarzbart's discussion with Banaczyk over how to transfer funds provided by the Jewish Agency, "Konferencja z Ministrem Banaczykiem . . . ," 20 September 1943, YVA—M2/72.

92. Jewish National Committee to Schwarzbart, 25 October 1943 (Parafraza No. 192), YVA—M2/265; Berezowski to Stańczyk, n.d., YVA—06/48a.10c. In November 1943 the Jewish National Committee reported that to date the Government Delegacy had transferred to it the sum of $40,000, far less than Jewish groups claimed to have sent for it. "Sprawozdanie finansowe Żydowskiego Komitetu Narodowego . . . ," 15 November 1943, AIP—PRML. 57. On amounts sent by Jewish organizations, see above, Chapter 1, n. 177.

93. "Konferencja z Ministrem Banaczykiem . . . ," 20 September 1943, YVA —M2/72. The earliest written accounting from official government sources in Schwarzbart's files of funds transmitted from abroad to Jewish organizations in the occupied homeland appears to be one dated 19 January 1945. "Zestawienie dokonanych wypłat Organizacjom Żydowskim w Kraju," YVA—M2/267.

94. "Konferencja z Ministrem Banaczykiem . . . ," 20 September 1943, YVA—M2/72. See also Schwarzbart to Banaczyk, 19 August 1943, ibid.

95. This was not the first time that Knoll had written the government-in-exile about Jewish matters. On an earlier memorandum, written in March 1940, see Engel, *In the Shadow of Auschwitz*, p. 65.

96. "Excerpt from a Memorandum by Roman Knoll . . . ," in Ringelblum, *Polish-Jewish Relations*, pp. 256–58.

97. Knoll's full description of Polish attitudes toward Jews, until the sentence quoted in the text, was as follows: "At this moment, Christian compassion for the tormented Jews is predominant in the Homeland; at the same time, however, a very strong animus prevails against the Jews in the eastern part of Poland. This is an aftermath of the period of Bolshevik occupation.

In the Homeland as a whole—independently of the general psychological situation at any given moment—the position is such that the return of the Jews to their jobs and workshops is completely out of the question, even if the number of Jews were greatly reduced. The non-Jewish population has filled the places of the Jews in the towns and cities; in a large part of Poland this is a fundamental change, final in character." He then added that "the Government is correct in its assurance to world opinion that anti-Semitism will not exist in Poland; but it will not exist only if the Jews who survive do not endeavour to return *en masse* to Poland's cities and towns."

98. He preferred "an East European territory for the future Jewish State in preference to Palestine, which is too small for the purpose, too exotic and arouses conflicts in the Arab world, and in preference to some tropical colony, to which the Jews will refuse to emigrate." He felt that such an idea could be presented in cooperation with "Jewish Zionist circles" and that it would thus be looked upon by "world public opinion" as having not "an anti-Jewish, but a philo-Jewish character."

99. On these risks, see above, Chapter 1.

100. See Olgierd Górka, "Notatka," 14 December 1943, HIA-PG, Box 702 (MSZ), File: Mniejszości Żydzi."

101. The Revisionists had split with the mainstream Zionists over several issues. They demanded, among other things, that the World Zionist Organization state publicly and unequivocally that the ultimate goal of Zionism was the establishment of a sovereign Jewish state in Palestine on both sides of the Jordan River (rather than an autonomous "national home") and that it promote mass Jewish immigration to Palestine (in contrast to the policy of selective immigration pursued by the Zionist Organization during the 1930s). See Schechtman and Benari, *History of the Revisionist Movement*; Shavit, *Jabotinsky and the Revisionist Movement*.

102. See Engel, *In the Shadow of Auschwitz*, p. 42, and "HaBerit haNichzevet," pp. 336–37. Jabotinsky had evidently felt a close ideological affinity with the prewar Polish regime. See Shavit, *HaMitologiyah shel haYamin*, pp. 15–62.

103. Engel, *In the Shadow of Auschwitz*, pp. 66–67, 110–12, and "HaBerit haNichzevet," pp. 338–46.

104. Engel, *In the Shadow of Auschwitz*, p. 112.

105. Engel, "HaBerit haNichzevet," p. 350.

106. Prominent among these were Marek Kahan, a Warsaw attorney who before the war had served as the Revisionist movement's liaison with various Polish government agencies, and Miron Szeskin, former head of the Polish Jewish veterans' organization known as *Berit HaHayal*. In October 1941 these two men had drafted a proposal for General Anders calling for the establishment of separate Jewish units in the ranks of the exile army. Anders had discussed the proposal with Ambassador Kot before rejecting it—not, as Lukas, in *Strange Allies*, p. 16, suggests, because of the general's commitment to the principle of integration in the ranks, but, among other reasons, be-

cause Kahan and Szeskin were close to Piłsudskist elements in the army whom both Anders and Kot regarded as politically unreliable. See Kahan interview; also Litvak, *Pelitim Yehudim*, pp. 227–29; Nussbaum, "'Legyon Yehudi,'" pp. 47–54. Kahan and Szeskin had indeed continued to maintain close ties with acquaintances from the prewar Polish army who held command positions under Anders, especially Gens. Michał Tokarzewski and Leopold Okulicki. Under the patronage of these generals the two men had assumed positions as unofficial advisors to the army's intelligence branch, preparing reports on propaganda matters and on the political situation in the Middle East. See, for example, M. Dogilewski to M. Heitzmann, 29 December 1943 (L. dz. 12790/43), AIP—A.XII. 3/40a; "Notatka o współpracy z organizacją rewizjoniści w Palestynie," January 1944, and M. Kahan, "Wrażenia z pobytu w Palestynie," 1 May 1943, HIA-Anders, Box 70, Document 139; and digests of reports by Szeskin, AIP—A.XII. 1/65. See also Kahan interview.

Other Revisionists from Poland who assisted Polish military intelligence were Menahem Buchwajc, a Kraków attorney, who supervised Jewish matters for the army's Document Bureau; Jan Bader, former editor of a Polish-language Revisionist newspaper and one of the authors of Jabotinsky's so-called evacuation program of 1936, who prepared several propaganda brochures for Polish military authorities; and Shimshon Juniczman, a former Revisionist Central Committee member, who served as an intelligence agent in Palestine. See Head of Political Department, Polish Ministry of National Defense, to Minister of National Defense, 10 November 1944, and Heitzmann to Zając, 10 November 1944, YVA—O25/72; M. Buchwajc, "Obserwacje i wrażenia z Palestyny," 20 May 1943, HIA-Anders, Box 70, Document 140; M. Buchwajc, "Żydzi polscy pod władzą sowiecką," AIP—KOL. 138/254.

107. See "Sprawa żydowska w Palestynie jako teren obserwacji polityki światowej mocarstw," 13 June 1943, HIA-Anders, Box 70, Document 158; Olgierd Górka, "Notatka," 14 December 1943, HIA-PG, Box 702 (MSZ), File: "Mniejszości Żydzi"; Kahan interview.

108. On the origins of the Irgun and its subsequent development, see Niv, *Ma'arachot haIrgun*.

109. This decision had led a minority faction, under the leadership of Avraham Stern, a former Irgun representative in Poland, to break away from the Irgun and to form a new military group known as Irgun Tseva'i Le'umi beYisra'el. This organization continued small-scale military actions against the mandatory authorities in Palestine until Stern's assassination by British security forces in February 1942. In early 1944 remnants of this group reconstituted themselves into Lohamei Herut Yisra'el, or Lehi. See Heller, *Lehi*, 1:83–110.

110. Cf. the words of Menahem Begin in July 1943: "A rescue regime must be established in Palestine immediately. There are still millions of Jews in Europe. But Hitler will destroy them as he retreats. . . . Nevertheless it is still possible to save them. The Balkans, Hungary, and certainly Poland as well are

territories for possible evacuation. . . . [We cannot] put off the war [against Britain] until tomorrow." Quoted in Shavit, *HaMitologiyah shel haYamin*, pp. 144–45. For a somewhat different view of the origins of the call to renew the armed struggle, see Sofer, *Begin*, pp. 63–67.

111. Memoirs of Aryeh ben Eliezer (MS), JI—P23/2/50 (hereafter cited as Ben Eliezer MS).

112. Ibid., P23/2/51.

113. See Sofer, *Begin*, pp. 58–61.

114. The episode of Begin's release from the Polish army is shrouded in legend. According to the version generally propagated by him and other Revisionists, it had first been proposed that he simply desert the Polish ranks, as many other Jewish soldiers who arrived in Palestine with the Polish forces had done (see below, Chapter 4). Begin, however, is said to have refused, on the grounds that "a deserter, even from an army that is not his own, remains a deserter and is unfit to stand at the head of a national campaign." Ben Eliezer MS, P23/2/52; see also Engel, "HaBerit haNichzevet," p. 333, n. 1. This story raises the question of why Begin and the Irgun, for whom the proposed revolt against the British had become their very raison d'etre and who in any case intended to operate illegally, would insist upon such legal and moral niceties in this case. Attempts by historians to penetrate Revisionist historical mythology have thus far not been able to elucidate this question. See Shavit, *HaMitologiyah shel haYamin*, pp. 125, 140–46. Kahan maintained more than forty years after the event that "difficult as it is to believe, there was nothing more involved [in this matter] than Begin's Polish sense of honor." Kahan interview.

115. T. Lipkowska "Współpraca polsko-żydowska na terenie Palestyny," 7 November 1943, HIA-Anders, Box 70, Doc. 149; Head of Intelligence Service to Head of Political Department, Polish Ministry of National Defense, 7 December 1943 (L. dz. 7024/KW.wyw.tj./43), AIP—A.XII. 3/40a.

116. Ben Eliezer MS, P23/2/52.

117. Ibid.

118. On the establishment of the Emergency Committee, see, inter alia, Wyman, *Abandonment of the Jews*, pp. 146–48.

119. Ben Eliezer MS, P23/2/54. Ben Eliezer continued by noting that "the public activities that we conducted in the United States, which consistently brought together thousands of American citizens, always generated an enormous response, mainly among the representatives of the overrun European countries who were in the United States at the time. They too were interested in mobilizing the power of the public on behalf of their own causes. As a result we were able to establish good contacts not only with American politicians and public figures but also with the representatives of the governments-in-exile, such as Poland, Czechoslovakia, Greece, and Yugoslavia." In reality, however, the Polish representatives in Washington, although undoubtedly impressed by the public attention that the committee obtained, were also

aware of the political difficulties involved in establishing too close a tie to it. See, for example, Ciechanowski to Polish Foreign Minister, 24 September 1943, HIA-PG, Box 700 (MSZ), File 851/e.

120. Ben Eliezer MS, P23/2/55–56.

121. "Notatka," [December 1943], AIP—KOL. 138/237; "Protokół z rozmowy odbytej . . . w mieszkaniu prywatnym Dr. Altmana," 1 December 1943, PC-Kahan. See also "Wysłannik 'Jewish Welfare Committee' w Ameryce—w Palestynie," [December 1943], AIP—KOL. 138/237.

122. Ben Eliezer MS, P23/2/56.

123. The proposal was explicitly discussed in this light; see "Notatka," [December 1943], AIP—KOL 138/237. Ben Eliezer, too, evidently took note of the Polish government's precarious position in formulating his idea. As he later wrote, "The Polish government-in-exile . . . had begun to lose its authority and strength following the departure of General Sikorski, who had been killed in an air accident." Ben Eliezer MS, P23/2/54.

124. Cable, Stroński to Kot, 3 September 1942 (no. 426), HIA-PG, Box 459 (MSZ), File 851/e; Tadeusz Kiersnowski, "Notatka," 7 October 1942 (Nr. 4985/Ia/42), AIP—PRM. 88/2. See also Engel, "HaBerit haNichzevet," p. 348.

125. The Revisionists made approaches to Tokarzewski through other channels in addition to military intelligence. One of their intermediaries was evidently Wiktor Drymmer, head of the Consular Department of the Polish Foreign Ministry during the late 1930s, who in that capacity had presided over the Polish government's effort to bring about the emigration of masses of Jews from Poland. In this context he had developed close relations with the Revisionist movement, which also sought to promote mass emigration. Drymmer had arrived in Palestine as a civilian refugee early in the war. See Korboński, "Unknown Chapter," pp. 376–77. On the emigration policy and Revisionist attitudes toward it, see, inter alia, Melzer, *Ma'avak Medini beMalkodet*, pp. 140–63, 319–38; Pobóg-Malinowski, *Najnowsza historia*, 2:807–21.

126. The contents of the order were reported in Head of Political Department, Polish Ministry of National Defense, to Minister of National Defense, 10 November 1944, YVA—O25/72. Begin was not actually discharged from the ranks but was merely granted a leave of absence for one year for the purpose of joining the delegation to the United States. Although the delegation never actually left Palestine, Marek Kahan, who played a role in securing Begin's release, has maintained that Begin was not recalled to service. Silver, *Begin*, p. 41; Kahan interview. On the other hand, Anders wrote in his 1946 memoirs that "at the head of the terrorist activity in Palestine stood a deserter from the Second Corps . . . , Begin." Anders, *Bez ostatniego rozdziału*, p. 201. It is extremely difficult to determine, on the basis of the documentary evidence that has been located until now, whether Begin was in fact regarded by Polish military authorities as a deserter. The document cited at the beginning of this note stated that Begin "is sought by the Polish and English authorities because of terrorist activity." This document, however, was prepared in

response to a British inquiry concerning known Irgun members who had entered Palestine with the Polish forces. The inquiry was made shortly following the assassination of the British minister of state in the Near East, Lord Moyne—an assassination actually carried out by Lehi, a radical Irgun offshoot (see above, n. 109), but in which Begin was suspected by the British of having had a hand. In this context the Polish authorities had an interest in maintaining that they did not countenance Begin's absence from the ranks. Another Polish document prepared in response to the same inquiry dealt with the status of two other Revisionist soldiers slated to join the delegation, Menahem Treller and Zalman Karasik. According to this document, these two soldiers had indeed never been ordered to return to the ranks, but this failure was attributed to the fact that "they are hiding, and as a result . . . it is impossible to present them with an order to report." However, the document specified that Treller and Karasik, unlike Begin, had been given an indefinite leave of absence and that for this reason they were not regarded officially as deserters. M. Heitzman to Gen. J. Zając, 13 November 1944, YVA—O25/72. It is possible perhaps to infer from this statement that because Begin did not receive an indefinite leave of absence, he could have been considered a deserter. However, not only do the same reservations about the timing of this document apply to it as to the document of 10 November, but no official document has as yet been adduced that refers specifically to Begin's status in the Polish army after 31 December 1943.

127. "Notatka" (see above, n. 121).

128. Ibid.

129. Lipkowska, "Współpraca polsko-żydowska na terenie Palestyny" (see above, n. 115).

130. Ibid. The author of this memorandum, Teresa Lipkowska, was the sister-in-law of General Sosnkowski. According to one testimony, she intervened personally with the Polish military leadership in Palestine on behalf of Ben Eliezer's plan. Kahan interview.

131. Shortly after this memorandum was composed, a series of articles in the weekly organ of the dominant Mapai party in Jewish Palestine explained that under no circumstances could Poland expect to recover all of its prewar territory and called upon the Polish government to adopt a conciliatory attitude toward the Soviet Union. If there was any flexibility in this stance, it was to be found only to the extent that the author of the articles expressed the hope that the Soviets would not insist upon retaining all of the territories captured in 1939 and would thereby do their part in promoting amicable Polish-Soviet relations. *HaPo'el HaTsa'ir*, 23 December 1943 (B[inyamin] W[est], "Rusiyah, Polin, veTschechiyah"); 27 January 1944 (B[inyamin] W[est], "Yahasei Polin-Rusiyah"); 10 February 1944 (B[inyamin] W[est], "Im haShinnu'im beHukat Berit-HaMo'atsot").

132. The invocation of Chmielnicki's name by the Soviets was also, in light of the state of Polish-Soviet relations at the time, undoubtedly a provocation directed against the Poles. The massacres of Jews had taken place as part of a

rebellion against Polish rule in the Ukraine, which had claimed many Polish victims as well.

133. Dogilewski to Polish information minister, 21 October 1943, HIA-PG, Box 801 (MID), File: "Referat Belgia, Holandia, Luxemburg, oraz Sprawy Żydowskie."

134. Reprezentacja, *Sprawozdanie*, p. 141.

135. Ibid., p. 145.

136. Ibid., pp. 145–47. Despite such loyal rhetoric, Strassburger appears to have been convinced of the validity of several of the Jewish complaints; at least he said as much in a cable to Adam Romer sent several weeks following the meeting. Among these valid complaints he noted "that one minister comes after another, discusses various matters, makes promises, goes away, and the matter is dropped." Cable, Strassburger to Romer, 9 January 1944, HIA-PG, Box 223 (MSZ), File 851-e/44: "Żydzi w Palestynie."

137. Reprezentacja, *Sprawozdanie*, p. 128. The Polish minister indeed lacked information. On the day after the meeting, he cabled Mikołajczyk and the Foreign Ministry as follows: "In Jerusalem I received the Representation of Polish Jewry, which complains that the assistance given by the government to the Jewish population in the homeland has been insufficient and has been distributed in discriminatory fashion in comparison with aid for the Christian population. [The Reprezentacja complains further] that thus far it has not been informed whether and how the sum of £25,000 that it transmitted this year from Jerusalem in two installments (£10,000 in April and £15,000 in October) for this purpose [of rescue] has been put to use. Please send me information on both matters." Cable, Strassburger to Mikołajczyk and Polish Foreign Ministry, 18 December 1943, HIA-PG, Box 223, File 851-e/44. This information was not forthcoming, and Strassburger had to request it again in a cable to Adam Romer on 9 January 1944 (see previous note). On 31 January 1944, Feliks Frankowski of the Foreign Ministry informed Strassburger that "the £25,000 has been received [but] is awaiting clearance and a means for spending it [*oczekuje się rozliczeń i sposobu zużycia*]." Cable, Frankowski to Strassburger, 31 January 1944, HIA-PG, Box 223, File 851-e/44.

138. Actually, a new nuance did appear in the discussion, one that seems to have been in keeping with the more optimistic evaluation of the future of Jewish-Soviet relations then being put forth in Polish military circles in Palestine. Strassburger claimed that the Soviets had been responsible for the small number of Jews evacuated from the USSR with the Polish armed forces, "because they feared anti-Soviet propaganda on the part of the Jews." Stupp interrupted, commenting, "This is very interesting, because up to now we have been hearing from the Polish side that the Jews were fraternizing with the Bolsheviks." Apolinary Hartglas, another Reprezentacja delegate, added that "something does not hold up here [*coś się tu nie klei*] . . . , because up to now the anti-Jewish atmosphere in the army has been explained by the argument that the Jews demonstrated a favorable attitude toward

the Bolsheviks." Strassburger abruptly changed the subject. Reprezentacja, *Sprawozdanie*, p. 146.

139. "Audiencja u Premiera Mikołajczyka," 13 January 1944, YVA—M2/80.

140. The assumption of the likelihood of Bund influence in a Jewish department supervised by the Labor Ministry probably stemmed from the fact that Labor Minister Stańczyk was a member of PPS and thus stood closer politically to the Bund than to any other Jewish group.

141. They subsequently raised it again through other channels and met with a similar although not entirely identical response. See below, Chapter 5.

CHAPTER FOUR

1. Virtually all sources, both Polish and Jewish, place the number of deserters at sixty-eight. See, for example, "Lista imienna" [a handwritten list of the sixty-eight soldiers, including serial numbers and unit assignments], 26 January 1944, YVA—M2/66; "Raport dzienny," 26 January 1944, YVA—M2/100; "Facts Concerning Attempted Disaffection among Jewish and Orthodox Soldiers in the Polish Army in Great Britain" [an explanatory pamphlet prepared by the Polish Foreign Ministry], HIA-PG, Box 227 (MSZ), File Z851/e: "Dezercja Żydów z Armii Polskiej, 1944"; untitled, undated statement beginning with the words, "W związku z dezercję [*sic*] pierwszej grupy żołnierzy-Żydów (68 żołnierzy)...," PC-Okręt, OF-11. Lukas, in *The Forgotten Holocaust*, pp. 137, 256, places the number at seventy-nine, citing a letter from Sosnkowski to the Polish president of 4 July 1944. The discrepancy in this letter is undoubtedly a typographical error; it is easily explained by assuming that the typist's right hand was positioned one key too far to the right when typing the figure. The Polish minister of defense, Marian Kukiel, once placed the number at only sixty—also most likely a typographical error. Kukiel to Gen. A. E. Grasett, British liaison officer to the Polish forces, 26 January 1944, HIA-PG, Box 227, File Z851/e.

2. Kukiel to Grasett (see previous note).

3. D. Allen, British Foreign Office, to Major Dru, British War Office, 24 January 1944, and attached minutes, PRO—FO 371/39480.C1087.

4. Komisja MON dla sprawy masowej dezercji żołnierzy-Żydów to Polish Defense Minister, 25 February 1944, HIA-PG, Box 227, File Z851/e. See also Schwarzbart and Tartakower to Kukiel, 19 January 1944, YVA—M2/100.

5. See Wasserstein, *Britain and the Jews of Europe*, p. 127. The Polish government had been stung previously by public complaints about the treatment of Jews in the Polish forces in Britain. See Engel, *In the Shadow of Auschwitz*, pp. 70–77, 87–88.

6. These reasons had to do most likely with the government's desire to fend off parliamentary criticism in the wake of the Tehran conference in Novem-

ber 1943. See Engel, "HaBerihah haHafganatit," pp. 192–94. See also Frank Savery to Tadeusz Romer (?), 13 April 1944, HIA-PG, Box 227, File Z851/e.

7. "Lista Nr. 1," [handwritten date of receipt 4 April 1944], YVA—M2/66, lists 136 soldiers by name. Most other sources place the number of deserters in the second group at 134. See, for example, "Sprawozdanie Ministra Obrony Narodowej o dezercji żołnierzy z wojska w Wielkiej Brytanii," n.d., YVA—O25/72.

8. The British warning appears to have been motivated by several factors. For one thing, the government maintained that should the 600 Jewish soldiers who remained in the Polish forces following the departure of the second group seek an arrangement similar to the one granted to those who had already deserted, the battle readiness of the affected Polish units, which were scheduled to take part in the upcoming invasion of France, would be impaired. See, for example, minute by D. Allen, 15 March 1944, PRO—FO 371/39480.C3386; Redman to Dixon, 22 March 1944, PRO—FO 371/39480.C3843. See also the remarks by Richard Law in the House of Commons, 6 April 1944, in Jędrzejewicz, *Poland in the British Parliament*, 3:471–72. There are also indications that some British officials worried that their willingness to accept deserters from another Allied force into their ranks might encourage similar defections by other disaffected minorities. See, for example, the confidential memorandum by Thomas Driberg, MP, 3 April 1944, HIA-PG, Box 226 (MSZ), File 851/e: "Żydzi w Armii Polskiej i dezercja Żydów." Moreover, shortly after the desertion of the second group the parliamentary debate over the results of the Tehran conference had come, from the government's standpoint, to a satisfactory close, meaning that the political considerations that had earlier encouraged it to go along with Polish desires regarding the soldiers no longer applied. See Engel, "HaBerihah haHafganatit," p. 194.

9. Proclamation by Polish Defense Ministry, office of the minister, 13 March 1944 (L. dz. 2345/W.Pol./44), HIA-PG, Box 227, File Z851/e. The order was to be read aloud before all units at assembly.

10. "Naczelny Wódz: Rozkaz Nr. 4," 20 March 1944, ibid. Sosnkowski appears in general to have favored attempting to remove the causes of the desertions as opposed to Kukiel's general tactic of placing the entire onus for the affair upon the deserters. As early as 26 January he wrote to Kukiel that in his opinion "the struggle against instances of antisemitism . . . is necessary both from a humanitarian and a general political perspective." Sosnkowski to Kukiel, 26 January 1944 (L. dz. 126/GNW/44), AIP—A.XII.1/65. On Kukiel's attitude, see below.

11. "Sprawozdanie Ministra Obrony Narodowej" (see above, n. 7).

12. "Lista żołnierzy-Żydów, przytrzymanych w dn. 30.III.44r.," YVA—M2/66.

13. According to official Polish statistics, there were 714 Jewish soldiers serving with the Polish forces in Great Britain at the beginning of 1943.

"Dane statystyczne dotyczące Żydów w Wojsku Polskim," HIA-PG, Box 227, File Z851/e.

14. "Sprawozdanie z przebiegu obrad 8-go Sądu Polowego . . . ," 24 April 1944, YVA—M2/100. See also untitled memorandum signed by Karol Kraczkiewicz, 4 May [1944], HIA-PG, Box 227, File Z851/e.

15. See "Memorandum on the Desertion of Eastern Orthodox Slavs (White Russians and Ukrainians) from the Polish Army," n.d., HIA-PG, Box 227, File Z851/e.

16. "Sprawozdanie Ministra Obrony Narodowej" (see above, n. 7).

17. Ibid.

18. Raczyński, for example, spoke of a "witch-hunt against Polish anti-Semitism." Raczyński, *In Allied London*, p. 213.

19. Jędrzejewicz, *Poland in the British Parliament*, 2:426–94.

20. Cable, Ciechanowski to Romer, 27 April 1944, HIA-PG, Box 227, File Z851/e; Ciechanowski to Congressman Emanuel Cellar, 27 April 1944, HIA-US, Box 1, File 2.

21. Wasserstein, *Britain and the Jews of Europe*, p. 128.

22. See Polonsky, *The Great Powers and the Polish Question*, pp. 29–30. See also Raczyński, *In Allied London*, p. 186: "Eden . . . warned us against returning a . . . hostile reply [to the Soviet demands regarding Poland's eastern border]. He made it abundantly clear that if we did so the British Government would . . . regard itself as having discharged . . . its obligation towards Poland."

23. See Polonsky, *The Great Powers and the Polish Question*, pp. 163–71.

24. See Babiński, *Przyczynki historyczne*, pp. 209–11; Ciechanowski, *Defeat in Victory*, pp. 258–59.

25. "Declaration by the Polish Government in connection with the crossing of the Polish frontier by Soviet troops," 5 January 1944, in *DPSR*, 2:123–24.

26. Polonsky, *The Great Powers and the Polish Question*, p. 173.

27. Ibid., p. 175. See also "Komunikat agencji TASS o oświadczeniu rządu Związku Radzieckiego w sprawie stosunków polsko-radzieckich," 11 January 1944, in *Stosunki polsko-radzieckie*, pp. 378–79.

28. "War Cabinet Minutes (Extracts)," 25 January 1944, in Polonsky, *The Great Powers and the Polish Question*, p. 176.

29. "Manifest demokratycznych organizacji społeczno-politycznych i wojskowych w Polsce," 15 December 1943, in *Stosunki polsko-radzieckie*, p. 371. Emphasis in original.

30. Ibid., pp. 369–70.

31. See Babiński, *Przyczynki historyczne*, pp. 213–19.

32. Indeed, in 1940, when similar charges of ill-treatment of Jews in the Polish forces had been brought to the attention of Parliament in less dramatic fashion, one MP had remarked that "the feelings of Poles toward Jews can only be paralleled by the feelings of Germans toward Jews." Engel, *In the Shadow of Auschwitz*, p. 71.

33. Szef Sądu Polowego przy D-twie APW to Szef Służby Sprawiedliwości APW, 18 October 1942 (L. Dz. 5/Sąd/42/Tjn), AIP—KOL.25/24. On the total number of Jewish evacuees, see Nussbaum, *VeHafach lahem leRo'ets*, p. 65.

34. "Notatka z przebiegu konferencji w M. S. Wewn.," 6 August 1943, AIP—PRM.114/3; "W sprawie dezercji Żydów z Armii Polskiej," [mid-1943], HIA-Anders, Box 71, Doc. 289; Łunkiewicz, Political Division, Polish Ministry of Defense, to Polish Foreign Ministry, 6 September 1943 (L. dz. 735/WPol/43), AIP—A.12/755/2; cable, Anders to Sosnkowski, n.d. (with covering letter dated 2 October 1943), AIP—PRM.114/13; memorandum by Kazimierz Chodkiewicz, Office of Chief of Military Police, Polish Ministry of Defense, entitled "Zestawienie zbiegów," 30 November 1943, AIP—A.XII.3/33; "Wyciąg z raportu Konsula Generalnego R. P. w Jerozolimie," 1 December 1943 (Nr. 52/Pl/9/43), AIP—A.XII.3/40a; Marceli Dogilewski to Marian Heitzman, Polish Ministry of Defense, 29 December 1943 (L. dz. 12790/43), AIP—A.XII.3/40a. Anders, in *Bez ostatniego rozdziału*, p. 201, claimed that "over 3,000 Jews left the ranks of the corps." There is no support for such a figure in any contemporary documents located to date; on the contrary, Anders himself, in his cable to Sosnkowski listed above, gave a figure of 1,000, and in a meeting with the Reprezentacja on 19 September 1943, of 1,500 deserters. Reprezentacja, *Sprawozdanie*, p. 134. The highest figure listed in any Polish source is 2,064 deserters as of 4 January 1944. See "Dane statystyczne dotyczące Żydów w Wojsku Polskim," HIA-PG, Box 227, File Z851/e.

35. Estimates of the number of Jewish soldiers taken out of the Soviet Union by the Polish forces range from 1,900 to 4,000. See Engel, *In the Shadow of Auschwitz*, p. 278. On the other hand, the number of actual deserters may have been less than that reported in any of the Polish estimates. Together with the soldiers, some 1,700 to 2,500 Jewish civilians had been evacuated from the USSR in 1942. A number of these possessed immigration certificates to Palestine and were anxious to take up residence in that country, but the governments of Iraq and Transjordan would not grant them transit visas across their territories for that purpose. Eventually an arrangement was made between Jewish Agency and Polish army officials whereby some of these civilians would be issued Polish military uniforms so they could cross Iraq and Transjordan and enter Palestine with the relocating Polish forces. In Tehran these Jews had also been given papers stating that they were to be discharged from military service. Evidently, however, this arrangement had been made without the consent of the British mandatory authorities, who had long worried that the presence of Jews among the Polish forces in Palestine would complicate their efforts to limit Jewish immigration into the country. The British apparently suspected that the Poles were assisting Jews to infiltrate the country illegally; when they received word that a transport of 133 Jews had arrived at the Polish military installations at Gedera and Rehovot, they dispatched a team to investigate. Upon hearing that British investigators were on the way to interrogate them, and perhaps fearing that

their immigration certificates might not be honored, all of the Jews simply took off their uniforms and walked out of the camp, as they had planned to do eventually in any case. The commanding officer of the Gedera camp, however, evidently not realizing the complexities of the situation, reported to the British investigators that the Jewish "soldiers" had deserted. In the opinion of the Polish commander of the Palestine sector, however, the Jews involved in this case could not be regarded as deserters. Gen. Wiatr to Kot, 19 January 1943 (L. dz. 176/Tjn/43/Of.Łączn.Pal.), AIP—KOL. 25/24.

36. Szef Sądu Polowego . . . to Szef Służby Sprawiedliwości (see above, n. 33). On the other hand, Jews do not appear to have deserted from Australian units stationed in Palestine.

37. "W sprawie dezercji Żydów z Armii Polskiej," HIA-Anders, Box 71, Doc. 289; Dogilewski to Heitzman, 29 December 1943 (L. dz. 12790/43), AIP—A.XII.3/40a.

38. "W sprawie dezercji" (see previous note).

39. The Jews of Palestine were involved at the time in a struggle to increase their numbers, in the face of British efforts to limit them. Numbers, they realized, stood to play a decisive role in the anticipated future battle over the political disposition of the country, and Jewish organizations were prepared to use illegal means to augment them. They thus had no compunction about aiding Jewish deserters from the Polish army. See Kless, *Gevulot, Mahteret uVerihah*, p. 133. For the testimony of a Palestinian Jewish activist involved in "smuggling Jews out of the Polish army and helping them settle in Palestine," see Dekel, *Shai*, pp. 300–304.

40. Szef Sądu Polowego . . . to Szef Służby Sprawiedliwości (see above, n. 33).

41. "Notatka z przebiegu konferencji" (see above, n. 34); "W sprawie dezercji" (see above, n. 37); Dogilewski to Heitzman, 29 December 1943 (see above, n. 37); letter to Teresa [Lipkowska], 28 November 1943, HIA-Anders, Box 71, Doc. 168; "Sprawy żydowskie w Palestynie," n.d. (L. dz. 8505), AIP—A.XII.3/40a; Polish Ministry of Defense, Armed Reconnaissance Division, to Director, Political Division, Polish Interior Ministry, 2 September 1943 (L. dz. 4753/P.W./43: "Sprawy narodowościowe i komuna w wojsku na Sr. Wsch.—omówienie sytuacji w m. maju br."), AIP—PRM. 114/7.

42. See Engel, "HaSichsuch haPolani-haSovieti," pp. 29–30. See also Reprezentacja, *Sprawozdanie*, p. 123. Among the examples of hostility noted by Jews were repeated instances in which Polish soldiers allegedly said in their presence, "Hitler did one good thing for Poland—he solved the Jewish question; and if a few of them remain in the country, we'll take care of them ourselves after we return." See the report prepared for the chief of staff by Miron Szeskin, one of the Jewish Revisionists who worked for Polish Military Intelligence (see above, Chapter 3), 20 September 1943, AIP—A.XII.1/65.

43. The reference is obviously to Mikhoels and Feffer.

44. "W sprawie dezercji" (see above, n. 37).

45. In his memoirs Anders contended that although "the desertion of such a large number of Jews, some of them well trained, left definite holes in the units," he made no effort to search for the deserting soldiers or to punish them, for he "did not want to have soldiers who were afraid to fight under [his] command." Anders, *Bez ostatniego rozdziału*, p. 201. Contemporary evidence, however, suggests that Anders was extremely concerned about putting an end to the defections and that he even advocated reprisal measures against the deserters' families, including revoking their Polish citizenship. Cable, Anders to Sosnkowski, n.d. (Nr. 244, with cover letter dated 2 October 1943), AIP—PRM. 114/13.

46. "Notatka z przebiegu konferencji" (see above, n. 34). All of the sources listed above in n. 41 either affirm the presence in the ranks of hostile feelings and actions toward Jewish soldiers in notable measure or do not deny the presence of such feelings. The only emphatic denial appears to have come from Anders himself, who at one point reported to Sosnkowski that "since we arrived in Palestine there has not been a single incident with the Jews against an antisemitic background." Cable, Anders to Sosnkowski, 2 October 1943, AIP—PRM. 114/13. The hostility in the ranks was frequently explained either as a reaction to the Jews' alleged treachery during the period of Soviet occupation or as a response to the desertions themselves.

47. The British White Paper of 1939 had severely limited Jewish immigration into Palestine, and the British government had been engaged ever since in a struggle to keep would-be Jewish settlers out of the country. See, inter alia, Wasserstein, *Britain and the Jews of Europe*, pp. 40–80. Even before Polish troops had been evacuated to Palestine, British officials had expressed apprehension that Jewish soldiers would remain there after the Poles had departed. See Engel, *In the Shadow of Auschwitz*, pp. 144–45.

48. See "Sprawa rewizji w kibucu Chulta [*sic*]," (hand dated 5 October [1943]), HIA-Anders, Box 71, Doc. 164; "Oficjalne sprawozdanie podane przez Agencję," hand dated 6 October [1943], HIA-Anders, Box 71, Doc. 162; "W sprawie rewizji w Ramat Hakowesz," n.d., HIA-Anders, Box 71, Doc. 165; cable (unsigned) from Rehovot for commander-in-chief and Romer, n.d. (Nr. 8911), AIP—PRM. 114/13; Anders to Mjr. Gen. D. F. McConnel, 24 November 1943 (Nr. 54/ADC/43), AIP—A.XII.3/40a. The raids also caused anger against the Poles on the part of Jews abroad. See Karol Ripa, Polish consul-general, Chicago, to Polish Embassy, Washington, 4 January 1944, HIA-PG, Box 801 (MID), File: "Referat Belg., Holand., Lux. oraz Sprawy Żydowskie."

49. Aleksy Wdziękoński, Polish consul general, Jerusalem, to unnamed addressee, 25 November 1943, AIP—A.XII.3/40a. See also "Wyciąg z raportu Konsula Generalnego R. P. w Jerozolimie," 1 December 1943 (Nr. 52/Pl/9/43), AIP—A.XII.3/40a. The Poles realized that they were being exploited by the British in an attempt to liquidate the Jewish military underground in Palestine, and they were not anxious to become involved in such an activity. See Frankowski to Wdziękoński, 22 January 1944, HIA-PG, Box 223, File 851/e.

50. Statement by Kukiel, 28 June 1943 (L. dz. 855/WPol/43), AIP—A.XII.1/65.

51. Cable, Kukiel to Anders, 5 July 1943 (L. dz. 893/WPol/43), AIP—A.XII.3/40a.

52. See, for example, "Notatka w sprawie zwalczania antysemityzmu w Armii Polskiej," 9 July 1943, AIP—A.XII.3/40a; "Instrukcja odnośnie zachowania się i postępowania żołnierzy polskich w Palestynie w stosunku do tamtejszej ludności żydowskiej," 1 August 1943, AIP—A.XII.3/40a.

53. "Rozkaz oficerski Nr. 6," 22 July 1943, AIP—A.XII.1/65.

54. "Protokół z posiedzenia Komisji Specjalnej Rady Narodowej . . . ," 5 January 1945 (testimony of Marian Heitzman, head of Political Division, Polish Ministry of Defense), and 25 January 1945 (testimony of Jerzy Flaum, officer in charge of Jewish affairs, Political Division, Polish Ministry of Defense), HIA-RN, Box 8, File 24 (2).

55. See Engel, "HaBerihah haHafganatit," pp. 179–81.

56. See the testimonies presented to the Special Investigating Commission of the Polish National Council at its meetings of 5–11 July 1944, HIA-RN, Box 8, File 24. See also the collection of letters presented by Jewish soldiers in the Polish army to the Committee for a Jewish Army, JI—H3A/3/75; Schwarzbart to Kukiel, 8 June 1943, YVA—M2/66.

57. "Protokół z posiedzenia Komisji Specjalnej Rady Narodowej . . . ," 5, 10 July 1944 (testimonies of soldiers Wilder, Zimmermann, Marber, and Geller), HIA-RN, Box 8, File 24.

58. "Protokół z posiedzenia Komisji Specjalnej Rady Narodowej . . . ," 5 July 1944 (testimony of Max Wald), ibid. Some soldiers even reported having contemplated suicide in the wake of confrontations with the so-called Rommel soldiers. For source citations, see Engel, "HaBerihah haHafganatit," p. 184.

59. Flaum testimony (see above, n. 54).

60. Heitzmann to Kukiel, 12 August 1943 (L. dz. 855/WPol/43), YVA—M2/66.

61. A copy of the newspaper is in YVA—M2/119; another is in HIA-Karski, Box 7. See also Flaum testimony (see above, n. 54).

62. See Heitzman to Kukiel, 12 August 1943 (L. dz. 855/WPol/43), YVA—M2/66: "Antisemitism, as a general phenomenon, organized and apparent from the outside, does not exist as a rule in the ranks of the army. However, instances of unfriendly and even hostile treatment of particular Jewish soldiers do occur. . . . There is an unfavorable attitude toward Jews that is quite widespread; wherever such an attitude exists, there will be outbursts."

63. Heitzman testimony (see above, n. 54). In this testimony Heitzman indicated that the Jewish representatives with whom he had met had accepted his suggestion and for a while had refrained from giving prominence to the question of the treatment of Jews in the Polish army. In one instance, he declared, he had actually been able to resolve the complaints of two Jewish soldiers without any adverse publicity for the Polish government.

64. See Engel, *In the Shadow of Auschwitz*, pp. 77–79, 93–94, 102–6.

65. Schwarzbart to Kukiel, 11 October 1943, YVA—M2/66.

66. See "Protokół z posiedzenia Komisji Specjalnej Rady Narodowej . . . ," 6 July 1944, HIA-RN, Box 8, File 24 (testimony of the soldier Bienenstok).

67. In October 1943 Lt. Jakób Brodt submitted the complaints of six Jewish soldiers to MP D. N. Pritt. See the correspondence on this matter in HIA-PG, Box 226, File 851/e. In November 1943 the soldier Fritz Bornstein approached MP G. R. Strauss, requesting his intervention with the Polish and British authorities on behalf of Bornstein's request for transfer to a unit under British command. See the correspondence in HIA-PG, Box 227, File Z851/e. On 2 February 1944, more than two weeks after the desertion of the first group, seven Jews submitted complaints about their treatment in the ranks to the Committee for a Jewish Army. The letters are located in JI—H3A/3/75. Of these seven soldiers, three eventually deserted with the second group and one with the third group, while three others remained in the Polish army for the duration of the war. Of the six soldiers represented by Brodt, only one left the ranks (with the second group); Brodt himself was released from the Polish army prior to the desertion of the first group. Bornstein did not desert; in March 1944 he was transferred to a British unit, evidently as a direct result of pressure from Strauss.

68. Synaj Okręt to Schwarzbart, 25 August 1943, PC-Okręt, OF-6. The letter demonstrates that Schwarzbart had been in contact with at least some of the most vociferous complainers about conditions in the ranks well before his visit and that he had worked hard at gaining their confidence; at one point the writer spoke of "a change in [the soldiers'] attitude toward your work" that had resulted from a deeper understanding "of the conditions under which you labor and of what your situation is." The writer also stressed that, to his mind and the minds of his companions, the situation in the ranks was getting progressively worse: "Not a day goes by in peace. . . . Our condition is without hope. In this situation of ours there does not appear to be anyone who even shows good will, let alone [a willingness to give us] the help that we need in order to ease our state."

69. See "Notatka P. Lipskiego," n.d., YVA—O25/71; "Sprawozdanie Ministra Obrony Narodowej" (see above, n. 7).

70. Tartakower and Schwarzbart to Polish Defense Ministry, 19 January 1944, YVA—M2/100. These two Jewish representatives informed the deserters of the government's position. On the reaction of the deserters, and on the attitude of the Jewish representatives toward the desertions, see below.

71. See, for example, "Rozmowa z Naczelnym Wodzem Gen. Sosnkowskim . . . ," 12 August 1943, YVA—M2/93; Heitzman to Kukiel, 12 August 1943 (L. dz. 855/WPol/43), YVA—M2/66; Sosnkowski to Kukiel, 26 January 1944 (L. dz. 126/GNW/44), AIP—A.XII. 1/65.

72. Kukiel to Grasett, 26 January 1944, HIA-PG, Box 227, File Z851/e. Kukiel knew quite well, of course, that the desertions in Palestine had been going on long before the Polish divisions were transferred to the front in

Italy and that none of his own investigators had ever suggested that fear of battle had been their primary motivation.

73. Ibid.

74. "Instrukcja dla prac Komisji," 25 January 1944 (L. dz. 1978/WPol/44), YVA—M2/66.

75. Stenographic protocols of the commission's sessions have not yet been located. Besides the commission's own final report there is only indirect evidence, in the form of testimonies, as to what exactly transpired during the sessions.

76. "Komisja MON dla sprawy masowej dezercji żołnierzy-Żydów," 25 February 1944, HIA-PG, Box 227, File Z851/e.

77. All quotations given here are based upon the Polish text of the report. An English version of the report was also prepared. In general it tended to mitigate some of the harsher conclusions of the Polish version regarding the character of Jewish soldiers and to embellish passages that placed the Polish authorities in a positive light. For example, the English version of this particular passage reads as follows: "It is notable that the mass desertion . . . was staged at a time when, after special orders had been issued by the Polish Army HQ, expressions of any anti-Jewish sentiment had disappeared."

78. Among the other causes adduced were "the loss by some Jewish soldiers of their families in the homeland and their plan to settle abroad permanently after the war"; "the uncertainty of the political situation in Poland, especially of its eastern territories and the concomitant lack of desire to return to former places of residence in these territories"; "an intention to acquire British citizenship through service in the British army"; "the influence of the political views of certain sectors of the Jewish community, which aim at the biological defense of the Jewish element"; and finally, "the unfriendly attitude of a certain portion of the Christian soldiers toward Jewish soldiers, expressing itself in isolated incidents and unpleasant remarks."

79. The report specifically singled out Jewish Polish citizens living in South America who had responded to recruitment efforts for the Polish forces that had been conducted earlier in the war, mainly in Argentina, Uruguay, and Brazil. No evidence was adduced, however, as to the number or percentage of Jews who had been recruited in these locations or to their number, percentage, and role among the deserters. On the South American recruitment campaign, see HL—G.D. Poland (Emigré Government), Army: Leaflets and Propaganda Material for the Poles in South America.

80. The same section of the report did acknowledge, however, that "expressions of satisfaction over the persecution of the Jews in the German-occupied territories, especially [when uttered] in the presence of Jewish soldiers, undoubtedly could cause them great pain." The implication, of course, is that such expressions were to be heard, at least on occasion, although the report never said so in as many words. The furthest the report went in admitting the existence of notable hostility toward Jews in the ranks was its statement that "isolated . . . outbursts directed against Jewish soldiers, which

in the specific current atmosphere of arousal could have been interpreted by them as acts of particular hostility dictated by antisemitic feelings, did take place."

81. See the (literally) thousands of pages of correspondence that Schwarzbart maintained on this subject with Jewish soldiers, Polish officials, and other Jewish agencies since 1940, YVA—M2/90–94, 101–11.

82. In addition to the files listed in the previous note, see D. N. Pritt to Polish Foreign Ministry, 6 October 1943, HIA-PG, Box 226, File 851/e; Aide-Mémoire by British Embassy to Poland, 16 November 1943, HIA-PG, Box 227, File Z851/e.

83. Minute by D. Allen, 7 February 1944, PRO—FO 371/39480.C1906. Of the soldiers to whose statements Allen reacted, two had already deserted, three were to defect with the second group, two with the third group, and three not at all.

84. "Letter received 4th February 1944, from Pte. S. Pomeranc from camp in Scotland, on behalf of the Polish Jewish soldiers who had come to London," JI—H3A/3/75.

85. Heitzman to Kukiel, 12 August 1943 (L. dz. 855/WPol/43), YVA—M2/66.

86. When Heitzman had reported on the commanders' views, he had added that in his view weight needed to be given also to the existence of "a fairly widespread antipathy toward Jews" in the ranks. Ibid. This opinion was not reflected in the commission's report. It is also interesting to note that the commission's report did not dwell upon the issue of Communist agitation. It does not appear to be possible to determine the reason for this lacuna, but it seems that in early 1944 the Polish leadership may not have deemed it politically advisable to raise this matter in a public document. See Engel, "HaBerihah haHafganatit," p. 190.

87. Schwarzbart Diary (English), 28 February 1944, YVA—M2/774. This comment, however, does not appear in the handwritten Polish manuscript (M2/754). Schwarzbart produced a typed English version of parts of his diary in the mid-1950s, and there are some discrepancies between it and the handwritten Polish text. Whether this particular addition was deliberate and represents a later invention of the diarist, or whether it is based upon some other text from the time in question, cannot be established.

88. See the various testimonies presented to the special investigating commission appointed by the Polish National Council, HIA-RN, Box 8, File 24.

89. "Memoriał w sprawie sytuacji żołnierzy Żydów w Armii Polskiej, przedstawiony Ministerstwu Obrony Narodowej," 9 February 1944, YVA—M2/66.

90. Quoted in Wasserstein, *Britain and the Jews of Europe*, p. 127.

91. Schwarzbart Diary, 1 February 1944, YVA—M2/754.

92. On the experiences of the soldiers of the first group during the five-week period in which the procedural obstacles were being cleared away, see Engel, "HaBerihah haHafganatit," pp. 191–92. During most of this period

they had been interned under guard at the Polish military depot at Tentsmuir.

93. Schwarzbart Diary, 17 January, 29 February 1944, YVA—M2/754.

94. Ibid., 16–17 January 1944. Schwarzbart met with the deserters together with representatives of the World Jewish Congress and the Board of Deputies of British Jews. The meeting had been arranged by Arieh Tartakower.

95. Ibid., 16–17 January 1944.

96. Ibid., 17 January 1944.

97. Ibid., 23 April 1944.

98. Reiss, *BeSa'arot haTekufah*, p. 239. For more on Reiss's mission to London, see below, Chapter 5.

99. "Protokół z posiedzenia . . . ," 20 February 1944, YVA—M2/92.

100. Schwarzbart and Tartakower to Polish Defense Ministry, 19 January 1944, YVA—M2/100. Schwarzbart regarded himself as the delegate of the Reprezentacja to the Polish National Council; Tartakower was nominally the head of the so-called American Branch of the Reprezentacja, which was in fact identical with the Committee on Polish Affairs of the American Jewish Congress.

101. Schwarzbart to Easterman, 18 February 1944, YVA—M2/92.

102. "Do żołnierzy Żydów w Armii Polskiej," signed by Schwarzbart, Tartakower, and Reiss, 24 February 1944, HIA-PG, Box 227, File Z851/e.

103. See "Protokół z posiedzenia odbytego . . . w lokalu Jewish World Congress [*sic*]," 20 February 1944, YVA—M2/92. There is, however, evidence that Tartakower did not maintain his position consistently and at times supported the refusal of Schwarzbart and Reiss to discuss such a possibility. See [Adolf] Dobkin and [Henryk] Weigensperg (in the name of the second group) to Tartakower, n.d. (with cover letter to Brodetsky, 19 March 1944), ibid.

104. See, for example, "Raport Dzienny," 29 January 1944, and "Conversation Easterman-Hall: Polish Jewish Soldiers," 28 February 1944, YVA—M2/100; Schwarzbart Diary, 28, 29 February 1944, YVA—M2/754.

105. Schwarzbart Diary, 25 April 1944, YVA—M2/755.

106. Schwarzbart Diary (English), 25 April 1944, YVA—M2/774. The comment about the "Jewish jungle" does not appear in the original Polish text. See above, n. 87.

107. H. Weigensperg to Brodetsky, 13 March 1944, YVA—M2/92.

108. Dobkin and Weigensperg to Tartakower, n.d. (with cover letter to Brodetsky, 19 March 1944), ibid.

109. On the establishment of the committee, see Penkower, *The Jews Were Expendable*, pp. 12–13.

110. Rosenberg to Helpern, 19 August 1942, JI—H3A/3/75. A Jewish battalion did not exist at the time. Rosenberg's complaints were typical of those of a number of soldiers: "I was born . . . in Lipowice, Poland, and came to Berlin as an infant six months old. I have spent all my life up till 19 years of

age in Berlin where I was driven out by the Nazis in 1938. I then came over to this country [Britain], where in October 1940 I joined the Polish Forces [because he was regarded by all parties concerned as a Polish citizen only]. Because I can't speak Polish I had difficulties in getting on at first. . . . After four months . . . I was arrested and charged with insulting the Polish state. This charge was quite false. . . . I was sentenced to 12 months imprisonment but . . . I was released after five months. . . . Since then . . . I have done my duty as a loyal soldier obeying every order. I have never absented myself even for one day for illness or any other reason. But in spite of all this my life was made impossible by my fellow soldiers. Every day they called me dirty Jew with every form of insults. One day when the wireless gave the news of the 40,000 Jews massacred by the Nazis in a gas chamber, they said to me: A good job! Poland will have less Jews. Another day a Polish soldier said to me, why are you here, we don't want you! If I were General Sikorski, I should drive you all out of our Army. Another time a Pole said to me: Wait until we get back to Poland, then we will not leave a single Jew alive. . . . I realised that I was among enemies, not friends. I . . . want to fight among my own people in a Jewish Battalion."

Rosenberg's name did not appear in the lists of the three groups of deserters in 1944.

111. Helpern to Sikorski, 25 August 1942, JI—H3A/3/57.

112. Memorandum by Helpern headed "The Jewish Army Committee and the Polish Jewish Soldiers," 25 April 1944, JI—H3A/3/75. Revisionist bodies in Palestine had also attempted to use the desertions of Jewish soldiers from the Polish forces there as an argument in favor of establishing separate Jewish units. See "Dezercja Żydów z AP," (with marginal annotation, "opracowanie Rewizjonistów"), n.d., HIA-Anders, Box 70, Doc. 162.

113. "The Jewish Army Committee and the Polish Jewish Soldiers" (see previous note).

114. "Letter received . . . from Pte. S. Pomeranc," (see above, n. 84). The group had evidently formulated this demand only after speaking with Tartakower.

115. "The Jewish Army Committee and the Polish Jewish Soldiers" (see above, n. 112).

116. The testimonies are located in JI—H3A/3/75. See also Helpern to the private secretary of the secretary of state [for foreign affairs], 7 February 1944, PRO—FO 371/39480.C1906; Helpern to Grigg, 23 February 1944, JI—H3A/3/48; "The Jewish Army Committee and the Polish Jewish Soldiers" (see above, n. 112).

117. Helpern to Grigg, 23 February 1944, JI—H3A/3/48.

118. "The Jewish Army Committee and the Polish Jewish Soldiers" (see above, n. 112).

119. On 20 March 1944 Helpern wrote to Pomeranc, "I have not heard from you for a long time, and I would like very urgently to see you." JI—H3A/3/75.

120. See Kukiel to Romer, 12 February 1944, HIA-PG, Box 226, File 851/e; Aide-Mémoire, British Embassy to Poland, to Polish Foreign Ministry, 22 February 1944, HIA-PG, Box 227, File Z851/e; Driberg, *Ruling Passions*, p. 202; Pritt, *Autobiography*, 2:201. On previous activities of these members of Parliament with regard to the situation of Jewish soldiers, see above, n. 67; also Engel, "HaBerihah haHafganatit," p. 179.

121. See the internal memorandum initialed "JW," n.d., attached to O'Malley to Romer, 30 October 1943, HIA-PG, Box 226, File 851/e. Cf. Pritt's comments in his autobiography: "Most of the emigré governments were pretty unrepresentative; their governments at home had been anti-Soviet, and they themselves were composed of politicians who had had the opportunity to escape, *and* had not thought it right to stop at home and fight underground against the Nazis; they had to be approved by the British Government, i.e. in substance the Foreign Office, which was 'thinking ahead' to have governments which might help to avert the 'menace' of Socialist rule within the countries concerned after the war." Pritt, *Autobiography*, 2:201n. Pritt also praised the Soviet Union for invading Poland in September 1939, thus preventing Hitler "from seizing . . . territories containing grain lands of infinite value to him, and from marching on to Rumania." *Autobiography*, 1:196–97.

122. They do not, on the other hand, appear to have actively sought publicity in order to embarrass the Poles. See below.

123. Schwarzbart Diary, 1 March 1944, YVA—M2/754. There is evidence to suggest that Driberg had thought to do so even before being approached by spokesmen for the soldiers. See ibid., 29 January 1944.

124. See the note by Frank Savery, British Embassy to Poland, 13 April 1944, HIA-PG, Box 227, File Z851/e.

125. Schwarzbart Diary, 28 February 1944, YVA—M2/754.

126. Driberg from the House of Commons, 3 April 1944, HIA-PG, Box 226, File 851/e. At the conclusion of the letter he explained what sort of support he required: "I shall feel obliged . . . to ask a question by private notice . . . and, if the answer is unsatisfactory, to ask leave to move the Adjournment of the House, under Standing Order No. 8, to discuss 'a definite matter of urgent public importance.' To obtain such leave, it is necessary that at least forty Members rise in their places in support of the Motion proposed."

127. Rathbone to Raczyński, 5 April 1944, HIA-PG, Box 226, File 851/e.

128. Raczyński to Rathbone, 5 April 1944, ibid.

129. Driberg, *Ruling Passions*, p. 202. See also Wasserstein, *Britain and the Jews of Europe*, p. 128.

130. Jędrzejewicz, *Poland in the British Parliament*, 2:427–29.

131. See the collections of cuttings in HIA-PG, Box 226, File 851/e, and WL—PC 210. See also Raczyński, *In Allied London*, pp. 209–10.

132. The protests are filed in HIA-PG, Box 226, File 851/e.

133. Savery to Romer [?], 13 April 1944, HIA-PG, Box 227, File Z851/e.

134. "Telefonogram [Romera] do Ministra Obrony Narodowej generała Kukiela," 14 April 1944, ibid.

135. "Notatka," 18 April 1944, ibid.

136. Górka to Polish Interior Minister, 24 April 1944, AIP—PRM. 142/13.

137. In fact, only one speaker during the entire debate directed any sort of a warning toward the Polish government, suggesting that if the Polish authorities could not properly control intergroup relations in the armed forces, Parliament would have to consider rescinding the extraterritorial authority under which Polish military courts could operate on British soil. Jędrzejewicz, *Poland in the British Parliament*, 2:427–73.

138. See "Raport z debaty parlamentarnej w dniu 5 i 6 kwietnia 1944r. (Sprawa dezerterów Żydów)," 13 April 1944, and Raczyński to Romer, 15 April 1944, HIA-PG, Box 226, File 851/e; Raczyński, *In Allied London*, p. 201.

139. "Raport z debaty parlamentarnej" (see previous note).

140. The substantiation that the report offered for its assumption was quite weak. In addition to proof by association, it could offer only the assertion that "Driberg's perfidious intention is concealed in the remarks that he made about 'constant and widespread instances of antisemitism.'" Ibid.

141. See, among others, "Notatka dla Pana Premiera w sprawie antysemityzmu w wojsku," n.d. (handwritten marginal annotation indicates that document was read by Mikołajczyk on 26 April 1944), and Mikołajczyk to Romer, 26 April 1944, HIA-PG, Box 227, File Z851/e; Maliszewski to Polish Information Minister, 1 May 1944, HIA-PG, Box 226, File 851/e. On the other hand, the government never adopted this position as its official explanation for the desertions. On 8 May Sir Owen O'Malley brought to Romer's attention charges raised by Driberg that a Polish colonel had told an audience in Scotland that the Jews had left the army under Soviet inspiration and had been paid £25 each by Soviet sources. When asked if the Polish government officially regarded this version of events as true, Romer replied that every Polish citizen had the right to his opinion and that in view of the hostility expressed toward Poland in the press over this issue, it was natural that Poles should think the desertions the work of forces hostile to their country. Romer, through Kukiel, also checked with the colonel in question, who claimed that he had been misunderstood. See O'Malley to Romer, 8 May 1944, and Romer to O'Malley, 5 June 1944, HIA-PG, Box 227, File Z851/e. O'Malley himself was evidently prepared to believe that "some outside influence was at work" upon the deserters; see O'Malley to Oliver Harvey, 9 May 1944, PRO—FO 371/39484.C6147. On the other hand, D. W. Allen of the Foreign Office wrote in a minute on 28 April 1944, "I know of no evidence that Soviet influence is behind the desertions and I think they can be explained without assuming it."

The actual extent to which the Soviets followed the situation of Jewish soldiers in the Polish army or tried to exploit the situation for their own propaganda purposes is impossible to determine definitively. In this connection it does seem relevant to point out that the story of the desertions was not extensively discussed in the Soviet press. The matter was mentioned only in scattered short news articles reporting Eden's responses to the parliamentary interpellations of 5 and 27 April and British press reaction to the trial of the third group. For example, in *Pravda*, see 6 April 1944 ("Zayavlenie Edena ob antisemitizme v pol'skoi armii"); 27 April 1944 ("Vystuplienie Edena v Palate Obshchin" and "Angliiskaya pechat' ob izdevatel'stvakh nad predstavitel'ami natsmen'shinstv v pol'skoi armii"). The organ of the Jewish Antifascist Committee published one article on the affair that concentrated on the public reaction to the desertions. *Eynikayt*, 25 May 1944 (S. Khaykin, "Antisemitizm in poylisher armey").

142. "Notatka . . . w sprawie antysemityzmu" (see previous note).

143. "Telefonogram [Romera] do Ministra Obrony Narodowej generała Kukiela," 14 April 1944, HIA-PG, Box 227, File Z851/e. This request might have been made in response to Savery's communication of a day previous, in which he stated that "His Majesty's Government feel it only right to warn the Polish Government that in spite of every desire to do so it may become difficult to restrain certain sections of public opinion, should it become known that what are considered, however unjustly, unduly harsh penalties have been imposed. It is therefore earnestly hoped that in any case the penalties imposed will not be such as could be represented or misrepresented to be disproportionate to the offences." See above, n. 133.

144. Romer to Kukiel, 21 April 1944, HIA-PG, Box 227, File 851/e. The Defense Ministry's investigating commission, in its report of 25 February 1944, had identified six instances of unacceptable behavior toward Jewish soldiers in the ranks and had recommended that the instances be investigated further with a mind to bringing the culprits to trial. However, there does not appear to be any evidence that prior to Romer's intervention such an investigation had been carried out.

145. Memorandum by Karol Kraczkiewicz, 14 April 1944, HIA-PG, Box 227, File Z851/e.

146. "Notatka," 18 April 1944, HIA-PG, Box 227, File Z851/e.

147. "Notatka . . . w sprawie antysemityzmu" (see above, n. 141).

148. "Interpelacja do p. Ministra Obrony Narodowej," 25 April 1944, YVA —M2/90. The interpellation was signed by four members of the Peasant Party, two members of the Labor Party, one member of PPS, and four non-party members. Neither of the two Jewish deputies was among the signers.

149. See above, n. 10.

150. "Protokół posiedzenia Rady Narodowej," 26 April 1944, HIA-RN, Box 4, File 13.

151. "Protokół posiedzenia Rady Narodowej," 2 May 1944, ibid. Adam Ciołkosz was appointed chairman of the investigating commission. Additional members were Witold Kulerski, Bronisław Kuśnierz, and Feliks Meissner, along with Schwarzbart and Szerer. At first, some members of the council objected to establishing a commission without first hearing the testimony of the defense minister. However, council chairman Stanisław Grabski, who had initially been opposed to the establishment of a commission, explained that Romer had asked him to do everything in his power to make certain

that Schwarzbart's motion was adopted without delay. Cf. Schwarzbart Diary, 26 April, 2 May 1944, YVA—M2/754.

152. "Posiedzenie Rady Narodowej," 10 May 1944, YVA—M2/96.

153. "Notatka dla Pana Ministra [Informacji i Dokumentacji], 27 April 1944, YVA—M2/100.

154. "Sprawozdanie z przebiegu obrad 8-go Sądu Polowego . . . ," 24 April 1944, ibid. There is no indication of the fate of the three remaining members of the group.

155. On the parliamentary discussions of this bill and Polish concern over them, see Engel, *In the Shadow of Auschwitz*, pp. 71–72.

156. Jędrzejewicz, *Poland in the British Parliament*, 2:485–88. See also "Notatka w sprawie interpelacyj dezerterów Żydów z W. P.," 29 April 1944, PC-Okręt, OF-9.

157. See Ciechanowski to Cellar, 27 April 1944, HIA-US, Box 1, File 2; cable, Ciechanowski to Polish Foreign Ministry, 27 April 1944, HIA-PG, Box 227, File Z851/e.

158. See previous note.

159. Cable, Ciechanowski to Polish Foreign Ministry, 2 May 1944 (Nr. 19), HIA-PG, Box 227, File Z851/e.

160. Unsigned Foreign Ministry memorandum, 28 April 1944, ibid.

161. Untitled memorandum signed by Karol Kraczkiewicz, 4 May [1944], ibid.

162. Ibid.

163. On 27 May, Romer complained to Kukiel that even the six Polish soldiers who had been named in the report of the Defense Ministry's investigating committee in February had not been brought to trial. Romer to Kukiel, 27 May 1944, HIA-PG, Box 227, File Z851/e. On 15 June, Kukiel replied that he was prevented from doing so by the terms of the amnesty that the Polish president had granted to the deserters on 12 May. Kukiel to Romer, 15 June 1944, ibid. On the amnesty, see below.

164. See the letter to Schwarzbart and Driberg signed by the deserters Rosenberg, Funder, Geller, Cymerman, Glatman, Barglowski, and Juliusberger on behalf of the entire third group, 9 May 1944, YVA—M2/92.

165. "Notatka dla Pana Ministra," 6 May 1944, HIA-PG, Box 227, File Z851/e. See also Romer's handwritten notes from the cabinet meeting of 5 May, headed "Sprawa dezerterów z Armii polskiej," ibid.

166. "[Decyzje] uchwalone na posiedzeniu Rady Ministrów," 11 May 1944, PC-Okręt, OF-12.

167. The Polish authorities, somewhat surprisingly, appear to have encouraged the British not to accept the soldiers. On 15 May an official of the Polish Foreign Ministry told F. K. Roberts of the British Foreign Office that in light of the recent amnesty decree the Polish government felt it essential that the British government restate its position against transfer. Roberts demurred, stating that the British position was already quite clear and that it would be repeated only under immediate provocation, such as a question in Parlia-

ment. "Notatka," 16 May 1944 (signed J. Weytko), HIA-PG, Box 227, File Z851/e. On the other hand, Karol Kraczkiewicz reportedly told Schwarzbart on 8 May that in preparation for the amnesty efforts were being made to insure that the British would accept the deserters should the soldiers continue to refuse to report to their units. Schwarzbart Diary, 8 May 1944, YVA—M2/755.

168. Text of resolution in HIA-PG, Box 226, File 851/e. See also Wasserstein, *Britain and the Jews of Europe*, p. 128.

169. Copy in HIA-PG, Box 226, File 851/e.

170. Raczyński, *In Allied London*, p. 213. On the various protest meetings, see the intelligence reports in HIA-PG, Box 226, File 851/e. Not all of the protests, though, were marked by a thoroughly anti-Polish tone. At a well-attended rally at Hyde Park on 28 May the rostrum was first occupied by a young Jew, calling himself a Zionist, who attacked the Polish government and army in a fashion that reminded a Polish observer of Soviet propaganda methods. However, after a short while, according to the Polish report, he was removed from the speakers' platform and his place was taken by the brother of MP Sidney Silverman. Silverman condemned the previous speaker as a Communist and a false Zionist, stating that although "among the Poles in England and the Polish government . . . there were antisemites," Jews should also remember that the Polish government had been the first source to transmit the news of the systematic mass murder of Jews by the Germans and was doing more than any other Allied nation to help the Jews. His speech was reportedly greeted with cries of "Bravo!" A. Serafiński to Polish interior minister, 3 June 1944, HIA-PG, Box 226, File 851/e.

171. "A Last Appeal," 19 May 1944, JI—H3A/3/75. Three weeks before, posters had reportedly been affixed to the door of the Polish Consulate-General in London, reading, "Warning. The imprisonment of Jewish-Polish Soldiers will be avenged. Irgun Zvai Leumi—Jewish National Military Organization." Raczyński, *In Allied London*, p. 203.

172. "Rescue Jewish Soldiers from Persecution in the Polish Army: Polish Government and Polish Commander-in-Chief Must Go," JI—H3A/3/75. The exceptions, of course, are rather significant.

173. The Security Division of the Polish Interior Ministry was especially concerned about the possible effect of a meeting held at Shoreditch Town Hall on 11 May, in which the various speakers had demanded not only the transfer of the deserters to the British army but also the immediate removal of Sosnkowski and Kukiel from their positions, the liquidation of the present Polish government as a "stronghold of fascism," and the placement of all members of the government in concentration camps for pro-fascist activity. M. Glaser to Polish Foreign Ministry, Information Ministry, and prime minister, 15 May 1944, HIA-PG, Box 226, File 851/e.

174. See the minutes of the commission's meetings in HIA-RN, Box 8, File 24.

175. See above, n. 78. On the other hand, only one soldier stated that

he definitely planned to return to Poland following liberation, whereas six indicated that they definitely would not return.

176. O'Malley to Romer, 17 July 1944, HIA-PG, Box 227, File Z851/e.

177. See the relevant correspondence in ibid.

178. See Heitzman to Jan Wszelaki, Polish Foreign Ministry, and Antoni Serafiński, Polish Interior Ministry, 24 October 1944, ibid.

179. Raczyński, *In Allied London,* p. 203.

CHAPTER FIVE

1. "Uchwała Rady Ministrów," 20 April 1944, HIA-PG, Box 227 (MSZ), File 851/e: "Rada dla Ratowania Żydów w Polsce."

2. The War Refugee Board was charged "to take all measures . . . to rescue the victims of enemy oppression who are in imminent danger of death." The board's mandate was thus not restricted specifically to assisting Jewish victims, although the enabling order did take notice of "Nazi plans to exterminate all Jews." On the establishment of the War Refugee Board, see, inter alia, Feingold, *Politics of Rescue,* p. 244; Wyman, *Abandonment of the Jews,* p. 209.

The creation of this agency undoubtedly encouraged Jewish leaders to press ahead with their demand that the Polish government establish a similar board; see below. Jewish leaders also pressed the British government to follow the American lead; see, for example, cable, Szerer to Churchill, 19 March 1944, JLBA—ME 42/4.

3. See above, n. 1.

4. Ibid.

5. This refusal had most recently been expressed by Mikołajczyk in his meeting with Schwarzbart and Tartakower on 13 January 1944. See above, Chapter 3.

6. "Communiqué for the Press issued by the Polish Government," 11 May 1944, HIA-PG, Box 227 (MSZ), File 851/e. The reference to the "Welfare Committee for the Jewish Population of Poland" undoubtedly signified the Council for Aid to Jews, which had been active, together with its predecessor body, for twenty months. The government's claimed sponsorship of this body had, moreover, not included earmarking specific funds for it, even though the council had been requesting such earmarking since October 1942. See above, Chapter 1.

7. Tartakower, "HaPe'ilut haMedinit," p. 177. Evidently some consideration was given to appointing Tartakower to a position in the Polish government, possibly as an undersecretary in the Interior Ministry. Proponents of this idea—among them Ludwik Seidenmann, a Jew serving at the time with the Polish Consulate-General in New York—maintained that such an appointment could be put to good use by Polish propaganda in the United States. Opponents, including Górka (who nonetheless expressed admiration

for Tartakower as a person), argued that there were already too many people in the Polish government dealing with Jewish affairs and that the government would be better served by having Tartakower in New York rather than in London. According to one account, Tartakower consulted various Jewish groups in December and found most of them opposed to the idea. Specifically, Nahum Goldmann is said to have warned that acceptance of such an appointment would complicate Jewish efforts to build bridges to the Jews of the Soviet Union—a goal that was more important in the long run than having Tartakower in the Polish government. See Seidenmann to Kot, 21 December 1943; Górka to Polish Interior Minister, 14 January 1944; and Górka to Polish Interior Minister, 20 January 1944, AIP-[EP], "Sprawy Żydowskie."

8. Reiss, *BeSa'arot haTekufah*, pp. 239–41. Actually, the Reprezentacja had not been the body that had sent Reiss; he was officially in London in the service of the World Zionist Organization and the Jewish Agency in order to facilitate coordination between the Palestinian and British headquarters of both bodies. The Reprezentacja, which a year earlier had tried to send Reiss to London on its own account, now gave Reiss the additional mission of attempting to organize rescue activities.

9. See above, Chapter 3.

10. See Górka's letter to the Polish interior minister, 5 January 1944, quoted in Reiss, *BeSa'arot haTekufah*, p. 241.

11. Olgierd Górka, "Notatka dla Pana Ministra Spraw Wewnętrznych," 3 February 1944, HIA-PG, Box 227 (MSZ), File 851/e. The suggestion that the special rescue department should be created within the Interior Ministry indicates that the agenda was drawn up without Jewish participation. Jewish spokesmen had consistently indicated their preference for a cabinet-level department or for one operating under the auspices of the prime minister's office; they had also considered the possibility of locating such a department within the Labor Ministry, but they had never spoken about the Interior Ministry as the desired locus for such an agency. See above, Chapters 1 and 3. This suggestion was to become a bone of contention between the Polish and Jewish sides in future talks.

12. Tartakower had pointed out that the World Jewish Congress had already scheduled a general conference on rescue for 7 May. He indicated that he was not averse to having the Reprezentacja summon a congress of Polish Jews in the United States toward the end of that month (in fact, he declared that the Reprezentacja would not require any funds from the Polish government to organize such a gathering). However, he made it clear that "at the Congress the Jews will expect a concrete statement from the Poles, without declamatory overtones, that will remove all still-existing suspicions that the government is playing politics [*że Rząd manewruje w swej polityce*]." According to the minutes, there was no reaction to this statement from the Polish side. See previous note. The idea of the congress never came up again in Polish-Jewish discussions.

13. According to Reiss, following the initial meeting (in which he had not

participated personally) he had suggested the establishment of a forum for coordinating the positions of the various Jewish bodies that were to be represented in the negotiations. Such a forum, consisting of, among others, Alexander Easterman of the World Jewish Congress, Berl Locker and Joseph Linton of the London Executive of the Jewish Agency, and Baruch Rosenthal of the World Zionist Organization, together with Reiss, Tartakower, and Schwarzbart, did meet from time to time during the course of the discussions with Polish officials. The forum opposed continuing talks about a congress of Polish Jews or about organizing pro-Polish propaganda among the Jews of the United States. It is thus plausible to assume that the initiative for drawing up the plan for a rescue department that was presented on 7 February came out of this group. See Reiss, *BeSa'arot haTekufah*, pp. 243–44.

At the same time pressure to take up the rescue question more actively had been directed toward the government-in-exile by the Polish National Council as well. On 31 January Emanuel Szerer had, with the support of eleven colleagues, introduced a resolution taking notice of the recent establishment of the War Refugee Board in the United States and calling upon the government "to create an organ . . . having as its purpose activity aimed at rescuing the mortally threatened victims of the German occupation . . . in cooperation with the newly formed American War Refugee Board." "Wniosek Nagły Dra Emanuela Scherera i Kolegów . . . ," 31 January 1944, YVA—M2/10. This resolution did not mention Jews specifically, although in its preamble it noted that "in Poland Hitlerite thugs are perpetrating the most horrible crimes, to which countless multitudes among the civilian population of our country, especially the Jewish population, are falling victim."

14. Olgierd Górka, "Notatka dla Pana Ministra Spraw Wewnętrznych," 7 February 1944, HIA-PG, Box 227 (MSZ), File 851/e.

15. "Plan Wydziału Ratowania Żydów Polskich przy Prezydium Rady Ministrów," n.d., YVA—M2/74.

16. The plan also included a list of the department's anticipated functions. This list was virtually identical to the list of functions eventually incorporated into the mandate of the Rescue Council. It was, however, the only part of the plan that was reflected in the enabling resolution that actually called the Rescue Council into being.

17. See above, n. 14. Kraczkiewicz indicated that his comments were strictly informal and personal, as he had no authority to represent the official position of his ministry.

18. Górka cautioned, however, that he could not commit himself to support any specific organizational structure for such activities until he had received appropriate instructions from the minister of the interior and the prime minister.

19. The text of this memorandum, the first of a series of lengthy missives from the Reprezentacja to the government-in-exile, is located in Reprezentacja, *Sprawozdanie*, pp. 13–21. Contrary to Reiss's assertion, it did not speak of "saving" Polish Jews; rather it asked the government to take certain steps

to improve the tenor of Polish-Jewish relations in the occupied homeland and elsewhere and to repudiate the approach of prewar Polish governments to the Jewish question.

20. The reference is to the discussions of November 1942–January 1943. See above, Chapter 1; also Engel, "The Polish Government-in-Exile and the Holocaust."

21. Tartakower and Schwarzbart to Mikołajczyk, 11 February 1944, YVA—M2/74.

22. Perhaps they were encouraged by the action of the National Council on 31 January, believing that politician Mikołajczyk might be more responsive to this body than would the civil servants with whom they had been meeting.

23. Górka to [Interior] Minister, 17 February 1944, YVA—O55/4.

24. At his third meeting with Jewish representatives, on 11 February, Górka had been told by Schwarzbart that no action to harness Jewish opinion in the United States to the Polish cause (something that Górka was visibly eager to begin) could be launched "without certain gestures on the part of the government, such as a political declaration by the prime minister [and] the creation of a department for the rescue of Jews." Olgierd Górka, "Notatka dla Pana Ministra Spraw Wewnętrznych," 15 February 1944, HIA-PG, Box 227 (MSZ), File 851/e.

25. See also Górka to Polish interior minister, 18 February 1944, AIP—[EP], "Sprawy Żydowskie." In this memorandum Górka indicated that a special broadcast to Poland instructing the population to do all in its power to save Jews was an urgent matter, and he commented that "it is permissible in this case to point out that Nazi barbarity is directed even more against Jews than against Poles."

Interestingly, a similar recommendation had been made at approximately the same time by Polish military intelligence in Palestine. Noting that several dozen Polish Jewish escapees had recently arrived in Palestine and had reported "a large-scale strengthening of antisemitism in Poland, and specifically . . . that the underground movement had not managed to take control of the situation and to counteract German antisemitic propaganda," the Document Bureau warned that the Jewish press was likely to distribute this information in the United States and comment on it widely. It thus urged that thought be given to issuing a proclamation to the homeland that "[Polish] denunciators [of Jews] and antisemitic thugs will be treated as Hitlerite agents [and that] sentences will eventually be handed down and carried out against a few of the most vicious denunciators," as well as to distributing abroad news of "the active struggle against antisemitism in the homeland and a demonstrative presentation of . . . antisemitism as the legacy of Hitlerism in the emigré press, including the military [newspapers]." See untitled document from Jerusalem, 14 February 1944, HIA-Anders, Box 71, Doc. 255.

26. At least no evidence of a response to it has as yet been located in any likely archival file. The lack of response is not surprising; the prime minister evidently shared the perception, current in many Polish circles since late

1943, that world Jewry was already moving spontaneously, as it were, in a pro-Polish direction and that concessions to Jewish interests were unnecessary in order to achieve Polish propaganda goals. On this perception, see above, Chapter 3. Górka, on the other hand, had been in regular contact with the Jewish leaders and was evidently aware that the spreading perception of other Polish politicians was not accurate.

27. Cable to government delegate (signed Orken), 21 February 1944, AIP —[EP], "Sprawy Żydowskie." The cable explained that "Hungary has already drawn politically in America upon its more lenient manner of treating Jews." See also Fiszman-Karińska, "Zachód, Emigracyjny Rząd Polski oraz Delegatura," p. 54.

28. Cable to government delegate (signed Orken), 21 February 1944, AIP —[EP], "Sprawy Żydowskie."

29. Olgierd Górka, "Notatka dla Pana Ministra Spraw Wewnętrznych," 5 March 1944, HIA-PG, Box 227 (MSZ), File 851/e. Reiss added that he knew of previous situations in which government orders had been carried out only partially by agencies in the homeland.

30. See above, Chapter 4.

31. See Great Britain, *Parliamentary Debates*, 397 H.C. Deb. 5 s, 3:696–99, 702, 710–11, 727–28, 730, 733–35, 737, 781–83, 788–89, 795 (22 February 1944); 3:861–62, 869–70, 891–95, 900, 913–14, 918–20, 936 (23 February 1944).

32. Cf. the words of R. M. Mack in ibid., 3:869: "The Minister of Information has told us that, as far as Poland is concerned, some of their literature and newspapers are not conducive to the successful prosecution of the war and the friendly relationship of our Allies and as a consequence had to be banned. I happen to know, and some of the Press also know, that the Polish Army makes very considerable racial discrimination among their men in this country and a great deal of suspicion must fall upon those responsible for that disgraceful state of affairs. . . . There are members of the Polish forces in this country who have literally threatened suicide because of the cruel discrimination that has taken place. Do we want to support a country with a Government of that nature? I most certainly would not."

33. Olgierd Górka, "Notatka dla Pana Ministra Spraw Wewnętrznych," 4 March 1944, HIA-PG, Box 227 (MSZ), File 851/e.

34. Górka offered no explanation for this position. Perhaps the government wished to avoid any action that might appear as a step toward the reconstitution of the government as demanded by the Soviets.

35. See above, n. 33.

36. Reiss is recorded as having stated, "From the discussions that we have been conducting we should like to take away a clear opinion as to what the government thinks about Jewish matters and what it intends to do. I stress that what is decisive for us is action, not a declaration. Until now the government has done nothing for Jewish Polish citizens, apart from [granting them] incomplete representation in the National Council; the Jewish community is

excluded from the creation of the state, but we are concerned today with saving the remnant of that community. Therefore we do not care about a declaration or about reconstructing the cabinet but about the establishment of a branch [*placówka*] that will be able to work independently and will have the means for carrying out that work guaranteed in advance. Everything revolves about the question, what means will the government give for this purpose and who will decide how these means will be used."

37. Olgierd Górka, "Notatka dla Pana Ministra Spraw Wewnętrznych," 13 March 1944, HIA-PG, Box 227 (MSZ), File 851/e.

38. In this regard Schwarzbart proposed that the council consist of three Jewish and three Polish delegates—the Jews to be appointed by the Reprezentacja, the Bund, and Agudas Yisroel; the Poles by PPS, the Peasant Party, and the Labor Party. He warned, though, that any attempt to name a representative of Endecja to the council would result in Jews taking a position of "unfavorable neutrality" toward its work. He also indicated that the Reprezentacja would have no objection to Manfred Lachs as executive director, "although the delegates from the Reprezentacja have differing individual opinions about this candidacy." Lachs, who had at one time served as Schwarzbart's executive secretary, had been suggested by Serafiński for the position.

39. Cf. Reiss's comments: "Between the project presented by the delegates of the Reprezentacja and the projected proposal of the Polish authorities is an enormous difference. It lies in the fact that the Reprezentacja wished through the establishment of an undersecretariat of state to bring about . . . a great act in relation to the Jews of Poland, [whereas] the proposed solution does not accomplish this [goal]. . . . Everything depends upon who carries out the assigned tasks and in what manner; for this reason a commission with an apparatus of a single civil servant is not to be regarded as an institution that will arouse confidence and give the conviction that . . . the matter of rescuing the Jewish population will be pursued with results. [I] do not agree with Prof. Górka's comparison of the stand of the Anglo-Saxon [British and U.S.] governments with that of the Polish government, especially because the representatives of Polish Jewry approach the Polish government in the matter of none other than Polish citizens alone." See above, n. 37.

40. Olgierd Górka, "Notatka dla Pana Ministra Spraw Wewnętrznych," 14 March 1944, HIA-PG, Box 227 (MSZ), File 851/e. The text of the actual proposal was not attached to this memorandum and has not been located.

41. Ibid. Szerer did object, however, to the inclusion of a representative of Agudas Yisroel in the proposed commission, on the grounds that that party was not represented in the underground Council for Aid to Jews. Górka appears simply to have ignored this objection.

42. In his memoirs Reiss explained the reasons for the Jews' acquiescence: "We went through no small amount of agonizing over whether to consent to the Polish government's proposal and to join the council that it intended to establish. We still did not believe that the tragedy [of Polish Jewry] was as

great as was to become clear later, that Poland remained virtually without Jews. We were convinced that their number was several times greater than it actually was; therefore we hoped that there was someone left to help. [We felt it our] duty to do so, and the institutions of the Polish government were the only way to establish immediate contact with the remnant of the Jews still living there. They were also the only way to transfer funds intended to assist the Jews or [to carry out] any possible rescue activity. . . . Cutting off contact with the Polish government would close an important channel—actually the only one—before us. This was our primary assumption." Reiss, *BeSa'arot haTekufah*, p. 250. Reiss truncated the time frame in this description so that he referred to Górka's proposal as a proposal of the Polish government as a whole.

The belief that many more Jews remained alive in Poland than was actually the case was supported by an estimate circulated by the Polish Information Ministry three days following the presentations of Górka's detailed proposal. According to this report at least 2 million Polish Jews had perished in the Nazi murder campaign, and fewer than 1 million remained alive in Poland. The document stressed, however, that these were minimum and maximum figures, respectively; the actual number of Jews dead and alive could not be determined with any accuracy. Untitled memorandum by Jewish Affairs Desk, Polish Information Ministry, signed by St. Kot, 16 March 1944 (L. dz. 3544/44), YVA—O55/4.

43. "Rozmowa z Ministrem Władysławem Banaczykiem . . . ," 28 March 1944, YVA—M2/141.

44. Tartakower, for one, appears to have believed that negotiations over the details of organization and funding would be completed fairly quickly. He returned to the United States shortly after the conclusion of his round of talks with Górka, leaving conduct of those negotiations in the hands of Schwarzbart and Reiss. On 2 April he wrote Schwarzbart, stating in matter-of-fact fashion that he expected that all of the necessary details had already been worked out. "Probably you have already reached an understanding regarding the Polish and Jewish candidates for the council that will be attached to the department," he added, indicating his belief that negotiations should by that point have reached a fairly advanced stage. Tartakower to Schwarzbart, 2 April 1944, YVA—M2/448.

45. Schwarzbart reported that immediately after his conference with Banaczyk he contacted Serafiński, who told him that the government's legal counsel had already given his approval to the wording of the proposal, having made "only formal" changes. Serafiński stated that he would now return the proposal to Banaczyk, "who had promised to call a special ad hoc meeting of the Committee on Homeland Affairs." "Rozmowa z . . . Banaczykiem" (see above, n. 43). If Serafiński's statements were true, then it seems meet to ask why it had taken two weeks to make "only formal" changes in the original wording of the proposal and why Banaczyk had not told Schwarzbart that he had promised to summon a special meeting of the appropriate committee

as soon as the bill was ready for presentation. Perhaps Serafiński had sensed Schwarzbart's impatience after his conversation with the interior minister and had tried to keep him from becoming discouraged.

46. See above, Chapter 4.

47. He had earlier advanced the argument that in U.S. public opinion sympathy toward Poland varied inversely with sympathy toward the Soviets, with a decline in one being matched by a proportional gain in the other. Strakacz to Polish Foreign Ministry, 8 April 1944, AIP—[EP], "Sprawy Żydowskie."

48. Strakacz also indicated that it would be most desirable to appoint Rabbi Yitshak Lewin of Agudas Yisroel to the directorship of the council. The Orthodox Jewish groups, he maintained, were "completely loyal to Poland," and their loyalty deserved repayment in the form of greater representation in government councils.

49. "Notatka dla Pana Ministra," n.d., initialed "KK," HIA-PG, Box 227 (MSZ), File Z851/e. A handwritten annotation instructed that this memorandum, dealing with the propaganda implications of the establishment of the Rescue Council, be filed under "Jewish desertions."

50. "Rozmowa z Prof. Górką," 13 April 1944, YVA—M2/74.

51. At the same time, the government also tried to tie the rescue issue to the desertions in another way. An internal Foreign Ministry memorandum prepared by Kraczkiewicz around 15 April noted that "the debate in the House of Commons [in response to Driberg's interpellation of 5 April] . . . inadvertently did ill service to . . . the relations between Poles and Jews. . . . The repercussions of the debate are making a fatal impression in Poland, where many Poles, at the risk of their own lives, are rescuing Jews from the Germans, without regard to their political convictions." Untitled memorandum bearing initials "K[arol] K[raczkiewicz], n.d. (handwritten date with initials J. Z[arański], 15 April 1944), HIA-PG, Box 227 (MSZ), File Z851/e. No doubt taking its cue from this observation, an English-language propaganda broadsheet about the desertions prepared by the Foreign Ministry warned the British public that "the publicity given to the whole affair is bound to produce a deplorable impression in Poland itself, where many Poles, disregarding the dangers involved, are actively rescuing Jews from the German executioners. The Jews, who have still survived in Poland, owe their lives to the protection extended to them at very great risk by friendly Poles, for persons harbouring Jews are punished by death." "Facts Concerning Attempted Disaffection among Jewish and Orthodox Soldiers in the Polish Army in Great Britain," n.d. (handwritten date 5 June 1944), ibid.

Such a suggestion was undoubtedly intended to caution Jews complaining about the government's handling of the desertions that their actions might have serious consequences for a very large number of their coreligionists. Indeed, at a press conference on 14 June 1944 Mikołajczyk announced that "between 800,000 and 900,000 Jews are still in Poland where they are being kept alive through aid being given to them by friendly Poles." *JTA Bulletin*, 15 June 1944. Mikołajczyk must have been aware at the time that those figures were greatly exaggerated; on 25 May 1944 Witold Bienkowski, a Polish underground official concerned with Jewish affairs, notified the government that, according to the best available estimates, some 200,000 Jews were in hiding among the Poles (along with 120,000 in camps and 90,000 in the Łódź ghetto, which had not yet been liquidated). Gutman, "Report of a Member of the Polish Underground," p. 106. Moreover, only two days before Mikołajczyk's statement a courier from underground Poland, Jerzy Jur (Lerski), had told the Rescue Council that official underground estimates reckoned the number of Jews left alive at 500,000 to 600,000 but that in his opinion this number was being deliberately exaggerated in the hope of obtaining more money from the government; in his opinion not more than 200,000 remained alive in Poland. "Referat por. Jura o sytuacji w Kraju," 12 June 1944, YVA—M2/74. Earlier Jur had made similar statements to the National Council; see "Protokół z posiedzenia Rady Narodowej," 2 May 1944, HIA-RN, Box 4, File 13–2. In actuality, even this estimate was too high; in February the Jewish National Committee had written Schwarzbart that only 50,000 were in hiding among the Poles and another 50,000 were in camps. Jewish National Committee to Schwarzbart, 22 February 1944, JLBA—ME 42/4. There is little possibility that Mikołajczyk had not been advised of any of this information prior to his press conference.

52. See above, Chapter 4.

53. For a description of the opening meeting, see Reiss, *BeSa'arot haTekufah*, pp. 250–54.

54. The council consisted of three Polish and three Jewish delegates. The Poles were all chosen from members of the National Council—Adam Ciołkosz of PPS, Witold Kulerski of the Peasant Party, and Stanisław Sopicki of the Labor Party. Emanuel Szerer, the Bund representative on the National Council, was selected to represent his group, but Schwarzbart yielded to Reiss as the delegate of the parties coalesced in the Reprezentacja. The third Jewish delegate, Abraham Babad, was a prominent member of the orthodox Jewish political party Agudas Yisroel in Britain. See Reiss, *BeSa'arot haTekufah*, p. 250.

55. Interior Ministry to Council members, 19 May 1944 (Nr. 827/44/Tjn./ Dz. Nar.), YVA—M14/f5.

56. "Statement of Władysław Banaczyk . . . ," 25 May 1944, HIA-PG, Box 227 (MSZ), File 851/e. Adam Ciołkosz also mentioned the desertion episode explicitly: "In times when every silly, unnecessary and injurious remark uttered in Polish barracks in Scotland is reverberating all over the world it become[s] . . . us Poles to bear constantly in mind that our compatriots in Poland deem it to be their most sacred duty to bring help to Jews hunted by the Germans. We must remind the world that the Polish nation should be judged primarily by the true qualities of its character, revealed in the very facts of organizing the Underground help for Jews in Poland." "Statement of Adam Ciołkosz . . . ," 25 May 1944, ibid.

57. Cf. Reiss to Tartakower, 14 June 1944, YVA—M2/436: "Unfortunately

I had to enter into a polemic with the minister [Banaczyk] on two points—the soldiers and aid in the homeland. I did this against my will, but I could not let those statements [by Banaczyk] go unanswered."

58. "Statement of Anzelm Reiss . . . ," 25 May 1944, ibid.

59. "Statement of Rabbi A. Babad . . . ," 25 May 1944, ibid.

60. "Statement of E. Scherer [*sic*] . . . ," 25 May 1944, ibid.

61. "Statement of Stanisław Sopicki . . . ," 25 May 1944, ibid.

62. See, for example, *Contemporary Jewish Record*, August 1944 ("Chronicle: Poland"); *American Jewish Year Book*, 46 (1944–45): 244–46. Both of these general discussions of Polish-Jewish relations mentioned the establishment of the Rescue Council only briefly, while concentrating primarily upon the desertion affair. See also *Jewish Chronicle*, 2 June 1944 ("Rescuing Polish Jews"), a brief article noting the council's opening meeting that, after naming the chairman and the three Jewish members, observed only that the council was "not a Government Department, but a social organisation." The daily Hebrew press in Palestine contained no notice of the council's establishment. The response of the general press, which had regularly reported developments regarding the desertions, was similar; none of the statements prepared for the press in advance of the opening meeting found their way, even in part, into the *New York Times* or the *Times* of London. The *Manchester Guardian* noted the council's opening meeting obliquely in a small item on an interior page; the report mentioned only that Szerer had used the occasion of the meeting to call upon the Allies to supply arms to the remnants of Polish Jewry, and it did not state that the council had been formed by the Polish government. *Manchester Guardian*, 26 May 1944 ("Jews in Poland: Appeal for Arms").

63. See Reiss, *BeSa'arot haTekufah*, p. 261.

64. See above, n. 51. As five of the six members of the Rescue Council were also members of the National Council, they had heard the courier's report before. It may be that the meeting with the courier was called mainly for the sake of having a meeting, in order to answer Reiss's recently expressed complaints about the council's inactivity. In a letter of 9 June to Adam Ciołkosz, who had been elected chairman of the council on 25 May, Reiss indicated that on 2 June he had requested that the council convene during the next week but that his request had been rebuffed. A forceful repetition of his request, he claimed, had met with a similar response on 8 June. Thus he wrote, "It is extremely unpleasant for me that at this early stage I must express my deep displeasure that two weeks have already elapsed from the day of the Council's ceremonial opening, yet until now we have not . . . made any efforts to begin effective assistance." Reiss to Ciołkosz, 9 June 1944, YVA—M2/74. Reiss wrote that he had been told that a meeting could not be called until Szerer, who had been assigned to draft a budget for the council, returned to London. He was scheduled to return 14 June. Still, however, a meeting was held, evidently in Szerer's absence, on 12 June, and as Reiss had requested, it considered a proposed formulation of the council's bylaws. See Reiss, *BeSa'arot haTekufah*, p. 254.

65. Cf. Kraczkiewicz's comments to Romer prior to the adoption of the resolution establishing the council: "During our discussions with Jewish figures . . . , the Jews attached great weight to mentioning in the text of the resolution some concrete sum provisionally designated by the government (until the problem was resolved through the normal budgetary procedure) for action to rescue Jews. It came out at the time that it would be possible to respond to that wish by assigning a certain quota from the budget of the Ministry of the Interior for purposes relating to the homeland [*na cele krajowe*]. This would be mainly a propaganda move, for as you know the disposition of funds for assistance to the homeland is dependent upon obtaining dollars. Now I see from the projected resolution that no quota is mentioned. Its absence undoubtedly weakens the impression of the resolution in Jewish circles. Could you not raise this question at the cabinet, pointing out the great propaganda significance of specifying a sum in the resolution designated by the government for assistance to the Jews in the homeland?" "Notatka dla Pana Ministra," n.d. (handwritten date of filing 26 April 1944), HIA-PG, Box 227 (MSZ), File Z851/e. An instruction in the margin indicated that this document was to be filed with papers about the desertion of Jews from the army—yet another indication of the close connection between the establishment of the Rescue Council and the desertions in the minds of Polish policymakers.

On the problem reflected in Kraczkiewicz's observation that "the disposition of funds for assistance to the homeland is dependent upon obtaining dollars," see below, n. 71.

66. "Uchwała Rady do Spraw Ratowania Ludności Żydowskiej w Polsce," 20 June 1944, YVA—M14/f40.

67. "Budżet na rok 1944: Część 12—Ministerstwo Pracy i Opieki Społecznej," JLBA—ME 42/8. The total budget of the ministry for 1944 was £9,426,560, making it by far the largest recipient of funds of any government department. Of this sum, in addition to the amount assigned for aid to the homeland, £3,783,050 was designated for aid to Poles who had been evacuated from the Soviet Union, £2,881,000 to Poles remaining in the Soviet Union, £878,470 to Polish refugees in Palestine, and £79,650 to Polish refugees in Great Britain. The remaining £1,340,390 were not specifically allocated.

68. Gross, *Polish Society*, p. 244. The conversion from the dollar amounts listed in the table is made at the rate of $4:£1. Extrabudgetary expenditures "related to the war" may even have reached as high as £12 million and more; see A. Romer to Schwarzbart, 26 August 1944 (L. dz. 4716/44), YVA—M2/80.

69. See Szerer to Leon Feiner ("Do Bundu w Polsce, na ręce Berezowskiego"), 21 July 1944, JLBA—ME 42/4. Szerer, who was charged with the task of drafting the council's budget, presented the following figures to the council on 30 June 1944: minimum monthly subsistence—100,000 persons @ $40/person = $4,000,000; providing 5,000 Jews per month with false

identity papers—$150,000; assisting 1,500 Jews per month to flee Poland @ $500/person = $750,000. He used a conversion ratio of 100 zł.:$1.

70. Ibid. Also Reiss to Schwarzbart, 12 July 1944, YVA—M2/431.

71. Ibid. See also Reiss to Schwarzbart, 13 July 1944, YVA—M2/436; Schwarzbart to Mikołajczyk, 18 August 1944, HIA-PG, Box 227 (MSZ), File 851/e; Schwarzbart to Reprezentacja, 21 April 1945 (Nr. 513/45, RTA 29/45), YVA—M2/802. The government explained that only dollars, not pounds, were of any value in occupied Poland and that it did not possess sufficient dollar reserves to supply the requested funds. Reiss to Gruenbaum, 17 July 1943, YVA—M2/431. Upon hearing this excuse, Reiss suggested that Jewish organizations would facilitate the exchange of the government's pounds for dollars. The government, however, does not appear to have acted upon this suggestion. In fact, the government does not seem to have been terribly interested in obtaining dollars for transmittal to the Jews in the occupied homeland. Even before the establishment of the Rescue Council, the World Jewish Congress had been exploring the possibility of "making dollars available for Jewish rescue work in Poland" through the U.S. War Refugee Board. John Pehle, director of the board, indicated that such a request would have to come from the Polish government. The message was relayed by Nahum Goldmann and Tartakower to the Polish government through Sylwin Strakacz in New York. The government, however, did not approach the board with the necessary request. See "Minute of Conversation with Mr. John W. Pehle," 31 March 1944, DRI—A1/117/1/106; untitled, unsigned memorandum (initialed "ef"), 24 April 1944, DRI—A1/117/2/68; untitled, unsigned memorandum, 12 May 1944, DRI—A1/117/3/27.

For details of the ongoing negotiations between the Rescue Council and the government over obtaining the promised allocation, which went on through April 1945, and of the government's ever-changing explanations as to why the funds were not delivered, see Reiss, BeSa'arot haTekufah, pp. 263–79.

72. Schwarzbart to Mikołajczyk, 18 August 1944, HIA-PG, Box 227 (MSZ), File 851/e; Reiss, BeSa'arot haTekufah, p. 262.

73. Quoted in Reiss, BeSa'arot haTekufah, p. 263.

74. Schwarzbart to Mikołajczyk, 18 August 1944, HIA-PG, Box 227 (MSZ), File 851/e. Earlier Schwarzbart had received a cable from Leon Kubowitzki of the World Jewish Congress in New York noting that the "conviction that Polish official financial assistance to Jews in Poland has been utterly inadequate results in the most unfavorable comments" by Jews. Kubowitzki to Pehle (requesting transmission to Schwarzbart), 25 July 1944, DRI—A1/117/7/73.

75. Reiss, BeSa'arot haTekufah, pp. 266–67.

76. Reiss to Schwarzbart, 2 August 1944, YVA—M2/431; Reiss, BeSa'arot haTekufah, p. 265. This request was evidently made in response to a suggestion to that effect by an emissary from the Polish underground named Stanisławski, who had left Poland in April 1944 and with whom Jewish spokesmen met on 7 July. See "Rezultaty rozmowy między inż. Reissem i

p. Stanisławskim," 7 July 1944, CZA—S26/1134; Reiss, *BeSa'arot haTekufah*, p. 264.

77. Reiss to Schwarzbart, 2 August 1944, YVA—M2/431. Reiss's comment: "After all, music and a little news are more important than efforts to do something to rescue Jews." On the other hand, Reiss had already been given the opportunity to broadcast to Poland at the end of May, and he was to do so twice more. Reiss, *BeSa'arot haTekufah*, pp. 255–56.

78. A. Reiss, "Sumarjusz," 7 August 1944, YVA—M2/74.

79. Ibid.; "Rozmowa [Schwarzbarta] z Premjerem Stanisławem Mikołajczykiem," 30 August 1944, YVA—M2/142.

80. "Rozmowa z Premjerem," (see previous note).

81. Ibid.

82. The precise figure is difficult to determine because of references to identical contributions in different documents. The figure of $1,727,363 is based upon comparison and collation of the following documents: Jacob Pat, Jewish Labor Committee, New York, to Janusz Żoltowski, Financial Counselor, Polish Embassy, Washington, 13 April, 22, 29 May, 21 July, 16 September, 18 December 1944, DRI—INV. 153/14; "Zestawienie dokonanych wypłat Organizacjom Żydowskim w Kraju," 19 January 1945, and Górka to Schwarzbart, 25 July 1944, YVA—M2/267; Reiss to Schwarzbart, 13 July 1944, YVA—M2/436; "Wykaz sum wpłaconych przez Joint," n.d.; "Wykaz sum dla Berez[owskiego] wpłaconych przez Reprezentację Amer. B[undu]," 26 October 1944; "Wykaz sum wpłaconych przez Komit. Rob.," n.d.; and receipts signed by Paweł Siudak, Polish Interior Ministry, 27 June, 1, 2 December 1944, JLBA—ME 42/5c. The principal contributors were the American Jewish Joint Distribution Committee, the Jewish Labor Committee, the American Committee of the Bund, and the Rescue Committee of the Jewish Agency for Palestine. Documents in the same files indicate that from the outbreak of the war through March 1944 these same organizations had transmitted no more than $600,000 via Polish government channels (although in mid-1943 they had discussed the possibility of sending more; see above, Chapter 3).

83. See above, Chapter 3.

84. A transfer of rescue funds generally began with a Jewish organization delivering a sum to the nearest Polish embassy or consulate. The organization would notify Szerer or Schwarzbart of the delivery. In the meantime, the Polish diplomatic office would place the money into an account maintained by the Polish Treasury in a commercial bank and notify the Treasury Ministry in London of the deposit. The ministry would then turn over the deposited amount in cash to either Schwarzbart or Szerer (or sometimes to both together), after deducting the costs of consignment and insurance. The Jewish representatives in turn would hand the banknotes to an official of the Polish Interior Ministry, designating the intended recipients in the homeland. The Interior Ministry was responsible for conveying the money physically to Poland. This process can be followed in the following docu-

ments, inter alia: Janusz Żoltowski, Financial Counselor, Polish Embassy, [United States], to Jacob Pat, Jewish Labor Committee, New York, 18 April 1944 (Nr. P. 4e/44), DRI—INV. 153/14; Kraczkiewicz to Szerer, 18 April 1944; Jarosław Luba, Polish Treasury Ministry, to Szerer and Schwarzbart, 16 August 1944 (L. dz. 686/7/Tjn/44/Kr. 3); and receipt from Paweł Siudak, Social Services Division (Wydział Społeczny), Polish Interior Ministry, 27 June 1944, JLBA—ME 42/5c. The Jewish representatives would check periodically with the designated organizations in Poland to ascertain whether the shipments of funds had arrived. See, for example, Szerer to Berezowski (Feiner), 3 February 1944, JLBA—ME 42/5c; Schwarzbart to ŻKN, 4 September 1944, YVA—M2/431. The Interior Ministry's transmission mechanism does not seem to have been terribly reliable; in January 1945 the Jewish National Committee informed Schwarzbart that it had not received any money since the previous April. See memorandum by Schwarzbart, 17 January 1945, YVA—M2/267. The following day Schwarzbart asked the Interior Ministry for an explanation of why the substantial sums that had been transmitted during this interval had not been delivered. Schwarzbart to Polish Interior Ministry, 18 January 1945 (Nr. 88/45), YVA—M2/267. No response to this letter has yet been found. See also the documents in Korzec, "The Government Delegacy."

85. The first deportations of Hungarian Jews from Subcarpathian Ruthenia and Northern Transylvania took place on 15 May 1944. Braham, *Politics of Genocide*, 2:604–5. For more on the Hungarian deportations, see below.

86. See above, n. 1.

87. The figure includes some 460,000 living within the borders defined by the Treaty of Trianon in 1920 and over 300,000 in the former Czechoslovak, Romanian, and Yugoslav territories annexed by Hungary in 1939–41. Braham, *Politics of Genocide*, 2:1143.

88. Hungary had entered the war as an independent ally of the Third Reich in June 1941. By early 1944, however, the Hungarians had given signs of seeking a separate peace with the Allies, prompting Germany to invade and establish a client government under the premiership of Döme Sztójay, former Hungarian minister to Germany.

89. Cable, Gerhart Riegner, World Jewish Congress, Geneva, to Stephen Wise, 23 March 1944, quoted in Gilbert, *Auschwitz and the Allies*, p. 184.

90. Quoted in ibid.

91. Ibid., pp. 185–86.

92. Quoted in Penkower, *The Jews Were Expendable*, p. 187.

93. "Rozmowa z Ministrem Władysławem Banaczykiem . . . ," 28 March 1944, YVA—M2/141. Hungary had been regarded as a relatively safe haven for Jews prior to the German occupation. Jews were, to be sure, subject to a certain amount of discriminatory legislation, and young Jewish men were conscripted into forced labor battalions for service on the Russian front (where perhaps as many as 42,000 lost their lives); but the Hungarian regime consistently abjured any "physical" solution of the Jewish question along Nazi

lines and refused to turn Jews over to German authority. On the Jewish policy of successive Hungarian regimes and on the forced labor battalions and their losses, see Braham, *Politics of Genocide*, esp. 1:140–249, 307–21, 2:1143. On the entry of Polish Jewish refugees into Hungary during the months prior to the German occupation, see below.

94. Szczerbiński to Polish Foreign Ministry, 3 April 1944, HIA-PG, Box 219 (MSZ), File 851/e: "Żydzi—różne kraje; ratowanie Żydów," Subfile: "Żydzi z Węgier."

95. In fact, he ventured, on the basis of "a series of small but highly characteristic incidents" he could determine that "the Germans have decided to scale back the physical extermination of the Jews" altogether. In his view Germany's pressing needs on the battlefield had resulted in policy decisions being made in accordance with the expressed needs of the German army, and the army, he noted, had traditionally preferred to keep Jews alive for service as forced laborers.

96. See E. Hutten-Czapski to Polish Embassy, London, 24 February 1944 (Nr. U/312/Z.II/W/44), HIA-PG, Box 188 (MSZ), File U312/Z: "Uchodźcy Żydzi w krajach europejskich," Subfile: "Żydzi na Węgrzech."

97. "Wyciąg z listu Delegata Rządu na Węgrzech," 7 December 1943 (L. dz. K.124/44), YVA—M2/414.

98. On this committee, see "Sytuacja uchodźców polskich na Węgrzech," 20 April 1943, HIA-Sokolnicki, Box 2, File: "Hungary's Political Position, 1943–44." The committee was also referred to at times in Polish sources as Komitet Obywatelski, which would have the same translation in English.

99. A. Wdziękoński, Polish Consulate-General, Jerusalem, to Polish Foreign Ministry, 7 February 1944, HIA-PG, Box 219 (MSZ), File 851/e. See also Sławik to Polish Minister of Social Welfare, n.d., YVA—M2/414.

100. For evidence of Jewish organizations bringing such charges, see, inter alia, cable, Rosmarin to Polish Foreign Ministry, 17 July 1943 (Nr. 47), HIA-PG, Box 188 (MSZ), File U312/Z; Isaac Weissman to Tadeusz Nowak, Polish Legation, Lisbon, 17 January 1944, YVA—M2/414.

101. See Banaczyk to Polish Foreign Minister, 21 January 1944 (L. dz. 115/44), and Stańczyk to Polish Foreign Ministry, 8 March 1944 (L. dz. 2776/44), HIA-PG, Box 188 (MSZ), File U312/Z. Sławik was also instructed to make certain that Jews received "the most forthcoming assistance" and was told that efforts were under way to raise more funds for his operation. Cable, Polish Foreign Ministry to Polish Legation, Bern, 22 March 1944 (Nr. 152), ibid.

102. See cable, Szczerbiński to Polish Foreign Ministry, 27 November 1943 (Nr. 294), and cable, Rosmarin to Polish Foreign Ministry, 4 February 1944 (Nr. 15), HIA-PG, Box 188 (MSZ), File U312/Z.

103. See the report on the testimony of two recent arrivals from Poland to Palestine, via Hungary, in Wdziękoński to Polish Foreign Ministry, 7 February 1944, HIA-PG, Box 219 (MSZ), File 851/e; also the marginal note by E. Przesmycki to Stańczyk and Polish Foreign Ministry, 8 March 1944

(L. dz. 2776/44), HIA-PG, Box 188 (MSZ), File U312/Z. Another reason for the Jewish emphasis on this approach was the existence in Hungary of a Jewish relief and rescue committee, which emphasized trying to smuggle Jews out of the country. See Braham, *Politics of Genocide*, 1:107.

104. See Braham, *Politics of Genocide*, 1:108. Braham regards these threats as nothing more than political sops to the parties of the right and states that beginning in late 1943 the situation of Jewish refugees actually improved. Nevertheless, Polish Foreign Ministry officials could act only on the basis of assessments of the situation to which they were privy, and these suggested that the situation of Polish Jews in the country was growing more precarious.

105. See above, n. 103.

106. [Signature illegible] to James Sommerville, U.S. Embassy to Poland, 17 February 1944; M. Budny, Polish Embassy, London, to E. A. Walker, British Foreign Office, 3 March 1944; and cable, E. Hutten-Czapski, Polish Foreign Ministry, to Polish Consulate-General, Tel Aviv, 30 March 1944 (Nr. 18), HIA-PG, Box 188 (MSZ), File U312/Z.

107. See Budny to Walker, 3 March 1944 (see previous note). Such thinking appears to have guided the Polish government earlier in dealing with the situation of Polish Jews in France. See above, Chapter 1.

108. Walker to Budny, 29 March 1944 (No. W/3583/3583/48), HIA-PG, Box 188, File U312/Z. Walker wrote, "As regards . . . Jews of Polish nationality, . . . we would probably be ready to accept them in Palestine, subject to security considerations. The latest developments in Hungary, however, will, I fear, make escape more difficult. As regards . . . non-Jewish Poles, . . . the prospects are not . . . very good, but we have reasonable hope that this may prove feasible in the not too distant future."

109. Czapski to Polish Embassy, Ankara, 17 June 1944 (Nr. 80); J. Weytko, Polish Foreign Ministry, to A. W. G. Randall, 15 July 1944; and J. Librach, Polish Foreign Ministry, to Rudolf Schonfeld, U. S. Embassy to Poland, 20 July 1944, HIA-PG, Box 219 (MSZ), File 851/e.

110. An orthodox Jew, Julius Kühl, served on the staff of the Polish Legation in Bern. He maintained contact with the representative of the American Union of Orthodox Rabbis in Switzerland, Isaac Sternbuch, who in turn received communications about the situation in Hungary from Rabbi Michael Dov-Ber Weissmandel, a leader of the Jewish underground in Bratislava who had recently escaped from a transport to Auschwitz. Kühl on several occasions had used the Polish diplomatic pouch to transmit messages about the condition of European Jewry. He was evidently also in contact with representatives of other Jewish organizations in Switzerland who had their own sources of information inside Hungary. On these channels, see Penkower, *The Jews Were Expendable*, pp. 183–92. The Polish memorandum of 3 June 1944 about the plight of Hungarian Jews (see below) was identified as having been "received by secret channels at the Polish Legation in Bern, Switzerland, from reliable Jewish sources in Budapest, Hungary." The source of the information was most likely Fülöp Freudiger, a leader of the Orthodox

Jewish community in Budapest. See Lewin, "Attempts at Rescuing European Jews," p. 13. In addition, Zionist delegates in Istanbul maintained contacts with a Zionist-led Jewish underground inside Hungary and with the Polish consulate-general in Turkey's largest city. See Porat, *Hanhagah beMilkud*, pp. 347–50.

111. See Gilbert, *Auschwitz and the Allies*, pp. 212–13.

112. Ciechanowski to Elbridge Durbrow, 3 June 1944, HIA-PG, Box 219 (MSZ), File 851/e. The three locations mentioned were indeed among the first to suffer deportation. See Braham, *Politics of Genocide*, 2:605, 614.

113. Quoted in Gilbert, *Auschwitz and the Allies*, p. 212. Brand's mission was an outcome of efforts made by the Assistance and Rescue Committee in Budapest, following the German occupation of Hungary, to bribe German officials not to deport Hungarian Jews to Poland. These efforts came to the attention of Adolf Eichmann, head of the SS unit that had been dispatched to Hungary to organize the deportations. Eichmann was indeed interested in discussing terms under which he might be induced to suspend deportations; evidently his superiors in the SS, including perhaps Reichsführer SS Heinrich Himmler himself, saw in such negotiations an opportunity to open contacts with the Western Allies, leading, perhaps, to the conclusion of a separate peace between them and the Third Reich. Eichmann, undoubtedly acting on orders from the highest echelons of the Nazi regime, had thus sent Brand—together with Grosz, who presumably knew the actual broader purpose of the mission—to convey to the Allies a proposal regarding the possible exchange of Jews for merchandise (including 10,000 trucks). The mission was an opening move in what Brand's SS dispatchers hoped would eventually develop into ongoing talks about ending the war on the western front altogether. For the details of this story, see esp. Bauer, *The Holocaust in Historical Perspective*, pp. 94–155.

114. On the responses of the Western Allies, see Bauer, *The Holocaust in Historical Perspective*, pp. 130–43; Gilbert, *Auschwitz and the Allies*, pp. 240–61.

115. Quoted in Gilbert, *Auschwitz and the Allies*, p. 254.

116. See J. Zarański to Romer, 23 June 1944, HIA-PG, Box 219 (MSZ), File 851/e, Subfile: "Żydzi z Węgier."

117. "Wyciąg z uchwały Rady Ministrów," 27 June 1944, ibid.

118. See, for example, cable, Czapski to Polish Embassy, Ankara, 17 June 1944 (Nr. 80), ibid.; Polish Foreign Ministry to Ciechanowski, 30 June 1944 (Nr. P.V./3/W/44), HIA-US, Box 12, File 6; Karol Maxamin to Polish Ministry of Social Welfare, 8 August 1944 (Nr. 797/VII-3/44), YVA—M2/414.

119. Romer to Kraczkiewicz, 27 June 1944, HIA-PG, Box 219 (MSZ), File 851/e, Subfile: "Żydzi z Węgier."

120. Górka to Polish Interior Minister, 27 June 1944, AIP-[EP], "Sprawy Żydowskie."

121. What was new in this information was the mention of Auschwitz as the site to which Jews from Hungary were being deported for killing. It was only a short time earlier that the name Auschwitz had begun to figure prominently

in discussions of the fate of European Jewry, as the result of testimonies by four Jews who had escaped from the camp in April and May 1944. See Gilbert, *Auschwitz and the Allies*, pp. 190–98, 231–39. The Polish government had long been in possession of information pointing to Auschwitz as a primary center for killing Jews, but it had not given such reports wide publicity. See, for example, "Wyjątek z opracowania Ministerstwa Spraw Wewnętrznych na pierwsze półrocze 1943," and cable from Wanda, 15 September 1943 (Nr. 623), SPP—3.16; cable from N, 3 May 1943 (nr. 78), HIA-Korboński, Box 1 Reel 2. See also Engel, *In the Shadow of Auschwitz*, pp. 201–2. Moreover, the government had recently been notified that 400,000 rather than 100,000 Jews had already been deported from Hungary to Poland and that the deportation of the remaining 350,000 was scheduled to begin the following week. Cable, Polish Consulate-General, Istanbul, to Polish Foreign Ministry, 25 June 1944, HIA-PG, Box 219 (MSZ), File 851/e, Subfile: "Żydzi z Węgier." It is impossible to determine precisely when this information was received in London. The government did pass it on to the Jewish Agency in London and to Nahum Goldmann in New York on 4 July 1944. See Górka to Kraczkiewicz, 4 July 1944, HIA-PG, Box 219 (MSZ), File 851/e, Subfile: "Żydzi z Węgier."

122. Actually the council had taken up the Hungarian situation even before the government had asked it to do so. Its first resolution, in fact, preceding even the request for £80,000, committed it to compiling a list of Polish Jewish refugees in the country, seeking the cooperation of the Jewish Agency in obtaining Palestine immigration certificates for them, and coordinating Hungarian rescue efforts with the War Refugee Board. "Uchwała Rady . . . ," 20 June 1944, YVA—M14/f38. A second clause in the resolution explicitly extended the scope of the council's concern beyond citizens of Poland alone by calling upon the Foreign Ministry to initiate a new common Allied warning that anyone from any country who facilitated the transport of Jews to the death camps would be looked upon as a war criminal and to contact the International Red Cross about assistance to the threatened Jews in Hungary.

123. "Uchwała Rady do Spraw Ratowania Ludności Żydowskiej w Polsce," 30 June 1944, YVA—M14/f46; "Uchwała Rady . . . ," 30 June 1944, YVA—M14/ff47–48. The concrete proposals included appeals for "energetic radio action in German and Hungarian" warning civil and military officials not to take part in any future murders, for the dropping of admonishing leaflets from the air over Hungary and Poland, and for the segregation of captured war criminals from other prisoners of war.

124. Romer [?] to O'Malley, 3 July 1944, and Romer [?] to Rudolf Schoenfeld, 3 July 1944, HIA-PG, Box 219 (MSZ), File 851/e, Subfile: "Żydzi z Węgier." The file copies of the letters are unsigned, but they were undoubtedly sent over Romer's signature.

125. Cable, Romer to Polish missions, Ankara, Bern, Lisbon, Stockholm, Vatican, 8 July 1944, ibid. The cable stated that 400,000 Jews had been sent from Hungary to Auschwitz and that "the deportations certainly aim at ex-

terminating the Jews of Hungary in similar fashion to what happened with the Jews of Poland."

126. For example, on 11 July the Foreign Ministry advised the Polish envoy in Stockholm that a Swedish representative in Budapest had temporarily returned home for consultations, and the ministry instructed the envoy to discuss with the Swede "means of counteracting the extermination action." Cable, Romer to Polish mission, Stockholm, 11 July 1944, HIA-PG, Box 219 (MSZ), File 851/e, Subfile: "Żydzi z Węgier." On 14 July, Romer asked the Polish delegate to the Vatican to urge the pope or the primate of Hungary to issue a public statement condemning the deportations, "for diplomatic pressure may prove to be too little, too late [*niedostateczny i spóźniony*]." Cable, Romer to Polish mission, Vatican, 14 July 1944, ibid. On 15 July, Jan Weytko of the Polish Embassy in London met with A. W. G. Randall of the British Foreign Office and pressed him for action regarding warning broadcasts and leaflets. "Notatka w sprawie akcji pomocy ludności żydowskiej," 15 July 1944, ibid. So too did Jan Librach of the Foreign Ministry with Rudolf Schonfeld at the U.S. Embassy to Poland. Librach to Schonfeld, 15 July 1944, ibid.

127. Easterman to Romer, 20 June 1944, ibid.

128. Reiss to Schwarzbart, 18 July 1944, YVA—M2/436.

129. Cable, Potworowski, Lisbon, to Polish Foreign Minister, 14 July 1944, and cable, [Michał] Sokolnicki, Ankara, to Polish Foreign Minister, 12 July 1944, HIA-PG, Box 219 (MSZ), File 851/e, Subfile: "Żydzi z Węgier."

130. On 15 July, Jan Weytko of the Polish Embassy to Great Britain spoke with A. W. G. Randall about three such proposals—broadcasts to the Hungarian people warning against participating in the deportations, dropping leaflets carrying the same message over Hungary, and supplying Jews with false passports issued by neutral countries. The last of these proposals had not been included in the resolutions adopted by the Rescue Council on 30 June, but it was clearly identified by Weytko as having originated with that body. Randall referred the first two suggestions to other government agencies and expressed doubt whether the third was practical. "Notatka w sprawie akcji pomocy ludności żydowskiej," 15 July 1944, ibid. See also Weytko to Randall, 15 July 1944, ibid. Ten days later, however, the Foreign Office notified Weytko that such action "would in principle meet with favourable consideration on the part of H.M.G. and could be discussed in detail as you suggest." A. Walker to Weytko, 25 July 1944, ibid.

131. See Braham, *Politics of Genocide*, 2:1067–85.

132. Ibid., 2:762–63.

133. See Kraczkiewicz to Polish Embassy, London, 11 August 1944, and Polish Foreign Ministry to Polish Legation, Stockholm, 16 October 1944, HIA-PG, Box 219 (MSZ), File 851/e, Subfile: "Żydzi z Węgier."

134. According to information gathered by the Polish Legation in Bern, El Salvador issued about 3,000 such passports, Honduras 400 to 500, Paraguay 200 to 250, and Peru some 100, with smaller numbers coming from Haiti,

Costa Rica, Chile, Venezuela, Ecuador, and Nicaragua. Cable, Ładoś to Polish Foreign Ministry, 25 July 1944, HIA-PG, Box 221 (MSZ), File 851/e, Subfile: "Paszporty/Vittel." There are also at least two testimonies that mention Guatemalan passports. Eck, "Rescue of Jews," p. 133. In addition to passports, officials of some of the states involved issued *promesas*—letters attesting to the bearer's citizenship and entitlement to a passport. See Eck, "Rescue of Jews," p. 138.

135. German authorities had confiscated a large number of passports that had been sent from abroad to Polish Jews no longer alive. They evidently decided to offer them for sale to Jews who might see in their purchase a possible escape from the constant fear and danger of hiding from the Nazis or posing as non-Jews. See Shulman, *The Case of Hotel Polski*, pp. 11–103; Eck, "Rescue of Jews," pp. 139–42.

136. See Eck, "Rescue of Jews."

137. See ibid., p. 137; Penkower, *The Jews Were Expendable*, p. 251; Gilbert, *Auschwitz and the Allies*, p. 123.

138. See Polish Foreign Ministry to Polish Interior Ministry (including a transcription of cable 187 from Bern), 17 May 1943, YVA—O55/3. The leading promoters of the passport scheme were Orthodox Jewish circles in Switzerland, who had a connection to the Polish Legation in Bern through Julius Kühl. See above, n. 110. See also Lewin, "Attempts at Rescuing European Jews," p. 4; Eck, "Rescue of Jews," p. 136.

139. See above, n. 134.

140. Ernest Frischer, Czechoslovak State Council, to Schwarzbart, 23 December 1943, and memorandum by Schwarzbart, 29 December 1943, YVA—M2/395.

141. The available documentation provides no definite indication of the thinking that animated the Polish government in this instance. It is known only that the Polish authorities requested that Jewish leaders be informed of the efforts they were making to have the passports recognized. See, for example, Kraczkiewicz to Schwarzbart, 19 January 1944, YVA—M2/395; cable, Kraczkiewicz to Polish Legation, Bern, 22 January 1944, HIA-PG, Box 221 (MSZ), File 851/e, Subfile: "Paszporty/Vittel."

142. See cable, Kraczkiewicz to Polish Consulate-General, New York, 22 January 1944; Peruvian Foreign Ministry to Oswald Kermenic, Polish chargé d'affaires, Lima, 28 January 1944; cable, Kraczkiewicz to Polish Legation, Bern, 9 March 1944; and cable, Kraczkiewicz to Polish Legation, Mexico, 9 March 1944, HIA-PG, Box 221 (MSZ), File 851/e, Subfile: "Paszporty/Vittel." It appears that the Polish government was not aware at this time which countries had issued passports to Jews in Vittel or how many Jews were involved. On 16 March 1944 Kraczkiewicz telegraphed the Polish Legation in Bern asking if it might be possible to obtain such information from Jewish representatives in Switzerland. Cable, Kraczkiewicz to Polish Legation, Bern, 16 March 1944, ibid.

143. Wasserstein, *Britain and the Jews of Europe*, p. 232. Cf. cable, Kraczkie-wicz to Polish Legation, Bern, 22 January 1944, HIA-PG, Box 221 (MSZ), File 851/e, Subfile: "Paszporty/Vittel."

144. Peruvian Foreign Ministry to Kermenic, 28 January 1944, and cable, Kraczkiewicz to Polish Legation, Bern, 9 March 1944, HIA-PG, Box 221 (MSZ), File 851/e, Subfile: "Paszporty/Vittel"; "Notatka w sprawie Żydów-obywateli polskich posiadaczy paszportów państw Ameryki Łacińskiej," 19 June 1944, YVA—M2/395. The Peruvian refusal did not arouse any pro-test from the Polish government. Cf. Polish Chargé d'Affaires Kermenic's response to the Peruvian Foreign Ministry: "He tenido el honor de recibir la carta de V. Excelencia con fecha 28 de enero 1944 por la cual Ella ha tenido a bien confirmar la entrevista que Ella me ha acordado el 27 del mes próximo pasado, y aprovecho de esta oportunidad para reiterar a V. Excelencia mi caluroso agradecimiento por los sentimientos de sincera y profunda simpatía que en el curso de esta conversación Ella ha tenido a bien manifestar para Polonia." Kermenic to Javier Conea Elías, secretary general, Peruvian For-eign Ministry, 6 February 1944, HIA-PG, Box 221 (MSZ), File 851/e, Subfile: "Paszporty/Vittel."

145. Testimony of Sophie Skipwith, former Vittel internee, sent by Potwo-rowski, Polish Legation, Lisbon, to Schwarzbart, 26 July 1944, and "Memo-randum Concerning Deportation of Jews from Vittel . . . ," 20 September 1944, YVA—M2/395.

146. See previous note. See also Eck, "Rescue of Jews," p. 149.

147. Cable, Polish Legation, Bern, to Polish Foreign Ministry, 1 April 1944 (received 5 April), HIA-PG, Box 221 (MSZ), File 851/e, Subfile: "Pasz-porty/Vittel."

148. Kraczkiewicz to Schwarzbart, 7 April 1944, ibid. Kraczkiewicz ex-plained that "even if such an exchange never comes about, such a declaration by itself might save the lives of these people."

149. Lewin, "Attempts at Rescuing European Jews," p. 11. In actuality, the first group of 163 Jews was in Drancy on 26 April; it was shipped to Auschwitz three days later. However, over 70 Jews remained in Vittel.

150. On 17 June 1944 the Polish Foreign Ministry received the following cable from Bern: "From April 20th no reliable news about the people for-merly at Vittel. United States Legation at Bern and Swiss Legation at Berlin could not obtain any information. About May 15th Auswaertiges Amt told the Swedish Minister that the 163 people he was inquiring about were de-ported in 'unknown direction.' An immediate offer of protecting powers to exchange some German citizens for those concerned may still help. Having Palestinian certificates they could go to Palestine straight from Portugal." Kraczkiewicz to Schwarzbart, 22 June 1944 (Nr. Z-851-e/paszp./44), YVA—M2/395. In reality, all Jews who had been removed from Vittel were dead by this time.

151. Cable, Polish Foreign Ministry to distribution list, 10 April 1944, HIA-PG, Box 221 (MSZ), File 851/e, Subfile: "Paszporty/Vittel." An exchange for

all of the threatened Jews appeared unlikely, largely because there were not enough German nationals in the Western Hemisphere who could be included in such a transfer. See Wyman, *Abandonment of the Jews*, pp. 276–77.

152. See Chałupczyński, Bogotá, to Polish Foreign Ministry, 23 May 1944, HIA-PG, Box 221 (MSZ), File 851/e, Subfile: "Paszporty/Vittel."

153. Kermenic to Polish Foreign Ministry, 1 May 1944, ibid.

154. Gérard Lescot, Haitian foreign minister, to Roman Dębicki, Polish legate, Havana, 22 May 1944, and Mirosław Arciszewski, Polish ambassador, Buenos Aires, to Polish Foreign Ministry, 31 May 1944, ibid. See also Shulman, *The Case of Hotel Polski*, p. 216.

155. See Chałupczyński to Polish Foreign Ministry, 23 May 1944, HIA-PG, Box 221 (MSZ), File 851/e, Subfile: "Paszporty/Vittel," quoting instructions sent by the State Department to the U.S. chargé d'affaires in Bogotá: "With reference to the view expressed, that although the proposed exchange of nationals would not become effective, the lives of the persons might be saved by a mere declaration on the part of the American republics, it appears from direct information from Berlin that an empty declaration would not be regarded as satisfactory by the German Government. . . . The Department of State is of course in thorough sympathy with the objectives in mind, but feels that the proposed method of approach may not be suitable at this time." See also Shulman, *The Case of Hotel Polski*, pp. 215–19.

156. "Raport Biura," 28 July 1944, YVA—M14/ff62–63; "Raport Lachsa . . . ," 2 August 1944, YVA—M14/f71.

157. Testimony of Sophie Skipwith (see above, n. 145).

158. "Aide-Mémoire Submitted to the High Commissioner for Refugees . . . ," n.d., YVA—M14/ff111–15; Lachs to Raczyński, n.d., YVA—M14/ff107–8; "Raport Lachsa . . . ," n.d., YVA—M14/ff100–106.

159. "Memorandum concerning Deportation of Jews from Vittel in April and May 1944," 20 September 1944, YVA—M2/395. See also memorandum by Lachs, 11 September 1944, YVA—M14/f125.

160. Note by Gruenbaum, 6 August 1944, YVA—M14/f88; cable, Gruenbaum to Schwarzbart and Reiss, 11 August 1944, YVA—M2/255.

161. So, too, did the World Jewish Congress. See World Jewish Congress to Rescue Council, n.d., YVA—M14/f85.

162. Schwarzbart to Mikołajczyk, 18 August 1944, HIA-PG, Box 223 (MSZ), File 851/e: "Żydzi w Polsce," Subfile: "Majdanek i inne obozy."

163. Text of appeal in HIA-PG, Box 219 (MSZ), File 851/e, Subfile: "Żydzi z Węgier."

164. Lachs to Raczyński, 2 October 1944, ibid.

165. Raczyński to British Foreign Office, 4 October 1944, and Raczyński to U.S. Embassy, London, 4 October 1944, ibid. Penkower, in *The Jews Were Expendable*, p. 205, notes that the government-in-exile also supported Jewish requests that the major Allies bomb the camp at Auschwitz.

166. Winant to Raczyński, 9 October 1944, HIA-PG, Box 219 (MSZ), File 851/e, Subfile: "Żydzi z Węgier."

167. Even earlier, the council had taken to appealing directly to the War Refugee Board for, among other things, funds, food, and medical supplies. Evidently the Polish government did not regard itself in a position to deliver these items. "Memorandum of the Council for Rescuing the Jewish Population in Poland, submitted to the War Refugee Board," 15 September 1944, YVA—M14/ff128–30.

168. See "Notatka dla Pana Ministra [Banaczyka], 20 February 1945, AIP-[EP], "Sprawy Żydowskie"; Schwarzbart to Ch. Perelman, Aide aux Israélites Victimes de la Guerre, Brussels, 19 April 1945, YVA—M2/802.

169. Schwarzbart to Polish Ministry of Social Welfare, 20 April 1945 (Nr. 508/45), YVA—M2/802.

170. "Rozmowa z p. Janem Bociańskim," 8 February 1945, YVA—M2/141.

171. Statement by the Rescue Council, 21 June 1945, YVA—M2/74.

ENVOI

1. Stalin to Churchill, 23 July 1944, in Polonsky, *The Great Powers and the Polish Question*, p. 208. Stalin remarked further, "The Polish Committee of National Liberation intends to set up an administration on Polish territory, and I hope this will be done. We have not found in Poland other forces capable of establishing a Polish administration. The so-called underground organisations, led by the Polish Government in London, have turned out to be ephemeral and lacking influence."

2. On the uprising, see Ciechanowski, *The Warsaw Uprising*.

3. Polonsky, *The Great Powers and the Polish Question*, p. 36. Poland was to be compensated by annexing substantial territories formerly belonging to Germany.

4. "Ambassador Winant's telegram to President Roosevelt . . . ," 23 November 1944, in *DPSR*, 2:473–74.

5. Mikołajczyk later explained the situation on the eve of his resignation as follows: "We were becoming increasingly isolated. The Big Three regarded us either openly or privately as *saboteurs* of their unity because of our refusal to yield on all points. My own cabinet felt that what I had agreed to represented too much of a compromise, though I explained to them that they were on the verge of being cut off from the Polish people by the threatened recognition of the Lublin group by all major Powers." Mikołajczyk, *The Rape of Poland*, pp. 104–5.

6. Churchill to Stalin, 3 December 1944, in Polonsky, *The Great Powers and the Polish Question*, p. 230.

7. Eden to Churchill, 1 February 1945 ("Conversations with Mr. Stettinius, Poland"), in ibid., pp. 240–42: "The time has probably gone by for a 'fusion' of London and Lublin, and the only remedy that we can see is the creation of a *new* interim Government in Poland, pledged to hold free elections as soon as conditions permit." Britain and the United States declined, however, to recognize PKWN as the new Polish government.

8. Romer to Polish prime minister, 4 October 1944 (Nr. Z.851-c/44), YVA —O55/4.

9. "Dekret Prezydenta Rzeczypospolitej . . . o zwalczaniu szerzenia niena-wiści do człowieka z powodu jego pochodzenia, wyznania lub narodowości," 14 October 1944, ibid.

10. There is no indication of any objection having been raised to it. In all likelihood, in the atmosphere of crisis that pervaded the work of the exile regime at the time, it was simply pushed aside.

11. Serafiński to Polish prime minister and all ministers, 20 November 1944 (L. dz. 1612/44/tj./AS/OF), AIP—A.21/5/3.

12. "Oświadczenie p. Premiera Arciszewskiego . . . ," 13 December 1944, HIA-PG, Box 223, File: "Żydzi w Palestynie." There is no documentary evi-dence to suggest that this statement was made only for public relations pur-poses or that it might have been anything but sincerely intended. Neverthe-less, it was subsequently used for public relations purposes. See below.

13. Polish Foreign Ministry to Rosmarin, 16 December 1944, ibid.

14. See, for example, "Sprawy Żydowskie w Palestynie," 19 June 1944, AIP —A.XII.3/40; "Akcja propagandowa i organizacyjna ŻPP wśród dezerterów na Środkowym Wschodzie," 22 November 1944, HIA-PG, Box 223 (MSZ), File: "Żydzi w Palestynie."

15. Górka to Polish interior minister, 29 November 1944, and 16 February 1945, AIP—[EP], "Sprawy Żydowskie."

16. Górka to Polish interior minister, 29 November 1944, ibid.

17. "Rozmowa z Ministrem Stanisławem Kotem . . . ," 25 October 1944, YVA—M2/142.

18. "Rozmowa z p. Markiem Celtem . . . ," 6 February 1945, YVA—M2/141.

19. *American Jewish Year Book*, 47 (1945–46): 400.

20. Quoted in ibid., p. 402.

21. As, for example, in the Reprezentacja's meetings with Stańczyk in Pales-tine in mid-1943 and in the negotiations over the establishment of the Rescue Council in early 1944.

22. This change was epitomized in the *American Jewish Year Book*, whose judgments tended to reflect a broad consensus of Jewish opinion throughout the world. In its summary of the twelve-month period ending in August 1942, it charged that "in spite of the declarations of equality, the Polish regime in exile, and especially the bureaucracy, is in fact still dominated by the pre-war anti-Semitic spirit." *American Jewish Year Book*, 44 (1942–43): 249. In contrast, its summary of the subsequent twelve-month period, written in September 1943, noted that "during the period under review the official attitude of the Polish Government-in-exile in London remained friendly to the Jews. This attitude has been demonstrated not only by the numerous pronouncements of government spokesmen with regard to the future constitution of Poland, but also by concrete actions." Ibid., 45 (1943–44): 311.

23. See Engel, *In the Shadow of Auschwitz*, pp. 69–80; above, Chapter 4.

24. This rise of Zionist influence among Jews during the war has been

analyzed with regard to American Jewry in Berman, *Nazism, the Jews, and American Zionism*.

25. Republic of Poland, Ministry of Foreign Affairs, *The Mass Extermination of Jews in German Occupied Poland*.

26. Again, this conclusion is offered exclusively as a proposition of fact, not as a judgment. The question of whether such a perspective is to be accepted or condemned is beyond the scope of this discussion. See above, Introduction.

27. The efforts that the government made to persuade Latin American states to confirm the validity of their passports held by Polish Jews in German-occupied Europe may represent a deviation from this generalization; insufficient documentation prevents determining whether or not these efforts were an exception.

28. Some officials below the top policymaking level evidently resisted coming to this conclusion, and toward the end of 1943 they were able to point to what they viewed as hopeful signs. They do not appear to have convinced any of their superiors in the government, however, and their own short-lived hopefulness was in any case dashed during the desertion affair.

Bibliography

The following is a list of sources cited in the notes, and not of all materials consulted in the preparation of this study.

ARCHIVES

1. Archiwum Instytutu Polskiego (formerly General Sikorski Historical Institute), London
   A.12   Ambasada RP w Londynie
   A.21   Ministerstwo Prac Kongresowych
   A.48   Kancelaria Cywilna Prezydenta RP
   A.XII   Władze Naczelne
   [EP]   Eaton Place Deposit (uncataloged)
   KOL. 11   Władysław Anders (formerly KGA)
   KOL. 25   Stanisław Kot
   KOL. 138   Wincenty Bąkiewicz
   PRM.   Prezydium Rady Ministrów
   PRML.   Prezydium Rady Ministrów, Sekretariat
2. Central Zionist Archives, Jerusalem
   J25   Reprezentacja Żydostwa Polskiego
   S25   Jewish Agency for Palestine, Political Department
   S26   Jewish Agency for Palestine, Rescue Committee
3. Diaspora Research Institute, Tel Aviv
   A1   Institute for Jewish Affairs, New York
   INV. 153   Adolf Berman
4. Histadrut Archives, Tel Aviv
   Minute Books, Council
   Minute Books, Secretariat
5. Hoover Institution Archives, Stanford, California
   Władysław Anders
   Jan Karski
   Tadeusz Komorowski
   Stanisław Mikołajczyk
   Poland. Ambasada US
   Poland. Konsulat Generalny New York
   Poland. Ministerstwo Spraw Wewnętrznych
   Poland. Rada Narodowa
   Polish Government
      Akta Ministerstwa Informacji i Dokumentacji

Akta Ministerstwa Spraw Zagranicznych
Michał Sokolnicki

6. Hoover Library, Stanford, California
   Government Documents, Poland
7. Jabotinsky Institute, Tel Aviv
   H3A   Committee for a Jewish Army
   P23   Aryeh ben Eliezer
8. Jewish Labor Bund Archives, New York
   ME 42   Emanuel Szerer
9. Private Collections (photocopies in author's possession)
   Marek Kahan
   Synaj Okręt
10. Public Record Office, Kew, London
    FO 371   Foreign Office, General Correspondence, Political
    FO 921   Minister of State, Cairo
    FO 954   Lord Avon
11. Studium Polski Podziemnej, Ealing, London
    3.16   Obozy koncentracyjne niemieckie
    56   Ministerstwo Spraw Wewnętrznych
12. Wiener Library, Tel Aviv
    PC 210   Press Cuttings. Polish Government-in-Exile
13. Yad Vashem Archives, Jerusalem
    M2   Ignacy Schwarzbart
    M14   Rada do Spraw Ratowania Żydów w Polsce
    O6.48   Rada Pomocy Żydom
    O25   Michał Zylberberg
    O55   Alexander Bernfes

INTERVIEWS

Marek Kahan, Tel Aviv, 17 March 1985
Jan Karski, San Francisco, 18 April 1982
Count Edward Raczyński, London, 17 November 1983

NEWSPAPERS AND PERIODICALS

American Jewish Year Book—Philadelphia
HaArets—Tel Aviv
Biuletyn Polski—New York
HaBoker—Tel Aviv
Congress Weekly—New York
Davar—Tel Aviv
Dziennik Polski—London
Eynikayt—Moscow

Forverts—New York
Free Europe—London
Jewish Chronicle—London
Jewish Frontier—New York
JTA Bulletin—London
Manchester Guardian
New Palestine—New York
News Bulletin on Eastern European Affairs (Yiddish)—New York
New York Herald Tribune
New York Times
HaOlam—Jerusalem
Palestine Post—Jerusalem
HaPo'el haTsa'ir—Jerusalem
Polish Fortnightly Review—London
Pravda—Moscow
Reconstructionist—Philadelphia
The Times—London
Der Tog—New York
HaTsofeh—Tel Aviv
Wolna Polska—Moscow
Zionist Review—London

OTHER PRIMARY SOURCES

Anders, Władysław. *Bez ostatniego rozdziału: Wspomnienia z lat 1939–1946.*
    Newtown: Montgomeryshire Printing, 1946.
Armia Krajowa w Dokumentach. 3 vols. London: Studium Polski Podziem-
    nej, 1970– .
Babiński, Witold. *Przyczynki historyczne do okresu 1939–1945.* London: B.
    Świderski, 1967.
Blumental, Nahman, and Kermisz, Józef, eds. *HaMeri vehaMered beGeto
    Varshah: Sefer Mismachim.* Jerusalem: Yad Vashem, 1965.
Bór-Komorowski, T. *The Secret Army.* New York: Macmillan, 1951.
Borwicz, Michał. *Arishe Papirn.* 3 vols. Buenos Aires: Unión Central Israelita
    Polaca en la Argentina, 1955.
[Cadogan, Alexander.] *The Diaries of Sir Alexander Cadogan, 1938–1945.*
    Edited by David Dilks. New York: G. P. Putnam, 1972.
Churchill, Winston S. *The Second World War.* Vol. 3, *The Grand Alliance.*
    Boston: Houghton Mifflin, 1950.
Ciechanowski, Jan. *Defeat in Victory.* Garden City, N.Y.: Doubleday, 1947.
The Crime of Katyn: Facts and Documents. London: Polish Cultural Founda-
    tion, 1965.
Dekel, Efraim. *Shai: The Exploits of Hagana Intelligence.* New York and
    London: Thomas Yoseloff, 1959.

Documents on Polish-Soviet Relations. 2 vols. London: Heinemann, 1961–67.

Driberg, Tom. *Ruling Passions*. London: Cape, 1977.

[Drohojowski, Jan.] *Jana Drohojowskiego wspomnienia dyplomatyczne*. Kraków: Wydawnictwo Literackie, 1969.

Engel, David. "The Polish Government-in-Exile and the Holocaust: Stanisław Kot's Confrontation with Palestinian Jewry, November 1942– January 1943—Selected Documents." *POLIN* 2 (1987): 272–301.

———. "HaYishuv biTekufat Milhemet haOlam haSheniyah baAspeklari-yah shel Dinim-veHeshbonot Diplomatiyim Polaniyim." *HaTsiyonut* 12 (1987): 401–21.

Foreign Relations of the United States, 1942. Vol. 2, *Europe*. Washington, D.C.: U.S. Government Printing Office, 1961.

Goldstein, Bernard. *Finf Yor in Varshever Geto*. New York: Unzer Tsayt, 1947.

Great Britain. Parliament. *Parliamentary Debates (Hansard): House of Commons Official Report*. 5th ser., vol. 397. London: His Majesty's Stationery Office, 1944.

Gutman, Ysrael [*sic*]. "A Report of a Member of the Polish Underground on Polish-Jewish Relations in Occupied Poland." *Michael* 6 (1980): 102–14.

Hirszfeld, Ludwik. *Historia jednego życia*. Warsaw: Pax, 1957.

Inter-Allied Information Committee. *Punishment for War Crimes: The Inter-Allied Declaration Signed at St. James's Palace London on 13th January 1942 and Relative Documents*. London, 1942.

Jędrzejewicz, Wacław. *Poland in the British Parliament*. 3 vols. New York: Piłsudski Institute, 1946–62.

Karski, Jan. *Story of a Secret State*. Boston: Houghton Mifflin, 1944.

Korczak, Różka. *Lehavot baEfer*. Merhavia: Sifriat Poalim, 1965.

Korzec, Paweł. "The Government Delegacy in Nazi-Occupied Poland and Funds for the Rescue of Jews—Selected Documents." *Gal-Ed* 13 (1993).

Kot, Stanisław. *Rozmowy z Kremlem*. London: n.p., 1959.

Kwiatkowski, Michał. *Rząd i Rada Narodowa R.P. w świetle faktów i dokumentów od września 1939 do lutego 1942 r.* London: Author, 1942.

Lubetkin, Zivia. *BiY'mei Kilayon uMered*. Tel Aviv: HaKibuts haMe'uhad, 1979.

[Meed]-Międzyrzecki, Władka. *Fun Beyde Zaytn Geto-Moyer*. New York: Workmen's Circle, 1948.

Mikołajczyk, Stanisław. *The Rape of Poland: Pattern of Soviet Aggression*. New York and Toronto: McGraw-Hill, 1948.

Nicholas, H. G., ed. *Washington Despatches, 1941–45: Weekly Political Reports from the British Embassy*. Chicago: University of Chicago Press, 1981.

Olszer, Krystyna M., ed. *For Your Freedom and Ours: Polish Progressive Spirit from the 14th Century to the Present*. 2d ed. New York: Frederick Unger, 1981.

Polonsky, Antony, ed. *The Great Powers and the Polish Question, 1941–1945:*

A Documentary Study in Cold War Origins. London: London School of
Economics and Political Science, 1976.
———, and Drukier, Bolesław, eds. The Beginnings of Communist Rule
in Poland, December 1943–June 1945. London: Routledge and Kegan
Paul, 1980.
Pritt, Denis Noel. The Autobiography of D. N. Pritt. 3 vols. London: Lawrence
and Wishart, 1965–66.
Publicystyka Związku Patriotów Polskich: Wybór. Warsaw: Książka i Wiedza,
1967.
Raczyński, Edward. In Allied London. London: Weidenfeld and Nicol-
son, 1962.
Reiss, Anshel. BeSa'arot haTekufah. Tel Aviv: Am Oved, 1982.
Reprezentacja Żydostwa Polskiego. Sprawozdanie z działalności w latach
1940–1945. [Tel Aviv, 1945].
Republic of Poland. List of Members of the Government and the National Council.
London, 1942.
Republic of Poland. Ministry of Foreign Affairs. The Mass Extermination of
Jews in German Occupied Poland. London, 1942.
Retinger, Józef. All about Poland. London: Minerva, 1941.
Ringelblum, Emmanuel. Polish-Jewish Relations during the Second World War.
Edited and with footnotes by Joseph Kermish and Shmuel Krakowski.
New York: Howard Fertig, 1976.
Slowes, Shalom. Ya'ar Katyn, 1940. Tel Aviv: Ma'ariv, 1986.
Stosunki polsko-radzieckie w latach 1917–1945: Dokumenty i materiały. Warsaw:
Książka i Wiedza, 1967.
Tartakower, Arieh. "HaPe'ilut haMedinit lema'an Yehudei Polin al Ademat
Amerika beMilhemet haOlam haSheniyah." Gal-Ed 6 (1983): 167–84.
Tendyra, Bernadetta. "Archiwum Prof. Stanisława Kota." Zeszyty Historyczne,
95 (1986): 140–51.
Tomaszewski, Jerzy. "Lwów, 22 listopada 1918." Przegląd Historyczny 75
(1984): 279–85.
[Zygielbojm, Szmul.] Zygielbojm-Bukh. Compiled by J. S. Hertz. New York:
Unzer Tsayt, 1947.

SECONDARY SOURCES

Adler-Rudel, S. "A Chronicle of Rescue Efforts." Leo Baeck Institute Yearbook
11 (1966) :213–41.
Arad, Yitshak. Vilna haYehudit beMa'avak uveKilayon. Tel Aviv: Sifriat
Poalim, 1976.
Arczyński, Marek, and Balcerak, Wiesław. Kryptonim "Żegota." 2d ed.
Warsaw: Czytelnik, 1983.
Avital, Zvi. "The Polish Government in Exile and the Jewish Question."
Wiener Library Bulletin 33/34 (1975): 43–51.

Bartoszewski, Władysław, and Lewin, Zofia, eds. *Righteous among Nations: How Poles Helped the Jews, 1939–1945*. London: Earlscourt Publications, 1969.

Bauer, Yehuda. *American Jewry and the Holocaust: The American Jewish Joint Distribution Committee, 1939–1945*. Detroit: Wayne State University Press, 1981.

———. *The Holocaust in Historical Perspective*. Seattle: University of Washington Press, 1978.

Beit-Tsvi, Sh. B. *HaTsiyonut haPost-Ugandit beMashber haSho'ah: Mehkar al Gormei Mishgeha shel haTenu'ah haTsiyonit baShanim 1938–1945*. Tel Aviv: Bronfman, 1977.

Berenstein, T., and Rutkowski, A. "Vegn Rateven Yidn durkh Poliakn bes der Hitlerisher Okupatsie." *Bleter far Geshikhte* 14 (1961) :65–104.

Berman, Aaron. *Nazism, the Jews, and American Zionism, 1933–1948*. Detroit: Wayne State University Press, 1990.

Braham, Randolph L. *The Politics of Genocide: The Holocaust in Hungary*. 2 vols. New York: Columbia University Press, 1981.

Breitman, Richard. "Auschwitz and the Archives." *Central European History* 18 (1985): 365–83.

Ciechanowski, Jan M. *The Warsaw Rising of 1944*. Cambridge: Cambridge University Press, 1974.

Cienciała, Anna M. Review of "In the Shadow of Auschwitz: The Polish Government-in-Exile and the Jews, 1939–1942." *American Historical Review* 94 (1989): 485–87.

Dawidowicz, Lucy S. "The Curious Case of Marek Edelman." *Commentary* 83 (March 1987) :66–69.

———. Letter. *Commentary* 84 (July 1987): 10–12.

———. *The War against the Jews, 1933–1945*. New York: Holt, Rinehart and Winston, 1975.

Duraczyński, Eugeniusz. *Kontrowersje i konflikty, 1939–1941*. Warsaw: Państwowe Wydawnictwo Naukowe, 1977.

———. *Między Londynem i Warszawą: Lipiec 1943–lipiec 1944*. Warsaw: Państwowy Instytut Wydawniczy, 1986.

Eck, Nathan. "The Rescue of Jews with the Aid of Passports and Citizenship Papers of Latin American States." *Yad Vashem Studies* 1 (1957): 125–52.

Engel, David. "HaBerihah haHafganatit shel Hayalim Yehudiyim meha-Tsava haPolani beAngliyah biShenat 1944: Parashah baYehasim bein Anglim, Polanim viY'hudim biTekufat Milhemet haOlam haSheniyah." *Yahadut Zemanenu* 2 (1985): 177–207.

———. HaBerit haNichzevet: HaTenu'ah haReviziyonistit uMemshelet Polin haGolah, 1939–1945." *HaTsiyonut* 11 (1986): 333–59.

———. *In the Shadow of Auschwitz: The Polish Government-in-Exile and the Jews, 1939–1942*. Chapel Hill: University of North Carolina Press, 1987.

————. "Jan Karski's Mission to the West." *Holocaust and Genocide Studies* 5 (1990): 363–80.

————. "The Polish Government-in-Exile and the Deportations of Polish Jews from France in 1942." *Yad Vashem Studies* 15 (1983): 91–123.

————. "The Polish Government-in-Exile and the Erlich-Alter Affair." In *Jews in Eastern Poland and the USSR, 1939–1946*, edited by Norman Davies and Antony Polonsky, pp. 172–82. London: Macmillan, 1991.

————. *Semantikah uFolitikah beTe'ur haYehasim bein Polanim liY'hudim*. Tel Aviv: Tel Aviv University Press, 1990.

————. "HaSichsuch haPolani-haSovieti keGorem beHityahasutah shel Memshelet Polin haGolah laSho'ah." *Shvut* 12 (1986): 23–42.

Fein, Helen. *Accounting for Genocide: National Responses and Jewish Victimization during the Holocaust*. New York: Free Press, 1979.

Feingold, Henry L. *The Politics of Rescue: The Roosevelt Administration and the Holocaust, 1938–1945*. New Brunswick: Rutgers University Press, 1970.

Fiszman-Kamińska, Karyna. "Zachód, Emigracyjny Rząd Polski oraz Delegatura wobec sprawy żydowskiej podczas II wojny światowej." *Biuletyn Żydowskiego Instytutu Historycznego* 62 (1967): 43–62.

Friedman, Saul S. *No Haven for the Oppressed: United States Policy toward Jewish Refugees, 1938–1945*. Detroit: Wayne State University Press, 1973.

Garliński, Józef. *Poland in the Second World War*. London: Macmillan, 1985.

Gelbard, Aryeh. *BeSa'arat haYamim: HaBund haRusi beItot Mahapechah*. Tel Aviv: Diaspora Research Institute, 1987.

Gilbert, Martin. *Auschwitz and the Allies*. New York: Holt, Rinehart and Winston, 1981.

Golczewski, Frank. *Polnisch-jüdische Beziehungen, 1881–1922: Eine Studie zur Geschichte des Antisemitismus in Osteuropa*. Wiesbaden: Steiner, 1981.

Gorodenchik, Rinat. "Berihat Tenu'ot haNo'ar miZaglembie, 1943–1944." M.A. thesis, Hebrew University of Jerusalem, 1986.

Gross, Jan T[omasz]. *Polish Society under German Occupation: The General-gouvernement, 1939–1944*. Princeton: Princeton University Press, 1979.

————. *Revolution from Abroad: The Soviet Conquest of Poland's Western Ukraine and Western Belorussia*. Princeton: Princeton University Press, 1988.

Gutman, Yisrael. "Jews in General Anders' Army in the Soviet Union." *Yad Vashem Studies* 12 (1977) 231–96.

————. *Yehudei Varshah, 1939–1943: Geto, Mahteret, Mered*. Tel Aviv: Sifriat Poalim, 1977.

————, and Krakowski, Shmuel. *Unequal Victims: Poles and Jews during World War II*. New York: Holocaust Library, 1986.

Halpern, Ben. *The Idea of a Jewish State*. Cambridge, Mass.: Harvard University Press, 1961.

Heller, Yosef. *Lehi, 1940–1948*. Jerusalem: Keter, 1989.

Iranek-Osmecki, Kazimierz. *Kto ratuje jedno życie . . . : Polacy i Żydzi 1939–1945*. London: Orbis, 1968.

Izek, Hersch. "Roosevelt and the Polish Question, 1941–1945." Ph.D. dissertation, University of Minnesota, 1980.

Janowska, Halina. *Polska emigracja zarobkowa we Francji, 1919–1939.* Warsaw: Książka i Wiedza, 1964.

Johnpoll, Bernard. *The Politics of Futility: The General Jewish Workers Bund of Poland, 1917–1943.* Ithaca, N.Y.: Cornell University Press, 1967.

Kacewicz, George V. *Great Britain, the Soviet Union and the Polish Government in Exile (1939–1945).* The Hague: Martinus Nijhoff, 1979.

Kalinowski, Piotr. *Emigracja polska we Francji w służbie dla Polski i Francji, 1939–1945.* Paris: Księgarnia Polska, 1970.

Karski, Jan. *The Great Powers and Poland, 1919–1945: From Versailles to Yalta.* Lanham, Md.: University Press of America, 1985.

Klarsfeld, Serge. *Vichy-Auschwitz: Le rôle de Vichy dans le solution finale de la question juive en France—1942.* Paris: Fayard, 1983.

Kless, Shlomo. *Gevulot, Mahteret uVerihah: Pe'ilut Tsiyonit-Halutsit biVerit haMo'atsot uKesharim im haYishuv baArets (1941–1945).* Tel Aviv: Moreshet, 1989.

Korboński, Stefan. *The Jews and the Poles in World War II.* New York: Hippocrene Books, 1989.

————. *The Polish Underground State: A Guide to the Underground, 1939–1945.* Boulder, Colo.: East European Quarterly; New York: Columbia University Press, 1978.

————. "[An] Unknown Chapter in the Life of Menahem Begin and Irgun Zvai Leumi." *East European Quarterly* 13 (1979): 373–79.

Korzec, Paweł. "Hidat Retsihatam shel H. Erlich uV. Alter biY'dei ha-Sovietim." *Gal-Ed* 10 (1987): 281–310.

————. *Juifs en Pologne: La question juive pendant l'entre-deux-guerres.* Paris: Presses de la Fondation nationale des sciences politiques, 1980.

Krakowski, Shmuel. *Lehimah Yehudit beFolin neged haNatsim, 1942–1944.* Tel Aviv: Sifriat Poalim, 1977.

Kumoś, Zbigniew. *Związek Patriotów Polskich: Założenia programowo-ideowe.* Warsaw: Wydawnictwo Ministerstwa Obrony Narodowej, 1983.

Landau, Moshe. *Mi'ut Le'umi Lohem: Ma'avak Yehudei Polin, 1918–1928.* Jerusalem: Zalman Shazar Center for Jewish History, 1986.

Laqueur, Walter. *The Terrible Secret: Suppression of the Truth about Hitler's "Final Solution."* Boston and Toronto: Little, Brown, 1980.

Lerner, Saul. Review of "In the Shadow of Auschwitz: The Polish Government-in-Exile and the Jews, 1939–1942." *Shofar* (Winter 1988): 36–37.

Levin, Dov. "The Response of the Jews of Eastern Poland to the Invasion of the Red Army in September 1939 as described by Jewish Witnesses." *Gal-Ed* 11 (1989): 87–102.

Lewin, Isaac. "Attempts at Rescuing European Jews with the Help of Polish Diplomatic Missions during World War II." *Polish Review* 22 (1977):3–23.

Lipstadt, Deborah E. *Beyond Belief: The American Press and the Coming of the Holocaust, 1933–1945.* New York: Free Press, 1986.

Litvak, Yosef. *Pelitim Yehudim miPolin biVerit-haMo'atsot, 1939–1945.* Tel Aviv: HaKibuts haMe'uhad, 1988.

Lookstein, Haskel. *Were We Our Brothers' Keepers?: The Public Response of American Jews to the Holocaust, 1938–1944.* New York and Bridgeport: Hartmore House, 1985.

Lukas, Richard. *The Forgotten Holocaust: The Poles under German Occupation, 1939–1944.* Lexington: University Press of Kentucky, 1986.

———. *The Strange Allies: The United States and Poland, 1941–1945.* Knoxville: University of Tennessee Press, 1978.

Mark, B. *Der Oyfshtand in Varshever Geto.* 2d ed., Warsaw: Yidish Bukh, 1963.

Marrus, Michael R., and Paxton, Robert O. *Vichy France and the Jews.* New York: Basic Books, 1982.

Melzer, Emanuel. *Ma'avak Medini beMalkodet: Yehudei Polin, 1935–1939.* Tel Aviv: Diaspora Research Institute, 1982.

Nedava, Joseph. *Trotsky and the Jews.* Philadelphia: Jewish Publication Society, 1972.

Niv, David. *Ma'arachot haIrgun haTseva'i haLe'umi.* 4 vols. Tel Aviv: Mosad Klausner, 1965.

Nussbaum, Kalman. *VeHafach lahem leRo'ets: HaYehudim baTsava haAmami haPolani biVerit haMo'atsot.* Tel Aviv: Diaspora Research Institute, 1984.

———. " 'Legyon Yehudi' o Ahizat Einayim?" *Shvut* 10 (1984): 47–54.

Pease, Neal. "New Books on Poles and Jews during the Second World War." *Polish Review* 33 (1988):347–51.

Penkower, Monty Noam. *The Jews Were Expendable: Free World Diplomacy and the Holocaust.* Urbana and Chicago: University of Illinois Press, 1983.

Perlis, Rivka. *Tenu'ot haNo'ar haHalutsiyot beFolin haKevushah.* Tel Aviv: Beit Lohamei haGeta'ot and HaKibuts haMe'uhad, 1987.

Pobóg-Malinowski, Władysław. *Najnowsza historia polityczna Polski, 1864–1945.* 3 vols. London: n.p., 1967.

Polonsky, Antony, ed. *"My Brother's Keeper?": Recent Polish Debates on the Holocaust.* London: Routledge, 1990.

Porat, Dina. *Hanhagah beMilkud: HaYishuv Nochah haSho'ah, 1942–1945.* Tel Aviv: Am Oved, 1986.

Prekerowa, Teresa. *Konspiracyjna Rada Pomocy Żydom w Warszawie, 1942–1945.* Warsaw: Państwowy Instytut Wydawniczy, 1982.

Redlich, Shimon. *Propaganda and Nationalism in Wartime Russia: The Jewish Antifascist Committee in the U.S.S.R., 1941–1948.* N.p.: East European Quarterly, 1982.

Schapiro, Leonard. "The Jewish Anti-Fascist Committee and Phases of Soviet Anti-Semitic Policy during and after World War II." In *Jews and Non-Jews in Eastern Europe,* edited by B. Vago and G. L. Mosse, pp. 283–300. New York and Toronto: John Wiley and Sons, 1974.

Schechtman, Joseph, and Benari, Yehuda. *History of the Revisionist Movement*. Tel Aviv: Jabotinsky Institute, 1970.

Shavit, Yaacov. *Jabotinsky and the Revisionist Movement, 1925–1948*. London: Frank Cass, 1988.

———. *HaMitologiyah shel haYamin*. [Kefar Saba]: Beit Berl and Moshe Sharet Institute, [1986].

Shulman, Abraham. *The Case of Hotel Polski*. New York: Holocaust Library, 1982.

Silver, Eric. *Begin: The Haunted Prophet*. New York: Random House, 1984.

Sofer, Sasson. *Begin: An Anatomy of Leadership*. Oxford: Basil Blackwell, 1988.

Sompolinsky, Meir. "HaHanhagah haAnglo-Yehudit, Memshelet Britaniyah vehaSho'ah." Ph.D. dissertation, Bar-Ilan University, 1977.

Steven, Stewart. *The Poles*. New York: Macmillan, 1982.

Szarota, Tomasz. *Stefan Rowecki "Grot."* Warsaw: Państwowe Wydawnictwo Naukowe, 1983.

Tal, Uriel. "On the Study of the Holocaust and Genocide." *Yad Vashem Studies* 13 (1979): 7–52.

Tec, Nehama. *When Light Pierced the Darkness: Christian Rescue of Jews in Nazi-Occupied Poland*. New York and Oxford: Oxford University Press, 1986.

Terry, Sarah Meiklejohn. *Poland's Place in Europe: General Sikorski and the Origin of the Oder-Neisse Line, 1939–1943*. Princeton: Princeton University Press, 1983.

Wasserstein, Bernard. *Britain and the Jews of Europe, 1939–1945*. London and Oxford: Institute of Jewish Affairs and Clarendon Press of Oxford University Press, 1979.

Wyman, David S. *The Abandonment of the Jews: America and the Holocaust, 1941–1945*. New York: Pantheon Books, 1984.

Zabiełło, Stanisław. *O rząd i granice: Walka dyplomatyczna o sprawę polską w II wojnie światowej*. Warsaw: Pax, 1970.

Zamoyski, Adam. *The Polish Way: A Thousand-Year History of the Poles and Their Culture*. New York and Toronto: Franklin Watts, 1988.

Zawodny, J. K. *Zum Beispiel Katyn: Klärung eines Kriegsverbrechens*. Munich: Verlag Information und Wissen, 1971.

Index

Jews from, 16–23; Allied statement on, 17; government-in-exile statement on, 17. *See also* Jews

Holocaust (television program), 3

Home Army, 12, 31, 33, 165, 168, 200 (n. 43), 229 (n. 108), 232 (n. 127); and arms for Jews, 22, 202 (n. 48)

House of Commons, 76, 110, 156, 173; and desertion affair, 128–29. *See also* British Parliament

House of Representatives, 110, 133. *See also* U.S. Congress

Hulda, 113

Hungary, 198 (n. 17); Polish Jews in, 84, 154, 158; Jewish policies of, 155–56, 158, 283–84 (n. 93); Poles in, 157

Ickes, Harold, 98

Intergovernmental Committee on Refugees, 164

International Red Cross, 71, 72

Iran, 21, 49, 60, 112, 217–18 (n. 9)

Iraq, 96, 112

Irgun Tseva'i Le'umi, 96, 97, 100, 125, 269 (n. 171)

Israel, State of, 9

Jabotinsky, Ze'ev, 95, 97

Jewish Agency for Palestine, 20, 34–35, 49, 64, 101, 195 (n. 1), 216 (n. 177), 218 (n. 13), 221 (n. 41), 239 (n. 27), 256 (n. 35), 271 (n. 8); Committee on Poland of, 20, 198 (n. 20); Rescue Committee of, 21, 86, 165, 282 (n. 82); and Polish government, 53, 60; and Soviet Union, 53–54, 60; and Polish-Soviet conflict, 60; on Katyn affair, 75; and Anders order, 87; and funds for Polish Jews, 93; asks for Polish underground action, 165; London Executive of, 272 (n. 13)

Jewish Antifascist Committee, 81

Jewish Anti-Hitlerite Committee, 56, 81

Jewish Committee for Aid to Soviet Russia, 103

Jewish Coordinating Committee, 228 (n. 107)

Jewish Fighting Organization, 202 (n. 48), 229 (n. 108), 232 (n. 127)

Jewish Labor Committee, 229 (n. 108), 282 (n. 82); and funds for Polish Jews, 93

Jewish National Committee, 155, 216 (n. 181), 228 (n. 107), 230 (n. 110), 278 (n. 51); complains about rescue funds, 93

Jewish Telegraphic Agency, 229 (n. 108), 241 (n. 51)

Jews: and Polish-Soviet conflict, 4, 27, 176, 177, 178, 239 (n. 27), 251 (n. 131); in Palestine, 13, 15, 16, 35, 46, 197 (n. 8); and news of Holocaust, 15–16, 196 (n. 8); demand rescue action, 16–23, 61; under German occupation, 25; reception of Red Army by (1939), 25; alleged influence over public opinion, 26–29, 75; in France, 29–30; responses to Polish overtures by, 34–35; in West, 39, 45; in underground, 45; in U.S., 48; in Soviet Union, 53, 83; respond to Sikorski broadcast, 74–75, 76, 77; and Katyn affair, 75; and Union of Polish Patriots, 81; and Mikhoels-Feffer mission, 82–83; and Maisky visit to Palestine, 83–84; in Hungary, 84, 155–58; and Anders order, 86–87; raise funds for rescue, 155; Arciszewski on rights of, 170; attitudes toward government-in-exile, 172–75, 177–78. *See also* Holocaust

Joint Distribution Committee. *See* American Jewish Joint Distribution Committee

Locker, Berl, 216 (n. 177), 272 (n. 13)
Lohamei Herut Yisra'el (Lehi), 248 (n. 109), 251 (n. 126)
Lublin, 42, 168, 169, 214 (n. 167)
Lwów, 34, 168, 171, 172, 239 (n. 31)

Ładoś, Aleksander, 162
Łódź, 46, 165, 232 (n. 122), 239 (n. 31), 278 (n. 51)

Maisky, Ivan, 83–84, 99, 222 (n. 48), 239 (n. 27)
Majdanek, 73, 244 (n. 69)
Mapai, 251 (n. 131)
Marlewski, Jan, 62, 227 (n. 93)
Mauritius, 228 (n. 100)
Mauthausen, 244 (n. 69)
Mecca Temple, 59
Meissner, Feliks, 267 (n. 151)
Meridor, Ya'akov, 96
Mexico, 47, 81, 217 (n. 9)
Mikhoels, Shlomo, 81–84, 99, 177, 238 (n. 20). *See also* Feffer, Itsik; Mikhoels-Feffer mission
Mikhoels-Feffer mission, 88, 102, 113, 242 (n. 57). *See also* Feffer, Itsik; Mikhoels, Shlomo
Mikołajczyk, Stanisław, 19, 21, 22, 33, 42, 45, 54, 76, 87, 110, 124, 131, 140, 154, 155, 165, 169, 170, 171, 176, 213 (n. 146), 216 (n. 177), 230 (nn. 111, 114), 232 (n. 127); and rescue of rabbis, 64; and ŻKN cable, 66–68; becomes prime minister, 80; and Rescue Council, 105–7, 143, 144; consents to border modifications, 168; resigns, 168; strategy toward Jews, 273–74 (n. 26); on numbers of Jewish survivors, 277–78 (n. 51)
Miller, Irving, 74
Molotov, Vyacheslav, 55
Moyne, Lord, 251 (n. 126)
Munkács, 158

Myerson, Golda, 239 (n. 27)

Narutowicz, Gabriel, 218 (n. 11)
Natanson, Stanisław, 57
National Council for Civil Liberties, 134
National Council for the Homeland, 110–11
Netherlands, 163
Neutral countries, 40, 42, 161; asked to give Jews asylum, 30
NKVD (Soviet People's Commissariat of Internal Affairs), 49, 56, 57, 79, 219 (n. 21), 225 (n. 72)
Normandy invasion, 136
North Africa, 115
Nowogrodzki, Emanuel, 224 (n. 68)
Nyíregyháza, 158

Okulicki, Leopold, 248 (n. 106)
O'Malley, Sir Owen, 122, 137, 266 (n. 141)
Oranienburg, 244 (n. 69)
Oświęcim. *See* Auschwitz
Ozorków, 232 (n. 122)

Pahlevi, 49
Palästina-Amt, 218 (n. 13)
Palestine, 49, 57, 60, 75, 239 (n. 26); Jews in, 13, 15, 16, 35, 46, 197 (n. 8); immigration to, 16, 256 (n. 35), 257 (n. 39); Hebrew press in, 19, 35; Soviet propaganda in, 35, 51–52; paratroopers from, 45; Mikhoels and Feffer on, 82; Maisky's visit to, 83–84; British mandatory authorities in, 96, 97, 100, 113, 221 (n. 41), 256 (n. 35); Jewish deserters in, 111–14; exchangees arrive in, 197 (n. 9), 198 (n. 20); refugees in, 205 (n. 75); Revisionist plans for, 247 (n. 101). *See also* Polish army
Pehle, John, 281 (n. 71)

People's Guard, 31–32
Peru, 163, 164
Pioneer Corps, 108, 126, 127
PKWN. *See* Polish Committee of
National Liberation
Pogroms, 193–94 (n. 25)
Poland: as primary site of Holocaust,
17; Second Republic, 48; reasons
for establishing killing centers in,
197 (n. 13). *See also* Poles; entries
beginning with "Polish"
Poles: treatment of Jews in hiding,
22; in France, 29–30; in Soviet
Union, 31; German actions
against, 32–33; in Hungary, 157.
See also Poland; entries beginning
with "Polish"
Polish army, 58; Jews in, 13, 25, 26,
49, 96, 112–13, 115–16, 136–37,
254 (n. 13), 256 (n. 35); desertions from, 13, 108–37 passim;
in Soviet Union, 25, 207 (n. 92);
evacuation from Soviet Union, 25,
31, 34, 256 (n. 35); intelligence,
34, 95, 99–100, 101–2; alternate
force established by Soviets, 79,
103–4; in Palestine, 95, 99–100,
101–2, 111–14; Revisionists in,
96; Document Bureau, 99, 102,
104; Begin's release from, 100;
analyses of Jewish attitudes by,
101–2; Rommel soldiers join, 115;
helps Jews reach Palestine, 256
(n. 35); recommends broadcast to
Homeland, 273 (n. 25)
Polish Civic Committee, 157
Polish Committee of National
Liberation, 168, 169, 171, 172
Polish consulates-general: New
York, 51; Jerusalem, 86, 105; Tel
Aviv, 170
Polish Defense Ministry, 45, 108,
122, 123, 130, 141, 173; establishes
Desk for Jewish Affairs, 115; and

desertions, 118–21, 133–34, 136;
notes army mistreatment of Jews,
267 (n. 143), 268 (n. 163)
Polish Democratic Party, 203 (n. 51)
Polish embassies: Kuibyshev, 31, 57;
Washington, 51, 66, 75, 82–83
Polish Foreign Ministry, 17, 24, 35,
43–44, 51, 57, 59, 130, 141, 236–37
(n. 165), 268 (n. 167); and rescue
of rabbis, 62–64; and evacuating
children, 65; and Mikhoels-Feffer
mission, 82; and desertions, 130–
31, 133–34, 277 (n. 51); and Jews
in Hungary, 157–59, 160, 161; and
Vittel internees, 163–64
Polish government-in-exile: Jews
allege discrimination in, 4; political aims of, 4; publishes information about Holocaust, 9–10, 17;
attitudes toward Jewish matters,
9–12, 24–29, 61–62, 68, 73–
74, 77, 78, 81, 88–89, 149–50,
157–59, 175–77; relations with
underground, 17–18; and proposed Ministry of Jewish Affairs,
21; and Polish Jews in France,
29–30; and rescue demands, 33–
46, 62–65; note of December
1942, 44, 46; demands retaliation against Germans, 44, 205
(n. 79); and rescue funds, 45, 92–
93, 154; reactions to Rudnicki
report, 51–52; and rescue order
(May 1943), 69–71; condemns
German atrocities, 72–73; reorganization of (1943), 80–81; and
Mikhoels-Feffer mission, 82–83;
analysis of Jewish attitudes by,
103–4; political position of, 103–
4; demands Polish administration
in liberated territories, 110; an-
nounces amnesty for deserters,
134; Committee on Homeland Affairs of, 145; Political Committee

of, 148, 149; and Jews in Hungary,
156–62; cooperates with Rescue
Council, 160; supports passport
schemes, 162–64; Rescue Council
dissatisfaction with, 167; jettisoned
by Allies, 169; ceases to play a role
in Jewish life, 172

Polish Information Center, 42, 74

Polish Information Ministry, 87, 88,
103, 242 (n. 51), 276 (n. 42); and
Mikhoels-Feffer mission, 82

Polish Interior Ministry, 24, 28, 141,
145, 146, 147, 150, 151, 157, 160,
169, 233 (n. 128), 269 (n. 173);
Division of Jewish Affairs in, 45–
46; and rescue of rabbis, 64; and
children's evacuation scheme, 65;
and rescue instruction, 69, 70,
71; and fund transfers to Poland,
282–83 (n. 84)

Polish-Jewish relations: public discussion of, 2–7; moral judgments
in, 2–13; Jewish presentations
of, 3; Polish presentations of,
6; semantics of, 12; in Polish
army, 112–13, 115–16, 136–37;
Polish-Soviet relations as factor in,
176–78

Polish Labor and Social Welfare
Ministry, 106, 141, 157; budget
of, 153

Polish Labor Party, 204 (n. 66), 208
(n. 105)

Polish legations: Budapest, 157;
Bern, 285 (n. 110)

Polish National Council, 19, 20, 28,
43, 47, 54, 61, 123, 124, 152, 170,
204 (n. 74); and desertions, 131–
32, 136–37; Jewish representatives
on, 155. *See also* Schwarzbart,
Ignacy; Szerer, Emanuel; Zygielbojm, Szmul

Polish National Party, 38, 275 (n. 38)

Polish Peasant Party, 204 (n. 66)

Polish Socialist Party, 90–91, 154,
204 (n. 66), 225 (n. 72), 253
(n. 140); on blackmail of Jews, 201
(n. 47); WRN faction, 203 (n. 51)

Polish-Soviet relations, 4, 27, 31, 39,
58; Jewish attitudes toward, 4, 239
(n. 27), 251 (n. 131); territorial
conflicts in, 26; Allied attitudes
toward, 26–27, 31; Poles try to influence Jews' attitudes toward, 27;
implications of desertions for, 111,
130–31; as factor in Polish-Jewish
relations, 176–78

Polish Telegraphic Agency, 75, 153

Polish Treasury Ministry, 282 (n. 84)

Polish underground, 4, 5, 28; trans-
mits news of Holocaust, 17;
relations with government, 17–
18; asks Allies for military action,
33; makes recommendations to
government about Jews, 38; aids
Jewish contacts with West, 45

Polish Workers Party, 31

Polo Grounds (New York), 81

Pomeranc, Seweryn, 126

Portugal, 21, 161, 205 (n. 75)

PPR (Polish Workers Party), 31

PPS. *See* Polish Socialist Party

Pritt, Denis Noel, 127, 260 (n. 67);
political views of, 265 (n. 121)

Rabinowicz, Yitshak, 222–23 (n. 49)

Raczkiewicz, Władysław, 19, 21,
22, 43, 76, 80; responds to
Schwarzbart, 24; gives amnesty to
deserters, 134

Raczyński, Edward, 19, 40, 41, 43,
44, 57, 62, 64, 65, 74, 125, 166, 210
(n. 119), 236 (n. 164); responds
to Schwarzbart, 24; and deportations from France, 29–30; and
Erlich-Alter affair, 58; and ŻKN
cable, 66–68; replaced as foreign minister, 80; and desertions,

Va'adat Ezra veHatsalah (Assistance and Rescue Committee), 159, 286 (n. 112)
Va'ad Le'umi (General Council of the Jewish Community of Palestine), 15
Van Passen, Pierre, 98
Vatican, 20, 22, 41, 43, 160, 161
Venezuela, 163
Vichy government, 29–30, 135
Vittel, 162–65

Waldman, Morris, 217 (n. 9), 245 (n. 81)
Wałęsa, Lech, 2
War Emergency Conference, 169, 170
War Refugee Board, 138, 142, 145, 164, 166, 281 (n. 71), 292 (n. 167)
Warsaw, 21, 42, 110, 115, 162; ghetto, 70, 73, 76, 203 (n. 55); uprising, 165, 168
Weissmandel, Michael Dov-Ber, 285 (n. 110)
Weizmann, Chaim, 40
Welles, Sumner, 222 (n. 48)
Weytko, Jan, 288 (n. 130)
White, William Allen, 98
White Russia, 4, 109
Wilno, 34, 37, 202 (n. 48), 239 (n. 41)
Winant, John, 166
Winds of War (television program), 3
Wise, Stephen S., 66, 90, 91, 92, 170, 213 (n. 157), 222 (n. 48), 229 (n. 108), 244 (n. 72)
Wolna Polska, 79
World Jewish Congress, 16, 24, 41, 66, 74, 90, 139, 161, 169, 170, 222 (n. 48), 229 (n. 108), 241–42

(n. 51), 245 (n. 81), 263 (n. 94), 271 (n. 12), 272 (n. 13), 281 (n. 74), 287 (n. 121); British Section of, 19, 82, 123, 124; rescue demands of, 20; and funds for Polish Jews, 93
World Zionist Organization, 19, 40, 95, 247 (n. 101), 271 (n. 8), 272 (n. 13)
Wouk, Herman, 3

Yad Vashem, 5

Zabiełło, Stanisław, 206–7 (n. 87)
Zagłębie, 198 (n. 17), 239 (n. 41)
Zamość, 33, 214 (n. 167)
Zionists, 21, 45, 46, 48, 75, 101, 106, 198 (n. 17), 226 (n. 90), 286 (n. 110); and Soviet Union, 51–54, 83, 174; goals of, 52; and desertions, 269 (n. 170). *See also* Labor Zionists; Revisionist Zionists
Związek Patriotów Polskich (ZPP; Union of Polish Patriots), 79, 81
Zygielbojm, Szmul, 20, 22, 66, 200 (n. 37); suicide of, 76; on aid for Jewish refugees, 205 (n. 75); on deportations from France, 207 (n. 90)

Żegota. *See* Council for Aid to Jews
Żołnierz Polski-Żyd, 116
Żydokomuna, 48, 54, 58, 61, 77, 81, 101, 103, 177
Żydowska Organizacja Bojowa (ŻOB). *See* Jewish Fighting Organization
Żydowski Komitet Narodowy (ŻKN). *See* Jewish National Committee